THE END
OF
The Conservative Era

BY ROBERT S. McELVAINE

Down and Out in the Great Depression:
Letters from the "Forgotten Man"

The Great Depression: America, 1929–1941

THE END
OF
The Conservative Era

Liberalism After Reagan

ROBERT S. McELVAINE

ARBOR HOUSE

New York

Designed by Robert Bull
Manufactured in the United States of America

10 9 8 7 6 5 4 3 2 1

Library of Congress Cataloging in Publication Data

McElvaine, Robert S., 1947–
    The end of the conservative era.

    Includes index.
    1. Liberalism—United States.   2. United States—
Politics and government—1981–   . I. Title.
JA84.U5M434   1987   320.5′13′0973   87-1005
ISBN: 0-87795-916-1

See pages 293–295 for song permissions.

IN MEMORY OF MY FATHER,

EDWARD McELVAINE,

1908–1985

My life has been a poor attempt
To imitate the Man
I'm just a living legacy
To the Leader of the Band
—DAN FOGELBERG

CONTENTS

PREFACE

Americans in the middle of the 1980s seemed obsessed with the desire for personal advancement. The most conservative president since Calvin Coolidge was a popular figure. He was doing his best to tear down the edifice of federal social programs that had been constructed by previous progressive administrations. Democrats were dispirited and many of them were suggesting that if their party hoped to win future national elections, it must move away from some of its traditional positions and become more like the Republicans.

The pages that follow argue not only that such a course would be disastrous for the Democratic party, but that the mid-1980s marked the beginning of the decline of the latest conservative era in our history. Despite appearances and despite the popularity of Ronald Reagan, the United States in the mid-eighties stood on the verge of a new age of progressive reform that is likely to dominate the late eighties and early nineties. Post-Reagan America will see a striking revival of liberalism, although the new reform movement will not be a copy of earlier periods of liberal change. Nor is the new agenda for reform likely to carry the unpopular name "liberal." Another label is needed, both to indicate important differences from earlier forms of liberalism and to win a hearing from a public that has been convinced it should not listen to anything called "liberal." In this book I describe an approach to public policy that I call the "New Progressivism."

But an analysis of and prescription for public policy is only one facet of this book. I believe that there exists a sort of Newton's Third Law of Political Attitudes that produces a reaction against the dominant mood at any particular time. The result is a pendulum that swings between eras in which a majority of Americans concern themselves with social problems and those in which most people turn inward to more personal concerns. In the mid-1980s the pendulum had swung as far to the right as it was going to go, and started its movement back in the other direction. Evidence of this shift was to be found in everything from public-opinion polls to rock music, movies, television, and mass-participation events staged to raise money and consciousness about hunger and homelessness.

That evidence was clear long before the Iran-Contra scandal began to undermine confidence in President Reagan. The manuscript of this book was completed before that debacle became known. Additions have been made to take Mr. Reagan's foreign policy disaster into account, but my basic argument is unrelated to the decline in the President's popularity in late 1986 and early 1987.

This book examines historical currents, popular culture, politics, and economics to offer an assessment of where we are, where we are going, and where we should be going. It is composed of equal parts of analysis, prediction, and prescription. Out of all this emerges a portrait of America in the aftermath of the Reagan years.

I owe more than the usual number of debts to people without whom the completion of this book would have been impossible. Charles Forcey, my mentor at the State University of New York at Binghamton, first introduced me to the concept of "waves" of reform in American history, a topic to which he has devoted many years of research. Lawrence W. Levine of the University of California at Berkeley opened up more fully for me the potential in studying popular culture as a means of understanding public attitudes. My colleague Ross H. Moore of Millsaps college provided me with a steady stream of newspaper and magazine clippings that greatly facilitated my research.

A large number of public figures gave generously of their time for interviews. Many of them also provided needed encouragement as the project moved along. Among them are Rep. Les Aspin, Gov. Bruce Babbitt, Sen. Lloyd Bentsen, Sen. Joseph Biden, Sen. Dale Bumpers, Patrick Caddell, Sen. Lawton Chiles, Gov. Bill Clinton, Rep. Tony Coelho, Gov. Mario Cuomo, Rep. Buddy Darden, former Assistant Secretary of State Patricia Derian, Sen. Christopher Dodd, Rep. Wayne Dowdy, Gov. Michael Dukakis, Rep. Barney Frank, Alvin From, Rep. Richard Gephardt, Richard Goodwin, Sen. Gary Hart, Rev. Jesse Jackson, Sen. Edward Kennedy, Sen. William Proxmire, Joseph Rauh, Gov. Charles Robb, Rev. Pat Robertson, Arthur Schlesinger, Jr., Rep. Patricia Schroeder, Sen. Paul Simon, Rep. Charles Stenholm, Rep. Morris Udall, and Rep. Jim Wright.

Representative Wayne Dowdy and his entire staff, including Elizabeth Byrd, Kerry McKenney, William Wright, John Pigott, Dean Pittman, and Toni Cooley, provided much assistance and a convenient base of operations on Capitol Hill. Kathy and Hugh Boyle of Rockville, Maryland, deserve special thanks for providing accommodation and friendship on my numerous trips to Washington.

Bill Albers of Washington; Carol and Charlie Boyle of Fayetteville, Georgia; Karen Carlley of Jackson, Mississippi; Hodding Carter, III, of Washington; Ned Chase of New York; Brad Chism of Jackson; Nancy and Jim Condangelo of Stoughton, Massachusetts; Jim Currie of Washington; Marcie and Earl Eidecker of Tucson, Arizona; Susan Garcia of Jackson; Anna and John Lee of Fayetteville, Georgia; Rose and Bob Lee of Mahopac, New York; Joan and Ron Marks of Long Valley, New Jersey; Joan and Charlie Meehan of Long Valley, New Jersey; Karen and Chuck Meehan of Landing, New Jersey; Susan and Brian Meehan of Belvidere, New Jersey; James Byron Morris of Houston, Texas; Linda and Michael Raff of Jackson; Elizabeth Ranager of Jackson; Eve and Harvey Saunders of Fulton, Missouri; and Elvin Sunds of Jackson also provided a variety of help.

Other members of the history department at Millsaps College — Frank Laney, Charles Sallis, and Adrienne Phillips—have been generous in their support, as has the college itself. My agent, Mel Berger, and my editor, Allan Mayer, deserve special thanks.

My father, Edward McElvaine, died while I was in the midst of this project. The dedication of the book does not begin to indicate my debt to him for the lifetime of boundless love and assistance he gave me. He and my mother, the late Ruth McElvaine, belonged to that nearly vanished breed, liberal Republicans, until Richard Nixon and Ronald Reagan convinced them that such a construction had become an oxymoron. They instilled in me the values that are evident in this book.

My greatest debts, as always, are to the members of my immediate family. My daughters Kerri and Lauren not only supplied much cheer to my life while I was working on the book, but also helped to guide me through some of the tangles of the current music scene. Allison, my youngest daughter, does not yet know much about music, but she is always a delight.

Nothing that I ever do would be possible without Anne. I owe her more than I could ever repay and more than words can say.

Robert McElvaine
Clinton, Mississippi
March 1987

The line it is drawn, the curse it is cast
The slow one now will later be fast
As the present now will later be past
The order is rapidly fadin'
And the first one now will later be last
For the times they are a-changin'
  —BOB DYLAN (1963)

INTRODUCTION:

"I Like Ron"

You know the good old days weren't
Always good
And tomorrow ain't as bad as it seems
—BILLY JOEL (1983)

An extremely popular, grandfatherly Republican with a quick smile and a knack for easing people's tensions is riding high in his second term in the White House. He won a resounding re-election victory over an old-style liberal from the nation's heartland, a man who is widely believed to have represented the last gasp of the dying New Deal coalition. The mood of the country is steadfastly conservative. Most Americans seem to be eager to live the good life; they appear to have forgotten that in the midst of visible prosperity poverty still afflicts millions of Americans. Or perhaps they are dimly aware of the poor, but they don't really care much about them. Most of the nation is concerned instead with personal advancement, new houses, fancy automobiles, and the gadgets of a new technology.

The family is the focus of the middle class. More people seem to be interested in religion than was the case a few years earlier, and television preachers have become very popular in some quarters. The president does not like to go to church, but his popularity with religious Americans is undiminished. He has been plagued with recurring health problems, which have added to his detached administrative style. He delegates much of his work to others. For a time he turned many of his duties over to a trusted aide who was sometimes called the "assistant president," but the aide was finally forced to resign after he was caught up in a scandal.

There are few signs of unrest. Teen-agers like wild rock-and-roll music and outlandish singers who place too much emphasis on sex.

1

Bleached blonde hair is popular among teen-age girls, as is dark red lipstick, and a hairstyle featuring a tail in the back has become a rage with some of the young. Action films starring tough-guy heroes are popular, as are science-fiction flicks featuring incredible alien creatures. Game shows and situation comedies dominate the nation's television screens. The campuses are generally quiet, and students are interested mainly in career preparation that will help them to make bundles of money. A small number of college students have shown discontent about racial oppression, but nothing more radical than sex and intoxication seems to hold any attraction for most of them, among whom Republicanism seems to be on the rise. Success and "living well" are the goals of most young people, and the way to achieve them seems to be majoring in business in college and then joining a corporation.

Concern about our educational system is widespread, and many fear that its inadequacies are hurting the nation's international position. There is much controversy over whether we should enter into a hugely expensive new space competition with the Soviet Union, but there are occasional hopeful signs of a possible thaw in relations between the superpowers. The attempts of antinuclear activists to stop atomic-bomb tests in the South Pacific have excited some opponents of the status quo, and actions taken against them and their ship have brought their movement considerable attention.

Democrats in Congress are holding their own and can often manage to block the proposals of the Republican administration. But the aging president's popularity remains great, despite the recession that occurred in his first term and the current signs of weakness in the economy. The vice-president has taken a number of foreign trips and carefully positioned himself as the heir apparent. Several Democrats appear keen to win their party's presidential nomination. Yet the mood of the country still seems conservative and the political climate does not look at all auspicious for liberals.

Many Democrats, in fact, are suggesting that their party should abandon much of its commitment to liberal causes and go with the conservative flow. The New Deal is no longer new, they point out, and promising to assist the poor is not going to win elections in an age of affluence. If the Democrats will move toward the Republicans, this argument goes, they will have a chance to win back disaffected voters who have deserted the party in the last two presidential elections.

Some intellectuals are deeply concerned about the nation's direction. One of America's leading novelists wrote to the defeated liberal Democratic presidential candidate:

> If I wanted to destroy a nation, I would give it too much and I would have it on its knees, miserable, greedy, and sick. . . . [In rich America] a creeping, all pervading, nerve-gas of immorality starts in the nursery and does not stop before it reaches the highest offices, both corporate and governmental. . . . On all levels American society is rigged. . . . I am troubled by the cynical immorality of my country. It cannot survive on this basis.[1]

Under the circumstances, anyone who would dare to predict that the dawn of a stirring era of liberal reform is imminent would appear to be a likely candidate for a rest home for senile political analysts.

Yet the time described in the preceding paragraphs is not the 1980s but the late 1950s. The president is Dwight Eisenhower, the powerful assistant president is not Donald Regan but Sherman Adams, the defeated liberal Democrat is Adlai Stevenson, the novelist is John Steinbeck, and just such a period of liberal activism *was* about to dawn. There are a number of indications that the same may have been the case in the mid-1980s. Appearances to the contrary notwithstanding, the American people may well be poised on the edge of a new age of liberalism.

Many signs that a return to liberal idealism may be in the air will be noted in the pages that follow. They were scattered in the mid-eighties, and some may not have seemed significant, but the same could easily have been said of the portents of a new reform era in the late fifties. Obviously there are great differences between the fifties and the eighties, but the similarities are also remarkable. The following talking blues, written by Akron United Rubber Workers Educational Director Joe Glazer and recorded in 1958 by John Greenway, for instance, has a distinctly eighties ring about it:

> I like Ike. He's a friendly guy.
> When things go wrong, he doesn't pine and sigh—
> No, that great big smile and friendly grin,
> Helps you forget the mess that we're in.
> I like Ike. Love that smile. Makes me feel so good.

Well, a pal of mine lost his job and his car
While Ike was out golfing, shooting for par;
Couldn't find a job for days and days,
But for good old Ike he had plenty of praise, he said,
"I like Ike. Love that smile. Makes me forget my troubles."

. . .

But Eisenhower loves this motley crew
That's doin' such a job on me and you;
He says, "I'm with 'em, every single man,
They're backing my dynamic conservative plan."
That Ike—he's a modern progressive.
That's a fellow that stumbles forward every time somebody
    shoves him.[2]

With a few name changes, this piece could be retitled "I Like
Ron" and would sound like it had been composed in the mid-1980s.

Of course history does not "repeat itself" in any simple way.
The sixties are not "coming back." Each new era of reform differs
substantially from those that preceded it. The New Progressivism of
the late 1980s and 1990s will pursue the same goals and values that
past liberal movements have sought, but it will employ new means
to reach those ends.

There is much evidence that American political and social
thinking moves in cycles, with periods of sentiment for liberal reform punctuated by conservative breathing spaces. In the former,
community values are dominant; in the latter, egoistic individualism
holds sway. As early in our history as 1841, Ralph Waldo Emerson
noticed the alternation between what he called "the Party of Conservatism and the Party of Innovation." Henry Adams in the late
nineteenth century and Arthur Schlesinger in the first half of the
twentieth century described cycles in American political and social
attitudes.

Arthur Levine has pointed out:

An emphasis on "me" is what differentiates periods of individual ascendency from periods of community ascendency. The ori-
entation of individual ascendency is hedonistic, emphasizing the

primacy of duty to one's self, while that of community ascendency is ascetic, stressing the primacy of duty to others. Individual ascendency is concerned principally with rights, community ascendency with responsibilities.[3]

Throughout our history, Americans have alternated between periods of reform and times in which people tired of thinking of social problems and withdrew into more personal concerns. The peaks of reform—in the American Revolution, the Jeffersonian era, the Age of Jackson, the Abolitionist crusade and the Civil War, populism and progressivism, the New Deal, and the New Frontier/Great Society—have taken place between times of inaction or reaction: the Federalist era, the "Era of Good Feelings" following the War of 1812, the 1840s and early 1850s, the Gilded Age of the late nineteenth century, the 1920s, the 1950s, and the late 1970s–mid-1980s. People grow weary of the activism of such leaders as Jefferson, Jackson, Lincoln, the Roosevelts, Wilson, Kennedy, and Johnson. But they also eventually become restless under the conservative regimes of the Adamses, Fillmores, Harrisons, Coolidges, Eisenhowers, Fords, and even Reagans.[4]

No period of reform in our history, with the exception of the Progressive era at the beginning of the twentieth century, has been sustained for more than a decade. There seems to be a limit on how long a majority of people will continue to be concerned with social problems. After several years of community-mindedness, much of the public tends to grow weary. People turn inward and leave the world's problems for others to worry about. The high hopes with which an age of reform usually begins inevitably outdistance the accomplishments of the reformers. Those who awaited the millennium are invariably disillusioned. Many of them conclude that if they cannot perfect the world, they might as well forget it and concentrate on improving their own lives.

"The fatigue factor is one of the main reasons why liberalism declines periodically," in the view of veteran liberal activist Joseph Rauh. "The most active workers get tired and decide that they haven't been able to achieve nearly as much as they wanted. . . . Many liberals come to feel that the great efforts that were made have not been appreciated. They're not going to try to do any more."[5]

As a liberal era wanes, cynicism displaces idealism, pessimism takes the place of optimism, and self-centeredness arises where a spirit of self-sacrifice had prevailed. The particular causes of these alterations vary according to specific historical circumstances. The last wave of liberalism in the 1960s was undermined by revulsion over the war in Vietnam, disgust with the alarming lack of candor exhibited by Lyndon Johnson and Richard Nixon, the scandals and corruption in the latter's administration, the "stagflation" that gripped the economy in the 1970s, and general doubt about the accomplishments of the "Great Society."

Some of those who had participated in the social movements of the sixties had become disillusioned by the time of Richard Nixon's resignation in 1974. Many of these once liberal "baby boomers" entered their chrysalises and emerged at the beginning of the next decade as Reaganite "yuppies." They were joined in the "me generation" by a younger group. The group (I leave the term "cohort" to the demographers) that came of age since the early seventies is different from that which preceded it into egoism. These younger self-centered Americans cannot accurately be said to be disillusioned. Before one can become disillusioned, one must first have illusions to lose. Those who reached the age of political consciousness in the seventies never had that opportunity. As James Simon Kunen, veteran of the 1968 Columbia University sit-in and author of *The Strawberry Statement*, put it in 1985: "They never had any illusions. They grew up in an America of assassinations, Vietnam, Watergate. We grew up in an America of Ike, togetherness, and tail fins. I think they never really expected anything of America. . . ."[6] Taking their cues from those who had come immediately before them and become disgusted with the developments of the Johnson–Nixon years, many Americans now in their twenties became cynical without first having believed in anything. They were a generation, like that of the 1920s described by Amory Blaine's famous words in F. Scott Fitzgerald's *This Side of Paradise*, "grown up to find all Gods dead, all wars fought, all faiths in man shaken."[7]

These conditions provide some of the basis for the assessment that a return of liberal idealism may not be far off. By the mid-1980s, America had been in an age of cynicism for at least a decade. There seemed to be nothing for the young to hold on to or believe in. They distrusted all institutions. Such cynicism was inevitable in the wake of the Johnson and Nixon presidencies, the growth of deceptive advertising, investigative reporting, and other phenomena of the sixties and seventies. Yet cynicism is an empty feeling. It satisfies none of the nobler desires of the mind or soul.

The young people who had grown up in this bleak atmosphere remained in the mid-eighties, on the surface, committed to the "me-generation" philosophy. But beneath the surface there could be detected a deep yearning for something outside themselves in which to believe and for which to work—a desire for a new idealism. The young of the eighties became, like their counterparts in the 1950s, "rebels without a cause"—or perhaps rebels in search of a cause.

There was also arising by the mid-eighties a post-yuppie generation. This rising generation, the vanguard of which was reaching college age, was not yet politically conscious when the wrenching experiences of Vietnam and Watergate came to an end. Accordingly, they lacked the reasons for cynicism that their elders had. "For the first time I'm proud to be a student," said one Berkeley undergraduate during the spring 1985 demonstrations seeking university divestiture from firms that do business in South Africa. "I'm proud to be an American student. It's like—maybe we're not all becoming yuppies."[8] These younger Americans are available for new liberal movements. All they lack is inspiration, something which a bold new Democratic leader could supply.

And if the rising generation of the eighties became caught up in idealism, it could become contagious. Those in their twenties, after all, were never inoculated against idealism. If liberalism were presented to them in a believable manner, they might yet be saved from self-centeredness.

Even the older baby-boom yuppies might still be redeemed. The Big Chill generation still feels guilty about its brie-chablis-BMW life and wistfully recalls the smashed ideals of its past. "So much was expected of this generation," pollster Patrick Caddell said to me in an interview, "but it has yet to accomplish much. The baby boomers are still anxious to fulfill their destiny."[9] The yuppie flirtation with Gary Hart's "New Ideas" in 1984 was indicative of their restlessness. Those in their thirties and forties are still susceptible to becoming "reillusioned." If they were offered something good and true to believe in, both the baby boomers and the younger voters could be wooed from Reaganism before the 1988 election. This is especially the case if the Democrats make it clear that such voters need not become ascetics in the process of adopting compassion.

Democrats should present the electorate with a New Progressivism that recognizes the need and right of the middle class to get ahead, but not by ignoring the needs of the poor.

It is unsurprising that the appeal of liberal calls for community and compassion has a limited life-span. But it should also be recognized that hedonism and egoism have their limits. The oscillations of public attitudes vary greatly because of differing historical conditions, but there can be little question that they have been an important force in America's development. Nor is this pattern without some predictive value. "We may expect the recession from liberalism which began in 1947 to last till 1962, with a possible margin of a year or two in one direction or the other," Arthur Schlesinger, Sr., wrote in a striking 1949 prophecy. "The next conservative epoch will then be due around 1978."[10]

The United States was in the latter stages of that conservative epoch in the mid-eighties. The "looking out for number one" mentality is ascendant. "This is not a time period," Joan Baez noted in 1985, "when people talk about sacrifices. This is a time when people talk about feeling good about yourself, about taking care of yourself first, . . . sitting in a hot tub."[11] Rock star Madonna hit the top of the charts in the spring of 1985 by proclaiming that she is a "Material Girl," "living in a material world," for whom "the boy with the cold, hard cash is always Mr. Right." Although there was some difference of opinion on whether these lyrics were intended to be satirical (a view supported by the video version of the song), if taken straight they would have made a good anthem for the Reagan administration.[12] Madison Avenue also reflected the acquisitive individualism that had become rampant: "Buick Century: It's one of the rewards you get for playing the game—and winning!" "Who says you can't have it all?" asked a ubiquitous Michelob Light commercial. "You're on your way to the top. You've always known where you're going." "I believe in Crystal Light, because I believe in *me!*" sang the performers in another catchy commercial tune.

This was depressing for those who longed for a greater spirit of community. "I've been around long enough that I've seen cycles come and go," Representative Morris Udall told me in 1985. "This is a rather sad time to be a liberal Democrat. Everything I've ever believed and worked for the last thirty years is under challenge by the Reagan administration. . . . Clearly the Democrats have to learn the difference between programs that work and programs that don't work. But we've also got an obligation to stand by our beliefs and wait for a better time," the Arizona congressman concluded.[13]

The situation is far from hopeless for liberals. The "better time" for which they wait is coming. By the late 1980s and early 1990s, we will be "due" for the pendulum to be swinging back toward a period of reform. There were already strong hints in the mid-eighties that the egoistic trend had bottomed out. Even the 1984 Reagan land-slide contained a few rays of sunshine. First, Mr. Reagan's coattails were virtually nonexistent. The Republicans did not do as well in Senate and House races as they did in 1980. Democratic losses in the House were minute given the presidential margin. (On the other hand, Republicans won nearly half of the nationwide vote in House races. The Democratic vote was distributed in a more advantageous way.) The gain of two Democratic seats in the Senate—along with a few other changes—produced a less conservative Senate than before the 1984 vote. Second, even as they were voting for Reagan, a ma-jority of Americans were shown by polls to disagree with him on many important issues. Third, and perhaps most significant, voters in California, Michigan, and Nevada rejected sweeping conservative tax-cutting referendums. The Jarvis tax-revolt movement, one of the most important harbingers of the conservative era, appears to have run its course, despite the passage of a few minor measures in 1986. That year a Gallup poll found that majorities ranging from 67 to 82 percent of the American people favored government subsidies for such things as low-income housing, mass transit, and preserving wil-derness areas. The same survey found 80 percent of its respondents favoring tax deductions for the rehabilitation of slum houses. The Democrats' net gain of eight Senate seats in 1986 was another indi-cation that Reaganism was not popular when divorced from the president's personality.[14]

Democratic politicians in the mid-eighties took note of these changes in attitudes and made the comparison to those that pre-ceded the last period of reform. "This second Reagan term reminds me so much of the second Eisenhower term that it's almost un-canny," Governor Michael Dukakis of Massachusetts told me in 1986. "People weren't *that* unhappy in 1960," he continued, "but I think there was a sense that it was time for something different, something new, some energy, just some vitality." Bruce Babbitt, the former governor of Arizona and an aspirant for the 1988 Demo-cratic presidential nomination, agreed. "There is a clear sort of cycle in American political history by which the progressive impulse runs its course and gives way to a time of consolidation—a kind of political settling process in which the momentum shifts to other areas of society. This inevitably sows the seeds of the next wave of progressive reform," Babbitt said. "Sometimes it almost scares me to think how much the current period is like the late 1950s. It's eerie."[15]

"I think," New York Governor Mario Cuomo has said, "that there is some validity to the cyclical theory and that the pendulum will eventually come back in what I consider the right direction. But I don't think we should wait for the natural swing. I'm convinced that we should grab hold of that pendulum and not let it drag us."[16]

Changes in public sentiment do not, as a rule, occur suddenly. "We have to recognize that we didn't get into this position overnight," Senator Lawton Chiles of Florida said in a 1986 interview. "We drifted into it over a long period, and it'll take us a while to get out. But when it finally turns, it'll probably turn much quicker than we anticipate."[17]

An era of reform builds slowly and fitfully. Signals are mixed during the years in which the dominant conservatism is decaying. And since those holding conservative attitudes are in power, appearances are likely to remain discouraging to progressives while the deeper public mood is actually shifting toward their values.

If we still saw around us in the mid-eighties ample evidence of the continuing "me generation," it was well to remember that the college students of the 1950s were called the "silent generation." Yet it was members of that generation of students who began to break the silence of the Ike Age in its last years and who led the sit-ins across the South in 1960, showing that some were ready to try to revive American idealism even before John F. Kennedy added his rhetoric to the cause.

To detect hints of the coming era of reform, one had to look very hard during Eisenhower's second term. Conformity, moderation, apathy, and affluence were the orders of the day. The spirit of the times seemed well summarized by a UCLA student who was asked what she wanted out of life. "Why, a good sensible life," she responded. "But, you know, of course not too darned sensible."[18] Moderation in everything—even sense—that was the silent generation's objective.

But such a mood could not last forever. There is among the American people a latent liberalism, a sense of compassion and sensitivity that is periodically submerged, but that eventually works its way back to the surface. Most liberals were in despair in the late fifties, much as they were in the mid-eighties. Yet the egoistic attitudes that gripped the country were self-destructive. General cynicism creates a need for belief. Young Americans in the late fifties began to find causes worthy of their commitment in the civil rights and antinuclear movements.

The signs of liberal revival were almost as shadowy in Ronald Reagan's second term as they had been in Dwight Eisenhower's. But, as the pages that follow demonstrate, they could be found. A few examples: socially conscious lyrics became prominent in rock music in the mid-eighties; numerous huge charity events, such as Live Aid and Hands Across America, showed that compassion and concern for others were becoming popular again; in 1986 inquiries to the Peace Corps were up by almost 1,000 percent.

The pace with which a new liberalism will grow cannot be said with assurance. We are talking about human history, not an astronomical phenomenon. All sorts of events and circumstances—the health of the economy, foreign adventures, the personal characteristics of political leaders, to name a few—will help to determine the timing and dimensions of the next era of reform. It is probable that the signs will be mixed in the late eighties, but the overall trend, contrary to the expectations of many observers, is likely to be one of conservative decline and liberal revival. The me era is rapidly giving way to a new "we era." The time is not far off when a new progressive politician will be able to inspire Americans as John F. Kennedy did in 1960, convincing them once more that we must "get this country moving again."

CHAPTER 1

Whatever Happened to the "McKinley Coalition"?

Catch a wave
And you're sittin' on top of the world
　—BRIAN WILSON (1962)

Why worry, there should be laughter after pain
There should be sunshine after rain
These things have always been the same
So why worry now
　—MARK KNOPFLER (1985)

"Realignment." In the wake of Ronald Reagan's overwhelming victory in 1984, this became the buzz word of American politicians and political analysts. Democrats trembled, but it brought a twinkle to Republican eyes. It came to occupy a position similar to those held by "backlash," "southern strategy," and "silent majority" in the late 1960s and early 1970s. In fact, realignment is another word for the same phenomenon that those earlier terms were employed to describe: the anticipated emergence of a Republican majority in American politics for the first time since the beginning of the Great Depression in 1930.

Several political observers confidently predicted just such a development during the presidency of Richard Nixon. In the late sixties, Kevin Phillips wrote at great length about *The Emerging Republican Majority*, dedicating his book to that putative majority "and its two principal architects: President Richard M. Nixon and Attorney General John N. Mitchell."[1] Whether these two men

12

were competent architects is open to question. What is not in doubt
is that they were, despite their wooing of "hard hats," not good
construction workers. Even before the edifice of their Republican
majority collapsed under the weight of the heavier structure they
built and called Watergate, the Nixon–Mitchell plan had fallen far
short of its objective.

The presidential election returns in 1972 certainly seemed to
confirm the belief that the Republicans had put together a new majority coalition, but in fact they had not. The Grand Old Party had
lost twelve seats in the House between 1969 and 1971, and gained
only one in the Senate in 1970. Even while Mr. Nixon was trounc-
ing George McGovern in 1972, the voters were showing no inclina-
tion in other races to abandon their long-standing preference for the
Democratic party. The GOP gained only twelve House seats and
lost two places in the Senate in 1972.

The Nixon scandals produced a dramatic shift to the Democrats
in 1974, when they won fifty-two seats in the House and four in the
Senate. Obituaries for the Republican party that had been published after the Barry Goldwater debacle in 1964 were dusted off
and reprinted. By the mid-seventies it was plain that Phillips had
been mistaken when he wrote that "1968 marks the beginning of a
new Republican cycle comparable in magnitude to the New Deal
era which began in 1932."[2] The Republican majority had emerged
stillborn.

It is undeniable, though, that Republicans have been winning
most of the presidential elections of late. Some analysts therefore
conclude that the predictions of Republican dominance were not
wrong, they were merely premature. NBC News polling consultant
Laurily K. Epstein said after Ronald Reagan's re-election: "The
changes in party identification evinced in 1984 indicate that a realignment is no longer incipient, but upon us."[3] If 1968 was not
1932, this argument holds, 1980 was. Richard Nixon was not up to
the role of being the Republican Franklin D. Roosevelt, but the part
is well filled by the nation's first Hollywood president. Realignment,
it is said, requires an inspiring leader to mobilize support for his
programs. FDR was such a leader; Nixon was not. We saw no
"Nixon Coalition" to replace that of Roosevelt, but after 1984 we
were told that the Reagan Revolution was underway and that realignment was finally doing what it was supposed to have done in
1968.

There are many reasons to doubt this analysis, the big Democratic victory in the 1986 Senate races least among them. Let us look at what has happened in terms of party identification. At the time of President Reagan's smashing victory over Walter Mondale in November 1984, a number of national opinon surveys found nearly as many Americans identifying themselves as Republicans as Democrats. The CBS News/*New York Times* poll taken immediately after the election actually found an even division between the parties, with 32 percent identifying themselves with each party and the remaining 36 percent saying they were independents. Such a surge in Republican affiliation was to be expected at a time when so many people were voting for the man at the top of the GOP ticket. But if it was actually only an election-time aberration, it was also to be expected that Republican identification would slip again fairly soon after the election. That is precisely what happened. By mid-January 1985, the CBS News/*New York Times* poll registered a four-point advantage for the Democrats. Other surveys between Election Day 1984 and February 1985 found the Democratic lead ranging from 10 (ABC News/*Washington Post*) or 11 (Harris) to 16 percentage points (Roper). By early 1986 polls that distributed independents with identifiable leanings showed that party identification was back to about what it had been at the beginning of Reagan's presidency: 49 percent Democratic and 41 percent Republican.[4]

These figures do not appear to be "convincing evidence that a sharp party realignment is taking place."[5] There was, to be sure, some erosion of Democratic support from the peak of the party's post-Watergate backing. A Gallup poll in 1977 found self-described Democrats outnumbering Republicans by more than two to one, 49 percent to 20 percent.[6] The GOP gains in the Carter and Reagan years are significant, but they amount to something far short of an historic national realignment. Perhaps the most convincing evidence is that in the midst of all the latest talk of an emerging Republican majority, the first advance polls on the 1988 presidential election, shortly after Reagan's 1984 sweep, pointed toward a Democratic victory. When the National Conservative Political Action Committee's Terry Dolan placed the names of George Bush and Gary Hart before a cross-section of voters in January 1985, Hart won, by 45 to 42 percent. A Gallup poll in February of the same year found Senator Edward Kennedy favored over Bush by 47 to 41 percent and a Harris poll two months later gave the Massachusetts

Democrat a two-point lead over the vice-president.[7] Of course none of these early polls assured a Democratic win in 1988, but they served to cast doubt upon the contention that the Reagan realignment was building a lasting Republican majority.

If there has been no realignment nationwide, though, the same cannot be said of the South. Democrats have been losing strength among southern white voters ever since 1948, when the inclusion of a civil-rights plank in the party's platform led to the formation of the States' Rights party, popularly known as the Dixiecrats, and the presidential candidacy of Strom Thurmond. At that point most white southerners could not yet bring themselves to vote for the party of Lincoln, but in the ensuing four decades (as, not coincidentally, the GOP has become less and less the party of Lincoln) more and more of them have followed Thurmond's path into the GOP. The transition was often accomplished in steps: first, defection from the Democrats to vote for Thurmond or, in 1968, George Wallace; then, voting Republican in presidential elections (as about half of all southern whites did as early as Dwight Eisenhower's first victory in 1952); then, voting for Republicans for the Senate and House; and finally, open identification with the Republican party.

In 1948 defections to the Dixiecrat ticket reduced Harry Truman's share of the southern white vote to 53 percent. The share of that vote going to Democrats has continued to drift downward, with the exception of the Lyndon Johnson landslide in 1964 and the native-son candidacy of Jimmy Carter in 1976. (And even Georgian Carter had to depend upon black votes to win in the region. Gerald Ford carried the white South by 52 to 46 percent.) Walter Mondale garnered a scant 28 percent of the southern white vote in 1984.[8]

But prior to 1984 most white southerners still identified themselves as Democrats, even while frequently marking their ballots for Republicans. As late as December 1983, Democratic pollster Peter Hart found 53 percent of whites in Alabama calling themselves Democrats and only 24 percent Republicans. Eleven months later, just before the Reagan avalanche, Democratic identification among white Alabamians had fallen to 29 percent and Republican allegiance had soared to 41 percent. A twenty-nine-point Democratic lead had been turned into a twelve-point Republican margin: a net shift of more than forty points in less than a year.[9] Now that *is* realignment. In the South as a whole, the *Los Angeles Times* exit poll in November 1984 found whites favoring the Republican party by

37 to 23 percent.[10] This has to be a cause for genuine concern among Democrats.

While religious fundamentalism and the possibility of personal political gain may be part of the motive for the Republicanization of the white South, there can be little question that the deeper reason is simply race. Race has always been the dominant factor in southern politics, and that, unfortunately, has not changed as much as it should have. What has changed is the name of the party of white supremacy. It used to be called "Democratic"; today its name is "Republican." White southerners may be conservative on other issues, but for many of them it is race that continues to overshadow all other concerns. They grumbled a bit, but did not desert the Party of the Fathers when Franklin Roosevelt introduced the New Deal. They began their serious defection only in 1948, when the Democratic party started to identify itself firmly with the cause of civil rights. The real disgust of the white South with its traditional party came in the sixties, when John Kennedy and Lyndon Johnson were seen to be forcing integration upon the region.

Even in the sixties and seventies, though, through the Humphreys and McGoverns, most white Southerners continued to call themselves Democrats. The percentage of Republicans grew over these years, but it continued to trail far behind the Democrats. Nor was it the "Reagan Revolution," pleasing as that was to some whites in the south, that led to the largest leap in Republican identification among them. The stampede toward GOP identification occurred not during the years of Reagan's tax cuts, military buildup, or attacks on the welfare state; it occurred in 1984. The disturbing conclusion seems inescapable: the man most responsible for the white South's headlong dash away from the Democrats was not Ronald Reagan, it was Jesse Jackson.

Many Democrats are aware of this problem, and some believe the best way to deal with it is through compromise. This does not mean, in the words of Democratic National Chairman Paul G. Kirk, Jr., that Democrats will attempt to "out-Republican the Republicans," but that they will move toward the center and try to avoid identification with more militant minority-group leaders. The rejection of Gary, Indiana, Mayor Richard Hatcher's candidacy for the post of vice-chairman of the national party early in 1985 seemed to be part of this strategy. Jesse Jackson accused Democratic leaders of rejecting Hatcher as a way of "proving they can be tough on blacks."[11]

Such actions, it is sad to say, may be needed to win the support of some whites. The questions that must be asked are: Is the price too high? When does legitimate compromise become appeasement and the sacrifice of the party's basic principles? Is such compromise necessary for a Democratic victory in a national election?

There is room for differences of opinion on the first two of these questions, but it is clear that there is some point at which the price becomes unacceptably high. The more interesting question is whether it is necessary to give in at all to the racial views of some whites. It is a rather startling fact that in the *ten* presidential elections since FDR died, the Democrat won a majority of the white vote only *once* (the Johnson landslide in 1964).[12] Yet Democrats won four of those elections.

Clearly it is possible to win without a majority of whites. The question then becomes how large a minority of white votes is necessary to win a presidential election. The bottom figure is probably about 45 to 46 percent. It would be a sad commentary on the nation if we were to conclude that such a percentage of white votes could not be obtained on a platform that continues to seek racial justice. In fact a majority coalition of blacks and progressive-to-moderate whites is still well within reach not only nationwide, but also in the South. Such coalitions have elected Democrats to high offices across the South during the past decade. They produced Democratic victories in 1986 Senate races in North Carolina, Georgia, Alabama, Florida, and Louisiana. They are unlikely to succeed if race becomes the dominant issue, as it often does when the Democratic candidate is black and as it did when Jesse Jackson was so prominent during the 1984 campaign. But if racial questions are not allowed to overshadow genuine issues, southern whites are willing to join with blacks to vote for progressive candidates—if the latter are white. The reluctance of white Democrats to vote for black candidates cannot be tolerated much longer. Whites who want black support must be willing to reciprocate, and if the 1985 election in Virginia and the 1986 election in Mississippi can be taken as indicators, perhaps they are ready to do so. When race does not become the leading issue, the biracial Democrats are still favorites to win most southern elections. Maintaining that coalition is essential to the future success of Democrats in the South. It will not be easy, but it can be done.

The outcome of the 1985 statewide elections in Virginia served to hearten Democrats and demonstrate that the party can still achieve remarkable success below the Mason-Dixon Line. The popularity of outgoing Governor Charles S. Robb helped Democrats sweep to victory in what has traditionally been one of the nation's most conservative states. Robb had built his great popularity by blending fiscal conservatism with social progressivism. He launched an education program that dramatically improved the scores of Virginia students on standardized tests and he appointed many times more blacks and women to positions in state government than had his predecessors. This moderately progressive record helped Democrat Gerald L. Baliles to a ten-percentage-point victory over Republican Wyatt B. Durrette. More notable were the four-point win by L. Douglas Wilder, the black Democratic candidate for lieutenant governor, and the smashing twenty-two-point win by Mary Sue Terry in the contest for attorney general. Mr. Wilder became the first black elected to a statewide office anywhere in the South since Reconstruction, and Ms. Terry became the first woman ever to be elected to a statewide office in Virginia. The following year voters in Mississippi sent Mike Espy to Congress and elected Reuben Anderson to the state's supreme court. These were the most significant victories for blacks in the Magnolia State in this century.[13]

It is plain from the 1985 and 1986 results that the realignment in the South does not mean that the region is irretrievably lost to Democrats. It merely means that there is genuine competition where there once was a solidly Democratic South. There is not yet a Republican Solid South, and there need never be one. The South has finally rejoined the Union politically. As in the rest of the country, affluent suburban whites in the South are likely to be Republicans, while the poorer residents of their region, white as well as black, will probably vote Democratic. In the 1984 presidential election, there was *no* significant difference between the outcome in the South and that in other regions. In the South, Walter Mondale received 42 percent of the votes; in each of the other three regions, he received 41 percent.[14]

If the South has become politically like the rest of the nation, and if the political realignment has been favorable to Republicans in that region, how is it possible to argue that there is not an emerging Republican majority nationwide? It is of course true that Ronald Reagan won a landslide victory in 1984, similar to that achieved by Franklin Roosevelt in 1936, which is usually taken to have signaled the emergence of a dominant "Roosevelt Coalition" that made the Democrats the majority party for nearly half a century.

But did the 1984 election herald the construction of a similarly dominant "Reagan Coalition"? It will be several years before we can be certain, but it seems highly unlikely that any such lasting Republican majority is in the works.

The rapid shifts in party preference that polls have found in recent years do not suggest a classical or permanent realignment because those shifts have been in both directions. Party loyalty has been in a long period of decline.[15] Gone in American politics are the days such as those in the 1890s described by Walter Dean Burnham:

> Little was to be gained by attempting to convert a large "floating" or independent vote, for the good reason that almost none existed. In this period there was no popular cultural support for the "independent" voter as the man who evaluated candidates and issues on the merits and arrived at an informed decision. On the contrary, such people tended to be scorned as "traitors," "turncoats," or corrupt sellers of their votes.[16]

To paraphrase Archie Bunker: You knew who you were then, Republicans were Republicans and Democrats were Democrats.

How different it is today. Those who *do* identify with a party are the ones who are obliged to explain themselves. The "normal" thing is to say, with at least a note of disdain for those who do otherwise: "I vote for the person, not for the party." Most polls now show self-proclaimed "independents" constituting approximately one-third of the electorate, sometimes outscoring either major party. But that statistic hardly plumbs the depths of nonalignment among American voters. At least another 20 percent shift their party labels often, as they move from candidate to candidate, or as the economy rises and falls. Three decades ago, half of all Americans expressed positive feelings about one party and negative feelings about the other. Political scientist Martin Wattenberg found that by 1980 that figure had fallen to 27.3 percent. Nearly three-quarters of all Americans have no strong loyalty to either party.[17]

What this seems to mean, as political scientists have been

pointing out for years, is that it is senseless to speak of "realignment" in the current American political context. Seymour Martin Lipset stated the case simply after the 1984 election: ". . . [N]o fundamental change has occurred, other than increased volatility. . . . There is as yet no evidence of a decisive partisan realignment, the white South excepted. . . . There clearly is still no majority party."[18] "De-alignment," not realignment, has been the leitmotif of American politics in the past few decades.

De-alignment has occurred largely at the expense of the Democrats because they had held the allegiance of a majority of voters since the New Deal. But if some substantial portion of the electorate has drifted away from firm adherence to the Democratic party, few of them have formed attachments to the Republicans. There has, in short, been some backsliding among the Democratic congregation, but little in the way of conversion to another political faith. Most of those who have withdrawn from the communion of Democrats have chosen to remain politically unaffiliated, although they will cast their ballots for one denomination or another on election days. It is precisely that conversion, which has not happened in recent years but did occur during the New Deal, that is the *sine qua non* of a historic political realignment.[19]

Part of the reason for de-alignment is certainly a degree of disenchantment with Democratic policies. But the extent of this dissatisfaction has often been overestimated. Opinion surveys throughout the "conservative" era of the late seventies and early eighties showed majorities of Americans to be in agreement with basic Democratic social and defense policies. The conclusion is in fact inescapable that a substantial portion of those who cast their ballots for Ronald Reagan in 1984 did so in spite of his positions on most issues, not because of them. "The Reagan victory of 1984," Cornell political scientist Theodore J. Lowi has correctly said, "was a personal victory—broad, nationwide, but shallow."[20]

More important in the de-alignment process have been several cultural and technological changes that have reduced the power of parties in general. Television is the most obvious and important of these. It has replaced the party organization as the main conduit through which information passes from a candidate to the voters. In addition, the general growth in cynicism and distrust of government associated with Vietnam and Watergate weakened bonds to political parties as it reduced confidence in politicians. (If presidents from both parties could lie to the public as regularly as Lyndon Johnson and Richard Nixon did, it was safest not to place much confidence in either party.) The cultural emphasis on individualism in the past two decades has also taken a toll on party identification. The acquisitive individualist wants no ties to organizations, least of all those that might call upon him to *do* something for them.

Finally, the very success of liberal Democratic social programs (that's right, *success*—I do not believe that we have been "losing ground," as I shall explain in the next chapter) has undermined the perceived need for party loyalty. Former Speaker of the House Tip O'Neill is among those who have noted that many Americans have been helped so much by Democratic programs that they can now afford to be Republicans. But that tells only part of the effects of the achievements of the liberal welfare state. Its protections have come to be taken for granted—although Ronald Reagan performed a valuable service in reminding people that they have reason to be vigilant about their "safety net," lest it be shredded. Voters old enough to remember what life was like before the New Deal still appreciate what the Democratic party did for them, and members of this "FDR generation" who cast their first votes during the 1930s remain more Democratic than any other age group.[21] Many younger voters have seen no reason to take sides on the issues of the New Deal because they accept its accomplishments as part of the nature of American life. Since those issues have continued to be the center of political debate in this country for the past half century, the parties have attracted less commitment from later generations of voters.

With little historic allegiance to either party, a general distrust of politicians, a premium on individual independence, and a tendency to rely on television as a way to judge candidates, voters have in recent years bounced back and forth between the parties. If this is worse for the Democrats than the position they enjoyed when the "Roosevelt Coalition" held sway, it is also a source of opportunity. The fluid political structure is one that can flow rapidly in the Democrats' direction. In fact there is reason to believe that the Republicans reached something close to their maximum possible support in 1984, and that any significant change will favor the Democrats. One way to put this is to point out that anyone who stuck with Walter Mondale in 1984 is not easily going to be swung over to the opposition. Those with firm attachments to the GOP constitute scarcely more than one-quarter of the nation's voters. The remainder can easily be attracted back to the Democrats—or repelled by the Republicans. Such shifts are most often associated with the state of the economy. Republican allegiance reached a peak in the second half of 1981, following the Reagan tax cut, but dropped precipitously in 1982–83 as the economy declined sharply. As the public perceived the economy to be regaining its health in late 1983 and 1984, Republican support again shot upward.[22]

One conclusion to be drawn is that there is nothing wrong with the Democratic party that a Republican recession would not cure. That is true, but such economic problems are by no means essential to a Democratic resurgence. Of all the past periods of liberal reform, only one (the New Deal) occurred during a depression. An economic collapse under a Republican administration would assure the Democrats of victory in the following election, but an economic decline is not a prerequisite to Democratic success. For political as well as ethical reasons, Democrats should not be seen as waiting for hard times. By November 1988 there may be negative reasons for a majority of Americans to vote Democratic, but it is the party's responsibility in the meantime to develop positive reasons for people to support it.

If, as I shall argue in these pages, the conservative swing in the American pendulum has been reversed, the natural questions arise of why Ronald Reagan won re-election by historic proportions in 1984 and why, at least until the Iran-Contra scandal, he remained so popular in his second term. The answers are not difficult to find. The greatest reason for Mr. Reagan's 1984 landslide was the popular perception that he had improved the economy. (This notion was in many respects mistaken, but it was very widely held.) Of those who believed that the economy was "beginning a long-term recovery" (43 percent of all voters), 92 percent voted for the president, according to the *Los Angeles Times* exit poll. Of those who thought the economy was "not really getting any better" (21 percent of voters), 87 percent supported Walter Mondale. The other cause of Reagan's popularity was his personality. In this quality, no one in Washington was close to him.[23]

A likable personality will not make up for an obviously poor economy, as Reagan's party found out in the 1982 elections, but it will cover a multitude of sins. In the case of Ronald Reagan, the sins covered by a smile and an "Aw, shucks" demeanor included what was generally acknowledged to be incredible ignorance of both domestic and international affairs, numerous policies with which a majority of Americans disagreed, a startling record of poor appointments to high positions in the executive branch, a larger contribution to the national debt than the combined total of all his predecessors, and the transformation of the United States from a leading creditor nation into the world's largest debtor, to name a few.

In addition to his personality, President Reagan was the beneficiary of an extraordinary quantity of good luck. The aphorism that holds that it's better to be lucky than smart might have been written about him. Luck and good timing are important in determining the success of American presidents. Andrew Jackson, Calvin Coolidge, and Franklin Roosevelt had them; Martin Van Buren, Herbert Hoover, and Jimmy Carter did not. Hoover and Carter were the only presidents in modern history who had the misfortune of seeking re-election in a year in which the national income was shrinking. It is not coincidental that they were also the only two elected incumbents to lose re-election bids since 1912.[24]

Mr. Reagan is a great admirer of Coolidge and Roosevelt—there's an odd couple for you, about the only things they had in common were luck and good timing—but it may be that a comparison with Jackson would be most instructive in assessing Reagan's role in American political history. For while it is most doubtful that he realigned party allegiance as FDR did, it is possible that Reagan set a new pattern for successful political candidates in much the same way that Jackson did. Prior to Jackson, all presidents had come from the educated, upper-class ranks of American society: the Virginia planters and the Massachusetts Adamses. Jackson changed all that drastically. He ran as a military hero, a man with very little education, but with an image as both hero and champion of the common man. This was shocking to some of Jackson's opponents, who continued to believe that the "better sort" (that is, the qualified) ought to be entrusted with responsibility for guiding the nation. Those who opposed Jackson formed the Whig party. At first they thought that the public would reject a man as unqualified as Jackson and prefer an intelligent politician. This view was proven wrong when Jackson was re-elected over Henry Clay in 1832.

The Whigs may have learned the new style of American politics slowly, but once they mastered it they employed it to their own advantage. Although they continued to represent the interests of the upper classes, the Whigs in 1840 nominated a military "hero" of their own, William Henry Harrison. He was perfect: he had a reputation for defeating Indians that had given him a nickname reminiscent of Jackson's "Old Hickory": "Tippecanoe." Moreover, Harrison was short on ideas. Whig leaders believed that they could persuade the foolish voters to elect the man, but that the party chiefs would then be able to control him.

The first part of the plan worked, but Harrison's death a month after taking office deprived the Whig leaders of a chance to implement the second part. The Democrats had established a new pattern with Jackson, but the Whigs cynically adopted it and began to make it their own. From that point on, the Whigs and their successors, the Republicans, nominated putative military heroes with striking regularity. Whenever either the Whigs or the Republicans thought that the outcome of an election was in doubt, they simply fell back on the formula, found themselves a military man—preferably one with a "heroic" reputation and a small intellect—and presented him as their candidate. The list is an impressive one: Zachary Taylor, Winfield Scott, John C. Frémont, U. S. Grant, Rutherford B. Hayes, James A. Garfield, and Benjamin Harrison. During the period when the Republicans enjoyed a solid national majority, between 1894 and 1930, this was unnecessary. But after the Democrats established themselves as the majority party, the Republicans fell back on the old formula one more time, turning to Dwight Eisenhower in 1952.

There have not been very many military heroes in recent American history, and it may be that the revolutionary effects of television have caused a fundamental alteration in American politics on a scale similar to that of the rise of the "common man" in Jackson's day. If this is so, perhaps Ronald Reagan will be the Republicans' Andrew Jackson: a symbolic leader with little of substance between his ears, the common man's hero, but now a celluloid rather than a military one.

Assuming for a moment that this may be the case, two questions presented themselves in Ronald Reagan's second term: Would George Bush play Martin Van Buren to Reagan's Jackson? And would the Democrats, like the Whigs in 1840, be tempted cynically to imitate the successful formula of their opponents? After the 1984 election, Walter Mondale's chief speech writer, Martin Kaplan, said that there were only two candidates who could have beaten President Reagan: Robert Redford and Walter Cronkite.[25]

Should the Democrats conclude not only that this was the case in 1984, but that it represents a permanent shift in the path to victory in American politics, their ideal candidates for a future national election would become obvious. How could the Republicans hope to match a Paul Newman–Meryl Streep ticket?

Whatever the merits of the Reagan-as-Jackson analysis, creating a new type of presidential candidate does not necessarily lead to realignment. Jackson's luck held out to the end of his second term, and the depression that resulted in substantial measure from his own ill-considered policies hit only after the hapless Van Buren assumed the presidency. The panic of 1837 ended whatever prospect there was for a "Jackson Coalition" making the Democrats a lasting majority.

There have been three genuine realignments in American politics since the Jackson Coalition failed to establish itself as dominant: in the 1860s, the 1890s, and the 1930s.

In the late 1850s and early 1860s, the new Republican party gained majority status in the North and essential parity with the Democrats nationally. Because of, first, the South's absence from Washington during the Civil War, and then the impediments the Democrats faced in the South during Reconstruction, the Republicans were able to maintain control throughout this period. In 1858 the Republicans (aided by another economic crisis, the panic of 1857) gained control of the House of Representatives and kept it for sixteen years. The twenty years after 1874 saw near-equality between the parties, and control of the House passed back and forth between them. In 1894 the Republicans won a solid majority of congressional seats and maintained control for sixteen more years. With minor exceptions, the Republican dominance that began in 1894 lasted until 1930. In that year, the Democrats regained a House majority, which they kept until 1946.[26] The Democratic majority that began in 1930 lasted until at least the 1980s.

The most recent realignment is plainly the one that enjoyed the greatest longevity. Since the majority that was built in the 1930s is often called the Roosevelt Coalition, it is natural to place great sig-

nificance on the power of FDR's personality in this historic transformation of American politics. And if the force of personality is the
key to partisan realignment, it would seem to follow that a politician
with Ronald Reagan's personal charm would make a likely architect
for a new majority coalition.

This is one of the reasons that so many people have been fasci-
nated by comparisons of Roosevelt and Reagan. Reagan himself
strove to get all the mileage he could out of identifying himself with
FDR. A *New York Times* editorial entitled "Franklin Delano Reagan" early in the 1980 campaign said Reagan was trying "to kidnap
Franklin Roosevelt."[27] Although he usually denied it because it was
politically embarrassing to him in later years, Reagan did admit to
having been "a very emotional New Dealer."[28] His admiration for
FDR was so large that Reagan did impersonations of the New Deal
hero and based his own political speaking style on Roosevelt's.[29]

It is clear that in terms of policy Reagan became almost the opposite of what Roosevelt (or, for that matter, Reagan himself) was in
the 1930s. Roosevelt's appeal was to the sort of people who rode in
boxcars; Reagan's was more to those who get around in Lear jets.
Even while Reagan was praising Roosevelt, he was attempting to
undo as much of the New Deal as Congress and the public would
permit him to. FDR biographer Frank Freidel has complained that
the New Deal president "should not be transformed into a Ronald
Roosevelt."[30]

Despite the great differences in the objectives of the two men,
there are important similarities between them. The most obvious
ones are in the area of personality. Both presidents had a quick smile
and a pleasant air about them. People liked Roosevelt, as they did
Reagan, almost without regard to his policies. Reagan's style, veteran reporter Lou Cannon has noted, "remained frankly and fer-
vently Rooseveltian throughout his life." David McCullough has
said that Reagan "sees Roosevelt as his 'kind of guy'—confident,
cheerful, theatrical, larger than life."[31]

Both men led charmed political lives, in which they were
praised for everything people liked, while the blame for all problems
fell on others. FDR was a "Teflon president" long before Teflon
was invented. After Roosevelt had won re-election to a second term,
he had the temerity to point out that "one-third of a nation" was
"ill-housed, ill-clad, ill-nourished." And in his re-election campaign
in 1984, Reagan continued to run against the "gov-mint," as he dis-

dainfully pronounced it, even after having been in charge of it for nearly four years. And Franklin Roosevelt was the first "media president," clearly deserving of the title "Great Communicator." He charmed radio listeners much as Reagan did his television audiences.

The stylistic similarities between Roosevelt and Reagan are large, and it is understandable that many observers have concluded that Reagan might be able to reshape American politics to the same extent that FDR did. "Like FDR," the *Wall Street Journal* contended in 1986, "Ronald Reagan is remolding the country's primary institutions and the principles of its economic life." The same year, *Time* suggested that "just as Franklin Roosevelt's ideas set the style that would dominate the next four decades of American politics," Reagan's policies might be doing the same.[32] But three factors make this most unlikely. The first two are fundamental differences between Roosevelt and Reagan. The third and most important is that personality has never been the decisive cause of a major political realignment.

Beneath the similar exteriors of Roosevelt and Reagan were two vastly different creatures. FDR was a pragmatist. He had general social and political goals toward which he worked, but he was decidedly nonideological. His lack of a coherent ideology made it easy for him to ride above criticism of his policies and advisers. Reagan also demonstrated a remarkable knack for letting his aides take the blame for blunders and for getting away with rapid foot-shuffling on unpopular policies, although his feet began to slow when the Iran arms deal became known. But Reagan, unlike Roosevelt, was at heart an ideologue. This put him at odds with the spirit of most Americans.

Ronald Reagan's ideology points up the second critical difference between Roosevelt and him. Reagan's antigovernment rhetoric was popular—so long as it was confined to rhetoric. In practice, most Americans reject the social Darwinism that the Reaganites espouse. The consequences of Franklin Roosevelt's programs were beneficial to a majority of Americans. There is much reason to doubt that the same will ultimately be said of the Reagan program. People may have liked Reagan's style almost as much as they liked Roosevelt's, but they did not agree nearly as much with his policies. Roosevelt offered the people a New Deal; Reagan's program might better be labeled the Raw Deal. One significant indication that Reagan's policies were not nearly as popular as Roosevelt's was Rea-

gan's failure to attract more voters to the polls. The accomplishments of Roosevelt's first term led some 7 million more voters to
cast ballots in 1936 than had in 1932. In sharp contrast, Reagan's
first term prompted scarcely any increase in the percentage of
Americans who chose to vote between 1980 and 1984.[33]

The final and most important reason why the Roosevelt analogy
does not mean that Reagan's presidency will result in a political realignment is that historic realignment does not occur as a result of
the personal impact of leaders alone. It certainly is not defined
merely by victories in presidential elections. Rather, a fundamental
realignment is marked by the massive conversion of voters from one
party to another. This simply did not happen in the Reagan years.
As the Roosevelt realignment took place between 1930 and 1936,
the Democrats gained House seats in each election: fifty-three in
1930, ninety-seven in 1932, nine in 1934, and eleven in 1936. A
comparison of these figures with those for the corresponding years
of the supposed conservative realignment ought to be sobering for
those intoxicated by the prospect of an emerging Republican majority. In 1978 the GOP gained eleven seats in the House. When Reagan was elected in 1980, his party picked up thirty-three seats. But
then it *lost* twenty-six in 1982 and regained a scant fourteen in the
Reagan landslide of 1984.[34] So the comparison of the four corresponding elections yields the following figures: Election I (1930,
1978): Roosevelt-era Democrats enjoyed a forty-two-seat advantage
over Reagan-era Republicans; Election II (1932, 1980): Democrats
plus sixty-four; Election III (1934, 1982): Democrats plus thirty-
five; Election IV (1936, 1984): Democrats minus three. The "bottom line" is that after eight years of "realignment" the Democrats
of the Roosevelt era had gained *138 more* seats than had the Reagan-era Republicans.

But, it might be protested, such a comparison is not fair. The
"Roosevelt" realignment began two years before Roosevelt was first
elected, and it clearly resulted from voter reaction against the party
in power when the Great Depression began. The Republicans in the
1980s had no such depression to help them win over voters. Just so.
That is precisely why the GOP is so unlikely to achieve a decisive
realignment.

External conditions are far more important than dynamic leadership in producing a major partisan shift. For all his charisma,
Roosevelt alone could not have manufactured the massive swing to

the Democratic party that took place in the 1930s. It was quite clearly the Depression that destroyed the public's faith in the Republicans and gave FDR an opportunity to build the "Roosevelt Coalition."

All three of the major partisan realignments since the days of Andrew Jackson were precipitated by immense crises: the conflict over slavery and sectionalism leading to the Civil War, the Panic of 1893, and the Great Depression. The decisive role external events play in bringing about realignment is clear when the political efforts of the two largest depressions in American history are examined.

The Democrats had just emerged from a long period of rough balance between the parties to win control of the presidency and both houses of Congress in 1892. This was the first time since the end of Reconstruction that either party had enjoyed undiluted control of the government. The Democrats' joy was short-lived, though. When the Panic of 1893—the worst depression America had yet experienced—struck, the Democrats absorbed the full blame. Even more House seats shifted party hands in 1894 than did in the other direction in 1932. As the people's anger and frustration turned against the Democrats, their president became the principal target. "I was a child of four during the Panic of '93," Walter Lippmann later recalled, "and [Grover] Cleveland has always been a sinister figure to me. His name was uttered with monstrous dread in the household. . . . And to this day I find myself with a subtle prejudice against Democrats that goes deeper than what we call political conviction."[35]

Grover Cleveland had perfected the part of national scapegoat long before Herbert Hoover replaced him as America's leading villain. Hoover as a Republican did more than any Democrat, save perhaps FDR, to make the Democrats a lasting majority. Russell Baker has recalled what his aunt told him in 1932: "People were starving because of Herbert Hoover. My mother was out of work because of Herbert Hoover. Men were killing themselves because of Herbert Hoover . . . " and so forth.[36] Franklin Roosevelt found it more congenial to run against the specter of Hoover than against his actual opponents in 1936 and subsequent elections. "We ought to be eternally grateful to Herbert Hoover, who has been our meal ticket for twelve years," New Dealer Tommy Corcoran told a Democratic meeting in 1944.[37]

Obviously Franklin Roosevelt's personality and programs were very important in the construction of a lasting Democratic majority. But realignments begin as negative, not positive, movements. They start as reactions against the party in power at the time of a national catastrophe. The presidential election of 1896 marked the beginning of more than three decades of Republican ascendancy, just as the presidential election of 1932 opened at least half a century of Democratic dominance. We speak easily enough of the "Roosevelt Coalition," but when was the last time you heard anyone mention the "McKinley Coalition"?

It might be more accurate to name the majorities resulting from historic realignments after those who became the symbols of what the majority rejected: the "anti–Jefferson Davis Coalition," the "anti-Cleveland Coalition," and the "anti-Hoover Coalition." Certainly Republicans after the Civil War identified themselves with Lincoln just as much as Democrats after the New Deal did with FDR, but they found more political advantage in reminding voters that the Democrats were the party of the rebellion, as mid-twentieth-century Democrats did by recalling that the Republicans were the party of the Depression.

The importance of economic depressions in this process may be even greater than has so far been indicated. In addition to the obvious role of the panics of 1893 and 1929, three earlier economic depressions came at crucial times in partisan shifts. The panic of 1837 nipped the Jackson coalition in the bud and the Whigs won the next election. The panic of 1857 joined with the sectional crisis to bring about a Republican congressional victory in 1858 and Lincoln's election in 1860. And the panic of 1873 may have had as much as the decline of Reconstruction to do with the ending of Republican hegemony in the mid-1870s, when the Democrats won the House in 1874 and Samuel Tilden had the presidential election of 1876 stolen from him. While it would be going too far to speak of lasting "anti-Van Buren," "anti-Buchanan," or "anti-Grant" coalitions, just such negative groupings were important in the years immediately following the economic depressions that occurred in the administrations of these presidents.

Surely there was in the late 1970s and early 1980s nothing similar to the Civil War or the depressions of the 1890s and 1930s to serve as the catalyst for an historic political realignment. Whatever Ronald Reagan's personal political magic, he had less with which to work in attempting to turn voters against the opposing party than did the molders of the emerging majorities of the 1860s, 1890s, or 1930s. Lacking such a catastrophe, the Republicans tried the next best thing and worked to convince the American people that everything was awful before Mr. Reagan took office in 1981. They have, in short, tried to "Hooverize" Jimmy Carter. What they hoped to build was not so much a "Reagan Coalition" as an "anti-Carter Coalition."

"Carter" doesn't look like a four-letter word, but for several years Republicans have been using it as one, and many Democrats cringe when the word is mentioned in polite company. The main GOP strategy in the 1984 campaign was to try to persuade voters that former Vice-President Mondale's first name was Carter, as in the "Carter Mondale administration," the "Carter Mondale grain embargo," the "Carter Mondale Olympic boycott," the "Carter Mondale hostage crisis," and so on. Many Americans may not have remembered clearly when Carter F. ("Fritz") Mondale was president, but as best they could recall, they weren't very happy.

All of this was terribly unfair to Jimmy Carter. He did not have Reagan's good luck or acting ability, but his substantive record in most areas compares favorably with Reagan's.

As Ronald Reagan knew, though, reality counts for little in politics. Impressions are almost everything, and in aiming for the public perceptions the Republicans desired, Jimmy Carter was the best ammunition available. Such is usually the case in modern negative campaigning. Barry Goldwater was the Democrats' greatest asset in 1964, and Lyndon Johnson was the same to the Republicans four years later. George McGovern and Richard Nixon were similarly useful to the opposing parties in 1972 and 1976. But in those cases the negative memories lasted for fairly short periods. If the Republicans can promote the Carter-as-Hoover myth sufficiently, they will have a banner they can wave at the Democrats for many years to come. They hope to create the impression that the "malaise" of the Carter years was something as horrible as the depressions that produced the last two major realignments. This Republican effort has succeeded with some people. "Since Carter left," a high-school senior in Indiana told David Broder in 1985, "it just seems like people feel better about themselves."[38] The Republicans desperately want us to believe that Ronald Reagan rescued the nation from a Carter disaster on the scale of the Great Depression. Should they manage to instill this false impression, they would have the raw material out of which a realignment might yet be assembled. They also, of course, possess in Ronald Reagan a personality and media manipulator capable of assisting greatly in the building project.

It seems more plausible to think that Carter will wind up having served a purpose for his political opponents on the level of a Van Buren or Grant (that is, providing a short-term advantage for the other party) than on the grand scale of Hoover. Indeed, a mid-1985 *Washington Post*/ABC News poll found that Carter had a remarkable 55 percent approval rating. Republican pollsters found just before the 1986 elections that most voters were unsympathetic to attacks on the former president. And voters in Idaho, Oregon, and Washington elected three former Carter cabinet members to statewide offices in 1986. Reagan's foul-up in Iran seemed to complete the rehabilitation of Carter's reputation. A December 1986 *Wall Street Journal*/NBC News poll found that twice as many Americans approved of Carter's Iranian policies as approved of Reagan's.[39] But even if the Republicans had been able to continue to employ Carter as their new "bloody shirt," they would have still faced serious, probably insurmountable, problems in trying to become the majority party.

Most important is that Reagan did not have an opportunity to put his program into effect. Since no genuine crisis preceded his election, his party was not able to seize complete control of the government, as the Republicans did in the 1890s and the Democrats did in the 1930s. The Reagan years have certainly seen important changes, but these were insufficient to produce the sort of fundamental alterations in American society undertaken in the New Deal years.[40] Without such changes, the public has little incentive to flock to the Republican ranks.

The second impediment to the creation of a Republican majority, even if the party is able to continue to tar its opponents with the supposed "Carter malaise," is that the GOP policies are neither very popular nor widely beneficial. Convincing voters that the other party brought on disaster will take the Republicans only so far. They must then persuade people that their party offers the better alternative. They may have the mason for the raising of a new Republican majority, and they may be able to make illusory bricks by Carter-bashing, but it is highly doubtful that they have the mortar.

Americans do not normally support extremists. Ronald Reagan was an exception to this rule because he was an extremist who did not seem like one. He was an extremist trained in acting and garbed in the clothing of a moderate. Without him, the Republican alliance between traditional conservatives and New Right ideologues may unravel rapidly. Without Reagan to mask their fangs, the extremists who joined him may lose for the Republican party millions of potential supporters. This possibility has struck fear into the hearts of moderate Republicans. (Yes, there are still such creatures extant, although they are clearly an endangered species.)[41]

The Reagan Coalition is an inherently unstable isotope (albeit no less stable than some of the combinations that composed the Roosevelt Coalition, such as blacks and white southerners). How long can full-fledged libertarians and traditional conservative businessmen who desire government assistance for themselves, if not for the poor, remain under the same roof with each other, much less with the Moral Majority types?[42]

The more fanatical element within the Republican party mistakenly believed that the voters in 1984 gave a mandate for their extremist programs. In fact, most of those who voted for Ronald Reagan were not thereby indicating that they wanted to turn Yellowstone over to Exxon and Yosemite to Walt Disney Enterprises, to return all women to the barefoot and pregnant status, to make Jesse Helms secretary of state, Dr. Strangelove national security adviser, Phyllis Schlafly secretary of health and human services, and Jimmy Swaggart chief justice of the Supreme Court, to pass a Social Darwinism Amendment to the Constitution, or any of the other pet projects of the lunatic right fringe. They were merely voting for prosperity and a smiling, pleasant seventy-three-year-old man.

The Reagan administration, however, began to fall victim to what Kevin Phillips has called "mandate hubris,"[43] a common malady in our political history. The record of American presidents who have won landslide victories in this century ought to have given the Reaganites pause. Warren Harding won 60.4 percent of the votes in 1920, but was neck deep in scandal when he died less than three years later. Franklin Roosevelt was endorsed by 60.8 percent of those who voted in 1936, but promptly lost much of his mandate by trying to "pack" the Supreme Court a few months later. In 1964 Lyndon Johnson crushed Barry Goldwater by taking 61.1 percent of the ballots, but he soon was so hated by a substantial portion of his countrymen for his escalation of the Vietnam War that he was unable even to stand for re-election in 1968. In 1972 Richard Nixon swept to a 60.7 percent majority, only to resign in disgrace in order to avoid impeachment less than two years later. Ronald Reagan's 58.8 percent of the popular votes in 1984 gave him the fifth-largest landslide in the twentieth century. And mandate hubris soon led Reagan and his aides into the arrogance that produced the Iran-Contra scandal.

Neither the external conditions nor the party's internal makeup and policies in the mid-eighties pointed toward a Republican realignment. Great popular victories do not necessarily constitute endorsements of party or program. Such landslides have sometimes preceded a party's loss of the presidency four years later, as was the case with Eisenhower's in 1956 (when he won 57.6 percent of the popular vote, nearly as much as Reagan did in 1984), Johnson's in 1964, and Nixon's in 1972.

The opportunity for realignment comes from highly negative external circumstances. The first reaction to serious trouble is to "throw the rascals out." In rejecting their old party after a bad experience, voters enter a sort of trial separation. If the newly favored party does a good job of wooing (and of pointing out the faults of the rejected mate), it may achieve a betrothal in the next presidential election, but consummation of the marriage requires a positive act. That has yet to occur in the current Republican courtship of the American voter. Ronald Reagan was a glamorous leading man with a great ability to whisper sweet nothings into the ears of the American people, but with him no longer the suitor, the electorate will want to know why it should maintain the liaison with his heirs.

Though handsomer than many of our presidents, William McKinley was no matinee idol. It is clear that the people who backed him in 1896 were voting out the party of that rascal Grover Cleveland, whom they believed had brought on a depression. The fact that McKinley's policies were much closer to Cleveland's than were those of his opponent, William Jennings Bryan, was of less importance to most voters than that Bryan belonged to the same party as Cleveland. Still, the time was ripening at the turn of the century for a new burst of reform. McKinley's policies would not have remained popular for long after 1900. Viewed from a long-term perspective, it was the Republicans' singular good fortune that just as the mood of the country was swinging away from conservatism and toward activism, McKinley was assassinated and replaced by Theodore Roosevelt, a man who was willing to join the people in their march into progressive reform. It was only by identifying the GOP with progressive policies that Roosevelt was able to confirm the realignment begun by the voters' rejection of the "Cleveland depression" in 1894 and 1896. This is another reason, along with McKinley's lack of stature, that we rarely hear of a "McKinley Coalition."

The Republicans were able to keep their majority status most of the time from 1894 to 1930 only because they shifted identities along with the public mood. Teddy Roosevelt gave them a progressive image when that was popular, but by 1920 the party had reverted to conservatism (actually many Republicans had never left it, but Roosevelt and a group of midwestern insurgents made it seem as if the party had) in time to reap the harvest of the post–World War I reaction.

If Americans in the mid-to-late 1980s were moving back toward a desire for active government, the Republicans' only hope to become the majority party was to make themselves appear progressive. That would be a tall order even for such a skillful political thespian as Ronald Reagan. It looked impossible for the nonprofessional actors in the party. George Bush, after all, was no Teddy Roosevelt. No one ever accused TR of placing his manhood in a blind trust.

A shift of the Republican party in a progressive direction, under the leadership of someone like Governor Thomas Kean of New Jersey, is possible, though highly improbable. Such a shift is the only hope the GOP has of gaining the ascendancy in the 1990s. If the Republicans remain under the dominance of the New Right, it is very likely that the United States will be led in the next decade by progressive Democrats.

CHAPTER 2

Keeping
the Faith

We made a promise we swore we'd always remember
no retreat no surrender
Like soldiers in the winter's night with
a vow to defend, no retreat no surrender
—BRUCE SPRINGSTEEN (1984)

To search for perfection is all very well
But to look for heaven is to live here in hell
—STING (1985)

" 'Liberal' is no longer a dirty word," proclaimed a *New York Times* editorial the day after the Democrats' good showing in the 1982 midterm elections.[1] Two years later many people—including a significant number of liberals—had to wonder if that assessment was correct. But if the Democrats seemed dead in November of 1984, they soon proved that they still had sufficient breath left in them to dig themselves a deeper grave.

In February 1985 the party's televised response to President Reagan's State of the Union address said to the American people—or that small fraction thereof that was tuned in—in so many words, "We don't know how to govern and we don't know what to do, so you tell us what you want us to do. We are listening."[2] That looked like the bottom, but worse was yet to come. A month later the Dem-

36

ocrats' Good Friday arrived. Members of the party's congressional delegation gathered at a West Virginia resort and listened to a group of "motivational experts" pronounce such pearls of wisdom as "It's in to be in and it's out to be out."[3]

This slogan may sound unarguable to some, especially Republicans, but it is actually the most dangerous prescription that the Democratic party could receive. An attempt to get "in" for no other purpose than to *be* in would amount to a complete sacrifice of principle. Moreover, it is the surest way to continue Democratic defeats. It would be folly for the Democrats to move closer to conservative, Republican positions. In a widely quoted speech at Hofstra University early in 1985, Senator Edward M. Kennedy called upon his party to "reclaim our rightful role, at the center of American politics." "We cannot move forward," he declared, "by running constantly to the right or to the left. . . . The answer is simply not more dollars and more spending." A few weeks earlier Senator Gary Hart told an audience at Faneuil Hall in Boston that the Democrats' "past achievements are not a cathedral in which to worship. . . . The party of change must change."[4]

Fine. But it is easy to push this worthy notion too far. Change is essential in a dynamic society, but that change should not be a cynical move toward what appears to be popular at the moment. (In fairness it should be noted that that is not what Senator Hart was suggesting.) New methods certainly ought to be explored, but Democrats would be ill-advised to alter their basic principles. Journalists and political pundits are notoriously overeager undertakers. They have buried the Republicans so many times that the GOP finally decided to appeal to the "born again" element in the electorate.

When the Republicans were pronounced dead in the 1960s, they did not move toward Democratic positions but away from them. They wound up winning four of the next five presidential elections. The year 1984 was the high tide of conservatism, as 1964 was of liberalism. It would be a tragic error for the Democrats to join the tide that is ebbing, rather than the one that is coming in.

There is no way to pretend that the terrible defeat the party suffered in 1984 was a good thing for the Democrats. But there is sometimes a good side to political banishment. It provides a time for the party out of power to re-examine its policies and redesign its approaches to make them more effective. This does not mean that the leaders of the opposition party alter their values or principles (although they ought to take the opportunity to reconsider them), but that they seek new and better means to reach their traditional ends. Being out of power also gives the rising stars of a party a great opportunity. The candidate who will resurrect the Democrats will be the one who does what Franklin D. Roosevelt did in the 1920s: resist the conservative flow, stake out a position as the leader of progressivism, develop new methods to achieve liberal goals, and wait for the next change in public mood to catch up with him and carry him into the White House. (I employ the masculine pronoun for stylistic purposes, not to exclude the possibility that such a progressive Democrat might be a woman.) Those Democrats who try to compete with the Republicans on their own conservative ground are doomed to failure. You can't out-Reagan Reagan.

The wise course is to do as FDR did in the twenties—and, from the other side, Richard Nixon did in the sixties—establish a position on the side of center toward which the party must go if it is to regain power. "Hamiltons we have today," Franklin Roosevelt wrote in 1925. "Is a Jefferson on the horizon?"[5] It is a question worth repeating six decades later.

"What future is there," TRB pointedly asked in the *New Republic* in 1985, "in the slogan, 'We're just like the Republicans, only less so'?"[6] Democrats who may be tempted to move in this direction would do well to inquire of Alf Landon where the mirror image of that stance got him in 1936. Or they might ask Richard Nixon—admittedly not an unimpeachable source—what his "I agree with Senator Kennedy on that" statements in the 1960 debates did for his candidacy.

New York Governor Mario Cuomo has seemed less willing than some other Democratic leaders to alter the party's progressive principles. He said in a speech at Yale early in 1985:

> It seems to me there comes a point where the eagerness to change can become an intent to pander . . . an intent not to lead, but simply to win. The unfortunate fact for those of us who prefer winning is that what is right is sometimes not popular, or at least not likely to get you elected; that sometimes the price of saying what you believe is to be rejected.

While acknowledging how the party's 1984 defeat had "created the temptation to be silent, to accept the victor's version of the truth,"

Governor Cuomo said that "even if all the pundits said that it was prudent to forget—that to deny these principles was the price of popularity—I would prefer to remember." "The principles I believe in," he declared, "are working, so I don't see any reason for abandoning them simply because the Republican candidate won the presidential election."[7] Mario Cuomo was putting in his bid to be the Jefferson on the horizon in the eighties, as Franklin Roosevelt had in the twenties.

In fact, even while the leading Democrats talked about the need for "new ideas," most of them were still keeping the liberal faith, though they often sought to avoid the "liberal" label. In his Boston speech, Hart endorsed "one of the purest old ideas," the belief that "society as a whole, through our government, has a moral responsibility . . . to achieve real justice . . . and assure the basic necessities of life."[8] The suspicion is hard to avoid that Senator Kennedy was also engaged in the venerable political practice of placing old wine in new bottles. This is a proven formula for success in American politics.

Americans are paradoxical. They love both the old and the new. One of the bases of Ronald Reagan's appeal has been his ability to identify himself with both tradition and innovation. A successful Democrat will have to find ways to do this, too. Liberals should point out that their principles are as old as the Ten Commandments and the Sermon on the Mount at the same time that they are calling them new.

Leading Democrats in the late eighties and nineties should do their best to identify themselves with "newness" while they are emphasizing "family" and "community" themes, with all their traditional connotations. Democrats have been saddled with the image of being tied to the past. That public perception is mostly, albeit not entirely, unjustified, but it must be broken if they are to win back the presidency.

Despite the aforementioned 1982 *Times* editorial, many Americans in the 1980s continued to think that "liberal" was a dirty word. Most politicians in the 1980s would much prefer to have the marital status of their parents questioned than be publicly called the L-word.[9] This was no overnight development. The term began to fall into disrepute at the height of liberalism's last period of success, the 1960s. Nor was this entirely the doing of conservatives. By the late sixties, many on the left, disgusted with the Vietnam War and impatient with the pace of social progress, were castigating liberals. Liberalism was not the victim of right-wing death squads; it committed suicide.

This should not have been wholly surprising. Liberals are by their nature susceptible to self-criticism and self-doubt. Unlike their opponents on both the right and the far left, liberals do not practice a "politics of certainty." Liberalism (if not always those who call themselves liberals) is tolerant. The liberal creed is one of open inquiry and of compassionate, pragmatic idealism. As such, it is close to the paradoxical basic beliefs of most Americans. "The spirit of liberty is the spirit which is not too sure that it is right," said Judge Learned Hand. "The spirit of liberty is the spirit which seeks to understand the minds of other men and women. The spirit of liberty is the spirit which weighs their interests alongside its own without bias."[10] "Liberalism," Milton Viorst wrote in 1963, "glories in the free play of ideas; the extremist deplores dissent. The liberal is constantly searching for new ways to meet new problems; the doctrinaire has a fixed dogma that provides the answers to all problems."[11] But because liberals do not claim to have all the answers, because they are not certain, because they admit that there might be better ways of doing things, they leave themselves open to attack by those who think they *do* have all the answers.

The preceding paragraph may give the impression that liberals do not believe in anything—or that they don't know what it is they believe in. This is not at all the case. Liberals have always had general goals that have defined who they are. These are summed up in such admittedly amorphous terms as "the common good." That has always been the liberal objective, from Thomas Jefferson's day to our own.

But throughout American history there has been much confusion over the meaning of "liberal." In the nineteenth century liberals generally agreed with the Jeffersonian concept that holds that "that government is best which governs least." If this belief were taken to define a "liberal" in the second half of the twentieth century, Ronald Reagan would have been one of America's leading liberals. But to the Jeffersonian, laissez-faire was not the goal of liberalism, it was merely a means to achieve the objective of the common good. The experience of Americans in the second half of the eighteenth century led them to see government as the primary threat to liberty and equality. This was true enough, since the oppressive government with which they were dealing in Great Britain was a blend of monarchy and aristocracy.

The notion that government was the principal enemy continued to guide liberals through most of the nineteenth century. They contended that all an individual needed was "a free field and no favor." Perhaps that was not too far from the truth for those who owned productive property and so were reasonably independent. But as the century progressed a growing percentage of Americans owned no productive property and so became dependent on others for employment. Under these circumstances, as industrialism swept across much of the country, liberals slowly began to realize that laissez-faire was not producing their goal. Rather, it seemed that the unfettered marketplace was yielding the greatest good for the smallest number.

Nor was government any longer the only potential oppressor. Great aggregations of capital seemed a more immediate threat to the common good than did possible abuses of government power. By the 1890s liberals were coming to understand that many of the fears of government developed under monarchy and aristocracy need no longer apply under a democratic government. In a democracy, liberals reasoned, government ought to be an instrument of the people, not their enemy. So during the Progressive era of the early twentieth century liberals underwent a 180-degree turn in their methods.

Conservatives, in the meantime, had seen that laissez-faire actually produced the sort of advantages for the few that had always been their goal. They therefore abandoned their Hamiltonian reliance on big government and began preaching the "natural" economy of the free market. Gleefully adopting the creed of social Darwinism, they argued that humankind is at the mercy of natural forces, forces with which we tamper at great risk. The only sensible approach was to let the natural forces proceed, determining who was "fit" and who "unfit." Economics, like biology, they said, is a science. Both might appear under Darwinian concepts to be rather dismal sciences, but in any case there is no room in a science for morality.

Liberals at the turn of the present century were also impressed with the accomplishments of scientists, but they took science in a different direction. If we could understand the workings of nature and begin to harness it for our own benefit, could not the same be done with society and the economy? If humans were prepared to intervene where the hand of Mother Nature had previously gone unchallenged, why should they allow the "invisible hand" of Adam Smith to control the economy without human guidance? Social scientists ought to be able to do in society what natural scientists seemed to be doing in their realm: discover the ways in which things operate, and "engineer" improvements.

To achieve this we needed an active government, committed to social betterment, headed by a charismatic leader who could inspire and mobilize the people to demand more from their government, and who could then place experts in charge of programs designed to promote the common good. The prototype of this active, committed liberal leader was Theodore Roosevelt.[12]

Liberals in twentieth-century America did not alter their fundamental goals; rather, they recognized that conditions had changed from the pre-industrial world and that the old methods were no longer working. Anything powerful enough to ameliorate great social ills is also powerful enough to be dangerous, and most liberals never lost sight of the potential for evil in big government. They have consistently opposed government power in matters of personal and political belief. Liberals are not unconcerned with economic liberty, but they have come to believe that the common good requires that social justice be given a higher priority than absolute economic freedom. Conservatives are—and always have been—on the other side of both questions. They are much more prone than liberals to limiting personal and political liberties, but they place the freedom of an individual to do as he pleases in the economic realm at the top of their concerns.[13] Social justice has held a lower priority for conservatives, from the days of Alexander Hamilton when they favored strong government as a means of protecting their economic privileges to the days of Ronald Reagan when they see government as an instrument of social justice and therefore as a threat to their economic position.

Conservatives and liberals have in this century traded means, but the ends they seek have remained consistent.

Liberalism in its finest sense understands that we live in an imperfect world. Marxists look forward to a state-controlled utopia, followed by the "withering away of the state." Right-wing ideolo-

gues believe that the state should be abolished first, and *then* a utopia brought about by the "Glorious Free Market" will ensue. Liberals have no such illusions. They know that the millennium is not
coming, not under Ronald Reagan or Daniel Ortega, not under the
Ayatollah Khomeini or Jerry Falwell, and not under the next liberal
Democratic president. The millennium is not coming, liberals
know, in 1988, in 1992 or—except on the calendar—in 2000. It is
not coming ever.

At its best, liberalism is a *mature* approach to social problems. It
realizes that there are no easy or permanent solutions, and the final
victory over all such problems will never be won. But liberals try not
to let that realization deter them. The struggle must be carried on,
anyway. We cannot make society perfect, but we can make it *better*.
That is our obligation. We should be proud of our past achievements, but we must never be satisfied with them. And we must
never delude ourselves into thinking that we are going to solve
everything. The process of maturation does not require one to abandon ideals, but to lower expectations somewhat.

Liberals do have a vision of a better society, one based on realism, reasonableness, and responsibility. They believe in cooperation,
community, conscience, and compassion. In his first inaugural address, Franklin Roosevelt condemned "a generation of self-seekers"
and called for "values more noble than mere monetary profit." "We
cannot merely take," he declared, "but we must give as well."[14]
This belief was at the core of the New Deal, and it remains a guiding principle of liberalism today.

Roosevelt's New Deal defined liberalism for more than half a
century. In the simplest terms, the New Deal represented the acceptance by the federal government of society's responsibility to aid
those who were unable to provide for themselves either because of
personal incapacity or the failure of the economy to create a sufficient number of jobs. It meant that the nation no longer would
completely stigmatize the individual victim of poverty and unemployment. The New Deal also committed the government to intervene in a positive way to try to make up for the inadequacies of the
marketplace and to protect the innocent from the mistakes of the
economy. (Arch-conservatives such as President Reagan would insist
that there *are* no inadequacies in the marketplace and that a free
economy *makes* no mistakes.) In short, the acceptance of the New
Deal indicated that the American people had finally decided that

moral considerations should have a place in the economy, that intervention in the economic process could be beneficial, and that we need not resignedly accept whatever happens as if it were dictated by the gods.

The belief that the economy should work on moral as well as economic principles continues to distinguish liberals from their opponents on both the right and the far left. Both those groups believe in their different ways that morality is irrelevant in economics. It is clear that the American people have long endorsed the idea that morality should play a part in the economy, as they have indicated by keeping the Democrats in control of Congress for most of the time since the New Deal, and as they continue to indicate by favoring social programs when they are asked about them in opinion surveys.

In the 1960s, Lyndon Johnson sought to outdo the hero of his youth, FDR. His goal was to complete the New Deal, not to escape its limits. Since Johnson's heyday, however, discontent with the No-Longer-New Deal has grown. Right-wingers in the eighties made much political capital out of lashing at liberals for being "out of step with the times" and practicing "antique politics of a bygone era." Liberals who thought that they had come up with few "new ideas" since the thirties—or at least since the sixties—and that many social problems remained unsolved, were too quick to accept such criticism. The policies of FDR and LBJ may be early antiques, but if so how then are we to label those of Calvin Coolidge, William McKinley, or Alexander Hamilton? The right-wing "supply-side" nostrums are so antique that they seemed new to everyone younger than Ronald Reagan.

But it was not the Reaganites who undermined confidence in liberalism. Self-doubt, arising in large part from the Vietnam War, had gripped liberals in the Johnson and Nixon years. Liberals were in disorderly retreat during the Carter administration. By the time Ronald Reagan proclaimed in his first inaugural address that "Government is not the solution to our problems . . . Government is the problem,"[15] many liberals were too tired and disillusioned to disagree.

With the liberal ranks thinned by desertion, the Reaganites had the battlefield to themselvs in the early 1980s. A new orthodoxy emerged in agreement with Reagan's conception of government as the problem. (Had not the government under two successive administrations, of different parties, repeatedly lied to us? Had not the government fought a seemingly endless war on the other side of the planet, at great cost in lives and dollars, for ill-defined purposes? Had not the government engaged in spying on its own citizens? And the litany could go on and on.) Small wonder that by 1980 63 percent of a national opinion sample agreed with the statement, "the government is run by people who don't know what they're doing."

Under these conditions, a party (the Democrats) and a political philosophy (liberalism) closely associated with government were bound to suffer a loss of popularity. It is critically important to realize, though, that it was the reputation of government, not the basic liberal belief in moral economics and social justice, that was declining. Even at the height (or depth) of Reaganism, clear majorities of Americans favored most specific social programs. In 1986, a CBS/*New York Times* poll found that 66 percent of a cross-section of Americans thought "the Government should spend money now on efforts similar to those of the Great Society programs to help the poor people in the United States."[16] It was the *idea* of government in general that people had come to oppose, not specific liberal programs or the concepts of compassion and community.

There are a couple of oddities about all of this. One is that the person who did the most damage to the reputation of the American government—and hence indirectly to the standing of liberalism in the public mind—was Richard Nixon, certainly no liberal himself. Ironically, through failure and disgrace Nixon came much closer to the conservative objective of undermining the American people's faith in government than he ever could have by succeeding in abolishing programs and impounding funds. Confidence in government—and in virtually all other institutions—fell noticeably during the Vietnam War, plummeted with Watergate, and continued to decline through the remainder of the 1970s.

The second and greater oddity about the opposition to government and the general acceptance of the idea that liberal programs failed is that, by and large, they did not. The widespread notion that government programs have wasted huge amounts of money and accomplished almost nothing is a myth.

The belief that liberals are "wimps" derives more, I think, from their unwillingness to stand up for their principles than from their nonaggressive foreign policy positions or their compassionate ("bleeding heart") domestic agenda. There is no reason to be ashamed of what liberalism has done. Its history is a noble one. If liberals have come to doubt this, all they need to do is ask the American people—or President Reagan.

When opinion surveyors ask Americans to rate their presidents, two names regularly head the list: Franklin D. Roosevelt and John F. Kennedy. Two examples: A *Newsweek* poll in 1983 asked a cross-section of Americans who, of all the presidents they have ever had, they wished were president today. Kennedy was the landslide winner, named by 30 percent of the respondents, with FDR a distant second at 10 percent, followed by Harry S. Truman at 9 percent. Incumbent President Reagan was named by only 8 percent. So 49 percent of this national sample chose a past liberal over the current conservative. When all those named by at least 1 percent of those polled are grouped as liberals or conservatives, 62 percent chose liberals (Kennedy, F. Roosevelt, Truman, Carter, Lincoln, T. Roosevelt, L. Johnson), while only 17 percent picked conservatives (Reagan, Eisenhower, Nixon, Ford, Washington). McKinley, Taft, Coolidge, and other leading conservatives failed to make the cut. What is more, this 1983 *Newsweek* poll left no doubt that the people who so strongly favored John F. Kennedy saw him as a liberal. Large majorities associated him with "concern for working people," "an effort to end racial injustice," inspiring young people to solve social problems, and "government taking an active role in solving problems."[17]

That was 1983. What about after President Reagan's huge "mandate" for conservatism the next year? In April 1985, 35 percent of those questioned in a Harris poll named FDR as the president who "most likely will be viewed as the best president in history." Second with 25 percent was JFK. Ronald Reagan ranked third on this list with 12 percent, followed by Truman at 9 percent. Five months after they had resoundingly rejected the liberal Walter Mondale in the voting booths, Americans indicated that they preferred one of three liberal presidents to Ronald Reagan by a margin of nearly six to one.[18]

Reagan himself understood the appeal of the liberal past better than many liberals did. In his 1984 campaign he persisted in identifying himself with political heroes of the American past. There was nothing out of the ordinary in that. What made it strange was that every hero that the Republican president named was a Democrat.

Mondale was angry at what he termed "grave-robbing." One of the few highpoints of the Democratic campaign came when, just after Reagan had been linking himself to the Kennedy legend, Mondale revealed bitter statements against John Kennedy that Reagan had made in a 1960 letter. More intriguing still were two characteristics that all the Democrats Reagan singled out for praise had in common. One was that none of them was alive to point out that Reagan had not approved of their ideas before. (It seemed, in fact, that the subliminal message the president was trying to convey was: "The only good Democrat is a dead Democrat.") The other trait is that all were liberals. When he picked the late Democrats to praise at campaign stops, the conservative president did not choose the likes of Grover Cleveland, John W. Davis, John J. Raskob, or Judge Howard W. Smith. Rather, he hailed Franklin Roosevelt, Harry Truman, John Kennedy, and Hubert Humphrey—liberals to a man.

Ronald Reagan was never noted for reading much, but he must have read the poll results on the popularity of liberal politicians. Today's liberals might find this interesting reading matter themselves.

The attack on liberalism has gone through stages, as the critics have grown more brazen. In the later seventies the conventional wisdom accepted as new dogma the belief that government action could do little to ameliorate social problems.[19] Hugh Heclo noted in 1981 that backing for the welfare state had declined: "Against a background of recurring fiscal crises, 'paying for services' has replaced 'fair shares for all' as the current political slogan."[20] If liberals were willing to agree, without significant protest, that their programs had not succeeded, conservatives were naturally emboldened to see how far they could push their advantage.

John Logue argued in 1979 that "the welfare state is inimical to freedom." "Welfare benefits are so high," he charged, that "they reduce the desire to work. There must be an incentive to work since people are fundamentally lazy. No one in his right mind will choose to stand on an assembly line eight hours a day if he/she can collect almost as much for doing nothing. Cutting off all benefits would reduce the number of unemployed."[21] This was standard conservative fare: that unemployment results more from an unwillingness to work than from a lack of jobs, so we should stop "coddling" the poor. It was the same sort of thinking that lay behind President Reagan's comment that he couldn't understand how people could be unemployed when there were twenty-five pages of "help-wanted" ads in the *New York Times* and *Washington Post.*

Yet early in his presidency even Mr. Reagan insisted that he wanted to preserve the "safety net" for the "truly needy." Some on the right wanted to go farther and in fact cut the safety net to ribbons. George Gilder, for example, contended that the welfare state was responsible for the destruction of the American family.[22]

It was left, however, to an obscure scholar from Iowa to make the ultimate test of how far the antiliberal argument could be taken. Charles Murray had written a pamphlet for the Heritage Foundation on the subject of "Safety Nets and the Truly Needy." In 1982 this piece, which indicated that doing away with poverty programs might help rather than harm the poor, caught the eye of William Hammett, head of the Manhattan Institute, a conservative think tank in New York. Here was just the case that many arch-conservatives wanted to see *someone* make. Hammett promptly offered to place the financial resources of his institute behind Murray if he would expand his argument into a book. He wanted something that could do for dismantling the welfare state what Michael Harrington's *The Other America* had done to inspire it.[23] If your religion lacks an up-to-date bible—and if your congregation is one of considerable means—you can hire someone to write one. Of course those who commission such scriptures will insist that the outcome fully support their creed.

It is not likely that Charles Murray's *Losing Ground: American Social Policy, 1950–1980* disappointed his patrons. Taking it as given that government social programs have not cured the economic and social ills of the poor, Murray goes on to argue at great length that those programs have *caused* most of the problems of the poor. His thesis is that a well-intentioned people, through government social programs, "tried to provide for the poor and produced more poor instead."[24]

As those who commissioned his book must have hoped, Murray rapidly became the Moses of the Mercedes crowd. It is easy to see why. While many people enjoy the benefits of greed, few feel entirely comfortable with its ethical implications. They want to live the good life, but they want also to feel good about themselves. Murray soothes their consciences by telling them that the elimination of social spending will not only lower their taxes and leave them with more of their high incomes with which to indulge themselves, but that it will at the same time help the poor. It may be better to give than to receive, but it is better still to tell yourself that you are giving *by* receiving. Presented with a choice between helping the poor through paying taxes for social programs and helping the poor by cutting off their welfare and using the money thus saved to dine at fine restaurants, your typical Reaganite prefers to say: "I gave at Maxim's."

Murray's basic argument is that the Great Society programs introduced in the 1960s increased the attractiveness of idleness and lowered the advantages of work, thereby creating a continuing dependent class. This is a contention that liberals cannot afford to ignore. If they are true to their own beliefs, liberals must not become dogmatic and insist that the methods used in the past should be immune from careful scrutiny to see if they are achieving their objectives. Murray's questions are valid, and liberals must address them. The problem is not with Murray's questions, but with his answers and the statistics he employs to reach them.

Charles Murray carried the Reagan proclivity for analysis by anecdote one step farther than the president did. Murray made up his own anecdote, the "case of Harold and Phyllis." Unlike Reagan's "Tale of the Welfare Queen" and similar parables, Murray's anecdote is not an isolated worst case from which misleading generalizations are made; Murray's case is entirely fictional.

Harold and Phyllis are a "typical" young, unmarried poor couple whom Murray places in similar hypothetical situations in 1960 and 1970 in order to "demonstrate" how incentives for work, welfare, and marriage were changed by the Great Society welfare expansion. He contends that in 1960 the incentives pointed the unfortunate young couple toward marriage and work, but by 1970 the "rules of the game" had changed to make living together on welfare while remaining unmarried the sensible way to go.[25] Murray makes his case very well. *Too* well, it turns out. The problems lie in two areas. First, the author is less than honest with his figures. Second, he fails completely to look for any sort of control on his hypothetical case, to see if the causes he has isolated can actually be held responsible for such problems as the alarming growth in out-of-wedlock births.

The first problem with Murray's imaginary couple is that he

considers them "typical," but places them in a state, Pennsylvania, in which the welfare benefits grew between 1960 and 1970 at a rate twice the national average. He compounds this bit of misleading calculation by failing to mention in his text which state he is talking about. He then omits the fact that the working poor were entitled to food stamps. By including food stamps in what they would receive if Harold were not working, but not including them when figuring their income if Harold were working, Murray distorts his comparison of the incentives for work versus those for welfare.[26] He pulls similar tricks elsewhere in his calculations. In figuring what Harold would make at a minimum-wage job in 1970, Murray emphasizes that his stated wages are "*before* Social Security and taxes are taken out," but he neglects to mention that, much less to emphasize it, when he is presenting Harold's 1960 wages, which Murray wants to appear more attractive than those of 1970.[27]

But this only begins to scratch the surface of the juggling and misleading selection of statistics in *Losing Ground*. Murray shows a graph of those receiving Aid to Families with Dependent Children (AFDC) as a percentage of all families, 1950–80, but neglects to explain what the markings on the "Percentage of Families Receiving AFDC Payments" axis represent. Each mark is in fact two-tenths of one percent, but the casual reader might easily think that each mark represents one percent, thus causing the increase in welfare families to appear five times larger than it actually was.[28] More important, the author does not tell us what the situation of Harold and Phyllis would be in 1980, even though his subtitle is *American Social Policy, 1950–1980*. He has good reason. Such a continuation of their saga would not tell the story Murray and his patrons wanted told. Whatever shifts in incentives may have occurred in the direction of welfare and away from work between 1965 and 1970 (and Murray certainly exaggerates them), the change was sharply in the other direction during the 1970s, when welfare payments fell far behind the inflation rate. By 1980 the mythical Harold and Phyllis would in some states have received 100 percent more income by his working at the minimum wage than by her going on welfare. Even in generous Pennsylvania, they would in 1980 have gotten one-third more income by working. Murray did not see fit to mention this fact because all the ills he wants to blame on social programs and the disincentives to work and morality they allegedly produced continued to rise rapidly in the seventies.[29] In that decade there was a 20 percent increase in the percentage of Americans living in families headed by women and a 73 *percent* rise in illegitimate births as a percentage of all births. Yet these same years saw only a 4 percent increase in the percentage of Americans living in welfare households.[30]

The startling increases in female-headed households, illegitimacy, divorce, and other social problems are genuine causes for alarm, and progressives must seek new ways to address them, but it is quite clear that they are not the results of liberal social programs. None of the many studies that have been conducted on out-of-wedlock births have found any connection between them and welfare payments. David Ellwood and Mary Jo Bane of Harvard concluded in 1984, after an exhaustive study, that "welfare simply does not appear to be the underlying cause of the dramatic changes in family structure of the past few decades."[31] Murray says that this particular study came out after his book was finished. Although his bibliography covers an impressive sixteen pages of small print, the other studies on this important subject are not to be found. Furthermore, as Christopher Jencks reminds us, "illegitimacy rose among movie stars and college graduates as well as welfare mothers."[32] Such pregnancies have also soared in southern states with pitiful AFDC payments and in affluent suburbs where welfare is, presumably, not especially enticing. To blame these larger social problems on welfare programs is to ignore the history of values in Western society since the 1960s. Charles Murray seems to be similar to the man in Paul Simon's 1969 song, "The Boxer," who "hears what he wants to hear / And disregards the rest."[33]

Losing Ground is about as reliable as an authorized biography. The Manhattan Institute and those it persuaded to join in financing Murray got what they paid for. The book's arguments became the manna of business conferences in the mid-eighties. Murray replaced George Gilder as the favorite academic in right-wing circles. Conservative groups no longer discussed how to dismantle the welfare state in order to help themselves; instead they could discuss how to dismantle the welfare state in order to help the poor. *Losing Ground* was employed to undermine the "moral foundations of a compassionate society."[34] As Meg Greenfield of the *Washington Post* put it in 1985, "No matter what kind of government effort you may argue for these days, in [the poverty] area . . . you are likely to be 'Charles Murrayed,' and that will be the end of the argument.

The simple invocation of the book's existence will be taken as an answer to the question."[35] Like the writing of the book, its impact was no accident. The Manhattan Institute spent much more promoting the book and Murray than a commercial publisher would for a similar nonfiction volume.[36] Whether or not minds can be bought, it appears that ideas, even pernicious ones, can be sold.

Murray's book fed such attitudes as that expressed in the spring of 1985 by an attorney for the company that supplies electricity to New Orleans. If the city took over the company, he said, it "would do sociologically destructive things, like give away electricity to poor people. It's like streetcars. Old people ride streetcars free."[37] This might not seem like a portent of the end of the civilized world, if we did not have Charles Murray to remind us that the indigent old folks would be better off walking.

What Murray did was to give a false aura of intellectual legitimacy to a set of socially destructive ideas. The sooner liberals forthrightly take the offensive against the notion that the poor were the casualties of the War on Poverty, the better for our society and for the best in American values.

The War on Poverty was very different from Lyndon Johnson's other war—this one was not an American defeat (although many Republicans do seem eager to run up the white flag in the conflict with poverty). Surely, though, it was something less than a total victory. There was no "VP Day" to celebrate the surrender of poverty. It might seem that the War on Poverty was more like the Korean "police action" than either Vietnam or World War II: a conflict with limited objectives resulting in a stalemate. But in fact it was much better than that. The truce line established when Ronald Reagan took command represented a considerable gain in territory previously held by the enemy, not a return to an economic thirty-eighth parallel. This must be understood if liberals are to regain the offensive. A return to the status quo ante bellum of the War on Poverty, such as that for which many defeatist conservatives are calling, would amount to a substantial retreat.

Before President Johnson pushed through his social programs, about one-fifth of all Americans lived in poverty. In the midst of the richest nation that the world had yet seen, malnutrition was common in some regions. A team of physicians reported:

Wherever we went and wherever we looked, we saw children in significant numbers who were hungry and sick, children for whom hunger is a daily fact of life, and sickness, in many forms, an inevitability. [Many of these children] were hungry, weak, and apathetic. Their lives were being shortened. . . . They were suffering from hunger and disease and, directly or indirectly, they were dying from them.

This was not a report from Ethiopia in 1985; it was a report on parts of the United States—the Bronx, Appalachia, the Mississippi Delta, and Texas—in 1967. The report of the team of doctors sent out by the Field Foundation that year led to massive increases in food stamps and child-nutrition programs. Ten years later the Field Foundation physicians returned to the same localities and found that it was "not possible to find very easily the bloated bellies, the shriveled infants, the gross evidence of vitamin and protein deficiencies in children that we identified in the late 1960s."[38]

In 1960 the United States suffered from one of the highest infant-mortality rates in the industrialized world: 2.3 percent of live births among whites and 4.4 percent among blacks. The gap between the rates for the two races had actually widened during the affluent Eisenhower years. The Great Society programs produced a marked improvement, with the infant-mortality rate for whites more than cut in half, down to 1.1 percent of live births in 1980, and that for blacks dropping to 2.2 percent. Particularly significant was the narrowing of the gap between the white and black rates (from 2.1 percent in 1960 to 1.1 percent in 1980). This indicates that the situation of black (often poor) infants was improving more rapidly than that of the society as a whole, which in turn strongly suggests the crucial role of Medicaid, the Special Supplemental Food Program for Women, Infants, and Children (WIC), and food stamps in the remarkable improvement. In some poverty-stricken areas, the infant mortality rate fell by 50 percent within four years of the beginning of government medical and nutrition programs.[39]

A similar story is told by the statistics on life expectancy. The mortality rate for men over the age of sixty-five *increased* in the years immediately before the establishment of Medicare. But in the decade after 1967, mortality rates for this group fell by 20 percent. Life expectancy for whites rose by 1.9 years during the fifteen years prior to 1965, but by 3.4 years in the fifteen years between the declaration of war on poverty and the Reagan cease-fire in that war. Non-white life expectancy went up by 3.3 years between 1950 and 1965, but by an additional 5.4 years between 1965 and 1980.[40]

No other government program expanded as rapidly in the years since 1960 as did Social Security. After adjustment for inflation, the average payment to retired workers approximately doubled between 1960 and 1980, while the mean for AFDC welfare payments *decreased* by 12 percent in real dollars. It was the elderly, not the younger poor, with whom we were being generous in these years. As a result, the rate of poverty among those over age 65 was cut in half.[41]

The list could go on and on. Children who participated in Head Start programs achieved on average a rapid seven-point increase and a lasting 3.5 point rise in their IQ scores. A long-term study in Michigan found that at age nineteen those who had been in the pre-school program were almost twice as likely as those who had not to be employed or in college or vocational school. Most telling of all, the percentage of Americans living in poverty was slashed by at least half in the years between the implementation of the liberal social programs of the sixties and 1980. By some estimates, the percentage of the national population in poverty declined from a range of 18 to 20 percent in 1960 to 4 to 8 percent in 1980.[42]

These are but a few of the accomplishments of what Ronald Reagan called "the failed policies of the past." It is of considerable interest to contrast these achievements of a discredited liberalism with those of the resurgent conservatism of the years since 1980. The percentage of children living in poverty shot up to 22.2 percent in 1983 from just over 16 percent in 1979. Part of this increase was undoubtedly due to such social factors as the increased number of divorces and the consequent rise in female-headed households. More than half of all poor children lived in families headed by women. But there can be no serious question that the Reagan cuts in "survival programs" for the poor—cuts which totaled at least $10 billion from 1981 to 1985—made the problem considerably worse.[43]

Infant-mortality rates have turned around and begun to increase again, as nutrition programs and Medicaid have been cut back. The United States has once again fallen behind other wealthy nations in this fundamental indicator of health and well-being. Early in 1985 the Physician Task Force on Hunger in America reported finding "a recent and swift return of hunger in America." These doctors found that the new rise in hunger, which left an estimated minimum of 20 million Americans chronically short of food, "can be traced in substantial measure to clear and conscious policies of the federal government." Between 1979 and 1983, the poverty rate in the United States rose by 3.5 percent. During the recovery year of 1983, the number of people below the poverty line *increased* by 1 million, bringing the total number of Americans in poverty to 35 million at the beginning of the "prosperous" election year of 1984. After the Reagan cuts, 15.5 million of those poor Americans were not eligible for food stamps.[44]

The only Reagan administration response to such dismaying reports from the battlefield was to blow their bugles for a more rapid retreat.

The "failed policies of the past" look a lot better from where I sit than do the "new" ideas of Reaganism. Although it was obvious that much remained to be done, Americans had a great deal of which they should have been proud in the successes of liberal social programs. The Republican policies are nothing more than a return to the days of shame before the 1960s—and, if we let them get away with it, before the 1930s.

In some respects the War on Poverty amounted to a domestic containment policy. With the huge growth in the workforce in the 1970s that resulted from the baby boom and the movement of more women into employment outside the home, simply managing to hold our ground against poverty would have been a significant achievement. But liberals were never content with merely "containing" poverty. As Dwight Eisenhower had pledged in 1952 with reference to communism, liberals promised to "roll back" poverty. Some of their promises were extravagant and raised hopes too high, but in fact liberals *did* roll back poverty in the sixties and seventies. Certainly they rolled it back far more than Eisenhower ever rolled back communism.

Liberals have been on the defensive for too long. Adversity can build character, and the Democratic defeats gave liberals in the party a good opportunity to re-examine their beliefs and policies. In their periods of dominance, conservatives do not advance the nation, but they can serve the useful functions of showing us that some past progressive programs have not worked as they were intended and reminding us that utopia has still not arrived. Liberals must constantly seek new ways of moving toward their goals. Particular liberal policies may be found wanting, and they ought to be replaced or reworked. But far too many liberals have overreacted to their recent troubles in presidential politics. Rethinking liberal approaches to compassionate government is wise, but the wholesale jettisoning of the concept would be political as well as moral lunacy.

The public is ready to endorse liberal values again, far more ready than timid politicians with liberal leanings but without the courage of their convictions. Throughout the Reagan years, significant majorities of Americans have favored retaining or increasing spending in such areas as health, education, and aid for the handicapped and the aged. Immediately after Reagan's huge 1984 victory, pollster Louis Harris found that his sample of the American people agreed by a margin of 56 to 40 percent that "under the Reagan administration the elderly, the poor, and the handicapped have been especially hard hit, while the rich and big business have been much better off." Harris concluded that, despite appearances, "the 1984 mandate includes a strain of compassion for the less privileged." The CBS News/New York Times postelection poll agreed. "There is no suggestion in this poll that the American public has grown more conservative during the four years of the Reagan administration," these opinion analysts found. "If anything, there is more willingness now to spend money on domestic programs and a better assessment of the social programs of the 1960s."[45] It appears that our political leaders may be lagging behind the sentiments of their supposed followers, as they have so often done in the past.

There is an innate decency in the American people. It is the task of liberals to call that decency forth. Our history has had many flaws, and we should not ignore them or try to hide them. But neither should we wallow in them. There is much in our nation's heritage—particularly our *liberal* heritage—of which we can be proud.

The first step in the revival of liberalism has to be that liberals themselves realize that their policies have accomplished much. There is no reason for reticence. As long as liberals seem to apologize for their beliefs they are likely to win few new adherents. The time for self-flagellation is over—the Republicans' lashing at liberals will surely suffice. This does not mean that liberals should claim that they have never made mistakes or that they are not willing to seek new methods to reach the common good. That is the essence of liberalism. When Franklin Roosevelt was asked why liberals are so often divided but conservatives seem to be united, he replied: "There are many ways of going forward, but there is only one way of standing still."[46] If they expect to get anywhere politically, liberals must stop hedging and boldly proclaim their pride in liberal values and accomplishments.

Pride in past accomplishments is necessary to reinvigorate American liberalism. But this in no way implies that all that is needed is to restore the policies of the Great Society. Each era of liberalism devises its own approaches to meet changed conditions. The Progressive era, the New Deal, and the sixties were not reruns of earlier ages of reform. They were inspired by the same broad values, but liberals in each period developed new ways to pursue those values. So it will be with the coming wave of liberalism.

The mid-eighties saw the beginning of a revival of liberal values, yet it was by no means certain that the word "liberal" would come back into fashion. Right-wingers had been so successful in creating negative associations with "liberalism" in the public mind that many liberal politicians in the eighties were wary of the label. Senator Edward Kennedy said to me in 1986 that "liberal" is "a code word." "I'm always prepared to defend my positions and values," he said, "but it's a code word that swings in meaning, in parts of the country and among individuals. I think you are going to have a more defined view in terms of 'progress.' " Governor Mario Cuomo agreed. "Why should you use a term that immediately puts you at a disadvantage with large numbers of people who could be won over if you got them to listen to what you're saying?" Cuomo asked me. "Why don't you use 'progressivism' ?" " 'Progressive pragmatism' is what I like to call it," the New York governor added.[47]

Although "progressivism" is in almost all respects a direct synonym for "liberalism," the public views the former term much more favorably. A 1985 CBS News/New York Times poll found that the "liberal" label had less of a negative effect than might have been expected. Only 17 percent of those surveyed said that the "liberal" label would make them think worse of a politician, while 15 percent said it would make them think better of him or her. The political effect of calling yourself a "liberal" in late 1985 appeared to be a wash. The "conservative" label, on the other hand, led 27 percent to think better of a politician and 13 percent to think worse of him—a two-to-one gain in favorable image. The radical right-wingers who had seized the "conservative" identity for themselves had made a wise move. "Populist," a term toyed with by politicians of both the right and left over the years, was the only label tested to show a clearly negative impact. By a more than a three-to-one margin (21 percent to 6 percent), respondents said the "populist" tag would make them think worse of a politician.

The stunning finding of the 1985 survey on the impact of political labels was that on the effect of the word "progressive." By a margin of 37 percent to 7 percent, Americans in this survey said they would think better rather than worse of a politician called a "progressive." This five-to-one favorable ratio was much better than the two-to-one favorable ratio for the "conservative" label. And the 7 percent unfavorable rating was only about half the 13 percent negative rating of "conservative." Even more striking is the fact that southern whites—a demographic group badly needed by Democrats and one that viewed the "liberal" label negatively by a margin of 26 percent to 12 percent—would favor a "progressive" politician by the remarkable ratio of 44 percent to 8 percent. Indeed, every demographic group in the published survey gave its highest favorable-unfavorable ratio to the "progressive" label.[48]

In view of its popularity, its history, and its basic meaning, "progressivism" is the best choice of labels for the new form of liberalism developing in the 1980s.

The outlines of what I shall call the New Progressivism were clearly emerging in the waning years of Reaganism. There was a surprising amount of agreement among Democrats on the basic vision and themes that they wanted to present to the voters in the late eighties and nineties.

The first ingredient in a winning Democratic theme has to be *optimism*. Almost all leading Democrats agree that, as Ted Kennedy put it, "reclaiming our heritage as the party of hope" is essential to the party's success. "If I had to pick one word for the late eighties and early nineties," Gary Hart told me, "it would be 'hope.'" Congressman Tony Coelho of California contends that people voted for Reagan and against the Democrats principally because Reagan offered them a positive message. "The fact that he's bullshitting them," Coelho said to me, "is irrelevant." Walter

Mondale made the same error that Jimmy Carter had in his 1979 "malaise" speech: he tried to convince people that they were worse off than they thought they were. "People want to feel good," Coelho says simply. "They don't want to feel bad; nobody wants to feel bad."[49]

America was built on dreams. As a character says in the 1982 film *Diner*, "If you don't have good dreams, you have nightmares." Ronald Reagan understood this, and Democrats in the mid-eighties began to as well. What they started to suggest is not that their party should compete with the Republicans in "bullshitting" the American public, but that Democrats must cease to be what Spiro Agnew—or William Safire—once said they were: "nattering nabobs of negativism."

Democrats want to offer the American people a hopeful, but realistic, vision of the future. Mario Cuomo believes that Democrats can take the Republicans' "talk of optimism and turn it against them. These are people," the New York governor told me, "who are defeatist and negative—they're seeking to drag down our aspirations. They're saying, in effect, 'We can't do it.' " President Reagan posed as an optimist, but what he was actually saying is that we are helpless when it comes to aiding the poor. His motto might be: "If at first you don't succeed, give up." He encouraged his followers to think that they, as individuals, can *have* it all, but we, as a society, not only can't *do* it all, we can't do much of anything in the way of social betterment.

The American people want an optimistic message. President Reagan worked this desire greatly to his political advantage. But what he offered was a limited, perverted sort of optimism. The attitude he elicited has been well described by Arthur Levine as "going first class on the *Titanic*."[50] It is a narrow, individual optimism about one's *personal* future embedded in a pessimism about the future in general. What New Progressives must do to counter this is to offer an optimism about American society—and humanity—as a whole. Liberals should remind Americans that the first-class passengers on the *Titanic* wound up in the same place as those who traveled more modestly.

It is time for liberals to start talking again about what we *can* do as a society, not what we can't, about what we *must* do, morally, for the less fortunate members of our society, not about which obligations we would prefer to ignore. Speaker of the House Jim Wright has a statement framed on his office wall that sums up the progressive attitude: "Don't tell me why it can't be done—show me how it can."

If some of our efforts to help the poor have not worked as they were intended to, should we, as the Republicans maintain, give up? Should we turn our backs on our fellow human beings who are suffering and say that this may be unfortunate, but there is nothing we can do about it?

If a machine does not properly do the task for which it was designed, do we conclude that no machinery works and go back to doing our work by hand? Of course not. We redesign the machine or build a new one. That is how progress is achieved. Yet when it comes to assisting the needy, the Republicans are asking us to return to the pre-industrial age. If they find that parts of the New Deal and Great Society have not worked perfectly, their only answer is to turn back to the days of Calvin Coolidge. They seem to have forgotten where those policies took us in 1929.

Although in general they have been much more successful than the Republicans would lead us to believe, it is true that some social programs have not worked out perfectly. But having *no* social programs has already been shown to lead to disaster. What we need to do is to take a hard look at the programs we now have, decide which ones are working well, which ones need changes, and which ones should be replaced entirely. In this way we will progress farther on the base we already have. That is the American way.

President Reagan eloquently repeated this American principle when he said after the tragic January 1986 explosion of the space shuttle *Challenger* that we would mourn the dead, but carry on with the exploration of space. Mr. Reagan and his followers have no trouble applying the American way to the space program, but when it comes to the struggle with poverty and social problems, they counsel giving up.

Governor Cuomo said:

I refuse to believe what the Reagan administration is trying to teach us, which is that America, having grown tired by her efforts to allow outsiders in, now has to sit back, exhausted, watching people play the cards that fate has dealt them—that's what he's telling us, really: "We can't help you. We have free enterprise, you get in there, you fight, you'll win, like me. And, if not, there must be some reason. God helps those whom God has helped. And if God hasn't helped you, who are we to presume on His will?"

In place of the wild optimism for those at the top and total pessimism for those at the bottom that has been the Reagan version of hope—a "new negativism" masquerading as optimism—most leading Democrats want their party to offer a realistic, commonsense optimism for the nation as a whole. Cuomo calls it "an America of great expectations."[51] Such a genuine optimism for all Americans should be more attractive than the Reagan brand of trickle-down optimism.

Closely related to the theme of optimism is that of *change*. From the time of the New Deal through the 1960s, Democrats were identified with innovation. "What's happened to the party in the last ten or fifteen years," Alvin From, executive director of the Democratic Leadership Council (DLC) told me in 1986, "is that the party that has always been the party of change and opportunity and progress and hope, has become the defender of the status quo." "I think you can't look like you're status quo," agrees Congresswoman Patricia Schroeder. "People want to change things, and the party has looked too much like it's fighting to preserve, to protect the status quo, to insure, to take the risk out of everything."

Most Democratic leaders believe it necessary to demonstrate that their party is not wedded to what Gary Hart called in 1984 "the old arrangements." "The basic Democratic instinct," Hart said to me in 1985, "is reform—change." "Our truest tradition," Senator Kennedy concurs, "is change." But many Democrats have become leery of innovation. Democratic liberals who, From notes, "had always been on the cutting edge of change, became the defenders of the status quo when their programs came under attack." He is right. And liberals who defend things as they are eventually cease to be liberals. When liberals fail to move forward, conservatives are given an opportunity to move backward and make it look like progress. At least they're moving, and Americans generally seem to prefer change to standing still. It is essential that a new, revitalized progressivism once again place itself on the cutting edge of change.

When Senator Hart said in 1985 that "the party of change must change," he made it clear that he did not mean that Democrats should abandon their traditional goals and values. What Hart and most Democratic leaders are saying is that new Democrats must be willing to discard those approaches that have not worked and seek new methods to reach the traditional liberal goals.[52] While old liberals want to continue to use the same outdated road map in their trip toward a better society and conservatives want to give up on the journey, New Progressives are realizing that some of the routes on the old map were dead ends and that new maps must be drawn and used.

Another way of emphasizing a commitment to change is to stress the need for *new ideas*. The trademark of Gary Hart's 1984 campaign has swept the party. Following Walter Mondale's debacle in November of that year, there were "a dozen or so people who ran for party chair," Hart points out. He contends that they were all saying the same thing: " 'This party needs new ideas and new leadership,' which," Hart told me with a laugh, "sounded remarkably familiar to me." Since then, Democrats running for all sorts of offices have been making use of Hart's theme. "The point is," Hart says, "we may have lost the nomination, but we won the party."[53]

In addition to offering hope and a commitment to change, many Democrats also understood that they must show voters that they have *confidence* in themselves and their beliefs. There may have been a bit less agreement among leading Democrats on this point than there was on others. Almost all the most prominent people in the party talked about the need to project an aura of confidence, but several attacked their own party's past to a degree that would have comforted Republicans. At the same time that some of these Democrats were calling for the projection of more confidence, they were apologizing for what their party had done in the recent past.

This was a mistake. To say to voters, as too many Democrats did in the 1980s, "We were wrong—tell us where you want to go and we'll take you there," is to demonstrate neither confidence nor leadership. Unlike being in love, being president may not mean, as Richard Nixon seemed to think, never having to say you're sorry, but the people want leaders who know where they're going and have confidence in the correctness of their course.

Many progressive Democrats realized that the party would never get anywhere until it regained its self-confidence and stopped apologizing. "One of the Democrats' major problems is their self-doubt," longtime liberal activist Joseph Rauh argued. "I think our principles are right and that'll be recognized in the end, but they won't be recognized by the people until the Democrats get over their own doubts about those principles." "We need leadership that will do what is right, without a sense of apology," is the way Jesse Jackson made the same point. Tony Coelho contended that almost all of the fourteen Democrats who lost their House seats in the Reagan landslide in 1984 were conservatives and "the reason they lost is that they apologized too much." Voters want leaders who believe in themselves, Coelho says. After reviewing the innovative ways in which past Democrats made use of government to help people, Mario Cuomo concluded: "And we didn't apologize for it. We boasted of it."[54]

Democrats of all viewpoints agree that *opportunity* must be a part of their party's new message, as it was central to the old Democratic appeal. When asked what vision his party should present to the American people, Congressman Richard Gephardt responded without hesitation: "One word: opportunity, underlined a hundred times and repeated a thousand times. Opportunity has been our tradition and our history, and I think it's the concept that we have to again assert to the American people." Senator Lawton Chiles of Florida similarly believes that what is needed for the Democrats to regain popularity and power is "a return to what has been our strength in the past, and that is that we were a party that certainly had a strong social concern and always wanted to be the party of opportunity, the party that allowed people to work their way up in the system."

Although he comes from what is usually seen as a different wing of the party from that of Gephardt, Chiles, From, and other members of the Democratic Leadership Council, Edward Kennedy emphasized the same point in 1986. "I think first of all we have to be the party that is perceived as, and in fact that offers the possibilities for economic growth, stability, and opportunity. President Kennedy said, 'the most important social program is a sound economy.'" What Senator Kennedy and other liberal Democrats have come to understand is that the achievement of their goals of social betterment for the poor is dependent upon a growing economy. Richard Goodwin, a speech writer for John F. Kennedy and an aide to Lyndon Johnson, points out that the whole liberal agenda of the 1960s depended upon "continuing economic growth, because as long as everyone was getting richer—Johnson always felt that was the key—they wouldn't mind helping others. When things get tight for them, they aren't willing to do that anymore."[55]

The renewed Democratic emphasis on opportunity and economic growth does not mean that Democrats are parroting their Republican adversaries. Republicans see growth as a substitute for social programs (that is, the trickle-down approach), while most Democrats see growth as a means to establish and maintain social programs that they hope will help people at the bottom have an opportunity to rise.

Most leading Democrats insist that the party must not abandon its *traditional values* and objectives. "You have to say," argues Gary Hart, " 'Here's what it means to be a Democrat, going all the way back to Jefferson and Jackson, and that's what makes us distinct from Republicans.' And *then* you have to say, 'But to achieve those values of justice and equality and opportunity, which *are* Democratic values, not Republican values, we have to have new policies, policies of growth.' " Al From of the DLC outlines the formula that has been successfully employed by Democratic governors across the nation: "Fiscal responsibility and discipline; traditional Democratic values as far as civil rights and opportunity and growth and civil liberties; progressive and innovative government in areas like education, economic development, and the environment; and an enormous willingness to take risks and try new things." This formula, with some variations, is one that all Democratic leaders believe will be successful on the national level.

New (or at least revamped) means to reach traditional Democratic ends—that was a theme repeated in the mid-eighties by Democrats from Charles Robb to Edward Kennedy. There was an understanding that the public still agreed with many, probably most, of the enduring liberal goals. " 'Liberalism' in general is unpopular," said Congressman Barney Frank, chairman of the Americans for Democratic Action, "but liberal issues are popular. We made the whole smaller than the sum of the parts." Those liberal issues have to once more be tied firmly to basic American values. "People are more interested in values than they are in issues," Jesse Jackson contended in a 1986 interview. Recent experience supports this view.[56]

In foreign policy, most Democratic leaders were in basic agreement with the new policy being outlined by Sam Nunn and Les Aspin. Few of the leading Democrats would take exception to Senator Kennedy's call for them to be "the party of strength and restraint." He pointed out that this combination was successful during his brother's administration, when the United States demonstrated strength in the Cuban missile crisis "and within six months, they had a test ban treaty. It's that combination of strength and negotiation in the pursuit of overall objectives that's the kind of policy we have to reclaim," Kennedy said to me.[57]

The broad themes upon which most Democrats agree should serve them well in coming elections. But the essence of the emerging New Progressivism is more fundamental than any of those themes. All Democratic leaders agree that the party must shed its image as a collection of special-interest groups and appeal instead to the common interests of Americans. This idea, however, goes far beyond simply creating a new image. It goes to the heart of the New Progressivism.

The thrust of this emerging liberalism differs from both conservatism and the old liberalism of the sixties. The public wants neither the extreme of laissez-faire nor that of collectivism. In the public mind, conservatives are generally identified as probusiness, antilabor, and antigovernment. They want to get government out of the way so that "unfettered free enterprise" can reign. For their part, liberals in the past were generally perceived to be prolabor and antibusiness. Both these old antagonists agreed that there were "sides" with sharply differing interests and that confrontation and conflict were natural. Certainly much of our nation's history supports such a view.

But we live in a new age, one in which we can no longer afford to be at each other's throats. The New Progressivism attempts to move beyond confrontation to cooperation. "We have to understand," Governor Bill Clinton of Arkansas says, "that while the myth of the individual 'lone ranger' is a part of our cultural heritage, that's not what cuts it in the kind of world we're living in. The people who work together are those who succeed."

Democrats believe strongly in "opportunity, in *real* opportunity, in the opportunity to become independent and self-sufficient," Massachusetts Governor Michael Dukakis told me. "And we think that it's a combination of private resources and public initiative that has to create that kind of environment." If you want to produce the sort of economic growth that is needed to sustain a public commitment to helping those in need, Dukakis contends that of necessity you have to have the active involvement of the leaders of business, labor, education, and the government.

Arthur Schlesinger, Jr., has come up with an effective way of putting this theme. Democrats, the historian and former Kennedy aide says, should speak of a *"concert of interests."* Mario Cuomo calls the same basic idea practicing "the *politics of inclusion"* rather than the politics of exclusion. The politics of inclusion, Cuomo says, "is a politics that never divides but unites; that never rejects but embraces; that never stoops to playing one side against another—group against group, state against state, region against region."[58]

None of this amounts to an abandonment of liberal principles. One of the things that distinguishes liberals from conseratives—and, generally, Democrats from Republicans—is that, as Governor Dukakis puts it, "When Democrats see an important social or economic problem out there, they're compelled to *do* something about it. They think it's got to be a combination of public action and private involvement that does it." New Progressives understand that people want to accomplish as much as they can as individuals, but they also recognize that the nature of a complex modern society is interdependence. While we seek to avoid one-way dependence, it is not possible to be independent; we have mutual responsibilities.

"We have to go to the *heart* of the message," Bill Clinton says, "which is: Those who have have to do for those who don't because we're rising and falling together. That's the argument. It hurts *all* of us. When you have a 25 percent high school dropout rate, it kills us all. When you have an adult illiteracy rate that's obscene, that hurts us all." Clinton thinks that people know this "down deep," but that Democrats have to bring those attitudes to the surface. "There is, in fact, a depression for certain segments of our people," Senator Bill Bradley of New Jersey says. "We must make that an issue, not of compassion, but an issue of conscience—don't feel sorry for other people, ask what this says about ourselves." "The argument we have to make," concludes Governor Clinton, "is that we need to do for others not only because it is right, it is also the selfish thing to do, because we are living in a day and age that rewards cooperation. And productivity comes in fact to those who cooperate best."

Mario Cuomo also articulates the New Progressive vision when he says that the "soul" of the Democratic party is the concept of community. "Those who made our history taught us above all things the idea of family. Mutuality. The sharing of benefits and burdens—fairly—for the good of all," he said in his 1983 inaugural address and again in his keynote speech at the 1984 Democratic national convention. "Feeling one another's pain. Sharing one another's blessings. Reasonably, honestly, fairly." "No family that favored its strong children—or that, in the name of evenhandedness, failed to help its vulnerable ones—would be worthy of the name. And no state, or nation, that chooses to ignore its troubled regions and people, while watching others thrive, can call itself justified."

"Family" is a fitting way to summarize the New Progressive objective. It implies responsibility, compassion, cooperation, and inclusion—all themes that Cuomo has repeatedly addressed. A family teaches responsibility, thinking of the future, obligations to each other, nurturing those not able to care for themselves. Governor Cuomo frequently points out that those who preceded us built an affirmative government that helped many of us to succeed. "At the very least," he declares, "the government of this generation should be able to do for those who follow us what has been done for us."

The vision of society as a family also allows Mario Cuomo to present his views in a way that voters find most attractive. He realizes that "people want to be told what government will do for them, not what we will do for someone worse off than they are." Therefore he strives to synthesize idealism and self-interest, to lead people to see that their futures are inextricably intertwined with those of others. "Jeremiah, more than two thousand years ago," Cuomo noted in our 1986 interview, "taught us that our own individual good is found in the good of the whole community." This combination of compassion and common sense will win majority support, but a straight "we want to help them" presentation will not. The interconnectedness of our society must be shown.

Of course cooperation is not always easy. Responsibility carries with it the necessity of some willingness to sacrifice. "The country will have to make up its mind whether we want to have a little present pain for future gain," is the way Bill Clinton puts it.[59] If it is made clear that the sacrifices are for the common good, for benefits that we will all enjoy, most people will be willing to make them. They will feel better joining in such a common effort that costs them something than they did in accepting what President Reagan offered them: a free lunch—free, that is, except for the costs to their consciences.

The conservative era from the late 1970s through the mid-1980s provided liberals with an opportunity to reassess their methods. Necessary adjustments in the liberal approach have begun to be made as a result of this reassessment. Most progressives now understand that they went too far in their reliance on the government to solve all social problems. Government participation is essential to finding solutions to our most pressing social problems, but the role of individual and community efforts in this process is similarly large.

Jesse Jackson believes that in the late sixties and early seventies the liberal movement

> got labeled with "free, but not responsible," "free without values," and became the dumping ground for every fringe protest formation. It was no longer just peaceful, nonviolent, disciplined, Gandhian-style demonstrations; it became free speech turned into license for obscenity, pornography, abortion, smoking pot. The liberal movement got trapped with all the decadent fallout and no values.

Whether such perceptions were justified is not the issue. It is undeniable that irresponsibility was linked in the public mind with "liberalism."

"The opponents of liberalism have attempted to use it as a label for permissiveness—no standards, no values, that sort of stuff," Governor Dukakis says. New Progressives are striving to get away from such associations. "I think the thing that caused the 'liberal' tag to go sour a little bit was this notion that we didn't care about those things [such as crime, drug abuse, and teen-age pregnancies] and weren't prepared to do anything," Dukakis contends. The New Progressivism must make very clear its commitment to its genuine values.

In 1986 former Virginia Governor Charles Robb called on his fellow Democrats to end their "conspiracy of silence" about the deterioration of life in minority communities. Surely racism was the original source of many of the social problems that plague these communities—and plainly racism persists in America and progressive dedication to combat it must not waver. But it is pointless to deny that the causes of the disastrous increases in illiteracy, violent crime, teen-age pregnancy, and drug addiction in these communities go beyond external racism. "It's time to shift the primary focus from racism, the traditional enemy from without, to self-defeating patterns of behavior, the new enemy within," Robb declared at Hofstra University.

What is needed is a new focus for the progressive approach to social problems. Bill Clinton maintains that Democrats must "rethink what we need to do about welfare and drug abuse, and the whole array of those social problems that are associated with disconnected people." This does not entail, as many Republicans would argue, that the federal government should halt its efforts and let these people fend for themselves. "We need a family policy which focuses on more spending on poor children and their pregnant mothers, more work for the mothers, and more responsibility to the fathers," Governor Clinton says.

The idea of social responsibility is *not* to lift responsibility from individuals, but to back them up and provide support for them, so that they can meet their individual responsibilities. The government must do as much as it can to assist those in need, but New Progressives are prepared to say to these people: "We'll do all we can to help you get in a position to help yourselves, but there's a limit to what government can do. You've got to change your values. If you don't choose to protect yourself and your family members from destruction, there's nothing a Democrat or a Republican can do for you."

The New Progressivism emphasizes a cooperative effort between government assistance and a heavy dose of self-help. A progressive president would be in a position to use the office, as Governor Clinton puts it, "as a bully pulpit for the regeneration of life and possibility for all the people who are being lost to these social problems." The New Progressive philosophy does not abandon the downtrodden to their own devices. It recognizes the social responsibility to aid them, but it also understands that individual responsibility must be encouraged. In the end, the fate of the underclass will be determined both by governmental initiatives and by the choice to survive and succeed being made by individuals and families and groups that the government can and should support, but cannot replace.

This New Progressive approach to social problems is not "blaming the victim." Rather, it represents a recognition that the victim must take an active role in overcoming his victimization. This is to be accomplished with a helping hand from the government, but it will succeed only if individuals and communities take a substantial portion of the responsibility upon themselves.

"The fundamental difference between a conservative and a liberal," Senator Christopher Dodd of Connecticut said in an interview,

> is that a conservative is anecdotal. The conservative guy will literally take his clothes off and say, "I'll give 'em to a homeless guy," if he knows who that person is and can relate to him. He will reach into his pockets in order to help out a neighbor. It's a very strong *personal* relationship. [That's] the reason why Reagan really does recite the litany of anecdotes—he can bring tears to the eyes of the most hardened conservative when he describes the plight of some black woman—forget that she survives only because of a federal program.

But conservatives refuse to believe that there are widespread social problems. Liberals, on the other hand, "have a hard time talking to their brothers and sisters about things. And yet they will sign petitions and march in the streets in the freezing cold over Nelson Mandela."[60]

Dodd's stereotypes of conservatives and old-style liberals are close enough to the mark that they help to point to the necessity of bridging the gap between these two attitudes. That is precisely what New Progressivism is all about. It seeks to understand the large social problems and to deal with them on both an individual and a societal level.

CHAPTER 3

The Roaring Eighties

You're driving with your eyes closed
You're drivin' with your eyes closed
You're drivin' with your eyes closed
You're gonna hit somethin'
But that's the way it goes
 —DON HENLEY, DANNY KORTCHMAR,
  and STAN LYNCH (1984)

We're living on good fortune
We're cheating all our friends
So tell me, oh tell me
Now where's it going to end
 —ROGER HODGSON (1984)

The perceived state of the economy was largely responsible for Ronald Reagan's landslide re-election in 1984, and the economy was the principal cause of his remarkably high ratings in public opinion polls during the first half of his second term. Yet there were many signs in the mid-eighties that the economy might not long continue to be the Republican party's best friend.

When Mr. Reagan campaigned for the presidency in 1980, he promised amazing results from his economic program. "Supply-side economics" sounded too good to be true. It was. Its proponents portrayed supply-side economics as a sort of magic bullet that would cure the ills of a seriously afflicted economy. Candidate Reagan proposed to cut taxes sharply, increase military spending enormously, maintain the social safety net for the "truly needy," bring inflation under control, stimulate economic recovery, and balance the budget. Fairy tales would not be fairy tales if they were not alluring, and the myth of supply-side economics was certainly that.

Painless panaceas are always popular, but it is wise to take a hard look at miracle cures offered by patent-medicine-peddling politicians. Although a majority of the American people were not willing to look very carefully at the content of Reaganomics, some politicians and economists did. The most telling early criticism came from a few of Mr. Reagan's fellow Republicans. John Anderson put it best during the 1980 campaign: "How can any president curb inflation, cut taxes, increase defense spending, and balance the budget all at the same time?" Anderson answered his own question: "It's very simple. You do it with mirrors."[1]

Anderson's retort scored a direct hit. The promise to accomplish all these contradictory objectives at once was ludicrous from the start. Vice-President George Bush, while campaigning against Mr. Reagan for the Republican nomination in 1980, referred to Reagan's plan as "voodoo economics." No one has yet come up with a more accurate description. The mirrors began to crack in Reagan's second term, and it became apparent that it would be difficult to avoid seven years of bad luck.

President Reagan tried to convince us of such fantastic ideas as that we could index taxes downward with inflation and expenditures upward with the same inflation and that the result would be a balanced budget rather than federal bankruptcy. It would have required a wizard to produce the results he promised, and Ronald Reagan proved to be no wizard. Rather, he was an illusionist, and in that craft he showed himself to be one of the most skilled practitioners the world has ever seen. It is natural that many people would like to believe the sort of illusions their president created for them. They sought in the 1980s, as their forebears did in the 1920s, a return to an imagined golden age of the past, described so well by Warren Harding as "normalcy"—an age that, like Harding's word, never existed.

Such a retreat into the past was, despite all the talk about the newness of supply-side theory, what the Republican policies were all about. They offered no long-term solutions to our genuine economic problems. "To retreat into our mythical past," economist Lester

Thurow has wisely said, "is to guarantee that our days of economic glory are over."[2]

Reaganomics posed as something new and daring. Daring it has been, gambling with the future of the American economy, but it was hardly new. Then-budget-director David Stockman put it succinctly in 1981: "Supply-side [economics] is trickle-down theory." The basic idea has been intentionally to redistribute income to the rich, to concentrate wealth and income in the hands of the few. "The hard part of the [1981] supply-side tax cut," Stockman told William Greider, was "dropping the top rate from 70 to 50 percent—the rest of it [was] a secondary matter. . . . the general argument was that, in order to make this [sharp cut for the top brackets] palatable as a political matter, you had to bring down all the brackets. But, I mean, Kemp–Roth was always a Trojan horse to bring down the top rate."[3] The purpose of the administration's program, Nobel Prize–winning economist James Tobin pointed out in 1981, was to "redistribute wealth, power and opportunity to the [already] wealthy and powerful and their heirs." The major goal from the start was to increase *in*equality. Self-interest, as economics journalist Robert Kuttner has said, was "successfully masquerading as a technical imperative. Ideology [had] appropriated the costume of value-free positive economics."[4]

Before the original tax and spending cuts were enacted, Stockman had carefully calculated their net effect on the 16.5 million Americans then living below the poverty line: 15 percent of them would gain, 34 percent would experience no change, and 47 percent would suffer a loss of spendable income. When the effects of increases in Social Security taxes and of "bracket creep" were added to the 1981 Reagan tax program, the poorest 60 percent of Americans were paying more in 1984 than they had been in 1980, but the richest 0.9 percent, those making at least $100,000 a year, enjoyed an average tax cut of 12.2 percent. The Trojan horse worked, and redistribution from the poor and lower middle class to the wealthy was effected as planned.[5]

The hope was that the concentration of wealth and income would result in increased investment. If you spread the money out among the many, this hoary argument contends, they will use it for such foolish purposes as buying food and paying the rent. But if you put more in the bank accounts of those who already have more than they know what to do with, they are likely to invest it. Eventually, if all goes well, some of the resulting wealth may leak down to those below.

Far from being new, this concept goes back to the beginnings of the American republic two centuries ago. The heart of Alexander Hamilton's economic plan was to concentrate wealth in order to stimulate investment and help start the industrialization of the nation. Hamilton favored a strong central government. For this reason the similarity between his program and that of Ronald Reagan may be clouded. It has long been recognized that twentieth-century liberals have used Hamiltonian means to reach Jeffersonian ends. What we have seen in the 1980s is an attempt by the Reagan administration to employ Jeffersonian means to reach Hamiltonian ends, that is, reducing the government in order to make the rich richer.

The trickle-down theory has arisen periodically throughout American history. Hamilton's Federalist economic policies were eventually taken up in somewhat altered form by such Whigs as Henry Clay and Daniel Webster. The trickle-down concept re-emerged in its Republican incarnation in the second half of the nineteenth century, and has in the past hundred years been most prominently associated with the names McKinley, Coolidge, and Hoover.

It was Calvin Coolidge whom Ronald Reagan most idolized. One of the new president's first commands upon taking office was to have a White House portrait of Thomas Jefferson replaced by one of Coolidge. A few months later, Reagan fully embraced the memory of his tight-lipped predecessor. He hailed Coolidge because he "cut taxes four times." "We had," the president continued, "probably the greatest growth of prosperity that we've ever known." In a 1978 radio talk, Reagan praised Coolidge's treasury secretary, Andrew Mellon, because he "succeeded in getting Congress to cut the highest bracket from the World War I high of 66 to 25 percent. There were no screams of protest about benefiting the rich," he incorrectly stated, "and very soon there was such an expansion of the economy and such prosperity for all. . . ." Mr. Reagan's selective study of history must not have told him about what became of that "Coolidge prosperity" less than eight months after the Yankee president left office in 1929.[6]

The course of events in the 1920s is most instructive in judging where Reaganomics may eventually take us. The parallels between the twenties and the eighties are striking. The president has never made any attempt to deny that his policies were modeled, at least in important respects, upon those of Coolidge and Mellon. They drastically reduced the tax "burden" on the rich. For a time this policy—along with such other developments as the automobile, radio, and appliance industries and the advent of credit buying—did produce the prosperity that Reagan talked about. But that prosperity was constructed on a foundation of sand. The Coolidge–Mellon tax cuts did not cause the Great Depression, but they did aggravate the basic problem in the American economy: maldistribution of income.[7]

Coolidge prosperity in the twenties was temporary and illusory, and Reagan prosperity in the eighties was actually far more so. Coolidge and Mellon set out to skew the nation's income distribution toward the top, but they did not do so by creating massive deficits. They did not spend trillions of dollars on the military. They did not turn the United States into a net debtor nation. They did not manufacture conditions under which the country suffered its worst trade imbalances in history. They merely exacerbated an already inequitable distribution of income and thereby helped to beget the worst economic collapse in modern history. The only protection we have against the recurrence of something as bad or worse resulting from Reaganomics is the array of social programs that act to counter the downward spiral of a depression, and the Reagan administration has spared no effort in trying to dismantle those safeguards.

The parallels between the twenties and the eighties are as disturbing as they are numerous. Many economists have noted the existence of long cycles in the economy. These Kondratiev waves, as they are called, register economic collapses at intervals of between 50 and 60 years. In 1986, the *Wall Street Journal* pointed to a remarkable similarity between the bull market of the late 1920s and that of the mid-1980s. The Dow-Jones industrial average followed a course between 1980 and 1986 that eerily paralleled the graph of the same index during a period fifty-eight years earlier (1922 to 1928). If the pattern continued, the surging market would reach the point corresponding to October 1929 in the fall of 1987. There was little reason to anticipate a collapse exactly "on schedule," but the policies of the Reagan administration were designed to duplicate the conditions of the twenties, and in this, at least, they were successful.

Farmers in the twenties suffered through depression while other sectors of the economy prospered. The same was the case in the eighties. Commodity prices deflated in the mid-eighties, as they had six decades before. Interest rates fell in the twenties, as they have in the eighties. Banks overextended themselves with dubious loans, weakening the entire financial system in both periods. A complex worldwide structure of enormous debt—Germans borrowing from Americans to pay reparations to other European countries, which in turn owed large wartime debts to Americans—provided the cracked foundation of Coolidge prosperity. Reagan prosperity in the 1980s rested upon similarly unstable underpinnings. From 1973 into the early 1980s, vast sums were transferred to oil-exporting nations. They returned much of their newfound wealth to Western banks, which promptly made huge loans to underdeveloped countries. Third-world debt exceeded $1 trillion by 1985. The Reagan administration's tax-cutting and military spending policies added to the problem by more than doubling the American government's debt to over $2 trillion. To this could be added mid-eighties figures of $1.5 trillion in American corporate debt and $0.5 trillion in domestic farm debt.

Few people familiar with the magnitude of the debt burden of the 1980s held out any hope that much of the principal of these loans would ever be repaid, at least without enormous inflation that would in real terms vastly reduce the debts. New loans were being made in the mid-eighties to enable third-world nations to meet interest payments on earlier loans. The world economy of the eighties is more interconnected than was that of the twenties. A serious hemorrhage anywhere in the world could cause the world's financial system to bleed rapidly to death.

Several other similarities of the Roaring Eighties to the period six decades earlier can be cited. Many Democrats joined with Republicans in their Coolidge era frenzy of tax cutting that slashed the top federal income tax rate from 65 to 25 percent. Almost exactly the same road was followed in the 1980s, when the highest rate was cut from 70 percent in 1980 to 28 percent in 1987.

Another disturbing parallel between the twenties and the eighties was the growing maldistribution of income. The share of national income received by the highest fifth of American families and unattached individuals rose from 43.5 percent in 1978 to 44.6 percent in 1984. The second fifth registered a more modest gain, from 24.0 percent to 24.3 percent. The middle fifth fell from 16.7 percent to 16.4 percent, the fourth fifth from 10.8 percent to 10.3

percent, and the poorest fifth from 4.9 percent to 4.4 percent. These changes were not nearly as dramatic as those recorded in the twenties, but they showed that Ronald Reagan's policies were doing what they were intended to do: redistribute income from the poor to the affluent. In the process, those policies achieved a dangerous reversal of the trend from the 1930s into the 1970s toward a somewhat better balanced distribution of income.

Americans were as confident of the future of the economy in the mid-eighties as they had been in the late twenties, when Republicans were proclaiming a "New Era" of eternal prosperity. Mergers resulted in a quickening pace of concentration of wealth and economic power in both periods. Perhaps most ominous of all the similarities between the Coolidge and Reagan eras was the blind faith of the nation's leaders in both periods in "the market." The result in both decades was a redirection of economic energies from wealth production to gambling. Fully three-fourths of the stock market gains registered in 1984 and 1985 were the consequences not of productive investment but of corporate takeovers. And both periods, steeped as they were in the ethic of self-advancement by any means available, were marked by unscrupulous and unethical practices by leading stock traders, resulting finally in large scandals.[8]

What came to be called Reaganomics in the eighties was not new. It had been tried and had resulted in disaster sixty years before. No one in the mid-eighties could confidently predict when a new collapse would occur, but if nothing were done to alter the course on which the Republican administration had set the economy, only the timing of a collapse, not its occurrence, would be in question.

The frightening parallels between the twenties and the eighties amount to a prophecy in the Old Testament sense: not a forecast of the inevitable, but a warning of what will happen if we do not change our ways.

"America is back!" President Reagan gleefully proclaimed from the hustings during his 1984 campaign. The slogan, along with "It's morning in America," formed the theme of his most effective television advertising. These phrases were meant to carry several messages, including a putative return to national strength, pride, and resolve in foreign and military policy. The most important area in which we were supposed to be "back," though, was our economy.

Surely most Americans in 1984 had the impression that the economy was back, and they voted accordingly. It is instructive to examine the extent to which the popular impression of economic resurgence was grounded in fact. Following the severe Reagan recession of 1982–83, it was not difficult to show an improvement in 1984. The recession was so bad that the upswing from it in 1984 produced a 5.8 percent rise in real per-capita disposable income. This was the sharpest such increase in an election year since an 11.4 percent jump in 1936 helped Franklin Roosevelt win by an even larger margin than Ronald Reagan did in 1984.

The notion of economic recovery in 1984 was based in large part on the drop in unemployment. This was real enough, but in judging whether America was back in 1984, it would be well to know the point of comparison. Where we were back to in unemployment in 1984 is where we had been when Ronald Reagan took office. In 1980 he called a 7.5 percent unemployment rate a "depression"; in 1984 he termed the same 7.5 percent unemployment rate "recovery." Yet the latter label was not unjustified. President Reagan's economic policies had helped to produce 10.8 percent unemployment at the end of 1982, the highest level since the Great Depression. In comparison to that, the seven-plus percent unemployment figures of 1984–86 constituted "recovery," but recovery from Reagan's own near-depression of 1982. The later Reagan figures represented no improvement over the end of the Carter administration.

In unemployment, America was back in 1984, back to where it had been under Jimmy Carter.

But even that gives the Reagan administration too much credit. There was a growth in the number of jobs after the bottom of the Reagan recession, but during the first Reagan term the gain in jobs was slightly more than 8 percent. During the preceding four years—that is, when the "failed policies of the past" were in the saddle under Jimmy Carter—civilian employment grew by 12.5 percent, a rate half again as fast as that achieved under Reagan. Moreover, employment should be examined qualitatively as well as quantitatively. The entire gain in employment in the Reagan years is accounted for by jobs in the service sector. Some positions so classified are excellent. There is little cause for complaint about the income levels of attorneys and physicians. But many of the service jobs pay the minimum wage for such activities as serving fast food. Employment in producing goods actually *fell* by 5.5 percent in Reagan's first term. According to some estimates, the nation lost more than two million manufacturing jobs in the first four Reagan years.[9] The unfortunate fact is that many of those who regained jobs after the 1982 recession were obliged to take less attractive positions at much lower pay than they had received before.

Of course Ronald Reagan did not cause this long-term alteration of the American economy. As long ago as 1973 the AFL-CIO warned that the United States was in danger of becoming "a nation of hamburger stands, a country stripped of industrial capacity and meaningful work . . . a nation of citizens busily buying and selling cheeseburgers and root beer floats."[10] Reagan was not responsible for starting the nation down this unhappy Frontage Road, but it is certain that his economic policies accelerated our momentum.

The Reagan administration's sympathy for the problems of those who lose their jobs was slight. Between 1979 and 1983, employment in Detroit declined by 11.5 percent, in Chicago by 6.9 percent, and in Philadelphia by 4.9 percent. When asked about the difficulties faced by people in old industrial towns and cities when factories close, Reagan suggested that people "vote with their feet." In a similar vein, Robert Ortner, the chief economist in the Department of Commerce, said simply: "People can commute."[11]

Credit must be given where credit is due, and while Ronald Reagan is not much of an economist, he is a great salesman. He found that economic problems could be "solved" by redefining what constitutes a problem. In the 1960s, unemployment levels of 5 percent led the government to enact programs for training and assisting the unemployed and creating jobs for them. A decade later, a jobless rate of 7 percent was considered a recession and prompted calls for vigorous government action. By President Reagan's second term, though, unemployment rates above 7 percent are called "normal" and "acceptable," or even a "boom." If you can get away with defining 7 percent unemployment as "full employment," you can cut back on benefit and training programs while 8 million Americans who are looking for work are unable to find it.[12]

From 1981 through 1985, real gross national product (GNP) grew by 12.6 percent. That sounds impressive until one compares this figure with the growth rate during the previous five years. In Gerald Ford's last year and Jimmy Carter's four years, real GNP increased by 23.2 percent. Ronald Reagan's supply-side miracle cure cut the rate of economic growth in half.[13]

There was genuine progress under Reagan in lowering inflation, but even here he helped himself along by redefining the problem. In 1971 an inflation rate of 4 percent was so alarming that it prompted President Nixon to institute wage and price controls in preparation for his re-election campaign. Under President Reagan the same rate of inflation was equated with complete price stability and seen as cause for rejoicing, not for ameliorative actions. Some economists went so far as to call the average annual inflation rate of 5.7 percent between June 1980 and June 1985 "disinflation."[14]

Four causes of the moderation of inflation stand out: the 1982 recession and the lingering higher rate of unemployment kept wages down; the Federal Reserve kept the money supply tight; the price of oil fell sharply; and the overvalued dollar made imported products cheap, keeping American price increases down. If Mr. Reagan wanted to take credit for the recession, he could make a good case. He did not, however, choose Paul Volcker to head the Federal Reserve (that was the work of the "incompetent" Jimmy Carter), and it is hard to see how he can claim a role in producing the world oil glut. Reagan's policies were instrumental in raising and maintaining the strength of the dollar, but that proved to be something of a mixed blessing.

In fact the portions of the Reagan economic program that seemed to work were not based on supply-side fundamentalism at all. The recovery of 1983–86 was led by a rise in consumer demand, which was stimulated by an old-fashioned Keynesian deficit, albeit one of quite unprecedented proportions. "You can't rack up more deficits than everybody since George Washington and not have *some* economic stimulus," Rep. Morris Udall points out. "If this president doubles the national debt to bring about recovery, does the next president have the right to triple it?" Arkansas Governor Bill Clinton notes that Reagan was able to make his demand-driven recovery "look Republican, because on the spending side he was emphasizing defense instead of social spending." "Ronald Reagan," Arthur Schlesinger has said, "is the first full-fledged Keynesian president we have had."[15]

When President Reagan proposed his 1987 budget, many members of Congress greeted it as if it were a social disease (only twelve Republicans in the House supported their president).[16] This is understandable because that is just what the Reagan budgets had become. Their effects upon American society are not unlike those of an epidemic, though a slowly growing one whose impact is not readily apparent in its early stages. A look at how this disease was originally contracted and at its incubation period during the early Reagan years makes clear the actual goals of Mr. Reagan's "second American Revolution."

What were the symptoms that indicated the need for the radical treatment the president prescribed? There was only one: the rapid growth of an apparently malignant tumor in the federal budget deficit, resulting in the nation being unable to maintain its economic balance. The cause of this malady is quite clear. The disease was contracted in the summer of 1981, when Mr. Reagan—with the assistance of many attending physicians in Congress—sharply reduced taxes and began a massive increase in military spending.

At the time, Reagan used his soothing bedside manner to assure us that a new miracle drug called supply-side economics would keep the illness thus inflicted upon the American body politic under control and, in fact, would soon bring the patient to lasting health. Some economic physicians said at the time that this was more akin to voodoo than modern medicine, but the president asked us to have faith. A prescription that would add to the imbalance of a patient already suffering from loss of equilibrium might seem to be odd medical practice, but the White House doctor assured us that his treatment would restore America's balance by 1984.

Unfortunately, the good doctor's prognosis proved to be in error. By the time of the 1984 campaign, the deficit tumor had grown far larger, but President Reagan now insisted that it was benign. It did not particularly concern him. It was, he said, only the "doomcryers and naysayers" who were predicting that the deficits would choke off recovery. Such talk, however, contrasted sharply with what Mr. Reagan had been saying throughout his political career: that deficits are an addictive Democratic drug, dependence upon which is the first step in a fatal process.

Had Ronald Reagan simply changed his mind about deficits? Had he, like Richard Nixon before him, become a Keynesian? During the campaign, this seemed possible, but afterwards the president reverted to his earlier attacks on deficits, and a more sinister explanation of his motives in creating those deficits at the outset of his presidency presented itself.

It became evident that the Reagan deficits were created as part

of a larger strategy to subvert federal social programs. David Stockman admitted as much to Senator Daniel Patrick Moynihan in
1981. "The plan was to have a strategic deficit that would give you
an argument for cutting back the programs that weren't desired,"
Moynihan explained in 1985 when he revealed Stockman's comments of four years before. "It got out of control." Moynihan indicated that Stockman was trying to convey to him the message: "I'm
not a dope; I don't believe in these tooth-fairy tales." But Stockman
was a good soldier. When he took the reins at the Office of Management and Budget in 1981, he fed the figures on Reagan's proposed
tax and spending programs into a computer programmed to model
the nation's economic behavior. When it accurately forecast that
the Reagan plans would lead to the worst peacetime deficits in
American history, reaching well over $100 billion in 1984 (the year
by which Reagan was pledging to balance the budget), Stockman
took bold action. He altered the computer program until it came
out showing that Reaganomics *would* work.[17]

It must be seriously doubted that Mr. Reagan and some of his
advisers ever believed in the magic of supply-side economics. It
seems that they had more common sense than many of us gave
them credit for. They apparently understood from the start that the
offspring that would issue from Mr. Reagan's marriage of large tax
cuts to drastic increases in military spending would not be a balanced budget, but record high deficits. By pretending that they had
faith in the supply-side doctrine, Mr. Reagan and his aides achieved
three goals: First, they won the election in 1980 and obtained passage of their program in 1981. Second, their huge deficits fueled a
Keynesian recovery in time to re-elect the President in 1984. Third,
the unprecedented deficits might help them to gain their most basic
objective: restoring the prelapsarian America of Calvin Coolidge.

What Mr. Reagan did was to practice a strategy of reaching his
political and philosophical goals by allowing things to get worse.[18]
"It's so shocking," Mo Udall told me. "Reagan so much wants to
eliminate government social programs that he's willing to double
the national debt in order to do it." The ballooning deficits swelled
the national debt to a point where servicing that debt ate ever-larger
slices of the federal budget. Annual interest payments on the national debt more than doubled in Reagan's first five years in office,
despite a substantial drop in interest rates. In 1985 we paid more
than $130 billion to service the debt. The Congressional Budget

Office estimated that the interest payments would rise to well over $200 billion a year by the end of Reagan's second term. Put another way, interest on the debt appeared likely to be larger in 1989 than the entire deficit was in 1985. Then, even if all current expenses were covered by revenues, we would still have a massive deficit, the only purpose of which would be to pay for previous deficits.

But how could we get to the point of paying as we go for current expenses, when the president remained adamantly opposed to any form of tax increase and to any significant reduction in military spending? There could be only one answer. The growth of the interest-payment portion of the federal budget created, as it was intended to, increasing pressure to cut social services. Mr. Reagan made use of this self-inflicted problem to argue for passage of the Gramm-Rudman deficit reduction bill at the end of 1985. Although many liberals backed that legislation in hopes that it would oblige the president to face reality by raising taxes and cutting military spending, it was Reagan's intention that the act would result in the virtual elimination of federal social programs.

Ronald Reagan has often linked himself to Democratic heroes of the past, particularly Franklin Roosevelt. One thing that these two very dissimilar presidents had in common is that they both pledged to balance the budget and instead greatly increased the federal debt. But when FDR broke his promise, it helped to make the New Deal; Reagan's repudiation of his pledge was central to his plan to unmake the New Deal and the welfare state constructed in the half century that followed it. Roosevelt's deficits were incurred to help the needy; Reagan's were planned to become an excuse to abandon them.

Reagan may have hoped for an epitaph to his presidency similar to the comment a Native American made late in the nineteenth century about his people's dealings with whites: "The white men made us many promises, more than I can remember, but they never kept but one; they promised to take our land, and they took it."[19] In Reagan's case, it would read: "Ronald Reagan made us many promises, more than we can remember, but he never kept but one; he promised to destroy the welfare state, and he destroyed it."

If we may return for a moment to the medical metaphor, the Reagan budgets pose a threat to American society similar to what AIDS does to one's body. The dismantling of the welfare state and the rising budget deficits are together slowly destroying the American society's immune system. When the next economic virus strikes, we will have few defenses. Ever since the days of FDR, governments faced with economic downturns have used fiscal policy to stimulate the economy and counteract the downward cycle. "But today," Senator Dale Bumpers told me in 1986, "writing $213 billion worth of hot checks in order to have a growth rate of 2.3 percent, you gotta ask: 'What do you do for an encore?' "[20] It will be exceedingly difficult to restore the economy's health with a massive increase in the deficit dosage. That would likely be a classic example of the cure being worse than the disease, with the medication killing the patient. With fiscal medicine unusable, pressure will become irresistible for the Federal Reserve to pump up the money supply. That way lies even higher inflation than we experienced in the 1970s.

The social welfare programs established over the years between the 1930s and the 1970s were economic vaccinations; they added to the economy's resistance to the serious illnesses that often threaten it. When a downward spiral started, increased payments for unemployment compensation, Aid to Families with Dependent Children, food stamps, and other such programs prevented demand from falling off precipitously and carrying the whole nation into deepening depression. The Reagan cuts in these benefit programs have left us more vulnerable to the sort of contagion that swept the economy in the early 1930s.

Like AIDS, the immune deficiency syndrome from which our economy now suffers—though as this is written still in a dormant stage—is *acquired*. We did not have it until President Reagan pushed his policies through Congress. In another similarity to AIDS, Reagan's weakening of the economy's immune system has few visible effects until another disease invades the organism. When the next recession hits—and hit it certainly will—we may find ourselves, like the AIDS victim, defenseless.

Hypocrisy, a cynic might say, is the mother's milk of politics. But there ought to be a limit. President Reagan has repeatedly made solemn pronouncements in favor of an amendment to the Constitution that would require a balanced budget. This was politics at its worst. What would Reagan have proposed to do if such an amendment were put in place? He absolutely refused to consider any sort of tax increase. He insisted that he had abandoned all plans to weaken the Social Security system. He wanted military spending to continue to grow. He never suggested repudiating the national debt.

If Reagan would not increase revenues and would not decrease expenditures in any of these areas, how *could* he balance the budget? His answer was always to get rid of the waste, fraud, and give-away programs. Neither the news media nor the Democrats were strong enough in pointing out that this answer is sheer nonsense, but there is no honest way to deny that it is. Of the entire federal budget of just over $1 trillion that Reagan proposed for fiscal 1987, he earmarked less than $100 billion for purposes other than the military, foreign aid, Social Security and other entitlements, and debt service. With a deficit in the range of $200 billion annually, it did not take a computer to discover the absurdity of the president's position. No matter how much waste, fraud, and abuse there may be in nonmilitary programs (and it is highly doubtful that there was nearly as much left as there was shown to be in military procurement), it is difficult to subtract $200 billion from $100 billion and come up with a positive number. Put simply, the *total elimination of all domestic activities of the federal government*—everything from welfare through the FBI and highway construction to the National Park Service—would not have been nearly enough to balance the budget in the Reagan years.

The president's only recourse might have been to seek a constitutional amendment repealing arithmetic. When one Reagan admirer in 1985 urged that the former actor's face be added to Mount Rushmore, a wag suggested that it would be more appropriate to "print his picture on an especially commissioned $200 billion bill."[21]

People in Ethiopia in the mid-1980s ate their seed grain, an understandable action when one is facing starvation. Relatively few Americans are hungry, but Ronald Reagan set the United States on a course of figuratively eating our seed corn. His creation of ever-larger debts that devour growing slices of the federal budget each year cannot help but reduce future consumption.

The signs of what was happening to the American economy in the 1980s were evident in the nation's trade and credit imbalances. Those who still said that the Reagan deficits were not a cause for great concern pointed out, as Paul Craig Roberts did, that "until

Reagan became president, political liberals had claimed for thirty years that 'the deficit doesn't matter because we owe it to ourselves.' "[22] He was right; liberals did say that. But there is a big difference in Reagan's deficits, and that difference is not what Roberts implied: that the deficits were the work of a Republican, so Democrats changed their tune. The difference is threefold. The size of the deficit under Reagan reached another quantum level from what it was during the thirty years to which Roberts referred. In a mere six years, Reagan ran up a larger deficit than had been amassed in the more than two hundred years of previous American history. A more important difference lies in the purposes for which the deficits were incurred. Deficits of a reasonable size are not inherently bad. If they are necessary to pay for essential social services, or if they are used for productive investment, they are entirely justifiable. Borrowing for capital expenditures, education, or training or for social services that will reduce expenditures in the future is wise; businesses undertake such borrowing all the time. The reasons for the Reagan deficits, however, are another matter. Trying to end social services and trying to make the rich richer by unnecessarily cutting their taxes do not amount to investing in the future. Quite the opposite.

The final difference between earlier Democratic deficits and the Reagan deficits is the most important of all. We no longer "owe it to ourselves." More than half the deficit in the 1980s is being financed by foreign investors. We are beginning to mortgage our future to foreigners, and it is they who will be collecting the interest and dividends for which we and our children must work to pay.

During World War I, as European nations at war liquidated their credits in the United States and began to borrow to finance their fighting, the United States moved from the status of net debtor to that of net creditor. America rapidly became the world's largest lender, and remained so from that time until the Reagan administration. Then in a space of a few years, as foreign capital poured into the country to finance the huge deficits, the United States became the world's largest debtor. We had grown accustomed to hearing of the profligate habits of such nations as Argentina, Brazil, and Mexico and of their consequent immense foreign debts. Under Reagan we exceeded them all. As we sternly told those nations to learn to live within their means, we went on an unprecedented credit-card buying spree of our own. It was a textbook case of "Do as we say, not as we do."

In the most basic terms, this historic alteration in the position of the United States in the world credit structure means two things for Americans. First, our economy can now be held hostage by foreign investors, who will be in a position to cause a collapse should they ever lose confidence in the United States as a favored place of investment.

The second problem we face as a result of becoming a net debtor is even more sobering. Prior to the Reagan reversal, the nation as a whole was able to consume more than it produced, paying for the difference with dividends and interest earned from foreign investments. For sixty-five years, from 1919 to 1984, Americans enjoyed this surplus income. As this is written in the mid-1980s, we are still consuming more than we produce, but we are no longer paying for it with interest and dividend earnings; rather we are going ever more deeply into debt to maintain our high levels of consumption. It is obvious that this practice cannot be long continued. Foreign investors have bought American securities, but this transfer of capital is no Marshall Plan. They expect to be repaid. In the future, we will as a nation be obliged to produce more than we consume, using the excess to pay interest and principal on the debts we are now running up. "In the next five years," Senator Lloyd Bentsen told me in 1985, "if we continue at the present trend, it'd be like every family [in the United States] assuming a second mortgage of $15,000 and not having anything to show for it." By 1990 Americans may be paying foreigners in excess of $100 billion a year in interest. People in this country will have to run faster just to stay in the same place and work harder to maintain even a declining standard of living. Bentsen pointedly asks what the American people will do if the International Monetary Fund ever has to come in and direct us to increase our exports and limit our imports, putting us in the same category as Brazil and Mexico.[23] One of the saddest aspects of this developing tragedy is that it need never have occurred. Its cause is not that Americans, still in many ways the richest people in the world, cannot afford to pay for what we get; it is just that we don't *want* to pay and our leaders in the Reagan years encouraged us to believe that we didn't have to.

A graphic representation of the American balance of international accounts since 1950 shows dramatically what happened in the Reagan years. The line hovers near the zero line of balance during most of the period, and is positive at the beginning of 1981.

Then an abrupt plunge carries the line into completely unprecedented and uncharted depths of negative numbers.

The trade deficit that grew out of the overvalued dollar was $123.3 billion in 1984 and $148.5 billion in 1985. As this is written it appears certain that the 1986 trade deficit will be even larger. What this amounts to is the export of millions of jobs. It means that even the "boom" of 1984 was not much of a boon to the American worker. The "substantial forward momentum" that President Reagan detected in the American economy in considerable degree benefited workers abroad. Approximately 8 percent of our purchasing power was stimulating industries in other countries, not our own. "We've created a lot of Japanese economic growth in the last couple of years," Governor Clinton said to me in 1986. Japanese growth has "almost all been due to exports, mainly to this country."[24]

Perhaps it is morning in Japan.

There is nothing wrong with tax reform. To be opposed to the abstract idea of reforming the tax structure that Jimmy Carter in 1976 termed "a disgrace to the human race" ranks with defacing the Statue of Liberty. But there is always reason to examine carefully the specifics of what poses as "reform." That word can mean almost anything, depending upon who is using it.

That the wealthy were the primary beneficiaries of Reagan's 1981 tax program cannot be seriously doubted. Their taxes were reduced sharply, and they were able to collect windfalls by lending at interest rates kept high by government borrowing. I have already noted that one consequence of the Reagan administration adding nearly $2 trillion to the national debt by the time its tenure ends is that the $200 billion we will soon be paying in annual interest will not be available for socially useful purposes. The other side of the coin is that besides not being available to help the needy, that money is going into the accounts of investors, most of whom are living well above the poverty line. The deficits that were caused in substantial measure by the first Reagan tax "reform" are quite literally taking from the poor to give to the rich. The amount of interest in the federal budget constitutes an immense public expenditure to subsidize the well-to-do, both in the United States and abroad. This should come as no surprise, inasmuch as this is the basic goal of Hamiltonian or supply-side economics.

What Ronald Reagan would really have liked to have is no taxation at all. In promoting his tax-reform proposals in a New Jersey
speech in 1985, the president held up a giant 1040 form with a large
red circle with a diagonal line across it: ban taxes. That has long
been his ideal.[25] Short of that, the next best thing, to his way of
thinking, would be to have a "flat tax" under which everyone paid
the same percentage of his or her income, regardless of how large
that income was. In the 1960s Ronald Reagan said: "We have received this progressive tax direct from Karl Marx, who designed it."
This preposterous notion is not one that Reagan outgrew. When a
reporter asked him in 1980 whether he had actually said that
progressive taxation was originated by Karl Marx, candidate Reagan
answered: "Well, it was. He is the first one who thought of it."[26]
This would have come as a considerable surprise to such Republicans as William Howard Taft, who was president when the Six-
teenth Amendment was passed by Congress, and Calvin Coolidge,
who spoke in 1924 in favor of one of the Mellon tax cuts. "The proposed bill," Coolidge said, "maintains the fixed policy of rates graduated in proportion to ability to pay. The policy has received almost
universal sanction. It is sustained by sound arguments based on economic, social and moral grounds."[27] Could it be that both presidents Taft and Coolidge—the latter Ronald Reagan's hero—were
conscious or unconscious dupes of the international Communist
conspiracy?
    Coolidge was arguing for lower rates on the rich, but the basis of
his argument was on wholly utilitarian grounds: High taxes could
not be collected. He specifically said that he was not arguing against
the belief that people with very high incomes *ought* (the word he
used) to pay very high rates. "I agree perfectly," Coolidge said,
"with those who wish to relieve the small taxpayer by getting the
largest possible contribution from the people with large incomes."[28]
Where Reagan parts company with Coolidge is that the current
president actually believes that progressive taxation is immoral (as
well as Marxian). Attorney General Edwin Meese, one of the president's closest friends and a man whose beliefs are almost identical to
Reagan's, said in 1982: "The progressive income tax is immoral."
Supply-side advocate Jack Kemp also argued that "abolishing the
steeply graduated income tax system in this country" would start a
revolution in the economy. Perhaps. But the results of a similar attempt in the 1920s were not encouraging.[29]

One of the primary purposes of the 1981 tax cut was to make the federal income tax much less progressive. Despite all the talk about its "across-the-board" nature, it gave bigger cuts—in terms of percentages as well as in absolute dollars—to higher-income taxpayers. Someone who was paying at a rate of 20 percent and got a 25 percent cut saw his tax rate cut by 5 percent (20 divided by 4), while someone in a 40 percent bracket gained a 10 percent cut (40 percent divided by 4). When the 1981 cuts were fully in effect in 1984, a couple earning $15,000 a year had their rate drop by 6 percentage points (from 21 percent to 16 percent), while a couple earning $200,000 enjoyed an 18-point reduction (from 68 percent to 50 percent).[30]

Knowing that the ultimate goals of Ronald Reagan are to reduce the functions of government to defending the borders and policing the people, to lower the taxes on the rich as much as possible, and to eliminate the progressive nature of the tax system, it made sense to look very carefully at any "reform" he proposed. William Safire has summed up the intent of Mr. Reagan's tax reforms: "make taxation painful."[31] The more painful taxes are made to seem, the less likely people are to pay them, and the less revenue governments at all levels will have to spend on social programs.

Parts of the Reagan tax-reform proposals were based on ideology and politics, not economics. In 1964, Reagan attacked "people who view the tax as a means of advancing changes in our social structure." In pushing his reform proposals in 1985, the president claimed that one of his objectives was to stop the use of the tax codes to "make social policy." It appears that Mr. Reagan may have suffered from hyperopia. He saw the social goals of tax proposals made by those far away from him, but was not cognizant of those closest to him. An incomplete list of the right-wing social agenda contained in the Reagan "tax reform" proposal of 1985 would include: (1) tuition tax credits for private schools, which would further undermine the public education system and increase class differences; (2) ending deductions for state and local taxes, which would reduce the ability of governments at those levels to provide social services, undermine the federal system, and possibly even accelerate the movement of population from the more Democratic regions of the Northeast and Midwest to the increasingly Republican Sun Belt; (3) elimination of the $1 checkoff on income tax returns to finance presidential election campaigns, a move that would benefit

the wealthier Republicans; (4) the original plan's proposal to penal-
ize two-income families, which White House communications
director Patrick J. Buchanan proudly called "a bias toward the traditional family" and which would also have been biased in favor of
wealthy families that could thrive on a single high income and
against lower- and middle-income families that need two incomes to
make ends meet.[32] But far be it from Ronald Reagan to try to make
social policy through the tax system.

The fact is that we cannot help but make social policy when we
amend the tax code. "Tax policy is social policy," economist Robert
Lekachman has rightly said. The only questions concern which
goals we want to pursue. For President Reagan they were, predict-
ably, the same objectives he had sought for a quarter-century. Nowhere was this more apparent than in his attempt to eliminate the
deductions for state and local taxes. This proposal quickly put the
lie to the president's claim to be a "federalist." After eliminating
revenue sharing, which provided federal money to states and localities, Reagan moved to cut their home sources of revenue. This is no
more federalism than was the Hamiltonian "Federalism" of the
early republic, a philosophy based upon the opposite of federalism
whose advocates seized the name because it was popular.

The proposal to end deductions for state and local taxes was intended to be the second blow in Reagan's assault on government.
The president sought to portray this change as a penalty on "high-
tax states," giving the impression that such states are wasteful "big
spenders." He said that deductibility amounts to a subsidy by low-
tax states of high-tax states.[33] The former charge is misleading in the
extreme; the latter is nonsense.

The "high-tax states" have earned that distinction for two reasons: they have a larger number of needy citizens per capita and
they are more willing to live up to their social responsibilities in
providing for them. State taxes can be equalized, as New York Governor Mario M. Cuomo told a hearing of the House Ways and
Means Committee in July 1985, when low-tax states want to take
their share of prison inmates, drug addicts, homeless people, and
welfare recipients. "How many do you want?" he pointedly asked
representatives of "low-tax states." "This notion that we [in the so-
called high-tax states] are manipulating our taxes so that we can attract more homeless, more criminals, more drug addicts, more welfare cases," Cuomo said, "is ridiculous."

The idea that low-tax states are subsidizing high-tax ones is laughable. Most of the high-tax states pay far more in federal taxes than they receive back in federal spending, while the opposite is the case with low-tax states, most of which have low per-capita incomes. this is as it should be; it is what the federal system is all about: the strong assist the weak; those who have more help those with less. "If you gave back to every state exactly what it contributed," Governor Cuomo pointed out, "you wouldn't need a federal Union."[34]

Tax reform had long been a liberal Democratic issue. The principal architect of the bill enacted in 1986 was Democratic Senator Bill Bradley of New Jersey. The legislation marked a definite improvement in the tax code, inasmuch as it removed some 6 million low-income people from the tax rolls, forced profitable corporations and wealthy people to pay some taxes, shifted a significant portion of the tax burden to corporations and, by closing loopholes, obliged the richest taxpayers to pay a higher *effective* rate than before. Little of this was intended by President Reagan, but he climbed on board Bradley's plan and attempted to take the credit for it.

There were also serious shortcomings in the 1986 Tax Reform Act. Most important, even with the closing of loopholes, the very rich were let off with a lower rate than they should be paying. The addition of one more bracket for people with high incomes would make the tax system fairer and more progressive, would help to cut the deficit, and would be a very popular move. An overwhelming majority of Americans believes that high-income people pay too little. The creation of another rate for the wealthy should be part of the New Progressive program.[35]

Short-term economic predictions are always risky at best. The long-term dangers in the economic course of the United States in the mid-eighties are another matter. It can be said with a high degree of certainty that disaster lurks somewhere not far down this path. The only hope for avoiding it is to change our course, and the longer we take to do so, the more difficult it will be to avoid twilight in America.

Ronald Reagan did not succeed in destroying the welfare state or Americans' social consciences, but he certainly changed the terms of debate and markedly narrowed the alternatives for Democratic economic policy. I can do no more here than outline a few of the ideas that progressives should consider in their struggle to develop policies that will be true to liberal social goals and at the same time help the nation and the world weather the economic crisis that seems to loom before us.

Many Democrats are still suffering from a reflexive obeisance to the god of Free Trade. There is no better teacher than history, but there is no worse guide if its lessons are misread. Two "lessons of history" have stood out more boldly than all others for the past two generations of American leaders. Both arose in the 1930s. The two evils to be avoided at all costs are "protectionism" and "appeasement." The former is associated with the names Hawley and Smoot, the latter with Munich. The first, history has allegedly taught us, causes worldwide depression; the second encourages aggressors and leads to worldwide war.

This is not the place to examine the merits of the lesson of Munich, but if liberals are even to begin to formulate an economic policy with some prospect of getting the United States out of the morass in which we now find ourselves, it will be necessary to rethink several of our most hallowed assumptions. Protectionism is a good place to start.

The Hawley-Smoot tariff of 1930 was part of a trade war that worsened the Great Depression. But if we leave it at that and draw the conclusion that *any* protection under any circumstances is a fateful step toward disaster, we make a serious error. Three points should be understood about Hawley-Smoot. First, it did not *cause* the Depression. Second, world economic conditions in the 1930s were vastly different from those of the 1980s. Third, Franklin Roosevelt found it necessary to operate behind tariff walls in order to try to cure the domestic depression without foreign interference that could have upset any New Deal attempts to achieve recovery.

The choice today is not between free trade and protection; it is among types of protection. Free trade might work well in a perfect world, but we have no prospect of living in such a world any time soon. We are dealing with a world economy in which everyone—including the United States—practices some form of protectionism. While Ronald Reagan (and most liberals) are seeking to restore the international world of David Ricardo, our competitors have gone farther back to borrow policies from the mercantilists.[36]

The history of free trade is instructive. Its strongest advocates in the nineteenth century were English; in the first half of the twentieth century, Americans were in the forefront of those preaching the gospel according to Richard Cobden. Today it seems to be the Japanese who most loudly hail the principles of the General Agreement on Tariffs and Trade (although, like their predecessors, they follow them rather selectively). It appears that while the benefits of free trade are supposed to be enjoyed by all, they are most obvious to the leading producing nation of each era. Americans who continue unreservedly to praise free trade when they have been surpassed by the Japanese do so at their own peril.

This is not to say that progressive Democrats should embrace a policy of erecting high tariff barriers whenever we see an American product threatened by imports. The sort of protection we need is not reactive and defensive; it should be innovative and offensive. Crude protectionism is indeed foolish and self-defeating, but there is such a thing as enlightened protection, and it can be combined with vigorous cooperative government action to assist American industry. What we need might better be called "promotionism" than protectionism.

Many of those who condemn protectionism believe that foreign competition will cause American wage rates to fall and that this is to the good. Do they seriously argue that American workers ought to be satisfied with the standard of living of workers in Singapore or Korea? Our relatively high wage rates can be an advantage. The greatest era of prosperity that we have ever experienced came in the high wage period that began during World War II and continued into the 1970s. High wages create high consumer demand. But if we are to enjoy the benefits of high wages, we must find ways to keep a sizable part of that demand at home. One of the reasons that even the massive deficits of the Reagan years failed to reduce unemployment to an acceptable level is that much of the demand that arose in this country as a result of both high wages and deficits was spent on imports. As Robert Kuttner has said, "the Keynesian pump leaks."[37]

The way to stop those leaks and regain control over our own economy is to develop sensible economic policies that will hold down the flood of imports and provide a degree of predictability that will encourage investment and modernization. This cannot be done by following the Reagan philosophy of laissez-faire. An active government is needed to take the lead in restoring America's competitive position in the world. We need not look at Japanese electronics to find an example of how an integrated program of cooperation among producers, financiers, researchers, and an affirmative government can produce a successful sector of an economy. As Gary Hart has pointed out, we have in American agriculture an example of what a "generally far-sighted, coordinated and cooperative approach" can accomplish.[38] Under such a program led by active government, American agriculture has been one of the marvels of the modern world. Its recent problems have come not from government intervention, but principally from an overvalued dollar, which destroyed America's ability to export agricultural as well as other products, and from the "promotionist" practices of other governments that provide export subsidies for their farm products.

It will be necessary for the American government to show the sort of leadership in industry that it once did in agriculture, if this nation is to avoid a permanent loss of strength in all industries from textiles through steel and automobiles to electronics and computers. We need coordinated efforts in research, training, public and private financing of promising ventures and ideas, job security, and continued high wage rates. Such policies could be developed by a modern version of the New Deal's National Recovery Administration. Cooperation of this sort would be denounced by some on the left as "corporate liberalism" and some on the right as "socialism," but in fact it would only be making use of our democratic institutions to promote the common good.[39]

Hart's call for a "high-technology Morrill Act," modeled on the legislation that created land-grant colleges, is a worthy idea for helping to restore America's competitive position.[40] But better-educated scientists and technicians will get us nowhere unless we also have properly trained workers who can feel reasonably secure in their jobs, sufficient investment, and some assurance of a market for the products of American industry.

Where all this differs from reactive, defensive protectionism should be apparent. Promotionism is a positive step. Tariffs were once used to protect "infant industries." Today they more often protect elderly industries that their managers, whatever their religious beliefs, have no desire to see born again. They prefer instead to grow decrepit behind higher and higher tariff walls. That crude sort of protection *is* folly, and that is the only kind we have been getting lately. When in future years the federal government offers some protection from excessive foreign competition, the companies that receive that protection must be required to modernize their plant and preserve workers' jobs, not continue their old practices, lay off workers, and use their profits to raid other companies. It has often been the latter practice, which Harvard economist Robert B. Reich has dubbed "paper entrepreneurialism," that the Reagan tax cuts have financed. Such shifting of assets may help a given company's ledgers in the short run, but it produces no new wealth and the nation as a whole derives no good from the rearrangement of ownership. Strings must be carefully affixed to any government assistance and protection.[41]

New ideas are needed, but old ideas ought not to be rejected merely because they are old. Just as a modern version of the National Recovery Administration might provide the sort of cooperative industrial policy that the United States needs to succeed in the world market, several other ideas from the 1930s deserve to be revived. One, long advocated by New York investment banker Felix Rohatyn, is a modified Reconstruction Finance Corporation, to provide desperately needed capital for new and rebuilding industries. Relatively small infusions of public investments could often stimulate private investors to join a promising venture. Such an effort would fit perfectly with the New Progressive emphasis on cooperation. Another idea worth reviving is that of the WPA, to provide work and some dignity to the able-bodied jobless and at the same time begin to rebuild public facilities that have been decaying since the demise of the first WPA. A new Civilian Conservation Corps could also combine worthy social and economic goals.

Retooling programs that have served as well in the past can be helpful, but liberals must realize that we are living in a rapidly changing world economy that demands new approaches. Our problems are not going to solve themselves. "Unleash free enterprise" may be a catchy slogan, but it does not add up to a program that has any chance of success. What that right-wing agenda amounts to is further cutting of social spending, reducing government regulation, and widening the gap between rich and poor in order to provide greater incentives. A strong case can be made that this is precisely the wrong prescription for our economic ills.[42]

Social spending should not be equated with throwing money away. If it is done properly, such spending amounts to investment in our most important resource: our people. Spending money on education is certainly not wasting it. Why is it that people who praise business practices and desire "more business in government" usually cannot see that, like businesses, the government ought to spend money to make or save money? Even if they require borrowing, such investments in education, retraining, industrial modernization, and research are prudent moves for the society, just as similar actions are for individual businesses. To look, as most right-wingers do, only at the current cost of social programs and not at the future benefits is an example of the short-term thinking that plagues American business and society today.

Liberals should explore ways in which social programs can be made more productive. They tend too much to promote dependence instead of making a sincere effort to help the needy individual progress. To the extent it proves feasible, we ought to try to transform unemployment insurance into a system of *employment assurance*. A revamped system could encourage companies to retain workers during recessions and to offer them retraining when their job skills become obsolete. A more flexible system of employment assurance has obvious advantages over the current setup, which offers those who lose their jobs nothing but a maintenance income and completely cuts them off if they take even part-time employment. Providing vouchers that can be used for retraining, relocation, or perhaps even for starting a small business would be part of such a flexible employment assurance program.[43]

Eliminating government "interference" is not the solution to our economic woes. As Lester Thurow has pointed out, many highly successful industrial nations, including West Germany and Japan, have far more economic regulation than does the United States. In particular, it would be wise to make it difficult for businesses to dismiss workers and encourage *productive* investments that are likely to lead to greater efficiency. Some regulations are useful, others plainly are counterproductive. Each should be judged on its particular merits, not by whether it fits one's ideology.[44]

The most pernicious of the right-wing assumptions about unleashing free enterprise is that a greater degree of inequality is needed to provide the incentives for businessmen and the goads for workers that will bring about economic progress. As John Kenneth Galbraith has wryly phrased this right-wing contention: "The poor need the incentive of lower benefits, while the rich require the incentive of lower taxes." This assumption is not supported by international comparisons. The gap between the top 10 percent and the bottom 10 percent of income recipients in the early 1980s was 36 percent less in West Germany and 50 percent less in Japan than in the United States. Those competing nations seem to find incentives without gross inequality. The assumption that increasing inequality is the key to economic progress is also disproved by the American experience. The disparity was greatest in the 1920s, and the maldistribution of income finally weakened demand to the point where the economy collapsed. One of the major factors in keeping our economy in relative prosperity in the postwar years was a less unequal distribution of income. This meant more purchasing power in the hands of those in the middle-income groups who would spend most of it on consumer goods. The conscious effort on the part of the Reagan administration to reverse the salutary lessening of maldistribution was among the more foolhardy policies of the 1980s.[45]

It is, of course, true that incentives are necessary. But the experience of other nations and our own past indicate that income differentials need not be huge to be sufficient. Saying otherwise merely feeds the socially destructive greed that has been promoted in recent years. *Lessening* inequality is the way to economic progress. Providing security for workers is likely to make them more productive.

We are living in an age when human resources are the most important asset a nation can have. Capital is exceedingly mobile, as multinational corporations regularly demonstrate. Raw materials can readily be moved around the globe, as can finished products to be sold in markets anywhere on the planet. In comparison, workers are relatively immobile, at least in an international sense. Some may reluctantly follow President Reagan's advice and vote with their feet by moving from Pittsburgh to San Jose, but their feet will not easily take them to Osaka or Hamburg.

If we realize this basic fact of the modern international economy, we should also see that the most important area for affirmative government action is in human development: trying to create a better-educated and more skilled and adaptable workforce. If we fail to do this, it is only a matter of time before the United States will begin a serious decline and Americans will be obliged to accept a lowered standard of living. The future can still be ours, but not if we do not alter our course and begin an active program of cooperation among government, business, workers, and consumers. This is the essence of the New Progressivism.[46]

To compete, American companies need not only well-trained

workers, but also workers who have a feeling that they are being treated justly, that they have a direct stake in the success of the company, and that their ideas, when worthwhile, will be heeded. All these requirements point toward the need for greater participation by workers in their companies' decision making, for a higher degree of job security for most workers, and toward workers owning larger portions of the companies in which they work. The government has many levers available to encourage moves in these directions, but both the Reagan administration and its predecessors refused to use them. Democrats would do well to work out proposals along these lines, emphasizing tax incentives and the use of union pension funds for direct investment in the companies in which the union members work. Not only would such proposals be good politics, but they could also be helpful to the nation.[47]

Progressives must demonstrate that the view popularized by right-wingers, that liberal policies are the cause of our economic problems, is fiction. One of the most often-repeated parts of the right-wing brief against social programs is that the sharp increases in taxes to pay for those programs destroyed economic incentives for the "productive" (that is, rich) members of society. In fact, however, the increase in tax rates during the sixties and seventies was extremely modest. In the 1950s the percentage of personal income going to income taxes rose from 7.2 percent to 10.8 percent. Between 1960 and 1980 there was a further increase to 12.9 percent, but the rate of increase was actually three times faster in the Eisenhower years than in the liberal years of the sixties and seventies. If we look at total taxes of all types, including Social Security levies, we find that between 1969 and 1980 taxes increased their share of the gross national product from 31.4 percent to 31.7 percent. Can anyone seriously suggest that a change of 0.3 percent was sufficient to alter the behavior of businessmen and investors markedly and to plunge the economy from prosperity into ruin? In fact the specific taxes that worry conservatives most—those on high incomes, corporate profits, and capital gains—had been drifting *downward* for a decade prior to 1981. Why then, one must ask, was there no supply-side boom before Reagan took office?[48]

Another right-wing contention is that high taxes and government regulation caused a damaging drop in investment. But nonresidential investment accounted for 9.5 percent of GNP in 1960 and 10.8 percent in 1979. Conservative critics of the welfare state also give the impression that American living standards declined in the 1970s. This, too, is simply wrong. Actually there was a 24.7 percent increase in real per-capita disposable income during the seventies.[49]

Perhaps things were not quite as bad as they seemed in the seventies, but only some of the problems were imaginary; others were real enough. While gross investment as a percentage of GNP did not decline, much of what was invested was not going into productive uses within the United States. Instead, it was used for foreign ventures or for corporate raiding at home. And the rise in real spendable income was not sufficient to keep pace with many other industrial countries. By 1980 the United States trailed Switzerland, Sweden, Denmark, West Germany, Luxembourg, Iceland, France, the Netherlands, and Belgium, along with a few Persian Gulf states, in per-capita GNP.[50] Americans might be better off in an absolute sense, but they were declining relative to the people of other industrialized or oil-rich nations. Moreover, income per household was not rising like per-capita income. And of course there was the high rate of inflation.

There were three basic reasons for the genuine economic woes of the United States in the 1970s, and none of them had much to do with liberal social policies. The first and most serious was the immense expansion of the labor force. As a result of the coming of age of the post–World War II "baby boom" generation and of the acceleration in the number of women seeking employment outside the home, nearly 30 million people were added to the work force between 1965 and 1980, an increase of 40 percent in fifteen years. Such a shock could not help but be detrimental to the economy. Since most of the new workers were young and inexperienced, it was to be expected that they would cause some lessening in productivity gains, that they would have a depressing effect on real income levels, and that with the number of workers increasing at a faster pace than the work to be done, they would contribute to inflation.

The flood of newcomers into the labor market caused serious dislocations, but it is remarkable that conditions did not get worse than they did. Employment did not expand rapidly enough to provide jobs for everyone, but the American economy did create 25 million new jobs in the fifteen years between 1965 and 1980. Liberal social programs not only did not cause the economic problems of the seventies, they helped prevent those problems from becoming much worse than they were. One example: the existence of Social Security made it possible for the vast majority of people over the age of 65 to leave the work force. Had they remained in it, the competition for jobs would have been far more vicious.

The fact that liberal programs were successful in creating an economy that nearly absorbed the vast numbers of new job-seekers in the sixties and seventies implies that such progressive policies could accomplish even more under the demographic conditions of the 1990s. In the next decade the rate of expansion of the work force will slow significantly, as the "baby bust" generation reaches working age. In addition, fewer women will be newly entering the work force in coming years, since such a large percentage of the female population is already working outside the home.

A second disruptive factor in the 1970s was a marked increase in the divorce rate. With a large portion of the American population living singly or in families with only one adult, income had to be divided among more households. It is not true that two can live as cheaply as one, but they can certainly live more cheaply together than they can apart. Divorce is the quickest route for a woman and her children into the ranks of poverty, and the traffic on this expressway looked like rush hour throughout the seventies.

The third major cause of the real economic problems of the seventies was the astronomical increase in the cost of energy. The Organization of Petroleum Exporting Countries upset the American economy in 1973–74 and again in 1979 and provided the single most important cause of high inflation.[51]

In short, the genuine economic problems of the seventies were caused by developments largely beyond the control of the American government. The liberal politicians of the sixties and seventies can hardly be held responsible for the reproductive decisions of people in the 1940s and '50s. Right-wingers would probably like to blame liberals for high rates of divorce, but it would be difficult to make the charge stick. And the oil sheiks presumably made their decisions for reasons that had little to do with America's social programs. In contrast to the economic woes of the eighties, many of which *are* the result of the actions of the American government, those of the seventies were for the most part not self-inflicted.

The first step for New Progressives to take in identifying an economic theme is to show voters that social justice and growth are *not* incompatible—in fact, that wise policies for social justice can induce growth. Republicans have shown themselves to be interested principally in growth while, at best, ignoring distribution and at worst promoting maldistribution. The party that would join policies of growth and equity would be in a position to gain widespread popular support. Such policies provide the most promising means of reuniting the disparate elements of the New Deal coalition.[52] If they remember their past, the Democrats should realize this, because they long *were* the party of both justice and economic expansion. While the Democrats were so perceived, the party enjoyed electoral success. The party held this image from the 1930s into the 1970s, and remained the majority party almost constantly, losing the presidency only to a national hero and when they were blamed for a disastrous military mistake.

The evidence that the Democrats have been the party of economic growth is striking. From 1930 to 1984, Democrats held the presidency for thirty-one years and Republicans for twenty-three years. When the annual growth rates, in constant dollars, for those years are examined a startling result is found. Over the thirty-one years of Democratic administrations, growth averaged 5.11 percent a year. In the Republicans' twenty-three years, growth averaged 0.80 percent per year. *The gross national product has grown on average more than six times faster under Democratic presidents than under Republicans.*[53] The failed policies of the past, indeed!

A clearer indication that policies of social justice are good for the pocketbook as well as the soul would be hard to imagine. If businessmen would be guided by their minds rather than their gut feelings, perhaps they would see that promoting the common good can also be in their own self-interest. That, in any case, is one of the basic tenets of the New Progressivism.

The path back to popularity on economic issues is clearly marked. If liberals care about the distribution of wealth—and certainly they should—they must make it clear that they are just as concerned with the *creation* of wealth. Voters must see progressive Democrats as people who are committed to equitably distributing wealth, not evenly sharing poverty.

It is often difficult in dim light to tell the time of day. Is it dawn or dusk? At the end of the Constitutional Convention in Philadelphia in September 1787, Benjamin Franklin watched George Washington get up from his chair, which was inscribed with a gilded half sun. "I have often ... in the course of this session," Franklin remarked, "looked at that [half sun] without being able to tell whether it was rising or setting; but now at length I have the happiness to know that it is a rising and not a setting sun."[54]

We are not yet in a position to make a judgment like Franklin's as to what sort of twilight the American economy is now passing through. If bold new policies are undertaken by an active, affirmative government, we can still expect to see a genuine morning in America. If the current policies are left unchanged, there is little doubt that the dim light that surrounds the economy today will soon give way to the beginning of nighttime in America.

CHAPTER 4

Boardrooms,
Not Bedrooms

You've gotta stand for somethin'
Or you're gonna fall for anything
   —JOHN COUGAR MELLENCAMP (1985)

Don't go changing, to try and please me
You never let me down before
   —BILLY JOEL (1977)

Many political observers contend that issues are virtually irrelevant to elections. This is another manifestation of the prevailing cynicism of the Reagan era. If liberals accept the notion that image is everything and issues are nothing, then they become no better than their opponents. Beyond this, though, the contention that issues make no difference in elections is wrong. Campaigns carefully based upon issues not only deserve to win, they *will* win.

Of course the way in which the issues are presented in also critically important, but the issues themselves should form the basis of any progressive campaign. A candidate and his/her staff should always know *why* they are in a race. Their goal has to be something more than just power. They need a vision of what they want to do for America and the world. Communicating that vision—and at least some of the specifics involved in it—should be the essence of the campaign. Candidates who clearly articulate a vision of America that appeals to the people will win.

Although issues ought to be the basis of any campaign, a laundry list of issues will excite few voters. A successful progressive presidential campaign must find a theme around which to build its presentation of the questions. Discussion of too many ideas leaves a campaign without focus. Thought needs to be given to a wide variety of issues, but all should not be given equal weight in the campaign. Candidates must have the courage to make choices. The unwillingness to make such choices was a serious deficiency among many liberals from the late 1960s into the 1980s. Former Arizona Governor Bruce Babbitt praises his fellow Democrats for "sticking up for the underdog," but charges that "we have got lost in our own toolbox. We have spent so much time polishing our instruments that we have forgotten what they are there for." Leading Democrats, Babbitt says, refused to set priorities. This amounts to "a kind of Gramm-Rudman syndrome in reverse," he told me in 1986, "—you add on to everything because you don't have the *guts* to substitute one thing for another." Those Democrats who adopted this posture, Babbitt said in a neat analogy, were preaching a "Brezhnev Doctrine of domestic politics: that every dollar and every program is forever, that revision—any revision, anywhere—is to be resisted to the end." Cornell political scientist Theodore Lowi has called the refusal to set priorities a policy of "to each according to his claim." "If everything is good to do," Lowi pointedly inquires, "is anything compelling?" Liberals cannot, Babbitt rightly insists, acquiesce in the "mindless moral equivalence" of Gramm-Rudman, "as if every federal program—from the life-and-death treatment of infants to the marginal improvement of our roads—were equally important."[1]

The refusal to make choices amounts to an abdication of responsibility. And responsibility is one of the key themes around which New Progressives should build their campaigns in the late twentieth century. The basic theme I would suggest for Democrats is "Community and Responsibility." Liberals should not shy away from their traditional concept of an affirmative government acting as a "balance wheel." That is what has made the Democratic party great, and if it were necessary to abandon the party's basic beliefs to win, there would be no point in winning.

Mario Cuomo brings audiences to their feet by talking about "the 'soul' of the Democratic party." He says he is proud to be a Democrat. "We're the party that proposes solutions to human problems." Republicans, on the other hand, are ready to give up on affirmative government. They say, in effect, "We tried throwing money at the poor; now let's try throwing money at the rich."

Pride in the traditional values of Democrats should be kept in the forefront of future campaigns, but justified pride should not be confused with self-satisfaction. In his standard speech of the mideighties, Delaware Senator Joseph R. Biden, Jr., pulled no punches in attacking Democrats—himself included—for the sin of complacency. This attitude carried with it an abandonment of the party's historic commitment to change. "After fifty years of success," Biden said, "we stepped back and gazed with a paralyzing self-satisfaction at our handiwork. We said, 'Don't change anything.' " "The Democratic party lost the liberty of its soul at the very moment that we stopped and turned back to admire our accomplishments." The result, Biden tells listeners, is that the party lost its vitality. "The Democratic party became a parched, fossilized shadow of its former self."[2]

The need for rekindling a commitment to responsibility was clearly seen by many Democratic party leaders of the mid-eighties. Former Virginia Governor Charles S. Robb told me that he was interested in proposals to instill in Americans "some feeling of the obligation of citizenship." He, like many other Democrats, leaned towards the establishment of a requirement for a year of public service for people in their late teens. Gary Hart frequently reminded listeners that genuine patriotism involves responsibilities. He called for Americans to have the courage to care for their country "in an age of cynicism, self-interest and materialism."

It is Hart's view that the reason that Jimmy Carter's calls for sacrifice in the last two years of his presidency (when he spoke of a malaise) did not work was that "he took a negative course, and that was all he had to offer." Instead of the basically hopeless Carter message, Hart wants to call, as Franklin Roosevelt did, for sacrifice combined with hope. "We can't *just* ask people to tighten our belts," Hart told me in a 1985 interview. "We've got to say, 'We'll tighten our belts *and* this will happen.' We need to present policies based upon the common good. It's not just that *you* as an individual should be responsible; it's that *we*, as Americans, for the sake of our country, have to be responsible."

The experience Lee Iacocca had in resuscitating the Chrysler Corporation led to a similar conclusion. Iacocca wrote in his 1984 biography that he is convinced that "most people, when called upon, will serve—so long as they're not being singled out to get the short end of the stick." "Equality of sacrifice is the key to getting people to cooperate for the common good," in Iacocca's view.[3]

The Reagan administration fostered neither a sense of community nor one of responsibility. It legitimated all of our baser impulses and preached essential *ir*responsibility. Ronald Reagan denied personal responsibility for any undesirable consequences of his actions. Everything that was wrong was someone else's fault, usually Jimmy Carter's. Reagan also led others to believe that *they* should not feel responsible for anything, either. His message was consistently that we are not our brothers' keepers. We could have everything we wanted, he told us, without sacrifice. We would have a stronger military, but we would neither have to pay for it nor serve in it. The budget would be balanced, but no one's taxes would be raised. Someone else's ox might be gored, but not ours. To some people, this was an attractive fantasy, but it was never more than that. The time has come to accept our responsibilities again. Our future depends upon such an acceptance.

Of course the idea of self-denial should not be pushed too far. People must be urged to be willing to sacrifice to an extent for the common good, but asking too much sacrifice, especially without a visible crisis to inspire it, is political suicide. The right balance must be found. Exhortation can never be a complete substitute for crisis in motivating people to sacrifice for the common good. The coincidence of enlightened self-interest and responsible cooperation should be the constant focus. New Progressives cannot allow them to appear to be irreconcilable opposites. Leaving the impression that decency and self-interest are incompatible was one of the worst mistakes that Walter Mondale made in his 1984 campaign.

What we need are policies that will be responsible toward the poor *and* that will not be harmful to middle-class people on the make. Those who have already made it do not need any help, although they get a lot of it from Republican administrations.

A key to the New Progressive approach to both domestic and foreign policy is *balance*. It is apparent that voters are not satisfied with what they perceive to be the thrusts of either party. That is one reason why they seem to prefer to have a Democratic Congress to check a Republican president. Most people believe that the Republican party lacks compassion, but that Democrats lack common sense. Accordingly, a Republican president prevents a Democratic Congress from spending too much, while the Democratic Congress prevents the Republican president from cutting too deeply into social programs. If the Democratic party can show the American people that it will be *both* fair and frugal, combining common sense with compassion, it will put itself in a position to win a solid and lasting majority.

If the proper way can be found to express this combination of common sense, compassion, and growth, the lower and middle classes can be reunited in the Democratic coalition. The contest, after all, is for the allegiance of the middle class. Democrats can count on the support of the poor (although not necessarily on their votes, unless the party can give them good reason to register and vote) and the Republicans can take the support of most of the rich for granted. When the middle class identifies with the rich, the Democrats lose; but if middle-class Americans see their interests supported by Democratic policies that also benefit the poor, Democrats will win.

New Progressives have to convince people in the middle class that there is more to life than owning a Mercedes. If America is to succeed, we certainly must concern ourselves with material growth, but we will fail if we do not at the same time remember our spiritual needs, which begin with a concern for the well-being of others, as well as ourselves. People can be made to see that helping others is not only right—a moral obligation—but that it is practical as well. Liberals should not seek to make people who have succeeded and like to live a good life feel guilty. The desire for success is natural and healthy. What progressives are concerned about is the *exclusive* quest for personal material gain. Those who think *only* about themselves *ought* to feel guilty. They should be asked to reflect upon the emptiness of an entirely self-centered existence and to join in a "New American Family," to restore our American sense of community, caring, and compassion.

Inasmuch as the essence of democratic government is self-government, we should encourage as much participation as possible. Most Americans feel powerless in affecting the institutions that dominate their lives. We cannot allow the complexity of modern problems to become an excuse for moving away from self-government. The party of Jefferson and Jackson must always seek to make democracy work more efficiently, even in today's high-tech society.

An overall theme for the New Progressivism might be called the *New Responsibility*, the *New Community*, or the *New American Family*. They all point to the same general vision for America's future, a vision that blends the best of the values for which liberals have always stood with the new approaches that progressives will employ to reach those traditional goals. The Reagan administration spoke a great deal about "family" values, but its policies actually went in the opposite direction. Families don't disown their weaker children; they don't encourage their members to try to get all they can for themselves and ignore the needs of other members. Families don't whitewash the truth; they teach their children to face reality. Families don't encourage their children to blame someone else for their mistakes. What would we think of parents who taught their children to think only of themselves, not to care for or about their brothers and sisters? What would we say about parents who advised their children to live in high style on borrowed money—or, worse, lived in high style themselves and left their children in debt as a result?[4]

One area in which liberals stand to benefit greatly because the public is already with them is that of civil liberties and individual rights. We need a proper mix of individualism and community: a community based upon individuals. We must always remember that the whole is the sum of its parts, not some mystical entity that is separate from and above the individuals who compose it. At the same time, though, we have to remember that we *are* a community, not an agglomeration of disconnected, self-centered individuals engaged in a Darwinian struggle for survival.

John F. Kennedy's famous statement in his inaugural address that Americans should not ask what their country would do for them, but what they could do for their country, was a necessary corrective to the acquisitive individualism of the 1950s. It certainly seems better than the Reagan philosophy, which could be stated: *Ask not what you can do for your countrymen—ask rather what you can get out of them.* But even the JFK formulation could easily be pushed too far, into losing sight of the importance of the individuals who compose the society. As private individuals, we must recognize our public responsibility, but public institutions must also recognize each individual's private rights.

The Republicans are on the wrong—and unpopular—side on these issues. Many right-wingers would like to ban Darwin from biology, the realm in which he properly belongs, but enshrine him in sociology, business, and international affairs, where he has no proper application. Progressives would keep him in biology, where his theories were intended to apply. Liberals see a proper role for the government in enforcing the community interest in such areas as protecting the environment, guarding consumers against adulterated food, fraudulent claims, harmful products, and the like, insuring bank deposits, inspecting automobiles and airplanes for safety, and numerous similar functions. Many right-wingers would abolish such government "interference" in the marketplace.

On the other hand, far too many of those who claim to be "conservatives" are unwilling to respect the rights of the individual to privacy, religious freedom, intellectual curiosity, political heresy, and general eccentricity. Liberal Democrats have long been the champions of personal freedom. The Republicans find themselves wrapped in deadly embrace with the social repression crowd of the "Religious Right." Most voters, especially younger ones, are tolerant of diversity and nonconformity. They oppose censorship, the mixing of church and state, discrimination against women, outright banning of abortion, the teaching of "scientific creationism," and the whole agenda of what used to misrepresent itself as the "Moral Majority." Walter Mondale took his most significant jump in the polls in the fall of 1984 when his television commercials linking the Reverend Jerry Falwell with President Reagan were aired.[5]

Right-wingers claim to be opposed to big government. They are not. They differ from progressives in their view of the purposes for which a powerful government should be used. They want government authorities to decide how people should pray, what people should be allowed to read or view, which styles of life will be acceptable, whose political views should be tolerated, when a person's constitutional protections should be infringed upon, which foreign speakers should be allowed to address American audiences, and so forth. The Federal Bureau of Investigation under the Reagan administration saw fit to have its agents make "friendly" calls upon American citizens who oppose intervention by this country into the affairs of Central American nations. Reaganites regularly had customs officials seize political writings of which they disapproved when American citizens attempted to enter the country carrying them. On several occasions, the Republican administration refused to allow foreign speakers whose views did not match the official United States government line to enter the country. The Immigration and Naturalization Service under Reagan used police-state practices to harass resident alien Palestinians in California. The Palestinians had broken no laws, but subscribed to unpopular political

views. The same administration threatened to withhold federal research funds from scientists who exercised their right of free speech
by disagreeing with the Reagan position on "Star Wars" technology.[6]

During the Reagan years, the "conservative" majority on the
Supreme Court handed down several unpopular rulings that weakened the liberties of American citizens. Probably the most notable
of these was the 1986 decision that upheld a Georgia law making it
a felony for consenting adults of the same or different sexes to practice sodomy. Although the Court's majority confined its comments
to homosexual practices, the law that was upheld carries a penalty of
up to twenty years in prison of heterosexual practices that some
polls indicate are engaged in by over two-thirds of adult Americans.
The decision reversed a long trend towards a greater respect for the
right of privacy and was clearly unpopular with a majority of Americans. A *Newsweek* poll after the decision found that by a margin of
57 to 34 percent Americans did not think that states should have
the "right to prohibit particular sexual practices conducted in private between consenting adult homosexuals." By an overwhelming
margin of 74 to 18 percent, respondents in this survey opposed state
regulations of consensual adult heterosexual practices. Most Americans not only wanted to get government off their backs, but to keep
government away while they were *on* their backs.

Few Americans support such intrusions on their basic liberties.
Most of them disapprove of pornography, but they value free ex-
pression more than they fear pornography, as the voters of Maine
showed decisively in 1986 when more than 70 percent of them rejected a referendum that would have made it a crime to sell or promote obscene material. These Yankees were not endorsing
pornography; they were supporting the First Amendment, a part of
the Constitution in which Attorney General Edwin Meese and
other Reaganites have never showed much interest.[7]

Similarly, it was with good cause that most Americans in the
mid-eighties became alarmed at the threat drug abuse posed to
American society. But this well-grounded concern did not justify
President Reagan's suggestion that practically everyone should
abandon constitutional protections of the presumption of inno-
cence, against unreasonable searches, and against self-incrimination
by submitting to "voluntary" urinalyses. As Senator Ernest (Fritz)
Hollings put it, this was carrying the administration's concern with
leaks too far.

Other signs were evident in the mid-eighties that the tide of public opinion was turning against repression and in favor of freedom. In 1985 the California Board of Education rejected more than twenty science textbooks because they "watered down" the teaching of evolution. Even in Texas, long a stronghold of fundamentalist textbook censors, the State Board of Education asked for several changes to strengthen the emphasis on evolution and move away from "creationism" in school science texts.[8]

Liberals simply do not believe that the personal convictions and private practices of adults are any of the government's business. Liberals oppose big government in such areas, and can accumulate much political capital out of making that clear. The right to personal freedom, to be different, to do as one pleases in matters that have no effect on others—these are the American liberties that must be protected from government.

The distinction between progressive and right-wing views of the proper functions of government can be stated simply: Progressives believe in affirmative government as a positive force; right-wingers believe in intrusive government as a negative force. Progressives believe that there are areas of personal morality in which the government should have no interest. The proper role for the government, as liberals see it, lies in making sure that what goes on in the nation's boardrooms does not subvert the common good, not in checking up on what goes on in our bedrooms.

The role of government in "family" issues has become a hotly debated topic in recent years. Many "conservatives" believe not only that government should prescribe religious practices, but also that it should proscribe some of the most personal choices that an individual is ever likely to confront. The most obvious such intrusion centers on the question of abortion. Right-wingers scored a major strategic victory when they laid claim to the "prolife" label. If one side in a controversy is "prolife," it seems to follow that the opposition must be "antilife." Of course this is nonsense, but terminology can sway the outcome of many debates.

Abortion is one of the knottiest moral questions in the modern world. No liberal should pretend that there is an obvious right and wrong side on the question. To do so is to be "proabortion" and to be associated with the stereotypical "you make 'em, we scrape 'em" abortionists. The sensible—and ethical—progressive position on abortion is "prochoice." Liberals who pride themselves on compassion should be able to see that abortion poses a dilemma. It is for precisely this reason that such a difficult moral decision must be left up to the woman involved, in consultation with her male partner, her religious adviser, and her physician. The government in a free society has no business imposing the moral conclusions of one religious group on the entire populace.

This does not mean that liberals are "proabortion," let alone "antilife." It means only that they believe that matters of conscience ought to be left to the individual and not dictated by the state. Many liberals sincerely oppose abortion under most circumstances, but they do not want to impose their beliefs on others. This is the position that, according to opinion polls, is held by most Americans. Many Republican politicians, though, have indicated that they oppose abortion in *all* circumstances, including rape, incest, and danger to the life of the mother. That extremist position will result, as it should, in a substantial net loss of votes.

Liberals must be careful in stating their views on this highly charged issue. They have to avoid the error Geraldine Ferraro made in 1984, when she said that she agreed with the Catholic church's position that a separate life begins at conception. Once that step is taken, it follows that the rights of that life must be protected and defended. It is better to leave uncertain the question of when a separate life begins, as in fact it is.

Few people will shift their votes on the abortion issue alone if they support a candidate for other reasons. In 1986, antiabortion candidates for the Senate and House who were unpopular for other reasons were almost invariably defeated by prochoice opponents. One suspects that many voters who cited opposition to abortion as a reason for supporting Ronald Reagan in 1984 actually backed him for reasons they could not articulate, but used abortion as a more reasonable explanation of their votes.

Many of the opponents of abortion are far more extreme than they may at first appear. They would outlaw birth control, too, if they thought they could get away with it. They cannot, yet, in the United States, but the extremists have had more success in exporting their repressive ideas. In 1984, the Reagan administration indicated that it did not support family planning for the third world and proceeded to deny funds to international family-planning organizations that did not disapprove of abortion, even when those agencies were using American funds only for birth control. In 1985, the Reaganites directed the Agency of International Development (AID) to fund groups that refused to inform women of any means of birth control other than the "natural" one. If right-wingers want to end artificial means of family planning abroad, surely they would like to do the same in this country. As the public comes to realize just how extreme some "prolifers" are, opinion is likely to shift even further in a liberal direction.[9]

The "social issues" dear to the hearts of some right-wingers may actually be among the greatest assets possessed by progressive Democrats in the late eighties and nineties. Fear of the intolerant "Christian Right" is widespread. Polls have shown young voters to be most liberal on social issues and especially nervous about the theocratic tendencies among some Republican allies. If Republican candidates are closely associated in the public mind with this crowd, it will be of great help to the Democrats. This is true despite the 1984 results, because in future elections the Republican candidate is not likely to enjoy Ronald Reagan's great personal popularity. Voters in coming elections will be more wary of a Republican who is backed by the religious Right.

Progressives make a serious mistake when they let their opponents claim the "family issues" banner. The right-wingers talk a great deal about families, but their policies are often detrimental to family life in America. Their concern for human life, as one wit put it with reference to President Reagan, "begins at conception and ends at birth." Cuts in child and maternal nutrition programs hardly help families. Progressives who are "prochoice" must make it clear that one of the choices—in most cases the best choice—is for a pregnant woman to have her child. The progressive way to facilitate this choice is not by outlawing abortion, but by following policies that make it possible for a woman and her child to get along. This requires not the right-wing negative intrusion of government prohibition but the liberal positive intervention of an affirmative government.

While the Reagan administration was saying things like "as the family goes, so goes our civilization," it was cutting federal funding for day-care assistance by 25 percent from 1980 to 1986. Since half the children under the age of one in America in 1986 had working mothers, slashing day-care funding does not seem to be a way to improve family life and stability.

Family issues are real enough. By the mid-eighties, one-fourth of all preschool children in the United States were living in poverty—the highest such proportion of poor children in any industrialized country in the world. The rate of teen-age pregnancy in the United States was the highest in the developed world, twice that of Great Britain and Canada, its nearest competitors. The rate of divorce in this country was also the highest in the world, nearly twice the rate of the second most divorce-prone nation, Sweden.

What can be done to solve these problems? As the cliché has it, talk is cheap, and "conservatives" are always attracted to the lowest-cost approach to domestic social problems. For this reason they talk. Progressives must make clear that they will do more than venerate families—they will actively seek ways to help them. The way has been pointed by Senator Daniel Patrick Moynihan of New York. In his 1986 book, *Family and Nation*, Moynihan noted that while government programs have done wonders in lifting the elderly out of poverty, poverty among preschool children is a national disgrace. In some cities nearly one-half of such youngsters live in poverty. Senator Moynihan has suggested raising the personal and dependent tax deductions, indexing child-welfare payments (the indexing of Social Security ranks with the establishment of Medicare as the two principal causes of the marked improvement in the economic position of the elderly), establishing a national standard for welfare for children, and engaging in a massive public education effort to reduce teen-age pregnancy and abortion. A bill introduced in 1985 by Congresswoman Patricia Schroeder of Colorado and others, the Child Care Opportunities for Families Act, embodies another sensible approach to family problems. The need for better, safer, and more reliable day care ought to be obvious. Although many conservatives prefer that women return to the home, there is little prospect of that happening. Most families are going to have to find ways to cope without a parent at home during the day. Strengthening child-care facilities is a way to strengthen the modern American family.

The same is true of requiring employers to provide job-protected maternity leave. In 1986, 60 percent of American women who worked outside the home still lacked such protection. In contrast, European nations provide an average of five months' maternity leave at full pay. Those who claim to be concerned about family issues but fail to support day-care programs and job-protected maternity leaves demonstrate their hypocrisy. The same could be said of those who decry the alarming incidence of teen-age pregnancy but oppose sex education courses in the schools and television messages about birth control. In fact, while right-wing politicians continued to oppose such measures in the mid-eighties, the public had left them behind. A 1985 Harris poll found that 78 percent of adult Americans favored the appearance of birth-control information on television. The following year, a survey in Mississippi, usually stereotyped as the most conservative state in the nation, found 70 percent of those polled to favor sex education in the schools.

The government can take important actions to improve family life in America. The proposals of both Moynihan and the backers of the child-care bill are worthy goals for a New Progressive family program, and they stand in sharp contrast to the empty platitudes of the conservative family advocates. Those who said we could not afford increased spending on family programs failed to understand that these programs are *investments*, not expenditures. Teen-age pregnancies are one of the greatest causes of poverty in late-twentieth-century America. Lack of early childhood education and day care contributes to delinquency, adult crime, and welfare costs. Failure to provide sufficient nutrition for children and pregnant women (by 1986, the Reagan administration and Congress had cut the WIC program to the point where it could serve only about one-third of those eligible for it) costs many times more in later health care, special education, and lost productivity than it "saves" in the short run. A twenty-two-year study of the Head Start program showed that it returned four dollars for every dollar spent.[10]

Investing in programs that help children and families meets the test by which the New Progressivism should measure all its policies: it is both hard-headed and soft-hearted. As an added bonus, such programs would be popular with the voters, a combination that is hard to resist.

Yet we should not fool ourselves into thinking that the actions of an affirmative government—necessary though they certainly are—will be sufficient to solve America's family problems. Senator Moynihan put it well when he said "a credible family policy will insist that responsibility begins with the individual, then the family, and only then the community." Liberals have not only to help people but to encourage them to help themselves. In this regard Reverend Jesse Jackson stands out among prominent Democrats.

"You must say no to drugs and no to liquor and no to babies having babies and no to violence," Jackson tells young audiences. "Your generation has a different kind of tension, a crisis in character. I've never known a generation before where babies are having babies, where there is so much violence, so much liquor drinking, so much drug consumption, so many youths in jail, so much youth dying." "You're not a man just because you can make a baby," Jackson tells young males. One of his favorite slogans is: "Down with dope; up with hope." He points out to minority youths that having the doors of opportunity opened to them does them no good if they are "too drunk to stagger through the door."

This is all very much to the good. Jesse Jackson may have an opportunity to do for blacks in late-twentieth-century America what John Wesley did for the English working class in the late eighteenth century: give them a code of life that can help them to improve their lot.

Jackson is, of course, under no illusion that a moral revival would suffice to solve the problems of those in the depths of poverty. That is the Republican argument. Jackson and most other Democrats know better. They are not going to blame the victim for his oppression. But Jackson took the lead in the mid-eighties among those Democrats who finally realized that an improvement in morality among the afflicted is a necessary portion of the solution. "Now if you don't talk about these ethical issues," Jackson told me in a 1986 interview, "by the time you get to budgetary matters, the ball game's over." He said, "Some people think, 'If we just had enough lumber, we could make a house.' Yes, but you can't make a *home* with lumber. A house is brick and mortar, but a home is a spiritual center."[11]

If New Progressives will blend self-help with affirmative government family policies, they will be able to take this key set of issues away from those who have so successfully exploited them in the conservative years, but never did anything about them.

Common sense and justice can be combined into an effective and popular New Progressive program on women's issues. There should be no backing away from the commitment to true equality between the sexes. Democrats must pass again and ratify the Equal Rights Amendment. Such an affirmation of equality is central to liberalism. One reason that the amendment failed of ratification in the past is that its hysterical opponents managed to convince people that it would mean something beyond equality. Most people favor the concept of equality, but equality is not the same thing as identity. Liberals can push with all their might for sexual equality without endorsing the idea that the sexes are or should become the same. People should be reminded that they learned in geometry that equality is not the same thing as congruence. The distinction is crucial, and making it could go a long way toward uniting most Americans behind a program of genuine equality. What worries most opponents of the women's movement is not equality, but the fear that all distinctions between the sexes will be eliminated, or at least blurred. Such a goal is unattainable as well as undesirable, but there is no reason why we cannot move to equality at the same time that we are accepting and even celebrating dissimilarities between women and men.

A great deal of passion has been whipped up over the issue of "comparable worth." In the abstract, the idea that jobs ought to be compensated on the basis of skills required and contributions to society is most attractive. As a practical matter, however, this is impossible. All the arguments over comparable worth are doing is needlessly dividing people and distracting them from combating the continuation of sex discrimination in employment. There are many instances of jobs that have lower pay scales because they are defined as "women's work." This is intolerable, and every effort should be made to remedy the situation. But this does not imply adoption of an unworkable across-the-board comparable-worth policy. Supporting the goal of pay equity while rejecting an extreme and unworkable theory fits into a common-sense New Progressivism.

A large part of the reason for the continuing low pay for women (who receive less than two-thirds of what men are paid)—is the outdated notion that men *need* more because they are supporting families. It has long been the case that most women who work outside the home do so because they, too, need the money. Few of them are just trying to occupy their time or make "pin money." But today there is even less justification for pay disparities on the basis of need. Nearly three-quarters of all women in the labor force are single, divorced, separated, widowed, or married to a man with a very low-paying job. Such women are burdened with heavy economic responsibilities. Their need for decent pay is every bit as great as that of most men.

While pushing for pay equity and the Equal Rights Amendment, liberals must defend affirmative-action programs, which have been under ferocious attack by the Republican administration. Affirmative-action programs are intended to make up for past discrimination. The eventual goal is to have a color-blind and sex-neutral approach to all positions, but it is grossly unrealistic to think that we can attain that so quickly after centuries of discrimination. This applies to both women and minorities. No retreat from the principle of correcting injustice can be accepted. Nor would it be politically expedient to do so. In 1985, a national opinion survey found that 75 percent of all Americans favored having a "federal law requiring affirmative action programs for women and minorities in employment and education, provided there are no rigid quotas."

Many other women's issues have been addressed in the proposed Economic Equity Act, introduced by a bipartisan group in Congress in 1985. The bill seeks to recognize the vastly changed conditions in American society. "The focus of this bill," Patricia Schroeder said, "is to say that the real world no longer looks like a Norman Rockwell painting." Included are proposed measures to provide women with better child-care facilities, retirement plans, health insurance, credit, and collection of child-support payments. Passage of these measures would go a long way toward fulfilling the promise of equality for American women.[12]

No set of issues more sharply tests the commitment of liberals to their values and principles than that concerning black Americans. For the first time since the civil-rights movement began to achieve its successes in the 1960s, there has been in the 1980s an administration in Washington that is clearly opposed to the concept of racial equality. There was more than a little reason to doubt the commitment of Richard Nixon to civil rights, but his administration never stood as blatantly against minority interests as did the Reagan administration.

Conservatives, many of whom were still firmly opposed to laws guaranteeing racial equality less than two decades before, suddenly saw in the 1980s the virtues of a "color-blind" society. They have been able to affect a seemingly righteous pose in favor of "equal opportunity" based upon "race-neutral" laws. In fact many of them have used this position to hide their satisfaction with the perpetuation of racial inequality. The recent conservative conversion to race neutrality parallels the conservative adoption of laissez-faire at the turn of the century. In both cases, those satisfied with the status quo came to realize that non-intervention was the best way to preserve their own privileges.

Ronald Reagan showed his true feelings on race on many occasions. He opposed the civil rights acts of 1964, 1965, and 1968. In 1966 he said "I would have voted against the Civil Rights Act of 1964," which he said was "a bad piece of legislation." This made his later claims to fervent support of the race-neutral concept enshrined in that law more than a little suspect. As president he supported the attempts of segregationist private schools and colleges to obtain tax-exempt status and initially failed to support an extension of the Voting Rights Act. Through lawsuits the Reagan Justice Department tried to force cities to abandon affirmative-action plans that seemed to be working well. Under Reagan, the Civil Rights Commission was politicized and became a mockery of its name.

Nothing could be clearer than the duty of progressive Democrats to oppose the Republican attempts to reverse the gains of the civil-rights revolution. Beyond this, though, liberals face difficult choices. Democrats must find ways to maintain the black support that they have enjoyed in the last two decades and at the same time win back enough whites to build a national majority. Democrats who support black rights can do little good if they fail to win power. On the other hand, abandoning blacks in order to win white support would be inexcusable. Most leading Democrats with whom I have discussed this problem believe that the solution lies in finding economic policies that can bring together the interests of blacks and poor and middle-class whites. This is an attractive solution, but it may be difficult to implement. Finding common ground will be necessary, but it cannot be done by ignoring the genuine problems that persist for minorities.

The record of accomplishment in American race relations since 1960 is remarkable. Liberals ought to be proud of their role in this transformation of American society to a point where our practice more nearly matches our egalitarian ethos. In the early 1960s, large parts of the United States were not very different from South Africa. Today few young Americans of either race can believe the conditions that existed here such a short time ago. This is, however, no reason for self-satisfaction. Something approaching genuine equality has been achieved by a small but growing stratum of middle-class blacks. But at least one-third of all blacks live in abject poverty, relatively no better off in an economic sense than they were before the civil-rights movement began. The plight of the black underclass constitutes the greatest challenge to the liberal vision of a just, prosperous, and compassionate America. These poverty-stricken, nearly hopeless people must be made part of the New American Family. Saying this is easy enough, but bringing it about will be exceedingly difficult.

The black ghettos of the nation's largest cities are another world, wherein life is vastly different from that known by middle-class America. More than half of all babies in these areas are born out of wedlock. In central Harlem, the figure is nearly 80 *percent.* Approximately two-fifths of black teen-agers in these ghettos are un-employed. As columnist William Raspberry has said, "to a frighten-ing degree the inner-city black male has been transformed from potential asset to active threat." "Neither the young men nor their women," Raspberry noted in 1986, "expect anything from them, except the role of drone." Living with the danger of violent crime is a daily way of life. Schools are often more holding tanks than places where an education can be obtained. Government intervention *can* help with some of these problems, but new approaches must be sought.

The only way real progress is likely to occur in the black under-class is through a change in the outlook of these depressed people. They have been down so long that they cannot see up. They are de-pendent and without hope, and it is difficult to blame them for this, since they have never had much cause for hope. Breaking the cycle of despair and dependence will, ultimately, depend upon the people in the underclass themselves, but government actions can create the conditions under which hope can be cultivated. The wound is deep, and the treatment will have to be radical.

An extraordinary amount of political courage is going to be re-quired to get this process started. Both black and white liberals will have to reject some of the policies that they have supported for years. Most of all, they will have to be ready to accept the give and take of criticism. Refusal to criticize an idea put forward by a black, simply because the source is a black person, is condescending rac-ism. If the horrors of inner-city black life are to be eased, new ideas must be produced, and this process will involve many disagree-ments. White progressives and blacks must be sufficiently mature to realize that disagreements do not prevent cooperation and friend-ship. If Jesse Jackson says something with which a black or white politician disagrees, there is no reason not to say so. Politicians of both races are not reticent when it comes to pointing out the errors of white politicians.

In order to win white support it is not necessary for progressives to dilute their commitment to blacks. It will, however, be necessary to show that liberals are not what much of the public now perceives them to be: indiscriminate defenders of every program on the books, regardless of its merits. Many liberal programs have been extraordinarily successful; a few have failed. To be taken seriously in their praise of those that have worked, New Progressives must be forthright in rejecting those that have not.

To oppose discrimination is not to be indiscriminate.

The solution to black economic problems does not begin with dismantling our social programs so as to provide the incentive of starvation in order to motivate the poor to work. They cannot work if there are no jobs. A genuine commitment to full employment is the first—and as I shall explain shortly, perhaps also the last—step toward improving life for the black underclass, and for many poor whites and others who suffer from chronic unemployment. This could be the New Progressives' most important "new idea." The idea itself, of course, is not new, but new methods to reach it could help to solve several problems at once. We currently guarantee our citizens welfare payments, but we don't guarantee them jobs. Why not guarantee all able-bodied citizens a job? This could be done on the Swedish model, with government-created jobs as a last resort, but with government subsidies to private employers who would offer jobs to the hard-core unemployed as the preferred method.

Conservatives have long gotten much mileage out of calling state anti-union-shop laws "right-to-work" laws. Like so many of their other carefully chosen labels, this is misleading, but it accomplishes their objective because it sounds uncontestable. New Progressives ought to call a new full-employment program the "Right to Work Act." This would be a far more accurate use of the language, and it would describe just what the proposal means.

A second part of the full-employment program would reverse the Reagan policies of penalizing the working poor. His budget cuts hit the working poor harder than any other group. President Reagan's cutbacks in fact did just what conservatives have always complained about: made work less attractive than idleness. It is true, of course, that idleness became less attractive because of the cutbacks, but work for the poor became even more *unattractive*. Presently we tax the wages of welfare recipients at a rate of 100 percent (that is, welfare payments are lowered by the amount a recipient earns).

Progressives should pledge to pursue policies that will make work more attractive than welfare, by maintaining at declining rates such benefits as Medicaid and food stamps and providing day care for people who move from welfare to work. Such an approach might begin to restore a bit of hope for advancement among the desperate people of the inner cities—and the rural poor as well.[13]

Social programs will continue to be an essential part of the strategy for betterment, but with some basic alterations. Social programs are medicines, and like any drug that produces desirable results, they can also have undesirable side effects. One such side effect, as with many drugs, is dependence. Just as in the case of a patient who would die without a habit-forming drug, it is obviously better to provide welfare for people who need it, even at the cost of making them dependent, than to let them starve without it. But too much of our welfare system has become a kind of methadone program in which the poor are provided with maintenance doses of addictive assistance, but with no real hope of recovery, of "breaking the habit."

Both FDR and his relief administrator, Harry Hopkins, understood the dangers of dependency. They saw work relief as far preferable to direct payments. "Give a man a dole," Hopkins said, "and you save his body and destroy his spirit. Give him a job and you save both body and spirit." That understanding was once at the heart of liberalism; it should be made so again. There is nothing that goes against liberal values in seeking to provide work rather than welfare for all able-bodied people. This may cost more at first then welfare does, but it constitutes another social investment that will pay handsome returns in the form of future savings and tax revenues.[14]

Several leading Democrats of the mid-eighties pointed toward innovative approaches to lift people out of poverty. Jesse Jackson proposed replacing the welfare system with a "human development system." The current system is a negative one "based on presuppositions that are very antifamily," he rightly argued. If a young woman in high school has a baby, there is often no day care available to allow her to go back to school and become employable. If she gets a job, she loses a dollar of welfare payments for every dollar she earns. And if the father joins the household, she loses everything. "There's no incentive to learn, to earn, or to stabilize families," Jackson told me in 1986. "That's a bad system." Charles Murray would agree. But unlike Murray, Jackson did not conclude that the bad system should simply be abolished. Rather, he said, the negative system "must give way to a system that's positive."

"Workfare" started as a conservative concept, punitive in nature and based upon the assumption that most people on welfare are lazy folks who just don't want to work. Massachusetts Governor Michael Dukakis took the idea of people working while on welfare and turned it into a liberal program based on the belief that many people on welfare *do* want to work. The Massachusetts Employment and Training Choices program, known as ET, provides welfare recipients who desire employment with job training and counseling, placement in jobs, mostly in the private sector, and assistance with transportation and day care. The goal is to make welfare recipients self-supporting. "We're not clubbing people off the rolls," said the Massachusetts employment security director. "We're giving them a stepladder out."

Governor Dukakis told me in 1986 that what he set out to do was to establish a program that would help people "lift themselves out of a condition of dependency." He based his approach on the essential New Progressive concept of cooperation between government and the private sector and sought to produce "independence and self-sufficiency *with* a helping hand." The result is a program that trains welfare people for real jobs, jobs with a future. "This isn't working off your welfare check picking up bottles," Dukakis says proudly. ET provides day care for the children of those in training and continues it for a time after they are employed. The program also maintains Medicaid benefits for its graduates during a transition period.

The results have been impressive. Between the inauguration of the program in October 1983 and early 1986, ET moved 25,000 people from the welfare rolls to private employment, and not solely to minimum-wage, dead-end jobs either. In mid-1986 the average starting wage for an ET graduate in the Boston area, according to the governor, was $6.30 an hour, nearly twice the federal minimum wage. There was some dispute over the correct figures for the reduction in welfare cases in Massachusetts in this period, but it was at least 4 percent. Critics point out that there was an economic boom during this time, and argue that this, not ET, was responsible for welfare recipients finding work. This contention seems plausible, especially when one considers that the Massachusetts economy has boomed more loudly than that of any other state. From late 1983 to early 1986, unemployment in Dukakis's state fell from 6.4 percent to 3.9 percent, the lowest figure in the nation. Yet there is strong evidence indicating that the improved economy would not in itself produce a reduction in welfare cases. "It just doesn't work that way," Dukakis pointed out. "The economy during my first term maybe wasn't quite as white-hot as it is now, but we went from 12 percent unemployment to 5 percent unemployment in three and a half years. We had 250,000 new jobs [in Massachusetts] in three and a half years—but welfare rolls went *up*" by about 10,000. And during the recovery of the mid-1980s, welfare caseloads in the largest welfare states increased by an average of 4 percent. A rising tide lifts those boats that are seaworthy, but it submerges craft that are mired on the bottom or riddled with holes. Dukakis made a strong argument that the difference between Massachusetts' experience in the eighties and its experience in the seventies and that of other states in the eighties was the ET program.[15]

Even so, programs like ET are never going to solve the problem of the culture of poverty among the urban underclass. The effort to salvage the lives of the most-motivated 5 to 10 percent of welfare recipients is worthwhile, but it will still leave the bulk of the problem untouched. And just what is the basic problem? The urban underclass is the legacy of segregation. Plainly, most blacks are not part of the culture of poverty, but that culture is a largely black culture that survives in the inner cities from which more successful blacks have escaped since the civil-rights revolution. Those who are left behind are left without positive role models, without middle-class restraints, without hope, and without work. The urban culture of poverty was not created by welfare programs, but those programs serve as its life-support system. It is a culture in which family life is almost nonexistent and in which only women with children but without husbands qualify for cash-support payments.

Out of the description of the problem comes the outline of the most plausible solution. That solution is in large part what I have referred to as the Right to Work Act: government-guaranteed full employment. This would not discriminate against males, childless women, or traditional families, as the current AFDC system does. A job at the minimum wage would be made available to every able-bodied American who wanted one. There would be no humiliating means tests, as there are in current welfare programs. As Mickey Kaus put it in a brilliant 1986 *New Republic* article outlining a similar plan, "if David Rockefeller showed up, he could work too. But he wouldn't."

Such a system will cost much more in the beginning than current programs, but it will be worth it. There is plenty of work that needs to be done. By refusing cash or cash-like relief to people physically able to work but at the same time offering them jobs (from which they could be fired if they failed to perform satisfactorily), a serious—perhaps a fatal—blow might be struck at the culture of poverty.

Such a program is of necessity a liberal program. It requires strong positive action by an affirmative government. It is morally right, it provides perhaps the only hope of solving the problem of the underclass, and it fits with what the public wants. A Right to Work Act should be the centerpiece of New Progressive social policy.[16]

Many other domestic issues fit into the general New Progressive theme of "community and responsibility." Education is a critical part of the New Responsibility. Nothing is more important to our future than education. It is obvious that the United States cannot remain the world leader if our young people's educational achievements do not improve. A 1985 study conducted by the Northeast Midwest Institute, a nonprofit research and education group, found that 60 million adult Americans were unable to read the front page of a newspaper. The report found 56 percent of adult Hispanics, 44 percent of blacks, and 16 percent of whites to be "total, functional, or marginal nonreaders." The costs of this deficiency are staggering in financial as well as human terms. Congressman Augustus F. Hawkins (D, California), chairman of the House Education and Labor Committee, estimates that the functional illiteracy of one-fifth of the adult population of the United States costs the federal government some $225 billion a year in welfare payments, crime, lost tax revenues, remedial education, and incompetence on the job. Another cost of the failure of our education system is the weakening of our national defense. Congressman Patrick Williams (D, Montana) has pointed out that so many American soldiers "can't even begin to read" that the Defense Department must spend $1,000 per page to convert the manuals for sophisticated weapons systems into comic books, in hopes that the illiterate soldiers will be able to comprehend them.

One of the major causes of the decline in American education in recent years is that our teachers have not been honored and rewarded properly for the service they perform. As long as we refuse to raise the salaries of our teachers to levels that are competitive with other careers open to bright and talented college graduates, we will not be able to attract sufficient numbers of dedicated and competent people into this most important profession for our nation's future. Unfortunately, we must face the reality that this is going to cost us money. Asking for higher teacher salaries is not serving a special-interest group; it is serving the common good in a fundamental way. That is why, even within the tight budgets that it will be necessary for the next Democratic president to submit in order to reduce the Reagan-era deficits, it will be necessary to propose a substantial increase in expenditures for education. That is the responsible thing to do.

As we responsibly raise teachers' compensation, we are entitled to insist that we get high-quality teaching in return. Any increase in educational salaries should be accompanied by plans to monitor teacher competency and skill, whether the National Education Association and the American Federation of Teachers like it or not. In the mid-eighties, both organizations were beginning to respond to public pressure on this point, anyway.

President Reagan talked about education, too. He had a three-point education program: cut funding for education, launch a teacher into space, and pray. Laying aside the tragic consequences of the second part of his plan, the Reagan approach hardly added up to a responsible way to deal with a national crisis.

Part of a responsible education program includes opposition to tuition tax credits for private and parochial elementary and secondary schools. Diversity is to be encouraged, but the destruction of the public education system—a real possible consequence of tuition tax credits—would result in the demise of one of the major institutions that bind Americans together and that support our democracy. If we attend separate schools based on different religious beliefs and ethnic backgrounds, where will our feelings of commonality and nationhood come from? The New Community cannot come into existence without a vital system of public education. Separate schools correspond to special-interest groups. They may have a role to play, but it is not the business of the national government to assist them. As in other areas, New Progressives should seek to promote the *national* interest, not the goals of special interests. In education this means a major commitment to improve the public schools, not undermining them with subsidies to the special interests represented by private schools.

That commitment has to be financial, but obtaining quality education will demand much more than money. A national commitment to education must have a strong federal component, especially in funding and setting national goals, but in the achievement of those goals the states should be left with much discretion. They have to find ways to encourage and reward excellence, to relieve teachers of clerical and administrative tasks that interfere with their teaching, to reduce class sizes, and to restore a sense of professionalism among teachers. The best ways to accomplish these objectives are not clear, and various state experiments will serve to speed the search for effective means.

In its constant quest to save money in the most worthwhile areas of government spending, the Reagan administration sought to place a "cap" on the amount of federal aid a college student would be allowed to receive. This would enable poor and middle-class students to attend state universities, but not leading private colleges. This is an odd and revealing stance on the part of politicians who claim to believe in the work ethic and rewarding merit. Its result would be to turn the best private colleges once more into the exclusive preserves of the offspring of the well-to-do, thus cutting off from the poor and much of the middle class one of the most promising routes for advancement. Attempting to keep the poor and middle class away from the schools reserved for the rich would not appear to be a step toward the "opportunity society" about which some Republicans are always talking (usually on C-SPAN).

It has long been an article of liberal faith that education provides opportunity and must be made as widely available as possible. Cutting student aid reduces hope for the very mobility that conservatives purport to champion. Access to education is the principal source of equal opportunity in modern America. The Reaganites reveal in many ways that their actual objective is not equal opportunity, but a return to a society based upon wealth and privilege. Nowhere is that goal more thinly veiled than in the administration's attempts to limit college opportunities. New York University President John Brademas pointed this out early in 1985 when he said that "Ronald Reagan's proposals for higher education represent, in effect, a declaration of war . . . on middle-income America."[17]

In education, as in so many other areas, responsibility and political advantage point liberals in the same direction.

It is important for the progressives to demonstrate to the voters that they can be "tough" as well as compassionate. The best place to show "toughness" is on the issue of crime control. An effective full-employment program would be one of the best ways to reduce crime, but liberals cannot kid themselves or the public into thinking that that is *all* that is necessary. It should always be remembered that it is more expensive to keep a person in prison than it is to send him or her to Harvard. Preventing crime through education and employment programs is much preferable to dealing with crime after it has occurred. But that does not alter the fact that there are a substantial number of dangerous people at large in our society. Our citizens have every right to expect to be protected from them. Certainly we need to address the causes of crime in our society, but the facts that a criminal may have grown up in poverty, was beaten as a child, or didn't get a proper education are beside the point in protecting our citizens now. Certainly we have to work on lessening the likelihood that today's young people will resort to crime, but those who are already criminals must be dealt with as they are. The feeling that led so many people to see Bernhard Goetz, New York City's subway gunman, as a hero is misguided, but the fear that was the source of this phenomenon is real and must be dealt with. Effective and tough proposals that treat constitutional requirements in a realistic rather than a strictly legalistic way—but which do not undermine those guarantees—are needed. This emphatically does not mean, as Attorney General Edwin Meese suggested in the mid-eighties, that only criminals want to see lawyers before talking with the police.

New Progressive calls for tougher action against criminals ought to be combined with a forthright demand for handgun control. The gun lobby is powerful, but in a national election the vast majority of voters will favor gun control and the National Rifle Association won't be able to hurt a presidential candidate as much as it can those running for lesser offices. (Taking on the NRA could also be one of several instances in which the Democrats show that they are capable of standing up for the public good against special-interest groups.) Far more important than these considerations, though, is the fact that real handgun control is an essential part of any effective program to limit crime. Nor is there any necessary conflict between the legitimate needs of sportsmen and the imperative need for handgun control. Senator Edward Kennedy attempted to show the way for such a common-sense compromise in 1985 by making a clear distinction between handguns and rifles. Restrictions on the former must be tightened, but there is no reason why a sensible compromise cannot meet the needs of hobbyists and sportsmen by making it easier to obtain rifles and shotguns for legitimate purposes. Supporting such a compromise would show that Democrats are serious about dealing with the problem of crime.

Other steps can be taken that will reduce crime. One is to improve prisons, not to make them "country clubs," but to turn them into institutions that teach literacy and basic job skills. Presently most prisons are educational institutions of the wrong kind: they teach inmates how to be better criminals. Prison reform is not popular, but it could be effective in reducing crime in the future. Court reforms are needed in order to make justice more swift and sure, and to prevent violent criminals from being freed on bail while appealing their convictions. A national victim-compensation program also deserves serious consideration, both because it is right and needed and because it would be popular. As in all areas, on crime progressives must show themselves to be "tough but fair," in contrast to the "tough and callous" right-wingers.

It is high time that we get away from the notion that being tough on criminals amounts to racism. Certainly an anticrime stance has been used by some as a code for racism, but that does not mean that those who oppose racism cannot also forcefully fight crime. Far more blacks are victims of crime than perpetrators. In 1985 the Bureau of Justice Statistics found that black males are six times more likely to be murdered than are others in the general American population. The Crime Risk Index, based on 1982 figures, found that 4 percent of all blacks were victims of violent crime, whereas 3 percent of whites were so victimized. A tough but fair approach to crime would be of clear benefit to most blacks (as well as the rest of the population), and it deserves strong support from liberals.

The American public is much more concerned, as it should be, about violent crime than it is about white-collar crime. But the record of the Republican administration on white-collar crime has been a disgrace. Progressives must emphasize plans to deal with street crime, but they have a right and obligation to demonstrate that they will not be as easygoing with upper-class criminals as the Reaganites have been. Some Republicans apparently believe in the concept of no-fault corporate crime, an attitude that is bound to undermine respect for the law. There may be victimless crimes, but there are no felonless felonies. White-collar crime is not as frightening as violent crime, but it sets a tone of disrespect for the law that is most detrimental to an orderly society. The cozy relationship between the Reagan Justice Department and the leading figures in E. F. Hutton, followed by a 1985 deal under which no one in the brokerage house was prosecuted for a massive check-kiting scheme that fleeced hundreds of banks, was most distressing. What the Republicans seem to be avoiding is making higher officials accountable for what goes on in their organizations. Here was another example of the doctrine of irresponsibility that pervades Reaganism. Liberals have to show that they will be tough on criminals of all types, no matter what their social position, and that they will hold those in positions of responsibility accountable for misdeeds over which they should have had knowledge or control.[18]

One of the clearest applications of the theme of the New Responsibility is in protection of the environment. Conservation comes from the same root as conservative, and once there was no contradiction between the two terms. Unfortunately this has no longer been the case in the Reagan years. An allegedly conservative administration gave us James Watt, Anne Gorsuch Burford, Rita Lavelle, and a host of lesser-known officials who saw their functions as protectors of our resources and environment as the opening up of as much land to private exploitation as they could in the shortest possible time.

Watt's view that the second coming of Jesus is imminent, so there is no need to conserve for future generations, provides one possible explanation for the Reagan administration's approach to the environment. The president's own opinions that trees cause more pollution than automobiles and that winds blowing across oil slicks in the Santa Barbara channel are good for the health of residents along the shore may also account for some of their actions.

Whatever the causes, the results are clear enough to stand out in a Los Angeles smog alert: Environmental Protection Agency head Gorsuch attempted to allow companies to buy and sell permits to pollute the air. The EPA also tried to eliminate the limit on lead in gasoline, a step that would save refiners an estimated one-tenth of a cent per gallon and likely cause significant increases in retardation of children. Robert K. Dawson's record of opening wetlands to private exploitation as acting assistant secretary of the army for civil works was so bad that the National Wildlife Federation broke a half-century-old tradition of not opposing presidential nominees to work against his appointment as permanent assistant secretary in 1985. In each of the 112 years prior to 1981, new land was added to the national park system. The first year of the Reagan presidency brought that proud record to a halt. Indeed, Mr. Reagan did not see fit to purchase any park land during his entire first term. As the president had said a few years earlier, "a tree is a tree; how many more do you need to look at?"

Those of us who, unlike James Watt, hope and believe that there will be future generations on this planet, have a clear obligation to preserve the air, water, land, resources, and natural beauty of the earth for those who come after us. Such responsibility goes against the grain of the Reagan ethos of consume and enjoy now and let the future worry about itself. But most Americans still believe, with most liberals, that strong environmental regulations are essential. A Cambridge survey in 1984 found that 56 percent of the American people thought there was not enough government regulation to protect the environment, while a scant 9 percent thought there was too much. Moreover, support for tougher environmental regulation grew steadily during the Reagan years, rising 21 points between 1982 and 1984. And, as Congressman Morris Udall told me in 1985, environmental protection is one of the issues most likely to help Democrats regain strength in the West, a region in which they sorely need to increase their support. Here, clearly, is another issue on which doing what is right and responsible is also good politics.[19]

A seemingly obvious area of social responsibility is the provision of a reasonable level of health care for all Americans. It is not obvious to everyone, though. In a 1979 radio talk, Ronald Reagan complained that "many liberal activists are using the UN proclamation [of 'The International Year of the Child'] as a moral mandate for new Big Government programs such as compulsory national health insurance and fully funded day-care centers." The UN declaration said that "the child shall have the right to adequate nutrition and medical care, including prenatal and postnatal care, to child and mother." Reagan balked at the reference to such basic necessities as "rights": "to speak of necessities such as medical care as 'rights' is . . . to say that it is the job of government."[20] So be it. New Progressives should not be reticent about proclaiming that nutrition and medical care are rights. That's just what they ought to be in a modern, wealthy, civilized society.

Liberals should reassure the American public that the Medicare system will be maintained and strengthened. In addition, we must strive to keep down the extraordinary rise in medical costs and to protect families against the costs of catastrophic illnesses. Maintenance of health insurance for those who lose their jobs is another desperate need that must be met through government intervention combined with the private insurance industry. And progressives must seek improvements in preventive health care. One way in which we can move toward this worthy goal is through improvements in nutrition programs. Anyone who thinks to save the government and the people money by cutting nutrition programs is a fool. "Better pay the butcher than the doctor," says a wise German proverb.

A 1985 study by the staff of the House Select Committee on Children, Youth and Families found that every dollar invested in the WIC program saves in the short run three dollars that would have been spent later for hospitalization of low-birth-weight babies. Even greater savings are, undoubtedly, realized over the lifetime of a person whose mother received proper nutrition during her pregnancy. The same study concluded that a dollar spent on childhood immunization saves ten dollars of medical costs of treating rubella, mumps, measles, polio, diphtheria, tetanus, and pertussis. The $180 million spent on a measles vaccination program has by itself saved an estimated $1.3 billion in long-term medical expenses that would have resulted from the disease.

This is common sense: "an ounce of prevention is worth a pound of cure." But common sense has been in short supply in the waning conservative era.

Americans are justly proud of the scientific accomplishments of our medical researchers. They are second to none. The same, unfortunately, cannot be said for our delivery of medical care. Improving health and nutrition programs and developing preventive medicine are not only morally responsible; they are also fiscally responsible.[21]

American agriculture in the mid-1980s found itself in its worst crisis since the Great Depression. The Reagan solution to this growing disaster was the same elixir offered for all ailments: unleash free enterprise. Mr. Reagan was never a careful student of history, so it was not to be expected that he would realize that it was unleashed free enterprise that put farmers in such dire straits in the late nineteenth century and in the 1920s and '30s.

The family farm is now even more endangered than the family. A large part of the farm problem is the result of the same cause that plunged American industry into hard times: the overvalued dollar. By raising the price of American farm products in foreign markets, the high dollar choked off much of the export trade upon which American agriculture depends. A responsible liberal fiscal policy would be helpful to farmers and manufacturers alike.

But more than a properly valued dollar will be needed to save the individual farmer. We must decide whether we think the so-called family farm is worth saving. Getting the government "off the backs" of farmers, as the Reaganites propose, will lead to the demise of the individual farmer. If we let the family farm become extinct, we will be completely dependent on corporate farms for our food. From the short-term economic viewpoint of consumers, this might not seem a bad idea. Agribusiness is assumed to be more efficient than the individual farmer. (This is not always so, but for many crops there are economies of scale that are beyond the means of individual farmers.) There are, however, other considerations. If corporate farming takes over American agriculture, will prices remain low? Will the consumer become beholden to a small group of corporations that will be in a position to set prices on the basic necessities of life?

If we are to maintain the farmers as well as their land, it will be necessary to revamp our federal farm programs. The key here is target pricing. This means that farm products are sold on the open market, but the farmer is guaranteed the cost of production for a certain amount of crop. If the market price falls below this target price, the government pays the farmer the difference. If the market price is at or above the cost of production, the government pays nothing. In order to make this system work without stimulating gross overproduction, recipients must be targeted as well as prices. Only active farmers, not absentee landowners, should be eligible to participate. And a limit should be placed upon the size of the crop for which payment will be made. Such a system would encourage individual farmers, assure an adequate food supply, and minimize the expense to the government.[22]

Ever since the mid-1930s, labor unions have been among the Democratic party's greatest assets. Recently, however, they appear to have become more of a political liability. When Republicans denounce "special-interest groups," the image they most often seek to evoke is that of a bloated, cigar-chewing union "boss." Many Americans have come to see unions as selfish groups that have no regard for the public good. In short, unions today are often perceived in the same light that corporations were seen in past eras of reform.

To be sure, there have been unsavory elements within the labor movement, and unions have not always pursued policies that were in the general interest. On the whole, however, organized labor has been the most progressive major institution in modern America. Unions have consistently championed social legislation that is beneficial to the neediest of our people. Those who think that labor unions are an unnecessary drag on free enterprise do not know or remember what life was like for American workers before the organization of the nation's basic industries in the late 1930s. Unions still have an essential role to play in the United States, and liberals ought to maintain a friendly relationship with them.

But good friends are not uncritical. Too often in recent years unions have stood in the way of progress. Some of their ideas have been counterproductive. Democrats owe it to workers, as well as to themselves, to point out where they think organized labor is wrong. Liberal politicians should never again place themselves in the position in which Walter Mondale found himself in 1984. Asked to give an example of an issue on which he disagreed with the AFL–CIO, Mondale was unable to answer for several days. Democrats need the support of labor, but labor even more needs to have sympathetic

Democrats in office. Union backing ought to be welcomed, but only on the basis of labor concluding that liberal Democrats stand for the values that workers hold dear, not on the basis of politicians endorsing the platform of the AFL–CIO.

If American workers are going to gain control over their working lives, and if the American economy is to survive in the fiercely competitive international marketplace, we will have to seek ways to reduce the conflict between labor and management. The most direct way to achieve this end is through increased worker ownership.

Worker ownership is a controversial idea, but a good one. Some will suggest that it is socialistic, but it is actually a means of making capitalism work better because it replaces the adversarial relationship between owners and workers with a cooperative relationship. Companies would continue to compete with one another as now, but a growing share of each firm would be owned by the workers, thus giving the employees a clear vested interest in the productivity and performance of the company. Various employee ownership experiments were underway in steel, mines, airlines, and other industries in the mid-eighties. There are many ways by which the government could spur such enterprises, including tax breaks and government contracts. It could also encourage the use of union pension funds to purchase stock in the companies that employ members of a given union. Here is a "radical" idea that could greatly help the nation in many ways, including improving our competitive position in world markets.

Traditional liberal Democratic positions on most domestic issues remained popular with a majority of Americans in the mid-eighties. Rather than retreating from these positions, New Progressives will have to show that they believe in them. They must be courageous about asking Americans to live up to the best values in their tradition, and they will have to blend those issues into a campaign theme that accurately and attractively presents their beliefs to the voters.

Plainly this does not mean telling voters that Democrats stand for "more of the same." Americans are never for that. They are always eager for change, which is why they keep swinging back and forth between liberalism and conservatism. When liberals have been in charge for a long period, they come to represent the status quo,

and the people turn against them not because the people have become "conservative" in the sense of wanting to keep things as they
are, but because they are discontented with the way things are and
they blame liberals for the problems. This does not long remain the
case. When discontent with things as they are arises again, and
American voters are once more receptive to that tried and true political slogan, "Had Enough?", it is conservatism against which they
turn.

Liberals cannot, however, afford simply to wait for this reaction
to happen. They should take advantage of their reverses in the Reagan years to sort out those programs that have been effective from
those that have not. Their praise for some social programs will be
more readily accepted if they can point to other programs that have
not been effective and that they would be willing to terminate.

It is also time to think of new approaches to our persistent problems. Several possibilities have been outlined in this chapter. Together, these issues can form the basis of a New Progressivism that
has the potential to sweep the country in the late eighties and early
nineties.

The theme of a New Responsibility, emphasizing a blend of
common sense and compassion, will mesh well with attitudes of a
large segment of the American public. People should be asked to
make limited personal sacrifices for the common good. That is the
American way. The best way to give form to the new idealism and
the need to work for the common good may be through pushing a
concrete proposal that demonstrates the need to get away from the
destructive "me-ism" of the past several years. Nothing could more
clearly show a commitment to reversing the self-centered individualism of our time and the building of a New Community than a proposal to establish a National Service Program. Such a program
would establish various options for a year or two of service in the
armed forces, in such existing organizations as the Peace Corps and
VISTA, or in a variety of national, state, and local community service and educational projects. Whether such service should be man-
datory or be encouraged by some sort of noncash incentives such as
college scholarships and job training is an open question.

The idea of a National Service Program, particularly a required
one, might seem too dangerous and "hot" politically to propose at a
time when so many Americans seem so egocentric. In fact, though,
it symbolizes what a resurgent liberalism would stand for: it would

embody the return of service, idealism, cooperation, community, character, and responsibility—precisely the themes that coming Democratic campaigns should stress.

New Progressives might also emphasize the reciprocal nature of citizenship by drawing up a "Bill of Responsibilities" to complement the Bill of Rights. I would not attempt to suggest here the wording of such a document, but it might include a recognition of our responsibilities to future generations, to protect the environment, to nurture and educate the young, to respect and care for the elderly, to protect and assist the weak and the ill, to tolerate those who think, act, or worship differently from us, to guard our liberties by respecting and protecting those of others, and to preserve peace.

New Progressives will remain among the foremost champions of the Bill of Rights, but the creation of a Bill of Responsibilities could demonstrate that they do not see membership in the New American Family as all take and no give.

CHAPTER 5

Positive Patriotism

Born in the U.S.A.
I was born in the U.S.A.
  —BRUCE SPRINGSTEEN (1984)

You measure peace with guns
Progress in mega-tons
Who's left when the war is won?
Soldier of misfortune
  —JACKSON BROWNE (1986)

As conservatives inflicted political damage on liberals in the late seventies and early eighties by persuading many Americans that liberals are big spenders who favor high taxes and unlimited giveaway programs, they were similarly successful in convincing voters that liberal Democratic defense policy consisted of running up a white flag. This popular perception was probably the single largest obstacle to Democratic success in the recent conservative era.

The notion that Democrats have been opposed to an adequate defense for the United States is, as Senator Dale Bumpers said to me in 1986, "a canard." "The truth of the matter," Bumpers insisted, "is that this country's defenses had not been let down." In 1984, Congressman Les Aspin notes, the Republican-controlled Senate supported 95 percent of President Reagan's defense proposals and the Democratic-controlled House voted for 91 percent. "The Democratic glass is almost entirely full," Aspin said. "But a huge proportion of the public magnifies this difference of 4 percentage points and perceives that there is nothing in the Democratic glass at all." The trouble is that when truth and perception do not coincide, people vote on the basis of the latter.

Part of the Democrats' problem with public perceptions of their stands on foreign and military policy in the Reagan years arose from the same source as their difficulties on domestic policy: Ronald Reagan's penchant for offering the public simple answers to complex problems. "We're for 'freedom fighters' in the third world." "The Strategic Defense Initiative will protect us from nuclear war." "The Russians are an 'evil empire.'" As long as President Reagan was defining the problems and claiming to have simple solutions, Democrats who tried to deal intelligently with international and security issues found themselves at a disadvantage in the public debate.

Another serious obstacle to improving the Democrats' public image on defense is the media's general disinclination to report on anything that does not involve a fight. This means that the public never hears much about the 90 percent of the Pentagon's requests that most Democrats support; it hears only about those items that the Democrats oppose. Since the Republicans seem to support almost everything the military hierarchy requests, the issues the people hear about are always those on which the Democrats are opposing a weapons system favored by most Republicans.[1]

The public impression in the eighties that the Democrats would not provide adequately for the national defense did not mean that most people fully endorsed the international and defense positions of the Reagan administration. As they did on domestic issues, most Americans seemed to agree on foreign and military questions with part of the Republican position and part of the Democratic position.

Most Americans are strongly opposed to war, but at the same time they do not want to see their country humiliated. They dread the possibility of nuclear annihilation, but do not trust the Soviet Union to honor arms-limitation agreements. They oppose governments that deny the basic human rights of their people, but want the American principle of support for human rights to be applied evenhandedly. They are disgusted with the excessive costs of military hardware, but want an adequate defense.

Out of these basic elements a sensible New Progressive foreign and defense policy can be fashioned. *Balance* is the most important concept in these areas, as it is in New Progressive domestic policy.

The starting point is for liberals to realize that there is nothing inherently wrong with a positive form of patriotism. The guide in patriotism, as in the rest of the New Progressivism, should be reason—common sense.

The trouble that most liberals have with patriotism is that so many of those who most loudly proclaim their patriotism are the sort who led Dr. Samuel Johnson to declare it "the last refuge of a scoundrel." The majority of self-proclaimed patriots are people who are, unknowingly, far more "un-American" than those they attack. Such pseudo-patriots do not cherish the freedom, fairness, and tolerance that are central to what America at its best stands for.

Progressives should unashamedly declare their love for the *ideals* that have been the basis of American society. These ideals were long an inspiration to people around the world who struggled for freedom and justice. They can once again become such an inspiration, if we will forthrightly proclaim them and do our best to adhere to them. We dare not neglect our genuine military needs, but a strong reaffirmation of American ideals would give us a great advantage in competing with a generally discredited communism for the allegiance of the aspiring people of the world. American ideals are this country's greatest strength. If we will make a sincere effort to live up to them, we will regain the respect of most of the world.

Our culture is a far better weapon than are our missiles in the struggle for the hearts and minds of the people of the world. "Unfortunately," French activist writer Regis Debray noted in 1986, "Americans focus more on Soviet military hardware than on their limited political prestige." This leads many Americans to greatly overestimate Soviet power, according to Debray, "as if power in history is the same as the force of arms! What myopia and shortsightedness. There is more power in rock music, videos, blue jeans, fast food, news networks, and TV satellites than in the entire Red Army."[2]

Debray is right, and progressives should demonstrate their patriotism by reminding our people of the extent to which American culture dominates most of the world. But while we should not overestimate the Soviets' power, neither can we afford to ignore their military threat.

A positive patriotism emphasizes what is best about American values. It does not denigrate other nations. This is a proper stance for liberals. It is necessary, though, if we are to be true to American values, that we be sharp-eyed patriots, not the blind "patriots" that the political right would like to make of all Americans. "My country, right or wrong" is the slogan of simpletons. It is antidemocratic and violates the ideals and goals for which the United States was formed. Indeed, had Americans in the 1770s followed this slogan, the nation would not have been founded. If we would be worthy of our ancestors who established this country and guided it through its perilous early history, we must always try to keep our nation on a course that adheres as closely as possible to the principles on which the United States was founded. Such a course plainly does not include the automatic acceptance of anything the government may do.

Bruce Springsteen has demonstrated the popularity of this sort of sensible patriotism. Those who know his songs only casually often misunderstand his message. "Born in the U.S.A." is no call for uncritical praise of everything that happens in the United States. Rather, it understands that love of one's country means loving its people, land, and principles, not necessarily all its leaders or all the policies and actions carried out in the country's name.

Like Springsteen, progressives should embrace a common-sense patriotism that expresses love for American values, not endorsement of everything a particular United States government does at a given time. To try to change the nation's direction when it gets off course is to be true to American ideals and so to be truly patriotic. Liberals—and all Americans—should be neither reflexive doves nor hawks. Instead, they should be eagles who examine each situation with sharp eyes and judge policy on the basis of our national values. Such a stance will help liberals to get away from the damaging image of being unpatriotic, of being the "blame-America-first crowd." New Progressives have an opportunity to lead Americans toward being righteous without being self-righteous.

Between the 1950s and the 1980s there was a curious reversal of roles between liberals and conservatives with regard to foreign policy. Through most of the twentieth century, from Theodore Roosevelt and Woodrow Wilson, through Franklin D. Roosevelt, Harry Truman, Adlai Stevenson, John Kennedy, and Lyndon Johnson, it was political leaders who took liberal positions on domestic issues, who were the leading advocates of prominent American participation in international affairs. Conservatives from Henry Cabot Lodge through Robert A. Taft usually opposed such foreign involvement. Traditional conservatives attempted to make realistic assessments of the national interest and to build a foreign policy on that basis. They opposed American participation in plots against foreign governments and in military campaigns to overthrow unfriendly governments. Such actions, traditional conservatives understood, violated American values and so could not be "conservative" in any meaningful sense of the word. Traditional conservatives also sought to avoid excessive spending for military as well as social purposes.

The New Right that emerged in the early 1960s and took control of the Republican party behind Barry Goldwater in 1964 reversed the foreign policy of traditional conservatives. "Conservatives" began to identify themselves with global adventurism. Convinced of the correctness of their position on all matters, politicians and intellectuals of the New Right launched a crusade both at home and abroad. Crusaders do not examine the national interest; they do not try to determine what the nation can afford to do. They intervene wherever they see "evil," at least wherever they see evil of a particular sort. Crusaders know, of course, that humans are tainted with original sin, so they do not expect to make the world perfect. They are interested only in fighting the Infidel. In the modern parlance, the Infidel is communism, the "Evil Empire" and its puppets. Some who are "on our side," such as South Africa or Chile, may be guilty of great crimes, but this is of no concern to the right-wing crusaders. The national interest may be poorly served by supporting tribal rebels in Angola with little chance of victory, but when such right-wing crusaders as Congressman Jack Kemp decided that the Angolan government was in the hands of the Infidel, they dubbed anyone who opposed that government "freedom fighters" and insisted upon American aid for the rebels.[3]

In the past it was likely to be liberal idealists who championed a bold, global policy of American intervention. This was especially true of the "macho liberals" of the post–World War II years, epitomized by John F. Kennedy and his declaration in his inaugural address that Americans would "pay any price, bear any burden, meet any hardship, support any friend, oppose any foe, in order to assure the survival and the success of liberty." Such statements were based upon an assumption of American omnipotence. That delusion got us into Vietnam, a cause that "conservatives" embraced only after liberals had become deeply involved.[4] Liberals made a serious mistake in believing that the United States had the *military* power to make the world over in our image. (The United States does have the *cultural* power and could have the *moral* power to lead much of the world to choose to become more like America, but attempting to remake the world militarily undermines these other American strengths.) What can be said in their favor, though, is that many liberals had sense enough to see that they were wrong about this and to shift toward the traditional conservative position of examining means and ends in light of the national interest, American values, and realistic cost-benefit analysis. "Conservatives," on the other hand, adopted something of the stance of the macho liberals at just the point when that position's disastrous consequences should have been becoming clear.

The trouble with the liberal reaction against the mistaken policies based upon a belief in unlimited American military power was that, like most positions rooted in reaction, it went too far in the other direction. The undeniable fact that the United States neither can nor should be the world's policeman was extended by some liberals to the assumption that *any* employment of force by this country beyond its borders was to be opposed and virtually *all* military spending should be halted. It is this image that liberals must alter if they are to win back the confidence of a majority of the electorate.

It is clear that the totally limitless sort of adventurism preached—although fortunately not practiced—by the Reagan administration is popular with voters only so long as it remains in the realm of rhetoric. Ronald Reagan was always good at striking poses, and that—along with massive military spending and duplicity on the question of negotiating with terrorists—was the essence of his foreign policy. The Reagan Doctrine, diplomatic columnist Philip Geylin has noted, might be "defined as looking and talking tough as distinct from acting tough." After a group of Americans who had been held hostage on a TWA plane were released in June 1985, President Reagan said: "Boy, after seeing *Rambo* last night, I know what to do the next time this happens."[5] The public accepted such wild statements from Mr. Reagan because most people understood that he rarely meant what he said. There were exceptions, such as the invasion of Grenada and the bombing raid on Libya, but on the whole President Reagan talked like Rambo far more often then he acted like him. If further proof were needed that Ronald Reagan did not mean what he said in foreign policy, the 1986 swaps of a Soviet spy for an American journalist and of American weapons to Iran for the release of hostages in Lebanon—both of which the President insisted were *not* swaps—left no doubt. Voters in coming years are not likely to be so sure that other Republicans do not mean what they say, and the public certainly no longer favors the sort of military expenditures that Reagan insisted upon.

This leaves a clear, positive position on foreign and defense policy for progressive Democrats. It is a position in some respects similar to that vacated by the traditional conservatives during the 1960s. It is *not* isolationism. Gary Hart chose a good name for a New Progressive approach to the world when he styled his foreign policy "enlightened engagement." We cannot withdraw from the world, but neither can we control it. If we believe in our values, we must also desire that what President Kennedy called "the success of liberty" be achieved everywhere in the world. Such a policy differs from the open-ended interventionism of both pre-Vietnam liberal internationalism and the Reagan administration in that it combines a realistic prudence with its universal moral values and objectives.[6] The New Progressive foreign policy should be based upon principle, but it must also understand the limits of American might and the connection between means and ends.

A New Progressive foreign and defense policy should recognize the wisdom of President Eisenhower when he said: "The problem in defense is how far you can go without destroying from within that which you are trying to defend from without."[7] What Eisenhower was warning of were the results of a lack of balance in our policies. The danger to which he referred can arise from several quarters. One is the destruction of freedom by a government obsessed with security concerns. The Reagan administration's 1985 acceptance of lie-detector tests for all people with access to classified information is an excellent example of this danger. A second danger is the militarization of American society; a third is the weakening of the social fabric at home through the transfer of funds from social programs to the military; and a fourth is the destruction of the American economy by excessive military expenditures. Even in America we *cannot* "have it all." Choices must be made and balances achieved between domestic and military needs, within each of these realms, between liberty and legitimate security needs, and between revenues and expenditures.

Progressives should take note of all the dangers in the policies advocated by the right-wingers and also point out the likelihood that their global interventionism will sooner or later get the country involved in another major war in the third world. American public opinion is decidedly against any such direct military involvement. A February 1985 *New York Times* poll found that only 19 percent of the American public believed that their nation's role in the Vietnam War was right, while 73 percent said it was wrong.[8]

It is easy enough for liberals to say what they are against in the area of foreign and defense policy. It is more difficult, but essential, for Democrats, as Les Aspin has said, "to be for something."[9] When Americans of the mid-eighties were asked in opinion polls which party they trusted on national defense, the Republicans won by large margins. This was not so much the result of popular approval of Republican policies as it was a consequence of the belief that the Democrats had no defense policy. Senator Joseph Biden rightly said in a 1986 interview that a substantial portion of the American people had come to believe that the Democrats had "lost their will. They wonder whether the Democrats would stop anywhere. They wonder whether the Democrats would *ever* call for the projection of force."

Former Virginia Governor Chuck Robb stated the obvious when he said to me in 1986 that the Democrats cannot allow themselves to "be perceived as lacking the will to defend our basic values and our freedom." In a speech later that year, Robb called for a foreign policy that "neither renounces nor relies exclusively on the use of force, a policy tempered, but not paralyzed, by the lessons of Vietnam." Both Biden and Hart concurred. His party, Biden told me, must get away from the " 'Vietnam syndrome'—this notion that the exercise of physical force or the threat of physical force is not an arrow in the quiver of our conduct of foreign affairs." Hart said that the Democrats had become an isolationist, antisecurity, antidefense party as a result of Vietnam. They had not been such before, and Hart indicated that it would be necessary to shed that image in order to regain the public's confidence.[10]

Shedding a relatively new image should entail more than simply returning to old positions. Progressives in the late 1980s and 1990s should develop a new, balanced foreign and military policy that differs in significant ways from those of the old cold-war liberals, the old conservative isolationists, the more recent liberal isolationists, and the new right-wing global interventionists.

The place to start the development of a New Progressive international policy is with the realization that military policy should always serve foreign policy, not the other way around, as sometimes seemed to be the case with the Reagan administration. "Our interests cannot be defended until they are defined," Gary Hart has sensibly pointed out. Ends must determine means, not vice versa, so progressives should begin by addressing the larger questions concerning the United States' role in the world and the goals that American foreign policy can realistically hope to achieve. Only after these goals are carefully defined does it make any sense to discuss what military capabilities are needed to achieve them.[11]

The basis of a New Progressive foreign policy is a rededication to the fundamental values in which Americans profess a belief. When Elie Wiesel accepted a Congressional Gold Medal from President Reagan in April 1985, just before Reagan was to journey to Germany to lay a wreath in a cemetery containing the remains of members of the Nazi SS, he summarized the essentials of what America at its best has been and should be: "the greatest democracy in the world, the freest nation in the world, the moral nation, the authority in the world."[12] The *moral* nation. The word "morality" has been so abused in recent years that there is an understandable reluctance to use it. Yet if we are to develop an American foreign policy worthy of our wholehearted support—and worthy of the heritage of the United States—we cannot get away from discussing morality.

The United States is still what Elie Wiesel said it was, but we have sometimes strayed from our principles. There are too many Americans who would surrender the moral high ground, who argue that we must be practical and "fight fire with fire."

There is a real danger that in opposing totalitarian nations we will be tempted to adopt their ways. We have seen this begin to happen in past confrontations with ruthless enemies. During Woodrow Wilson's crusade to "make the world safe for democracy," many basic freedoms of the American people were curtailed. While we fought Hitler's racist concentration camps, our government put into "relocation centers" American citizens whose only crime was their Japanese ancestry. And in Vietnam numerous incidents such as the massacre at My Lai demonstrated how easy it is to slip into the tactics of those we oppose. Colonel Kurtz, the Marlon

Brando character in the 1979 film *Apocalypse Now*, articulated this process when he warned that we could not compete with the Viet Cong because they were prepared to do what we would not. They are decent people who love their wives and children, he said, but they will not hesitate to cut off a child's hand to teach villagers a lesson. If we would not do the same, Kurtz indicated, we would lose. "It's judgment that defeats us," he said.[13]

In fact it is judgment that distinguishes the moral from the immoral. What the United States lost in Vietnam, in addition to nearly 60,000 American lives and hundreds of billions of dollars, were its self-confidence and its reputation in the world as "the moral nation." The latter was one of America's greatest sources of strength. Regaining that reputation would be worth more to our national interests than a trillion dollars worth of military hardware. Indeed the moral, humanitarian content in our national policy might be usefully contrasted to military hardware by calling it the "software" of foreign policy. This is not to say that we do not need military force to support our moral positions. As is the case with computers, both the hardware and the software of foreign policy are each useless alone.

To insist that we strive to be a moral nation is, of course, to hold our own actions to a higher standard than we expect of others. This is as it should be. Saying "the Communists do it" is no justification for adopting any policy or tactic. Undoubtedly holding ourselves to a higher standard makes it more difficult for us to do certain things in the world, but this insistence on a high standard is ultimately our greatest source of national greatness and strength. When we mine the harbors of another nation, we are not, as Tom Wicker of the *New York Times* has put it, meeting "sound American standards of behavior." Neither is sending weapons to Iran while admonishing other nations not to do so.[14]

To fail to live up to our own standards of behavior is to invite a further erosion of those standards. Historian Henry Steele Commager has noted the relevance for international relations of a classic statement made by Supreme Court Justice Louis D. Brandeis a half century ago:

> In a government of laws the existence of the government will be imperiled if it fails to observe the law scrupulously. Our government is the potent, the omnipotent teacher. For good or ill it

teaches the whole people by its example. If government becomes a lawbreaker it breeds contempt for law: it invites every
man to become a law unto himself. It invites anarchy.[15]

Some conservatives have complained of liberals who allegedly
postulate a "moral equivalence" between the United States and the
Soviet Union. Perhaps some people who call themselves liberals
have held such a preposterous view, but the most serious proponents
of a policy that amounts to "moral equivalence" are those on the
right who contend that we must use the means employed by the
Communists in order to fight them. A State Department official
once told Patricia Derian, assistant secretary of state for human
rights and humanitarian affairs in the Carter administration, that
"the United States has nothing to gain by acting on principle."[16] If
we believe that, we not only abandon our values, we also lose our
greatest source of strength. We *are* different from dictatorships, but
if we forget the differences and start behaving the way they do, we
will become like what we say we despise. In the process, we will lose
the very reason for our opposition to dictatorships.

There can be no serious question that the Soviet Union represents the greatest threat to the values that most Americans believe
in. Progressives must make clear that they understand this and are
prepared to meet the Soviet challenge. This does not mean that we
cannot do business with the Soviets or with other dictatorships. It
simply means that we enter negotiations with them without illusions, with our eyes open, and with an understanding of whom we
are dealing with. It means that our dealings with them must be
based upon our common interests, not upon trust. Right-wingers
may be wrong about most things, but they are on target when they
say you can't trust the Soviet leaders. Progressives should not be reticent about this plain fact.[17]

We cannot have an effective foreign policy without a credible
military force with which we can back up our principles. Nor can we
have an effective foreign policy if we do not follow our professed
principles. To condemn Communist abuses while winking at the
same sort of actions among our "friends," or, worse, to turn around
and undertake some of the same tactics we denounce the Soviets
for, is a real sign of weakness.

A genuinely *democratic* foreign policy should be a goal of the
Democratic party. A revival of idealism includes a return to the

much-maligned but quite effective human-rights emphasis of the
Carter administration. His human-rights policy is one of the few
things that people remember favorably about Jimmy Carter. It
caught the imagination of Americans and became part of the vision
of the nation. But human rights were de-emphasized in the foreign
policy of the Reagan administration.[18]

There is an important middle ground in foreign policy to be
claimed between the Democratic left that sees the faults of right-
wing dictatorships but fails to say much about abuses in Communist nations, and those Republicans who are quick to point to horrors in Communist countries but readily cozy up to any savage ruler
who boasts of his anticommunism. The best course for us as a nation and for the Democratic party and its candidates is to avoid both
these positions. While some Democrats are busy attacking South
Africa but saying little about Poland or Afghanistan, and while
many Republicans are wringing their hands about the Gulag but are
silent about Pinochet and apartheid, New Progressives should link
the abuses on the opposite extremes and condemn them equally.
This is sensible, it is morally correct, and it would in all likelihood
be politically advantageous.

Practicing what we preach is not easy. The preference of some
American policymakers for "friendly" dictators is understandable.
Dealing with dictators is quicker and easier than dealing with democratic institutions. You can call up a cooperative dictator and get
what you want overnight. There is no need for public debate, or
even for thinking a policy through and assessing its effects on the
people of the other nation. Aside from the inherent moral objec-
tions to supporting dictatorship, such a course does not serve long-
term American interests. We may get what we want out of an
undemocratic leader for many years, but then one day we wake up
to find him overthrown and the hostility of the people of his country
focused on the United States for having supported the oppressive
government. Iran is the clearest instance of where this sort of mistake can lead.

As former Assistant Secretary Derian noted in a 1985 interview,
"you cannot have a foreign policy where you only consider the head
of state or the government and not what's happening among the
people." Why do many Americans seem to think that we must have
openness and discussion of public policy, and democratic decision
making, but people in other parts of the world do not need such
procedures? Unless we subscribe to the racist view that "there are

some people who are culturally and genetically unsuited for democracy," we cannot do anything less than support human rights and democracy around the world. This usually would not entail military intervention. Except in cases where the evil to be opposed was great and the prospects were good for achieving at a reasonable cost a government both more democratic and more popular than that it displaced, such intervention could not be justified. In short, military intervention to promote our values should be acceptable to progressives, but only in those cases that meet both the test of clear need and that of practicability. Grenada may have met those tests; Angola and Nicaragua do not. We must always be careful not to violate our professed belief in self-determination, but we should also realize that the established government in a dictatorship does not amount to self-determination.

Human-rights considerations should be given an explicit place in the formulation of policy, so that we develop a foreign policy that reflects what we teach our children about ourselves as a nation.[19]

Is it asking too much that a liberal Democratic foreign policy should promote liberal values and encourage democracy? We might yet find ways to make "the free world" a meaningful term.

A foreign policy based upon the values we teach our children leads to certain specifics. It means that we should push for human rights and democracy around the world, and refuse to align ourselves with such brutal groups as the Khmer Rouge, even if they are fighting against a government backed by the most powerful enemy of democracy, the Soviet Union. It means as well that we must strive to combat hunger and poverty around the world. These enormous problems have to be approached in a realistic manner. We cannot expect to bring about the millennium overnight—or ever. What we can insist upon is that American foreign policy will attempt to improve the living conditions of people in underdeveloped countries.

We must commit ourselves to conquering hunger. This is a moral obligation of all the wealthier nations. A proposal made by House Speaker Jim Wright represents a good starting point. Wright suggested that the United States and the Soviet Union each place 10 percent of their military budgets into a trust fund to be used to fight world hunger, disease, and illiteracy.[20] This proposal should become a central feature of New Progressive foreign policy. The

United States should challenge the Soviet Union—and other developed nations—to join us in such a swords-into-plowshares effort, both because it could make a significant contribution to the struggle to provide a decent standard of living to people in the third world and because it would put us on the right side in the effort at arms reduction.

A serious "war" on world hunger can be effective, but only if it is combined with all-out efforts at long-term economic development and population control. More food aid will be needed, along with conservation, improved technology in the third world, and changes in government agriculture policies. But all this will accomplish little if, as is projected, world population doubles in the next four decades, reaching close to 10 billion. Ninety percent of the projected growth is anticipated in the third world. By the end of the century, there are likely to be nearly one billion people on the continent of Africa.[21]

Nothing short of a monumental advance in population control will be sufficient to prevent future famines on a much broader scale than those the world has recently witnessed. Much of American aid to underdeveloped nations should be channeled into population control, an objective with which most Americans are in agreement. Yet the Reagan administration, under the sway of right-wing ideologues, substantially *reduced* funding for international population-control agencies. The opposition to such groups as the International Planned Parenthood Federation began in the abortion controversy, but many "right-to-life" advocates are also opposed to birth control. "We don't think government should fund artificial birth control," said Robert G. Marshall of the American Life League early in 1986. That is plain enough language. The reasoning of those right-wingers who do not base their opposition to birth control on religious grounds is interesting. A theory called "supply-side demography" arose in the 1980s. Its adherents argue that population growth is not a threat because, as the conservative American Enterprise Institute for Public Policy Research said in a study on the subject, "every baby comes equipped with two hands as well as a mouth." Ye of little faith might wonder at the wisdom of encouraging unchecked population growth, but some supply-siders in the eighties came to see that it is every bit as sensible as encouraging production and letting demand take care of itself.[22]

Birth control, especially in the poor nations, is essential to the future well-being of humanity. For the long run, it is even more important than food. (But, as Harry Hopkins liked to point out during the New Deal, people eat in the short run. Both food assistance and birth control are needed if we are to have any hope of defeating recurring famines in the underdeveloped world.) This is another good example of an issue in which morality and popularity coincide, and Democrats have an opportunity to speak up for what is both right and politically advantageous.

One of the most striking features of the Reagan administration's foreign policy has been its proclivity for going it alone. On one issue after another, the Republican government has taken positions (and sometimes actions) without consulting the allies of the United States. It had little use for the United Nations, thumbed its nose at the World Court, and withdrew from the Law of the Sea Treaty. When American navy planes forced an Egyptian plane to land in Italy in 1985 without consulting either country, though both are American allies, President Reagan proudly proclaimed: "We did this all by our little selves."[23]

Such statements were politically popular within the United States. (Although it was not at all popular when the Reagan administration, all by their little selves, traded arms to Iran for hostages and sent the profits to the rebels in Nicaragua.) Most Americans prefer to think that we can do as we please around the world. A New Progressive foreign policy should modify, but not completely reverse, this approach. A great power, especially one that seeks to base its foreign policy upon the values of liberty and democracy, cannot allow itself to become the captive of sometimes fainthearted allies. Yet multilateral positions and actions are, as a rule, preferable to unilateral stances.

Obviously the United Nations and other international organizations have fallen far short of what was expected of them. It would be foolish, however, to react to this disappointment by discarding the entire concept of international cooperation. This is an example of the difference between those who continue to seek new ways to succeed and those who give up when something does not work as it was supposed to. The alternative to continued attempts at international cooperation is international anarchy. That way lies almost certain economic disaster and an increased danger of nuclear war.

154 ROBERT S. McELVAINE

Liberals should frankly recognize the failures of international organizations, and not abjure unilateral actions when they may be necessary. But they should also maintain a commitment to international cooperation, understanding that such cooperation is not only desirable, but in a nuclear world it is essential to survival. In short, "going it alone" may sometimes be necessary, but it should be a last resort, not the normal course it seems to be to Rambo Republicans.

One would have thought that the clearest lesson to be learned from the United States' tragic experience in Indochina was that our country is not omnipotent. We may be rightfully interested in events and conditions everywhere in the world, but our ability to influence them has to be carefully assessed before we contemplate unilateral action.

An innovative idea in the area of international cooperation that is worth pursuing is the establishment of an international organization of democratic nations. Such a body would have strict criteria for membership and would be prepared to expel nations that strayed from democratic values and practices. It would not be intended to replace the United Nations, which should continue to serve as an inclusive organization that can sometimes lessen tensions. An international association of democratic nations might help the United States to avoid taking unilateral stands on so many issues. It would also represent a means of blending a liberal commitment to American values with a practical form of internationalism. Surely it is worth a try.[24]

The toughest part of pursuing a foreign policy based upon democratic values is finding viable democratic forces to support in the third world. In too many cases the choice seems to be between despotisms of the right and the left. Conservatives readily argue that we must back anti-Communist dictatorships or see more nations fall under Communist tyranny. Liberals oppose the same right-wing dictators, but too easily assume that anyone who is against the tyranny of the right is in favor of democracy. It would be a much simpler and more pleasant world if this were true, but pretending that it is will not make it so. Like Ronald Reagan, much of the American public may prefer to ignore complexity, but it must be faced if we are to develop an effective foreign policy.

American support for *either* a government or its opponents

should be based upon the demonstrating of a commitment to democracy. This means withdrawal of support from such regimes as those in South Africa and Chile, but it does not involve a reflexive endorsement of anyone who opposes those despotisms. Opposition groups, like established governments, should be expected to earn American support positively, not be given it by default because of the negative features of those they oppose.[25]

In practice such a policy would mean that in many cases the United States would support neither side in an internal conflict, but would instead hold out its potential support as an incentive to both sides to become more democratic. Our standards must be genuine but flexible. We should not expect a government or an opposition group to be perfect before we offer support, but we should judge them against absolute standards and also against each other. There is sometimes a clear choice between opposing groups, even if neither of them is sufficiently democratic to suit us.

One of the places where this policy should be applied is South Africa. The failure of the United States long ago to reject the white government in that troubled land has left us in a difficult position. Many South African blacks have mistakenly come to associate communism with freedom. The association of the white government with the Western bloc has served to discredit Western values among the country's blacks.

The Reagan administration's policy of "constructive engagement" with the Pretoria government was a failure. Part of the reason is that the American government was "engaged" with only one side in the South African struggle. Dealing simultaneously with the African National Congress would have put the United States government in a position to mediate the dispute at the same time that it would have put some distance between America and the system of apartheid.

The other cause of the failure of the Republican policy of constructive engagement is that many officials in the Reagan administration did not view apartheid as an especially great evil. This was indicated in 1985 when the president made the incredible statement that the South Africans had already eliminated most forms of segregation that had existed in the American South prior to the civil-rights movement.

The failure of many Republicans, from the president on down, fully to appreciate the evil of apartheid is curious. (By 1986 a substantial number of Republicans did begin to come around on the question of breaking ties with the South African government, but almost all those who continued to support the Pretoria regime were Republicans.) Republicans have traditionally insisted that they are great champions of liberty. They have contended in domestic policy that economic security must be sacrificed for the greater good of free enterprise. The price of regulation to protect against risks, they often argue, is too great because it is paid in a loss of liberty. Full stomachs, they say, are no substitute for freedom.

If they truly believe this, if these are not simply the self-serving arguments of the well-to-do who hide behind the slogans of liberty, why don't they practice what they preach with regard to South Africa? There, many right-wingers are quick to point out, blacks may not be free, but they are economically better off than their counterparts in most black-run countries in Africa. This argument is akin to asserting that American slaves were better fed than African tribesmen and therefore slavery was not an evil.

If Republicans want us to accept their sincerity when they claim to be true believers in liberty, let them demonstrate their belief by placing a higher premium on liberty than security in South Africa as well as in the United States. That many of them do not signals not only their lack of commitment to liberty, but the great import that they place upon short-term world politics. As in so many other cases, right-wingers have been willing to tolerate flagrant abuses of human rights in South Africa because the government there is "friendly" to the United States. This argument is both morally bankrupt and short-sighted from a practical viewpoint. The longer we identify ourselves with the repressive regime in Pretoria—a regime whose days in power are clearly numbered—the more likely we make it that the new government will be unfriendly to American interests and values.[26]

The inconsistency of those on the right who value liberty above economic well-being in most of the world but reverse those priorities for South African blacks is matched by those on the left who are often willing to wink at the undemocratic practices of "socialist" governments while saying that living standards have improved even if liberty has not. Such leftist apologists, like their counterparts on the right, reverse their argument when it comes to South African blacks. In this case alone, it seems, many leftists place a higher premium on freedom than on economic gain.

There are no easy answers in South Africa, and liberals should not pretend that there are. Maximum pressure should be kept on the white government to dismantle apartheid and negotiate a sharing of power. Communications should be kept open with popular black leaders and attempts made to convince them to stay out of the Soviet orbit and to establish true democracy when they take over.

Why is it that an administration that thought constructive engagement with the South African government would be useful in altering unpalatable policies in that country refused to try the same approach in the case of Nicaragua? As with South Africa, the Reagan administration's engagement in Nicaragua has been with only one side. The difference is that in this case the side chosen is not the government but the violent opposition. President Reagan insisted that economic sanctions against South Africa would only worsen conditions for the majority of people there and cause the government to become more repressive. Yet in the case of Nicaragua he went far beyond sanctions and hired a guerrilla army to terrorize the unpalatable regime. Perhaps this should be called "destructive engagement."

The Sandinista government has been guilty of many gross violations of human rights. There is no point in whitewashing its activities. The question, though, is how to improve conditions for the people of Nicaragua. Supporting the Contras, whom Mr. Reagan likened to the Founding Fathers of the United States but who are apparently guilty of at least as many atrocities as the Sandinistas, does not seem the best way to achieve that objective. It leads us to subvert our own values, as in the cases of the terrorism training manual the CIA wrote for the Contras and the secret diversion of funds to the rebels at a time when this was prohibited by American law. And American support for the Contras pushes the Sandinistas further into the Soviet camp and provides them with a rationale for building and maintaining a large military force and a repressive regime.

The Contra war in Nicaragua is the most prominent example of a supposedly new concept in military tactics: "low-intensity conflict." The idea is to keep American participation far in the background and let local guerrilla bands do the fighting, with American technical and financial assistance. The hope is to turn the tables on the Communists. Where the United States overtly used to assist right-wing regimes in power to fight Communist-backed insurrections, now the Soviets will have to aid left-wing regimes against American-backed rebels. The Reaganites insisted that this policy of low-intensity conflict differs from the counterinsurgency tactics of the Kennedy administration. But the only difference seems to be who controls the government and who backs the rebels.[27]

A major question about low-intensity conflict is what happens when the group you are backing loses. When the Soviets were on the insurgent side, it was not difficult for them to abandon unsuccessful rebels, since they had never made any public commitment to them. But the United States government has discovered that covert actions are not compatible with democracy. So the Congress openly votes to send aid to insurgent groups. If the latter do not succeed—and few knowledgeable observers in 1986 gave the Contras much of a chance of succeeding—what comes next? Does the United States raise the ante by committing American forces, making it a "mid-intensity conflict"? And since the Soviets are more openly committed to governments in power than they were to insurgents, how do they react to direct American intervention? A "high-intensity conflict" is the last thing any of us wants in the nuclear age.

The American people have been strongly on the liberal side of Central American issues. Throughout the mid-eighties, polls showed two-to-one majorities opposing aid to the Contras. This was true even in a survey that asked whether the United States should "help people in Nicaragua who are trying to overthrow the pro-Soviet regime there."[28]

Simple opposition to aiding the rebels does not, however, constitute a satisfactory response to the Nicaraguan situation. As Les Aspin put it, "We're right on the policy, we're right on the politics, but it still adds up to the overall impression that we're not *for* anything."[29] By all means, we should keep up economic pressure on the Nicaraguan government, and the military option should be discouraged. If we were to open negotiations with the Sandinistas, the United States might yet be able to use its engagement with the Contras to mediate a settlement that would be in the best interests of the people of Nicaragua and the entire region. This could be accomplished only if we made it clear to the Contras that failure to negotiate in good faith and accept a reasonable settlement would result in a complete end to any United States support for their cause and if we could convince the Sandinistas that we were prepared to accept their continuing place in a more democratic government.

But what if such an approach fails, or if the Sandinistas invade their neighbors or invite the Soviet Union to construct a submarine base in Nicaragua? Progressives must make clear that there is a limit to their patience and that they will use force if necessary. "Certainly, if any nation in the region were to allow itself to become a new Soviet base," Gary Hart said in 1986, "we would be compelled to take any action necessary, including the use of military force, to remove those bases." Joe Biden argued that same year that when it comes to protecting vital American interests in this hemisphere, we should not be "constrained by what is a limited version of international law that in fact technically precludes us from taking actions that appear to be in our interests." Biden cited John F. Kennedy's actions in the Cuban missile crisis as an example of what he was talking about.[30]

Statements such as Biden's are troubling because we should be making every effort to build up international law, not violate it ourselves. But as long as it is understood that the sort of actions he is talking about would be taken only in extreme situations of clear threats to vital American interests, he is right. A New Progressive foreign policy would resort to force only after other options had been exhausted, and would seek international action before taking unilateral steps. But progressives have to make clear that there is a point at which they would use force to protect vital American interests.

One essential thrust of a New Progressive defense policy is to point out that throwing money at military contractors is not necessarily a way to improve our national defense. We must demonstrate our strength and resolve, but that does not mean, as Mr. Reagan once said, having "an unrestricted arms race," because "the U.S. could not possibly lose, given our industrial superiority." He apparently thought that if we kept wasting money on unnecessary arms the Soviets would have to do the same, and they would go bankrupt before we did! As Les Aspin put it, Reagan's idea is "to spend the Russians into the Stone Age"—and ourselves along with them.[31] That is not a responsible defense policy. (Nor is its basic premise correct. It is true enough that the United States is far wealthier than the Soviet Union, but our people expect a much higher standard of living than the Russians do. This means that the

Soviet government can get away with devoting a greater part of their resources to the military than can an American government.)

The Republican party embraced the military establishment earlier and more tightly than it did the "Christian Right." This alliance has benefited the party in recent elections, but it may prove an embarrassment in the near future. One senior administration official complained in 1985 about the closeness of the Reagan White House to military contractors. "We don't have any obligation to defend white-collar criminals who are ripping off the defense budget," he declared. "We ought to distance ourselves from them."[32] But it will be difficult for Republicans to separate themselves from what has proved to be a symbiotic entanglement.

It seems odd that a president who built a career assailing "big spenders" chose as one of his top cabinet members the biggest spender in history, Secretary of Defense Caspar Weinberger.

Given the Reagan administration's determination to spend unprecedented amounts on the military, largely for the purpose of spending the Soviets into the ground, fraud, waste, and abuse were almost certain to result. The goal of spending $1.6 *trillion* on the military in five years virtually guaranteed that greedy contractors would be tempted to grab all they could get away with. None of us can really comprehend numbers in the trillions. One way to get an idea of a trillion is to look at one of those signs at a McDonald's restaurant that tells us how many hamburgers the chain has sold. In 1985 they read, "Over 50 Billion Sold." This means that in all the McDonald's outlets in the world, in all the years since the company first went into business, by 1985 it had sold only *one-twentieth* of a trillion hamburgers.

If you are determined to spend in the trillions, you are going to attract the sort of businessmen who sell $748 pliers, $600 ashtrays, and $640 toilet seats. And your procurers, in trying to spend that much money, are likely to write specifications for coffeepots on airplanes that can continue to brew during crashes and in situations where the G-force is great enough to kill everyone on board.

The list of Defense Department waste could be extended indefinitely, and the examples are too well known to bear detailed repetition here. The prize, as far as I have been able to determine, goes to General Dynamics, which charged the government $7,417 for an alignment pin worth three cents. That comes out to a tidy profit of 24,723,233 percent. We all have to make a living, after all, and no price is too high to defend ourselves from communism.[33]

If the Pentagon were just wasting money, it would be bad enough. In fact, the bloated budgets and ties between military contractors and senior officials in the Defense Department have led to such corruption that we have purchased defective weapons that would in the event of war endanger the lives of American troops. The classic example of this sort of travesty was the Sergeant York antiaircraft gun. At a cost of $6 million each (for a total of $4 billion), Ford Aerospace was providing the army with sophisticated, computer-guided weapons that were demonstrably less effective in shooting down planes than were traditional antiaircraft guns fired by skilled human gunners. In June 1985 the Army falsified information about a test of the Sergeant York. A videotape was produced, purporting to show the gun destroying drone planes. Later it was learned that the drones had actually been destroyed by explosives placed on them before takeoff and detonated by radio signals from the ground. If only we could persuade the Soviets to place such explosives and American radio detonating devices on all their planes, the Sergeant York might do its job.[34]

The outcry over this deception and the general ineffectiveness of the Sergeant York led to its cancellation in August 1985. The public is left to wonder how many more high-tech Edsels are still being sold to the armed forces and at what risk they are placing our servicemen and women.

Any Democratic candidate who cannot use such tales as effectively as Ronald Reagan employed his "welfare queen" anecdotes for so many years should not be allowed to present the party's case to the jury of voters. But Democrats must be careful to indicate that they are opposed to waste, not to defense. The distinction is crucial, and it is one to which most of the electorate will respond.

The first half of the 1980s saw a complete turnaround in public opinion on defense spending. According to a *New York Times* poll in 1981, 61 percent of the American public favored an increase in military spending while only 7 percent wanted the Pentagon's budget cut. Four years later, at the start of Mr. Reagan's second term, only 16 percent still wanted to give the military more money and 30 percent favored decreasing defense spending. In March 1985, a *Washington Post*–ABC News poll found 53 percent of its sample in favor of making "substantial cuts" in military spending. In the five years between 1981 and 1986, another *Washington Post*–ABC poll found that support for increasing military funding fell from 72 percent to 22 percent.[35]

Paying hundreds and thousands of dollars for screws, nuts, bolts, and hammers, as the Republican Pentagon did, is not a responsible defense policy; it amounts to criminal neglect of a public trust. A majority of the electorate had come to realize this by 1986. The way is open for Democrats to offer a responsible alternative. Progressives can point out that building extremely expensive, highly technical military gadgets faster than we can train people to operate them is not a responsible defense policy. Building new weapons when we don't have spare parts to keep current ones operational is not a responsible defense policy. Wasting billions of dollars on a bomber—the B-1—that was expected to be obsolete by the time it reached full production is not responsible. A stronger defense is to be achieved by concentrating on the more advanced Stealth bomber.

Choices among expensive weapons must be made, but President Reagan and his Pentagon refused to do so. More than a quarter-century ago President Eisenhower warned of the consequences of such an abdication of responsibility. "Some day," Eisenhower wrote in a letter to his friend Swede Hazlett,

> there is going to be a man sitting in my present chair who has not been raised in the military services and who will have little understanding of where slashes in their estimates can be made with little or no damage. If that should happen while we still have the state of tension that now exists in the world, I shudder to think of what could happen to this country.[36]

By the mid-eighties we had seen the culmination of Ike's fears in unprecedented deficits, weakened social programs, and a $2 trillion national debt.

Waste, fraud, and abuse in the Pentagon do not have to be tolerated. When Harry Truman was in charge of a Senate committee overseeing military procurement during World War II, he clamped down on the crooks who were trying to enrich themselves by cheating the taxpayers and endangering the lives of American servicemen. "If you were listening in on the Senate committee hearings of your dad," Truman wrote to his daughter in 1941, "you would understand why old Diogenes carried a lantern in the daytime in his search for an honest man."[37] The Truman committee performed a great service in the 1940s. We need another such committee. And we need someone like Harold Ickes, secretary of the interior and head of the Public Works Administration during the New Deal, as secretary of defense. Ickes made sure that the public got a dollar's worth of benefit out of every dollar he spent. Progressive Democrats should pledge to find someone like him to head the Pentagon in the next administration.

What have we gotten for our expenditure of nearly two trillion dollars on the military since Ronald Reagan took office? It is clear enough that some of us—the stockholders of General Dynamics, for instance—are more secure. It is much less certain that the nation as a whole is significantly more secure than it was before the massive increases (which amounted to a 41 percent rise in real defense outlays during Mr. Reagan's first term). If we look only at expenditures, it seems that we must be far more secure than we were. What is important, however, is not input but output, as conservatives are quick to point out in regard to social programs. Chuck Robb was one of the many Democrats of the mid-eighties who criticized the Republican approach to defense for being more concerned with input than output. "Their ability to demand quality control," Robb said to me, "is, at best, suspect."

"We've allowed Weinberger to say that a 5 percent growth or a 3 percent growth is what makes for good defense," lamented Senator Lawton Chiles in a 1986 interview. This, he rightly contended, is nonsense. "You've got to look at what comes out at the bottom end, and you've got to look at what your defense *strategy* ought to be, and it's not necessarily that you have all these strategic weapons piled on top of each other." Congressman Richard Gephardt made essentially the same point. "There's an ability now to talk about efficiency in the military, rather than just throwing dollars at it," he told me. He said he thought most Americans had come to understand that the Reagan approach had not worked and had not bought us more security. Gephardt also believed that people were beginning to understand that economic strength "is probably more important to national security than military hardware." "The acid test of the military," defense analyst Jeffrey Record sensibly noted in 1984, "is how effectively it performs on the battlefield, not how much money it can wring from politicians in peacetime."[38]

Fortunately, we have not had any significant opportunities to test the Reagan military on the battlefield, but there is little evidence by most measures that there has been an improvement in defense that is anywhere near commensurate with the spending increases. One of the few areas in which there has clearly been an improvement is in the number and quality of recruits into the volunteer military. Part of this is attributable to the surge of "patriotism" associated with the Reagan presidency and part is the result of higher pay scales. It is generally agreed, though, that the major source of the improvement in military personnel was a sharp increase in unemployment in 1981–83. Ronald Reagan's most effective contribution to improving the nation's military may well have been his recession.

In areas other than personnel, however, there has been little gain resulting from the huge Reagan expenditures. Les Aspin found at best "minuscule improvements" in military preparedness after Mr. Reagan's first term. Although the budget for weapons purchases soared by 91 percent from 1980 to 1984, one-third of all military equipment inventories actually declined during that period. "Is Ronald Reagan doing with defense what he accused previous administrations of doing with social welfare—just throwing billions of dollars at the problem and then the statistics show that poverty remains rampant?" Aspin asked pointedly late in 1985.[39]

A New Progressive defense policy should look at output, not input, and should measure our security in terms of clearly defined objectives. The Reagan administration seemed to have no grand strategy. It learned nothing from the experience of Vietnam and still dreamed of American omnipotence. Secretary Weinberger said in 1983 that the administration's "long-range goal is to be capable of defending all theaters simultaneously."[40] No wonder he wanted to keep increasing spending. This goal is simply unrealistic. It would require devoting far more of our national effort and production to the military than even the Reagan administration seemed prepared to do. Certainly it would require several times more military spending than a majority of the American people are willing to support. And it would require the one thing that Mr. Reagan refused to ask of the American people: sacrifice. But even massive sacrifice could not achieve Weinberger's objective. "This crowd," Dale Bumpers said of the Reaganites, "is violating what Frederick the Great once said: if you try to be strong everywhere and be able to fight everywhere, you'll wind up being weak everywhere."[41]

Progressives need to define a strategy that is achievable through the devotion of a reasonable portion of our resources. Priorities must be set; choices must be made. Purchasing more advanced technology is not always a wise course. Quite often high-tech weapons are too complex for troops in the field to use effectively. Even if they are workable, they are often so expensive that they cannot be bought in sufficient quantity to provide for an adequate defense. An advanced, computerized tank may be marginally better than a less advanced version, but if the high-tech tank costs twenty times as much, we would be much better off with twenty of the old model than one of the new.

All weapons systems should be carefully examined to see if they will actually provide more security. The MX missile may at first glance appear to be a way to improve our defenses and make us safer. In fact, it is just the opposite. Placing these missiles in silos that cannot withstand a direct hit makes them useless for anything but a first strike. We have no intention of ever launching a first strike. Deploying the MX missiles is doubly irresponsible. Not only is it a waste of more billions of the taxpayers' dollars that could be better spent on genuine defense needs, social needs, or reducing the deficit, it is also a way to destabilize the nuclear standoff with the Soviets and bring the possibility of nuclear war closer. A "Peace-keeper" it is not. Yet Mr. Reagan once said: "Some of my best friends are MX missiles."

At the heart of a truly responsible defense policy should be strong conventional forces to supplement the nuclear deterrent we already possess. This will help to assure that we will never have to face the terrible choice that could confront us under the Republican policy: whether to resort to nuclear weapons if our conventional forces are overpowered. Building up our conventional forces and providing sufficient stockpiles of conventional weapons to sustain a fight of more than a few weeks duration are ways to reduce the likelihood of nuclear war and therefore in fact constitute a peace program and an essential part of a responsible defense policy.[42]

We need, as Sam Nunn, Gary Hart, Les Aspin, and many other Democrats have been saying in recent years, a leaner, better organized and more effective military. "More is better" is not the proper slogan for the nation's defense, even if it is for defense contractors. Yet that is the only defense program that the Reagan administration ever presented.

"There is an increasing concern in this country," Dale Bumpers said to me in 1986, "that we've spent these hundreds of billions of dollars on increased defense and we're no better able to fight today than we were before—that what has in fact happened is that we've been 'taken in' by throwing money at that problem."[43]

The most controversial portion of the Reagan military program has been the Strategic Defense Initiative, or "Star Wars," idea. It is a most seductive proposal. Who could oppose the idea of protecting ourselves with a defensive system that will shoot down enemy missiles? This seems clearly preferable to the current protection against nuclear war, mutually assured destruction (MAD). Now the superpowers hold each other's populations hostage. Under SDI, President Reagan tells us, only missiles, not people, will be targets.

Who, then, could prefer MAD to SDI? The answer, I think, is anyone who looks carefully at the SDI proposal.

The "Star Wars" idea is even more wasteful and destabilizing than the MX missile. It has three fundamental flaws. First, most scientists familiar with the technological problems agree that a system that would protect most of the American population is utterly unfeasible. One example should suffice: it would require at least two thousand space shuttle flights to deploy an "umbrella" system such as that envisioned by President Reagan. On NASA's most optimistic predictions, sixteen shuttle flights per year will be possible. So if the space shuttle were used for nothing else, it would take *125 years* to put a Star Wars system into space. As Admiral Richard Truly, the administrator of NASA's space shuttle program, told me, there is "no way" that the shuttle could deploy SDI.[44]

Even if such a defensive system were made operational and was 95 percent effective, that might mean that the Soviets would get "only" 1,000 warheads through to their targets, essentially destroying our nation. Indeed, a defensive system that was 95 percent—or even 99 percent—effective would merely provide the Soviets with an incentive to build many more offensive weapons, so that the 1 to 5 percent of their warheads that got through would be a larger absolute number. Does anyone really believe that a "leakproof" defense can be created?

Former Secretary of Defense Robert McNamara has said that he believes that American technology is capable of developing the hardware for Star Wars, "But the question is: What good will it do you? What good is it if [the Soviets] will merely seek to develop better offensive weapons?" This is precisely what the Russians promise to do if the United States proceeds with Star Wars. They claim that they can take countersteps, such as dummy missiles and coated rockets, that would, at a cost of "1 or 2 percent" of the SDI system, turn the American space defense system into "useless junk."[45] That assessment should not be taken too seriously. SDI obviously frightens the Soviets. What they fear most is that the system might put the United States in a position to launch a first strike. There is little reason to expect thay any American government would do this, but increasing Soviet fears is a step towards greater danger, not more security. Even if SDI scares the Soviets, that's no reason why it should not scare us, too. It is one of the paradoxes of the nuclear age that when your enemy becomes more insecure it decreases your own security as well.[46]

In fact most advocates of Star Wars do not claim that it could cope with a huge number of enemy missiles, some real, some dummies. Although they do not often mention it in public, most SDI supporters admit that for their plan to be workable it will be necessary to have an agreement between the superpowers to reduce substantially offensive nuclear weapons.[47] This is a desirable goal, but one that can be achieved without bankrupting the nation by building a space defense system.

For anyone who does imagine that a 100 percent effective system is attainable—and the explosion of the space shuttle *Challenger* and the Chernobyl nuclear accident in 1986 reminded us of how foolish it is to think that any piece of machinery, no matter how high its technology, is foolproof—another major problem arises. If the defensive system were 100 percent effective, it would leave the Soviets at our mercy, and they might well conclude that their only option was to launch a first strike against us before the "Star Wars" system was operational.[48]

Star Wars is, as Mr. Reagan said, a "dream." Like most dreams, it cannot stand the light of day. Therefore it has been placed under more than the usual secrecy that surrounds weapons systems. Several key elements in the original plan did not work out in tests, but scientists who work on the project were prohibited, under threat of imprisonment, from telling the American people of any failures. A couple of top officials in the program quit because of this gag rule.

What the public hears is carefully managed "news" about the experiments. It is unsurprising that such statements from the Pentagon always speak of "spectacular" results and "breakthroughs." Mr. Reagan did not want his dream disturbed by reality. Reality in this case may well have been defined by a scientist on the project who said, "instead of a weapon we have a toy."[49]

Nor did President Reagan want the public to realize too soon just how much his dream will cost. The Pentagon set out to spread the contracts for SDI research and development to as many different companies and areas as possible, so as to create a broad constituency of interest groups that are tied to the program and can help it survive when the cost becomes clear to the public. That cost has been estimated at $1 trillion to develop and deploy the system and then $200 billion per year to maintain it.[50]

What we have in SDI is an unprecedentedly expensive system that may or may not work, but can never be tested and so could not be relied upon for our defense, which the Soviets can probably counter at a fraction of its cost, and which if it did work perfectly might lead directly to nuclear annihilation. Star Wars amounts to an extremely dangerous trillion-dollar boondoggle.[51]

One of the major problems with Star Wars is that it relies on machines to prevent war. For all its apparent MADness, Mutually Assured Destruction relies on the self-interest of the superpowers to prevent war.[52] So far it has worked well, and there is little reason to think that it will not continue to do so. It is highly unlikely that either side will ever choose to launch a nuclear attack, at least as long as it knows that it and most, if not all, of the world would be destroyed in the process.

The problem with MAD is the constant danger of accidental war. With more than 50,000 nuclear weapons on the planet, the possibility that the final "The End" will be written on the story of humankind is always with us. That is a major reason for seeking sharp mutual reductions in nuclear weaponry.

Arms control is both essential and overwhelmingly popular. President Reagan appeared to be in a position to achieve an historic agreement to limit nuclear weapons. His position on this issue was analogous to those of Dwight Eisenhower in ending the Korean War and Richard Nixon in opening contacts with China. Reagan's credentials as a hawk were such that he would have a much easier time than would a Democrat in getting the approval of the American public and of Congress for an arms-control treaty. Such an agreement is infinitely more important than partisan politics, and all Americans hoped that he could do it.

He faced particular obstacles at home that made such an agreement difficult, even if the Soviets proved cooperative. At the time of the Geneva summit meeting in 1985, many defense contractors were reported to view the possibility of a 50 percent cut in nuclear weapons by each side as "ominous." Mr. Reagan got into bed with the military-industrial complex, which saw genuine arms control as the greatest threat to its own self-interest.[53] It is important for New Progressives to push vigorously the concept of an American interest that supersedes all special interests. There is no case where the national interest is more in conflict with a special interest than on the question of arms control.

There was also growing doubt by 1986 about whether Ronald Reagan was really serious about wanting an arms control agreement. He rejected all Soviet offers for a mutual ban on nuclear tests and he announced his intention to exceed the arms limits in the unratified SALT II treaty.[54]

"Nuclear war must be removed from the realm of what is considered acceptable discussion or practice," Senator Albert Gore, Jr., has said, "as such things as human sacrifice and slavery have been. We must get beyond nuclear war—have it unconditionally rejected by all countries."[55] We can all endorse this objective, but we should understand that fine words and treaties are not enough. The Kellogg-Briand Pact outlawed war scarcely more than a decade before World War II began. *Practical* measures to prevent the use of nuclear weapons must be found.

One such practical step that could be taken in nuclear arms control negotiations would be the elimination of multiple-warhead launchers and their replacement with single-warhead "midgetman" missiles. Such weapons provide deterrence, but since it is necessary to use two warheads for each target in a first strike to be sure the target is eliminated, a first strike would be utterly insane if both sides had a similar number of single-warhead launchers. Deterrence without the danger of a first strike—that is a far more responsible defense than the exotic and expensive Star Wars fantasy. The single-warhead midgetman missiles move in the opposite direction from the MX and Star Wars, toward greater stability and safety. This should be a major thrust of a New Progressive defense program.

Administrations since that of John F. Kennedy have seen a complete ban on testing nuclear weapons as a desirable goal. Ronald Reagan disagreed. He rejected the Soviet gesture of a unilateral test ban in 1985–86 as a "propaganda ploy." One reason for Mr. Reagan's opposition to a test ban was that he believed that nuclear tests would be necessary to develop Star Wars. But an end to testing would be a much better step toward general security than SDI. Democrats in the mid-eighties indicated a willingness to pursue a mutual, verifiable ban on all nuclear tests. This is an eminently sensible position. Such a ban would put us at no disadvantage to the Russians and would make the use of the weapons less likely.[56]

A general reduction in the number of offensive nuclear weapons is to be earnestly sought. This would not only provide a safer world, but would also save enormous amounts of money that could be spent on innovative programs to deal with our social problems and to reduce the deficits that threaten to cripple our economy. During the later years of the war in Indochina, opponents of the war frequently spoke of a "peace dividend" that would be available when the war spending ended. For a variety of reasons that dividend never materialized to any considerable extent. It seems certain, though, that a sharp reduction in nuclear weaponry would provide a most useful "arms control dividend."

By combining morality, human rights, a realistic assessment of our capabilities, a commitment to democracy around the world, an emphasis on a lean, strong conventional military force, an insistence on strict accountability from defense contractors, and a sincere effort to reach meaningful arms-control agreements, New Progressives can develop a positive patriotism that will be true to American values and that will be attractive to the electorate.

CHAPTER 6

Say Good-bye
to Hollywood

He's a walking contradiction
Partly truth and partly fiction
   —*KRIS KRISTOFFERSON (1974)*

He thought he was the King of America
But it was just a boulevard of broken dreams
A trick they do with mirrors and chemicals
   —*DECLAN MacMANUS (ELVIS COSTELLO) (1986)*

"The 1960s," columnist George F. Will has asserted, "were God's gift to conservatism."[1] In one sense, he is correct. In that same sense, the Reagan administration has been God's gift to liberalism. The Lord moves in mysterious ways. So does history.

What were perceived as the excesses of liberalism in the administration of Lyndon Johnson, along with widespread opposition to some of the actions of blacks and the youth culture (whose activities in the late sixties many Americans associated with liberal "permissiveness"), combined with dismay over the course of the Vietnam War to give conservatives an opportunity to gain the upper hand politically. The tide began to turn toward conservatism as early as 1968,[2] although the conservative triumph, temporarily slowed by Richard Nixon's disgrace, did not occur until 1978. By that time right-wingers had gained control of the debate to such a degree that even Nixon and Watergate were converted from liabilities into assets. If government was corrupt, why not eliminate as much of it as possible, they argued.

The excesses of the Reagan administration provide progressives

171

in the late eighties and early nineties with as much of an opportunity as those of the Johnson years gave to conservatives in the late sixties. The extreme policies of the right are one of the major reasons why the pendulum of public attitudes was beginning to swing back in a liberal direction in the mid-eighties. The principal difference from the situation in the sixties is that LBJ, who was never skillful at presenting himself on television, had personally become very unpopular by 1968. Democrats who thought that the contradictions in Ronald Reagan's policies would ever catch up with him and make him unpopular were deluding themselves, at least until the president's swap of arms for hostages began to scrape his Teflon off.[3]

The man is a master of seduction, possessed of what Richard Sennett has called, in another context, "narcotic charisma."[4] Liberals in the mid-eighties finally had to accept what was for them a bitter reality: the probability that Ronald Reagan was still going to be personally popular on the day he left office. Most people, Mario Cuomo says, "will always *like* Reagan, but they will not *respect* him; he's not the kind of idea you can get your arms around."[5] Perhaps not, but the public was reluctant to turn on him. Once this unpleasant fact had been recognized, progressives could look for ways to assure that the president's personal popularity would not transfer to his party's future nominees. It is both possible and necessary to attack President Reagan's policies and his party without personally criticizing him.

Understanding what it is that made President Reagan so popular is the first step toward assuring that another Republican will not repeat his mastery over the Democrats. Clearly it was Reagan's personality, not his policies, that won the support of so many people. Central to his popularity was his Panglossian optimism. The president almost always told people what they wanted to hear. It is understandable that they responded favorably to this technique. As Connecticut Senator Christopher Dodd points out, when given a chance to telephone either of two doctors, "one of whom will tell you that you have a terrible disease and the other will tell you that everything is fine, human nature says you will call the one who will tell you what you want to hear."

Senator Dodd made an interesting comparison. Reagan, Dodd asserted in a 1986 interview, "is the reincarnation of Hubert Humphrey.... Old Hubert, God bless him, used to get up and talk about feeding the entire world. When was the last time you heard anyone get up and say he was going to eliminate *all* nuclear weapons? Some people used to laugh at Humphrey, but people *like* that kind of message, and Reagan is very good at it as well. He talks about things in *sweeping* terms."[6]

Like the late Minnesota senator and vice-president and many other Americans, Mr. Reagan is a dreamer. His dreams may sometimes be absurd, but people appreciate the fact that he is still willing to dream. It was once liberals who "dreamed the impossible dream." When they did, a majority of Americans went along with them. In the early 1980s, they followed Mr. Reagan's very different dreams. Until the Democrats articulate a dream of their own—a vision of the future such as the New Progressivism outlined in these pages—they will have trouble competing with Republicans who adopt Reagan's vision.

There is nothing wrong with dreaming. The trouble with some of Mr. Reagan's dreams is that they are completely contradicted by common sense. There comes a point where dreams become hallucinations. At that point they cease to be guides to the future and become instead impediments to progress.

Complementing President Reagan's dreamy optimism has been the simplicity of his vision. Ronald Reagan is, as Anthony Lewis has neatly put it, "a man of convictions, not facts." People have accepted this and seem to be willing to forgive almost any ignorance or confusion on his part. Ronald Reagan understands less about the complexities of major political issues, former Virginia Governor Chuck Robb says, "than anybody who's ever served in that office, at least in recent history." He "has such a strong compass, even though it has just a few simple guideposts, but it's so obviously a critical part of the man that people will forgive him for *all kinds* of things he doesn't know or understand and they'll forgive him for a number of positions they don't agree with because they respect his adherence to basic values that they know are unshakable. It's not a very complicated presidency." Reagan's values, Robb notes, "are *so* simple that we worry about his ability to truly comprehend some of the factors that others of us worry about from time to time."[7]

And well we should worry. Mr. Reagan has simply dismissed any facts that contradict his preconceived view of the world and he has readily accepted as truth any assertion, no matter how undocumented or farfetched, that conforms to his ideology. He has often continued to repeat as "facts" statements that have been shown to be false. Knowledge is a threat to his convictions, and he prefers to remain free from knowledge rather than risk sacrificing his convictions. His sources of information have ranged from the *Reader's Digest* and airline magazines to the publications of the John Birch Society.

David Broder once said that Reagan "is the living refutation of Francis Bacon's aphorism that 'knowledge is power,'" and commented on the task that confronts his aides, "of watering the arid desert between Reagan's ears." Anthony Lewis has referred to the "Vacuum at the Top" and the "Hollow Center," and said that the President is "Out to Lunch." There is no need to cite chapter and verse of the transgressions against truth that gave rise to such assessments. The voluminous evidence has often been catalogued.[8] The Iranian debacle simply served to force onto the public's consciousness a realization of Reagan's sloth and ignorance. Those characteristics had long been plainly visible to all who dared to look.

As David Broder has concluded, Ronald Reagan has shown that "conviction is power."[9] The president's ungrounded convictions were politically powerful because he so firmly believed them and had the ability to persuade people to follow him.

The conservative movement had not had a salesman with Ronald Reagan's abilities in several decades, but his contribution to selling their cause went beyond his communication skills. A large part of salesmanship lies in making your product attractive. The product conservatives were offering to the American people before Reagan was about as attractive as ginger root. Conservatives kept telling people that they must face reality, that they could not expect to get something for nothing, that they must accept a pay-as-you-go philosophy. They condemned liberals for promising more than they could deliver, for leading people to believe that they could obtain things without effort. Anyone on Madison Avenue could have told them that this was no way to market their product.

As it happened, though, it took someone from Hollywood to transform the conservative message into a gadget that chops, dices, slices, waters the garden, feeds the pets, and makes snow cones for the children. Reaganism is the sort of product that could be sold on cable TV for $19.95 (plus shipping and handling): "And if you call in the next five minutes, you will also receive, absolutely free, two digital watches, a genuine diamond ring, a set of carving knives, and the state of Nevada! Use your MasterCard or Visa. Dial 1-800-. . . ."

Reagan understood that pain is a difficult item to move. Instead he sold, as Gary Hart put it, "a shallow—at best shallow, if not phony—cost-free brand of patriotism."[10] It sold a lot better than the old conservative wares. Mr. Reagan offered us something for nothing: a strong military without a draft or high taxes; plenty of energy without conservation; higher defense spending, an adequate safety net for the truly needy, and a balanced budget, but it won't cost you anything. You can have the good life without sacrifice. In fact, not only will you not have to pay for any of this, but we'll actually *lower* your taxes! Conservatives used to warn us that there is no such thing as a free lunch, but Ronald Reagan went beyond reversing that. He offered the gullible American consumer a *rebate lunch.*

Ronald Reagan's ability to mesmerize much of the American public was brought into focus by an Argentine who said to Congresswoman Patricia Schroeder in the middle 1980s,

I never want to hear an American ask the following question again: "How can Argentina, which has a strong middle class and is in a temperate zone, and everybody's well educated, *ever* have voted for people like Juan and Evita [Peron] and others who ran the country right off the cliff? *Now* you know. They sold magic. You [in the United States] have been very lucky. You haven't had politicians who sold magic in the past, but you've got one now!"[11]

Like many effective salesmen, Ronald Reagan's background was in acting. Long before he entered politics, he knew how to produce a tear in his eye and a choked voice when talking about traditional values. Any good actor can turn on emotions on command. This has nothing to do with one's true beliefs. Although Mr. Reagan gets misty about family values, he and his four children have been involved in nine marriages and the children rarely communicate with him or among themselves. Jesse Jackson was not far from the mark when he said to me in 1986, "Reagan is *in fact* the most antifamily president we ever had."[12] Such reality never hurt the

President's standing with those who cherish family values, because he *seems* like a good family man. He rarely sees his grandchildren, but he has photos of them around when he gives speeches. He talks about God, although he never attends church. His audience is impressed with the props and the spoken lines. And why shouldn't it be? That's what the art of film is all about.

It is unsurprising that Mr. Reagan never seems concerned when his lines fail to match reality. In the world of the motion picture, as John Kenneth Galbraith has reminded us, "the script has an imaginative dimension of its own; the script *is* the reality."[13] This insight is essential to an understanding of Ronald Reagan. As a professional actor, he is uninterested in reality. One of the consequences of this is that the president's vast ignorance neither bothers him nor does him much harm in terms of public esteem. For most of Mr. Reagan's presidency, the public found his script more beguiling than it did the tragic or pedestrian reality of life. Out out, damned fact!

"Let Reagan be Reagan" is a slogan without meaning. There *is* no Reagan. It is possible to let Reagan be George Gipp or to let Reagan be Drake McHugh, but don't ask Reagan to be Reagan.

Well, maybe that's not quite fair. "Ronald Reagan found out who he was by whom he played on film," contends University of California political scientist Michael Rogin.[14] A Reagan persona was developed over the years, and that is the role that Ronald Reagan plays. It is not entirely clear who created the part. Perhaps it was Nancy Reagan or her stepfather, Loyal Davis. It may have been his employers at General Electric. Certainly the group of directors who collected on his set after "the Speech" in 1964 helped to refine the role. Clearly this "Ronald Reagan" character, developed in the 1950s and '60s, became Ronald Wilson Reagan's favorite part.

Like almost all of this actor's previous roles, "Ronald Reagan" is an upbeat characer. The fact that the president is playing this part accounts for much of his optimism. Reagan the actor insists upon scripts with happy endings. Since the script is all that matters to him—all that is "real" to him—he always expects happy endings in everything he does. He thought that the budget would be balanced without sacrifice not so much because he believes in magic or voodoo, but because sad movies always make him cry.

Like any good trouper, Reagan tries to give the audience what it wants to hear. This does not mean that he makes a conscious practice of lying. Rather, as James Reston has noted, "often he does not mean anything except that what occurs to him might be popular with whatever audience he's addressing."[15]

It is to be expected that someone who blends his real life into a Hollywood fantasy will be more concerned with spoken lines than with action. So it has been with Ronald Reagan. In both foreign and domestic policy, his motto seems to be: "Speak loudly and carry a small stick." He loves to use tough-guy language, especially from celluloid heroes. Some of his favorite lines were borrowed from the likes of Clint Eastwood ("Go ahead, make my day!") and Sylvester Stallone.

But the tough talk was rarely matched by action. There has been a kind of "hyberbole gap" in his administration. President Reagan repeatedly promised "swift and certain retaliation" against terrorists, but because—with the exception of his 1986 air strike against Libya—he could find no way to carry out this threat effectively, he usually wound up following the same course for which he used to malign Jimmy Carter. And in the case of American hostages in Lebanon, he went far beyond Carter by trading arms to Iran to obtain the hostages' release. Reagan was forever threatening to veto "budget-busting" legislation and he frequently complained about the Congress's spending habits. Yet in his first term he exercised his veto power on an average of only seven times per year. This is the second lowest rate of vetoes per year in modern American history. It seems that few of Mr. Reagan's days were made for him.[16]

Conservatives who have been viewing "Reagan—The Movie" have generally seemed content to listen to the president's dramatic readings. Not long ago, it was liberals who were more impressed with style than substance, but as in so many other areas, in presentation Mr. Reagan seized the liberal style and most conservatives were willing to keep buying theater tickets.

Ronald Reagan is that marvelous American paradox, the pragmatic ideologue. His destination—the restoration of Coolidge's America—was unalterable, but he has been prepared to take any route, no matter how circuitous, to get there. He gets what he can at a given moment, trims when he has to, and then comes back later to get the rest.

The tenacious pursuit of one's ideological goals should not be confused with moral commitment. Indeed, ideology can sometimes get in the way of morality. President Reagan *talks* about morality, but he sees morality only in terms of good American free enterprise versus evil Soviet communism. When he agreed in the spring of 1985 to visit a cemetery containing the remains of members of the Nazi SS, Reagan completely failed to see the moral implications of his symbolic act. Instead, he placed everything into the contemporary ideological conflict. The West Germans are now "good guys," so we can forget what the Nazis did in the not-so-distant past. Mr. Reagan went so far as to say that the SS murderers "were victims just as surely as the victims in the concentration camps." I'm OK, you're OK, and the Nazis are OK. It's just the Commies and the evolutionists and those who oppose school prayer who aren't.

The division of the world into simple categories of "us" and "them" also accounts for the administration's willingness to tolerate human-rights abuses by dictators who are American allies, although the pragmatic side of Reagan's mix of ideology and pragmatism has led him to abandon "our SOB's" when their positions in their own countries became hopeless, as happened in both Haiti and the Philippines early in 1986. The Reagan division of the world into "us" and "them" also permitted him to condemn abortion but remain almost completely silent about the bombings of abortion clinics, and to condemn terrorists in the Middle East while mining harbors in Nicaragua and secretly shipping arms to Iran.[17]

Ronald Reagan's moral confusion is also evident in the corruption that has been so widespread in his administration. The names are familiar enough: Raymond Donovan, Rita Lavelle, Anne Gorsuch Burford, Michael Deaver. Former members of the Reagan administration and of the president's campaign staff went on to collect huge fees from businesses and foreign governments as "consultants"as they peddled "access" to high places. But the public never seemed to be concerned.[18]

In one respect, the degree of corruption and "sleaze" in the Reagan administration should not have been surprising. There was scarcely any corruption in the early New Deal because those who were involved were believers in affirmative government who saw federal positions as public trusts and would not tolerate anyone who used such a position for personal enrichment. "Idealists," Arthur Schlesinger, Jr., has noted, "have many faults, but they rarely steal." The Reaganites, in contrast, have always seen the federal government as an enemy. Moreover, their philosophy holds that each person should be out to help himself and not worry much about the general good. It is natural that people with such beliefs would be more likely to become involved in corruption.[19]

But the president's lack of moral commitment goes further. Mario Cuomo scored a direct hit when he said, "I think the worst thing Reagan has done is that he's made the denial of compassion respectable." At the same time Reagan and his followers have tried to convince the American people that the government is automatically their enemy—something hostile to their interests, inefficient, corrupt, and to be resisted wherever possible. This not only precludes active, positive government, it also furthers the atomization of American society. It undermines any sense of community, any understanding that some things can best be achieved cooperatively, just as others are best done individually. The president sees government and taxes as evils; he shows no understanding that there ought to be a sense of community and that people should use the government as a means of meeting community responsibilities. To say, as Edwin Meese did, that "the progressive income tax is immoral" is not only to indicate the administration's concept of morality, it is also to encourage tax dodging and a general shunning of responsibility.

"What he can't see, or doesn't want to," the *St. Petersburg Times* said of Reagan in 1985, "is that the government and the country are one. When the government is hurt, so is the economy. So are the people." Ronald Reagan and those in his party who think as he does do not understand that the United States is a single nation, a community. "Why should the woman in Albuquerque, New Mexico, pay to subsidize transportation in the Northeast?" Mr. Reagan asked in a 1985 television address. As Senator Joseph Biden points out, such statements indicate that the president doesn't understand America: "The reason why that woman in Albuquerque has any water to drink, the reason why when she turns on her spigot water comes out in that desert, is because the taxpayers in Pennsylvania, New York, Connecticut, Massachusetts—the ones who *need* that transportation—pay taxes. *That's* why!" Biden insists that Americans have always said: "If part of us are in trouble, the strength of the rest of America will come to help." We must realize, the Delaware senator said in his standard speech of the mid-1980s, "that what we need most is one another; the only person who doesn't need anyone is the person who has everything. . . . We are one country, with one destiny."

Mario Cuomo made the same point in 1985: "If California has forest fires and they don't have enough firefighters, we [in New York] are very proud of the fact that we send our people to California to help. That's federalism. When the South had to be rebuilt after the Civil War, we used the wealth of the nation outside the South to do it. That's how our American Union works." Despite his patriotic rhetoric, Ronald Reagan never seemed to realize this. "The Reagan Republicans are a Calvinist clergy," Arizona Governor Bruce Babbitt neatly said in a 1985 lecture at Yale. "They're all for faith, but not good works."[20]

And yet there is a great irony in the apparent success of Ronald Reagan's crusade against government. If, as I have argued, Richard Nixon through his failures succeeded in advancing the conservative goal of discrediting government, it may well be that Reagan's apparent success will subvert his goal. By making government seem to work, the Reaganites reduced dislike of the government even as they tried to persuade people that government is a menace. As *Newsweek* columnist Robert J. Samuelson has said, Reagan "deplores government but has restored confidence in government." The irony is extended by the real possibility that the Gramm-Rudman law, intended by its authors to reduce the function of government to defending the borders and—perhaps—delivering the mail, will ultimately have the effect of showing middle-class Americans that they do need the government.[21]

The Reagan revolution has been harmful to the nation, but it remains an incomplete revolution. And it may well prove to be self-destructive.

Magician. Snake-oil salesman. Actor. Whatever we choose to call Ronald Reagan, he will be a tough act to follow. When I asked Senator Dale Bumpers whether he thought that anyone else the Republicans might put up would be able to sell the American people the sort of contradictory messages that Reagan has peddled so successfully, he said: "I'll go you one better: I don't think *Ronald Reagan* will be able to sell those ideas by the time he leaves office. If he continues to be as intransigent as he has been in his economic philosophy, the thing is going to cave in on his head. Unless a few of those guys like Bob Dole and Bob Packwood and Pete Dominici—who know better—can prevail on him, Ronald Reagan has a very good chance of leaving office discredited."

Logic indicated that Bumpers was correct, but when it comes to Ronald Reagan, we had seen luck triumph over logic too many times to think that it might not happen again. It is uncertain as this is written whether the Iranian fiasco will do permanent damage to Reagan's prestige, but few who had seen him rebound in the past would be especially surprised to see it happen again. It seems clear, though, that even if the economy does not take a nosedive in the late eighties, future Republican candidates will face serious obstacles that Reagan was able to avoid. It is almost axiomatic that the person who attempts to follow someone who managed to escape blame for almost all problems is going to have to answer for the genuine problems of his predecessor.[22]

The inevitable problems of trying to find someone who is up to the challenge of succeeding a man who has gone beyond politics to become a "father figure"—problems experienced by Richard Nixon as he attempted to follow Dwight Eisenhower in 1960—will be multiplied for the Republicans in Reagan's wake. By the 1980s, the Republican party had become unstable. Ronald Reagan may be the only leader capable of holding together the unlikely alliance of libertarians, genuine conservatives, right-wing repressive religious fanatics, and middle- and working-class Americans who gave him large victories in two consecutive national elections. These groups disagree on far more than they agree on. There were many signs in the mid-eighties that they would soon turn on each other.[23]

The nature of the Republican split is in the eye of the beholder. Representative Jack Kemp has said the division is between "New Testament Republicans and Old Testament Republicans." It was clear that Kemp wanted to be seen as the leader of the former. Yet the "New Testament" group is itself fractured and in constant danger of shattering. The New Right united behind Reagan, their dream president, but he satisfied them more with rhetoric than with getting their visions written into law. Reagan himself has noted that some "conservatives" prefer to "jump off the cliff with all flags flying" rather than to recognize what is politically possible. He used his charm to keep such jumpers from open mutiny, but as the scramble for the succession intensifies, they will demand from would-be Republican leaders strict adherence to their program.

As the New Right and the religious Right become more insistent in their demands, traditional conservatives and libertarians will grow more uncomfortable with their Republican allies. It is a safe bet that before long these uneasy bedmates will be at each other's throats.

Those who have congregated under the Reagan banner do not form a congregation. The Republican party, as George F. Will has noted, "has taken in many new adherents, a lot of whom do not like each other." Many businessmen and "yuppies," he correctly said, "are Republicans because they love tax cutting, deregulating, hell-for-leather economic growth." Most of these younger, economically oriented Republicans are liberal on social issues. They are most unenthusiastic about the repressive agenda of the hard Right. Some on the religious Right are doing their best to appeal to such younger Republicans on the make. Reverend Jerry Falwell, for instance, has proclaimed that "material wealth is God's way of blessing people who put him first." And there is a group of Pentecostal ministers, led by Kenneth Copeland of Fort Worth and favored by Pat Robertson of Virginia Beach and the Christian Broadcasting Network, that preaches a "prosperity Gospel" that promises the faithful that God will make them rich. Despite such appeals, however, most of the young, upwardly mobile set would still prefer to worship Mammon directly and keep the snooping right-wingers out of their personal lives. The differences between these segments of the Reagan coalition will be almost impossible to compromise, and they are nearly certain to bubble to the surface soon.[24]

The most visible—and vocal—members of the Reagan Coalition are the right-wing extremists, both the avowedly religious and those who concentrate on specifically political objectives. Some of these people are no doubt sincerely concerned about the erosion of traditional values in our society. But most of the leaders of these

hard-right groups are kooks and extremists whose aspirations scare
most Americans. They congregated around President Reagan without damaging his popularity because most people did not believe
that Reagan really shared their views. The president has enjoyed the
best of both worlds. The right-wingers took his statements seriously
and forgave him for his lack of action on their "social issues," while
mainstream Americans dismissed his hard-right rhetoric and concentrated instead on his pleasant personality, which does not seem
that of an intolerant fanatic.

But can anyone else accomplish Reagan's feat of pleasing both
of these naturally antagonistic groups? If Democrats have their Jesse
Jackson problem, Republicans have a potentially more damaging dilemma in Jerry Falwell, Pat Robertson, et al. In Reagan's second
term, George Bush found himself in deadly embrace with the chief
of God's army—who found it necessary to bury the irritating title
"Moral Majority" in an organization newly dubbed the Liberty
Foundation—and "700 Club" host Robertson became ever more
deeply involved in GOP politics.

Opinion polls in the mid-eighties indicated that Jerry Falwell
was the most unpopular public figure in the United States. The
1984 Election Day *Los Angeles Times* exit poll asked voters about
the Reverend Falwell. Only 16 percent of the respondents rated him
favorably, while 46 percent had an unfavorable opinion of him.
Even among Reagan voters, Falwell was not liked. A 1985 survey of
Reagan voters found that 44 percent viewed him unfavorably, while
29 percent approved of the right-wing evangelist. On his home turf
Falwell fared no better. Just before the 1985 Virginia elections, the
Richmond Times-Dispatch conducted a poll in that state that indicated that only 8 percent of those sampled were "more likely" to
vote for a Falwell-endorsed candidate, while 51 percent were "less
likely" to support someone he backed. Some Republican candidates
in the South tried to use Falwell's support to win the backing of his
followers, but to keep knowledge of that support from the wider
electorate. This approach does not work, though. "You cannot keep
it a secret," a religion professor at the University of Virginia says of
a Falwell endorsement, because "it's too precious to the opposition."[25]

What is most frightening about the religious Right is their intolerance. They practice the "politics of certainty." "And you never
ask questions," as Bob Dylan once reminded us, "when God's on

your side." Firm in this belief, they conclude that tolerating those who do not share their views amounts to compromising with Satan. They make it clear that what they want is to establish a "Christian nation." Mario Cuomo says that when Ronald Reagan made the statement in 1984 that "this is a Christian nation" he started people thinking about the issue. Reagan, Cuomo points out, had to spend three months trying to back away from the statement, but people began "to focus on the question: 'Do you really want this, even with a good man like Reagan, do you *Christians* want this to be a "Christian nation"?' And everybody said, 'No!' That's an important issue."[26]

People have reason to fear the goals of the political fundamentalists. The example of Iran ought to be enough to give any thinking person pause. If not, a sufficient number of most disturbing statements have been made in recent years by Christian fundamentalists in this country. Television preacher James Robison, who gave the opening prayer at the 1984 Republican national convention in Dallas, has defined an anti-Semite as "someone who hates Jews more than he's supposed to." Jimmy Swaggart of Baton Rouge, one of the most popular of the television evangelists, has called Catholicism a "false religion." "Muhammad is *dead,* but Jesus is alive," Swaggart shouts from his stage, "He's *alive.* He's *alive!* GLORY!" Swaggart, whose weekly television audience is estimated to be 9.3 million, denounces the Supreme Court as "an institution damned by God Almighty." Reverend Falwell went to South Africa, liked what he saw, urged Americans to buy krugerrands and invest in companies doing business there in order to support the white regime, and denounced Nobel Prize–winning Bishop Desmond Tutu as "a phony."

Pat Robertson must be taken more seriously than some of the other television preachers. To begin with, he comes from a different background from that of most of his competitors in the TV evangelism business. Robertson was born into the upper crust—and into politics. He is the son of former United States Senator A. Willis Robertson. Pat won a Phi Beta Kappa key at prestigious Washington and Lee University and, after a stint in the marine corps during the Korean War (during which, some of his colleagues assert, Robertson used his father's influence to avoid combat duty), graduated from the Yale Law School. He failed the New York bar exam and joined with two friends to launch an electronic parts business. Soon Robertson had a conversion experience and lived for a time as a church worker in a black neighborhood in Brooklyn. In 1961, by his own account, God told him to buy a small UHF television station in the Virginia Tidewater. The Lord has long been more detailed in his conversations with Robertson than He is with most mortals. Robertson says that God instructed him to pay precisely $37,000 for the station. God also told Robertson to buy a 685-acre plot near Virginia Beach. "I want you to buy the land," Robertson quotes the Lord in one of the conversations the two hold regularly. "Buy it *all*." On another occasion, God told Reverend Robertson to buy an RCA transmitter. Now there's an endorsement that the RCA marketing people ought to be able to use.

In the early years Pat Robertson's venture into electronic Christianity faced many difficulties (the result of "satanic oppression," he states matter-of-factly). He continued to expand and eventually founded the Christian Broadcasting Network. But in 1981 CBN was on the ropes. Its steady diet of religious programming could not compete with secular stations. So Robertson decided (presumably at the direction of God) to replace most of his religious shows with old movies and reruns of wholesome sitcoms. Whether the Lord actually said to him "Bring back the Beaver and Eddie Haskell" is unclear. In any case, CBN's ratings went up, and Robertson's operations have prospered ever since. Today Robertson lives in a mansion valued in excess of $400,000 and travels in a private jet.

Robertson's political potential should be neither dismissed nor overestimated. Surely a majority of the electorate—or even a majority of Republican primary voters—would not support a man who speaks in tongues (that is, goes into a trance and utters unintelligible spiritual messages) and engages in faith healing. September 1985 was one of several occasions on which Pat Robertson claims to have used his close association with God to turn hurricanes away from the Virginia Tidewater. As Hurricane Gloria approached, Robertson said: "In the name of Jesus we command you to stop where you are and move northeast." When I asked him about this the next year, Robertson told me that he never claimed to have turned the storm around by himself. "We had half a million people praying," he said. "And when you pray for something and it happens, you usually credit God."[27]

Then there are the fundamentalists who believe that Armageddon is imminent, that God is on our side, that the devil is in league with the Soviets, and that nuclear war is the "lake of fire" referred to in the Book of Revelation. The possible consequences of this belief are too stark to require elaboration. Yet President Reagan himself has repeatedly indicated that he counts himself among those who believe that Armageddon may be coming soon—or at least that it *is* coming.

The influence of the hard Right in the Republican party is not confined to "Christians." The assortment of extremists who have become prominent in Republican ranks since 1980 includes racial "purists," neo-McCarthyites, people who see Secretary of State George Shultz as a dupe of the international Communist conspiracy, who see the handicapped as victims of their own evil ways, and who see assistance for battered women as a conspiracy by "pro-lesbian, hard-core feminists."

Roger Pearson, a man who believes that the "purity" of the white race must be protected against "inferior genetic stock," has called for "breeding back the 'ideal' types," and has advocated support for neo-Nazi organizations, has promoted himself with a 1982 letter signed by President Reagan. The letter hails Pearson's "substantial contributions to promoting and upholding those ideals and principles we value at home and abroad." In 1985 the Reagan administration appointed a woman named Marianne Mele Hall to the $70,000-a-year position of head of the Copyright Royalty Tribunal. Then it was revealed that she had helped to write a 1982 book called *Foundations of Sand.* The volume said that blacks want to be on welfare "so they can continue their jungle freedoms of leisure time and subsidized procreation."[28]

Although Ms. Hall claimed that these were not really her views and she resigned the position, the question of why the Reagan administration kept finding such kooks to appoint remains. One cannot help but suspect that statements such as those made by people on the fringes of the Reagan administration come close to the privately held views of the president and many of his right-wing supporters.

Patrick Buchanan, who served a stint as President Reagan's director of communications, is a skilled McCarthy-like hatchet man. He labels those who disagree with the administration's support of Contra rebels in Nicaragua as people who choose communism over democracy. Buchanan may be the most grating of the neo-McCarthyites, but his approach permeates the administration. The right-wing ideologues, as Haynes Johnson of the *Washington Post* has said, "turn facts upside down and recast every losing fight as having been caused by sinister ideological forces—by the 'liberals' out to do in true 'conservatives.'"

In the summer of 1985 a group of hard-rightists held a conference in Washington and called it "The State Department Held
Hostage." The conference's chief organizer, Richard Viguerie, publisher of Conservative Digest, proclaimed: "My No. 1 objective is
the removal of George Shultz." The reason? "In country after country," Conservative Caucus chairman Howard Phillips charged,
"Shultz is making deals with the devil at the expense of the United
States." A rather serious charge—or else sheer nonsense. The hysterical Right that has grown like a tumor on the Republican party
represents the latest manifestation of a recurring American phenomenon that historian Richard Hofstadter called "the paranoid style in
American politics." Like such predecessors as the Anti-Masons, the
Know-Nothings, and the John Birch Society, today's right-wing extremists believe in the existence of a mysterious conspiracy that
thwarts them at every turn.[29]

The Reagan administration's penchant for choosing right-wing
extremists was also evident in the 1985 appointment of Dr. Eileen
M. Gardner to the staff of Secretary of Education William J. Bennett. Believing as she does in reincarnation, Dr. Gardner thinks that
anyone who suffers from a handicap is being punished for transgressions in a past life. She called for the elimination of special programs
for the handicapped because they are "selfish" and "counterproductive." Her argument seems to be that if only we could get all those
selfish paraplegics off the public assistance rolls, we could give more
to the altruistic, truly needy defense contractors.

Like Ms. Hall, Dr. Gardner quit. But no one in the Reagan administration expressed a word of embarrassment over either appointment, and some New-Right activists saw both as martyrs
sacrificed to the liberal enemy. Moreover, the administration
showed its attitude toward the disabled by embarking on a wholesale removal of hundreds of thousands of people from the lists of
those receiving disability payments from Social Security.[30]

In June 1985 the Reagan Justice Department held up a grant to
the National Coalition Against Domestic Violence because a "conservative" named Patrick McGuigan asserted that " 'pro-lesbian,
hard-core feminists' might be among those helped by programs for
battered women." Any administration that listens to an argument
like that is paying far too much attention to fanatics.[31]

And then there was Lieutenant Colonel Oliver North, a man
considered far out even by some members of the Reagan administration. North was allowed to conduct secret military operations and

determine American foreign policy in critical regions of the world. The president called North a "national hero."

But the fanatics are not satisfied. They never will be. They demand absolute "purity" from candidates who seek their support, the more so since they have grown accustomed to power. Paul Weyrich of the misnamed Committee for the Survival of a Free Congress has criticized Congressman Jack Kemp—who seems conservative enough to the uninitiated—for supporting limited sanctions against South Africa's repressive government (apparently something no member of a "Free Congress" ought to do) and for only *voting* "right" on abortion and school prayer, but not *talking* enough about these issues.

Another group at the American Enterprise Institute—considered to be in the mainstream of the "conservative" movement—professed horror in the mid-eighties at what they called the "birth dearth." Their worry is that the fertility rate in the United States and other Western nations is too low. What's wrong with that, you ask? "Only large populations have tax bases broad enough to support the defense systems that are the basis of national power and security," according to Benjamin Wattenberg and Karl Zinsmeister. What their argument boils down to is this: We need to ban abortion and birth control to be able to pay for Star Wars. Their slogan could be: "Make love so that we will be able to make war."

Since these gentlemen believe that larger populations are the key to world power, they must expect Mexico to be the rising superpower of the twenty-first century. The kindest word one can think of for the argument that we should try to increase our population is insanity. But in the mid-eighties such loony notions were receiving respectful consideration in "conservative" journals.[32]

As the fanatics of the hard Right push Republican candidates ever farther towards the extreme right, they virtually guarantee the destruction of the Reagan Coalition. These kooks on the Right are on a course that will discredit "conservative" Republicans in the late eighties to as great an extent as the kooks on the Left discredited liberal Democrats in the late sixties.

Opinion polls consistently show that the positions on "social issues" favored by the New Right are unpopular with a majority of Americans. They are especially anathema to the young, upwardly mobile set that has been attracted to Republican economic policies.

Conservative columnists Rowland Evans and Robert Novak are among those who have pointed out that such voters "dislike governmental intervention in morals as much as [they do] in markets." But one New-Right leader told Evans and Novak that if the Republicans pandered to this group, "we would be a party of greed and sex."[33] That may be just what some "yuppies" are looking for.

No one can justly accuse the Republicans of the Reagan era of pandering to sexual desire, but plainly they have been appealing to greed. Jimmy Carter admitted to lusting (after women) in his heart—every man does, he noted—but said that Jesus would forgive him. The Reaganites say it is all right to lust after wealth with your whole person, not just your heart. They seek no forgiveness for this lust because they think none is needed. They are the sort who believe that the way to contribute to the poor is to throw (imported) beer cans out the windows of their Porsches as they drive along, thus giving the poor an opportunity to pick them up and sell the aluminum. This may be the meaning of the "conservative opportunity society."

These Republicans argue, Tip O'Neill has said, that the way to achieve the American dream "is to go it alone, to forget about those less fortunate. This new morality says that the young should forget about the old, the healthy should ignore the sick, the wealthy should forget the poor." O'Neill is right when he insists that "this is an alien philosophy to our country. We believe in hard work, in getting ahead, but we also believe in looking out for the other guy."

Reagan Republicans see those who work at public service jobs for less than they could make in private business as fools. Some portion of the public shares that view, but it is doubtful that anyone will be able to sell it to a majority of the electorate after Reagan is gone.[34]

It is not that the lifeboat mentality was invented by Ronald Reagan. Narcissism was clearly on the rise in the 1970s, as Christopher Lasch made clear in this 1978 book, *The Culture of Narcissism*. Many Americans, distressed at the complexities of the modern world and at their own positions of relative comfort on a planet plagued with poverty and oppression, and fearful that the abundance upon which that life was based was under threat, began to turn inward. Some were attracted to various therapies that emphasized the individual over everything else. These therapies give the practitioner, in the words of Peter Marin, who studied them in the mid-seventies, "a retreat from the worlds of morality and history, an unembarrassed denial of human reciprocity and community." In est (Erhard Seminar Training), people are told that the individual will is God and that one's will completely determines one's fate. Therefore those who are poor and hungry are so because they *wish* to be; the people in Hiroshima *wanted* to have an atomic bomb dropped on them; people who are raped or murdered *will* these events upon themselves. Thus a moral vacuum is created. Followers of such therapies are provided "with a way to avoid the demands of the world, to smother the tug of conscience."

Est is only one of many such self-centered therapies and cults that became popular in the 1970s. All variations of the "human potential movement," Marin pointed out, shared an alluring simplicity, the doctrine that "truth is identical to belief," the abolition of shame and guilt, "the refusal to consider moral complexities, the denial of history and a larger community, the disappearance of the Other, the exaggerations of the will, the reduction of all experience to a set of platitudes." People who joined these groups "wanted someone to set matters right again, to tell them what to do, and it did not matter how that was done, or who did it, or what it required them to believe."[35]

Here, in the mid-1970s, in an intensified form, was a blueprint for America in the Reagan years. Obviously most Americans never went to the extremes of the human-potential-movement adherents, but its characteristics as listed by Marin show striking similarities to the message Ronald Reagan brought to the nation at large in the 1980s. Reagan stands, as journalist Sidney Blumenthal has said, for "consumption without guilt." The president is "the avatar of a new age of narcissism, where the pursuit of happiness has been reduced to the ruthless pursuit of money. What hedonism and unbridled capitalism have in common," Blumenthal argues, "is the repudiation of the social contract." He might have added that they also share this characteristic with the human-potential therapies.

Republicans are right to reject collectivism; where they make their mistake is in confusing any notion of reciprocity or community with collectivism. When this is done, notes Leon Wieseltier in the *New Republic*, "all that remains is an irredentist individualism. The view that an unimpeded market automatically produces justice is rather a specific version of the hidden hand. It is the hidden hand in the shape of a fist."[36]

Ronald Reagan managed to glove that fist nicely, but most Americans are not ready for a permanent repudiation of the social contract. The egoism that propelled Reagan is likely to produce a violent crash for the next Republican who tries to sell the same philosophy, probably without the pretty Reagan packaging.

Most Americans realize that "the notion that pure selfishness results in the common good just isn't so." They still have a basic generosity, but as Berkeley sociologist Robert Bellah says, they "are baffled as to how to translate it into something that won't be distorted. If New Progressives can show that decency and self-interest *are* compatible, if they can synthesize ideals and self-interest and make people see that helping others is not only right—a moral obligation—but that it is practical as well, they can win over a majority of Americans.[37]

The Reagan Republicans never seem sure what to call themselves. "Conservative" is the term they most frequently, albeit inaccurately, employ. Some of the Republicans have adopted another name from American political history: "populist." The choice of this label by people who seem generally to favor the rich is most curious.

Nineteenth-century populists were identified by their demands for a progressive income tax, government regulation of industry, the nationalization of public utilities, railroads, and banks, and the use of a flexible currency to bring about "easy money," that is, inflation. Georgia populist Tom Watson once told whites and blacks: "You are kept apart that you might be separately fleeced of your earnings." Nineteenth- and early-twentieth-century populists made it clear that they were for the common people and against "the Interests." William Jennings Bryan took over the populists' crusade for flexible currency in 1896 after giving a speech in which he said to those who wanted to maintain the gold standard, "You shall not crucify mankind upon a cross of gold."

Those Republicans who have in recent years expropriated the name "populist" sought a regressive "flat tax" that would take as large a percentage of the income of the poor as of the rich. While Reagan has tried to camouflage the regressive nature of his tax cuts, Republican "populist" Jack Kemp boasts about the regressivity of his proposals. He forced the insertion into the 1984 Republican platform of a statement saying that the party "pledges to continue our efforts . . . to eliminate the incentive-destroying effects of graduated tax rates." The new populists propose to end virtually all government regulation of business and industry. It was one of their leading lights, Mississippian Trent Lott, who advised the Reagan administration to push for tax exemptions for segregated schools. This might be translated to: "We will fleece the government of its revenues that we might keep you separate."

Most incredible, such Republican "populists" as Kemp favor a return to the gold standard. This is, first of all, a way to help make the rich richer by protecting their assets against inflation. It is also a further attack on government because it would take away from the government both the responsibility and the means of maintaining stability in the economy. Wild fluctuations in currency values certainly have not been good for the world economy, but gold is not the answer. Better management, through international cooperation, is the only solution. A return to the gold standard would be to deal with currency problems in the same way the Gramm-Rudman Act dealt with budget deficits: abdication of responsibility. Like the misguided budget reduction law, the gold standard would turn over our fate to something over which we have no control, in this case the amount of a particular metal that happened to be available in the world.

Jack Kemp insists that enactment of his proposals on taxes and gold would unleash a golden age of prosperity. If he had majored in history rather than physical education at Occidental College, he might know what happened when we last tried such a supply-side program in the 1920s.[38]

People who call themselves populists advocating the gold standard—poor Bryan must be spinning in his grave.

There are, however, some traits that the new populists have in common with their earlier namesakes. One is a rejection of complexity. Populists of any stripe have always sought simple answers. Like their predecessors, those who label themselves populists today are likely to believe that conspirators are responsible for their troubles. Populists have generally tended to be anti-intellectual, although the modern Republican version may be more so than were the original populists, who arose in Texas in the 1880s. President Reagan saw fit to characterize those who opposed his 1985 tax reform proposal (which had little in it that deserved to be called "populist") as "heavy-browed intellectuals." So if favoring ignorance over knowledge makes one a populist, perhaps some of those claiming that name today deserve it. But what about opposition to "the Interests"? In 1985 Congressman Newt Gingrich (R, Georgia), one of the leading Republican "populists," told the College Republican National Committee that the Grand Old Party must be transformed into the "Grassroots Opportunity Party." It must represent the common man and be "down home," Gingrich told the enthusiastic gathering of young populists after they had finished their candlelight dinner of steaks followed by amaretto soufflé. Many of the congressman's followers, who shouted "Newt! Newt!" were dressed in the modern neo-populist uniforms: tuxedos and full-length gowns. One wonders whether Imelda and Ferdinand Marcos were populists, too.

In claiming that the administration's tax-reform plan was rooted in populism, Secretary of the Treasury James Baker said in 1985 that populism is "opposed to elitism, opposed to excessive concentrations of power and oriented toward fairness." This statement was cheered by the Houston Chamber of Commerce, which thereby made plain its opposition to elites, "the Interests," and people with concentrated power.[39]

Today's Republican populists are so much more tolerant and inclusive than were the populists of an earlier day. Today, John D. Rockefeller and J. P. Morgan could be populists and join in the fun of searching out elites and Interests to castigate.

The Christian Right, the hard Right, the repressers, "me" Republicans, "populists." We all know that the once numerous species called *Republicanus moderatus* is almost extinct. But one might wonder where that ancient and until recently powerful species *Republicanus conservativus* fits into the new GOP taxonomy.

The fact is that genuine conservatives are no longer very powerful in the Republican ranks. Conservatism means what the word implies, but few of the Reaganites have shown much interest in conserving what they found in American society and government. Political scientist James MacGregor Burns has listed the elements of the conservative tradition established by Edmund Burke in the late eighteenth century:

> . . . the organic view of society, compelling a national and social responsibility that overrides immediate class or group [or, we should add, individual] interest; a belief in the unity of the past, the present, and the future, and hence in the responsibility of one generation to another; a sense of the unknowable, involving

respect for the limits of man's knowledge and for traditional forms of religious worship; a recognition of the importance of personal property as forming a foundation for stable human relationships; personal qualities of gentility, or gentlemanliness, that renounce vulgarity and conspicuous display and demand sensitivity to other persons' needs and expectations; and an understanding of the fact that while not all change is reform, stability is not immobility.[40]

By this definition, Franklin Roosevelt may have been a conservative, but not Ronald Reagan or most of those who today call themselves conservatives. There are, to be sure, many Republicans who still subscribe to these conservative principles, but their voices are rarely heard in the party's councils, which are dominated by right-wing radicals who fall short on almost every one of the qualities listed.

Neither Reagan nor most of his followers demonstrate any appreciation of history. They certainly show no concern with future generations, as they practice a most unconservative policy of fiscal irresponsibility that could be called "beggar thy children." The attitude of many of them toward the needs of others might be summed up by Commodore Vanderbilt's motto: "The public be damned!" And their approach to conspicuous display is quite the opposite of conservatism: "If you've got it, flaunt it!"

Those genuine conservatives who remain in the Republican ranks are becoming restless. Benjamin J. Stein, who served as a speech writer for presidents Nixon and Ford, wrote early in 1986 of the dismay among traditional conservatives. He had thought that "Republicans stood for conserving what was best and most lasting in our free society. They were against adventurism and experimentation for its own sake. They conserved a way of life I appreciated." No longer is this the case under the radical right that has taken over the party. "Today's 'Republican' politics," Stein charges, "is a revolution directed from the top, aimed not at preserving society but at convulsing and reorganizing it in line with the personal, idiosyncratic goals of a few people. This is not Republican practice. It is a Cultural Revolution against many of the basic values of American society and against common sense."[41]

Former Delaware Governor Pierre S. ("Pete") du Pont IV is an example of a conservative in the new GOP. His name makes him suspect among the New Right, who fear that anyone whose money is more than a generation old might not be sufficiently in favor of helping those on the make to accumulate new fortunes. It makes little difference to the new breed on the Right that the du Ponts' credentials in opposing every modern social program since the start of the New Deal are impeccable. Moreover, Pete du Pont was educated at Exeter and Princeton, and the supply-side "populist-conservatives" are understandably leery of anyone with a good education (Pat Robertson being a classic example of the exception that proves the rule). "Many conservatives feel that anyone who has been near an Ivy League school is suspect," said Senator Paul Laxalt, in a statement that shows just how much the New Right has altered the meaning of the word "conservative."[42]

Most of the true conservatives remained loyal to the GOP during the Reagan years. They had no immunity against Mr. Reagan's seductive charms. It is most questionable, though, whether they will stick with a party under the domination of the religious Right, the hard Right, the "me" Republicans, or the neo-populists, whichever of those groups succeeds in seizing control of what used to be the party of Lincoln.

Where will the Republicans be without Ronald Reagan to lead them and to smooth over the great fissures that divide them? "I think they're in trouble without Reagan," answers Mario Cuomo. "I think they're in *big* trouble, even without a strong Democratic candidate." The New York governor thinks that anyone else will have a very hard time selling the right-wing message and the denial of compassion. "He's done that not with the power of his argument, but with his geniality, with his ostensibly non-menacing attitude, with his lack of belligerence," Cuomo contends. "I don't see anybody doing it as well. He places a kind of velvet glove over the harshness of his philosophy. . . . I think when you take him away, the harshness is revealed. Take him away and leave the world to study his policies through [Patrick] Buchanan and what have you? He [Buchanan] starts calling you a neo-socialist and says you're not a traditional family because your wife is working. He's mean and hard."

Ted Kennedy told me in 1986 that he thought the rising crop of Republicans is a weak one. "No matter what you might think of their politics," the Massachusetts senator said, "Nixon and Reagan were *good* political candidates—very *effective* candidates—and I don't really think that the Republicans have got anything in their stable [now] that can compare with those two."

Many Republicans are aware that it will not be easy to transfer President Reagan's personal popularity to other candidates. Reminding sanguine members of his party of what happened at the end of the last two-term presidency, that of Dwight Eisenhower, Pete du Pont has warned that the GOP should not try to rest its case "on eight years of peace and prosperity." Eisenhower, like Reagan, had become a father figure, beloved without regard to his policies. Yet after eight years of Ike's smiles, Americans were ready to "get this country moving again." "We have to offer a message for the future," du Pont cautioned in 1986, "rather than just promising more of what we've had."[43]

It is certain that the struggle for the Republican succession will become bitter. In the early stages of a party's national dominance, its adherents are so happy to have their people in power that they soft-pedal their internal differences. But as time goes by, the various factions within a victorious coalition become more arrogant and assertive. The New Deal coalition fragmented rapidly after FDR's death; the same is very likely to happen to the Republican coalition without Reagan to lead it. Republicans showed how much they feared this when they launched an utterly hopeless campaign to repeal the Twenty-second Amendment in time to allow President Reagan to seek a third term. Those behind this effort demonstrated a clear lack of confidence in other potential Republican leaders.

As the party of government since 1980, the Republicans will find it increasingly difficult to do what they do best: run against the government. And as the party of government, the Republicans have attracted all sorts of conflicting interest groups such as those that have plagued the Democrats in the past.

Conservatives in the mid-eighties were running out of ideas. Their think tanks had become stale, and they seemed to be losing confidence. George Will, himself a leading conservative, even suggested in the summer of 1986 that that season might someday be looked back upon as the beginning of the conservative decline. By the fall of that year, Will was listing areas in which we need affirmative government.[44]

The conservative era crowned by the Reagan presidency appeared to many in the mid-eighties to be establishing itself for a long run. In fact, however, it was already fading.

CHAPTER 7

Never
Surrender

Take these broken wings
And learn to fly again
　　—RICHARD PAGE / STEVE GEORGE / J. LANG (1985)

With a little perseverance you can get things done
Without a blind adherence that has conquered
some . . .
So if you're lost and on your own
You can never surrender
　　—COREY HART (1985)

Although the trend in social attitudes in the mid-eighties was in a liberal direction, many obstacles must be overcome if the New Progressivism is to prevail in the late eighties and nineties. Foremost among these are several difficulties that have plagued Democrats in recent national elections.

Democrats suffered greatly in 1984 from the public perception that the party was dominated by "special interests." Walter Mondale's campaign was the ultimate example of how to woo special-interest groups sufficiently to win a nomination, but in the process to destroy any chances of winning the general election. Mondale was seen by the public to be jumping through hoops set up by various constituencies. His attempts to appease them left him with the image of being weak, malleable, and "unpresidential." The problem, as Congressman Barney Frank has pointed out, was not so much with Mondale's positions as with "the perception that they were not taken out of conviction—that they were merely a series of concessions wrung out of the Democratic leaders by mutinous militants." The result of the demands made on Mondale by the interest groups was that the whole of the Democratic platform seemed to be less than the sum of its parts. Voters agreed with many of the positions Mondale took on the issues, but not with the way they saw him reaching those positions. The Democratic party has long believed that government should serve as a broker among interest groups. The trouble with this is that interest-group politics degenerates into narrow conflicts that weaken the fiber of national unity and turn politics into a selfish scramble for favors.

The national Democratic party in which interest groups developed such power became, in the view of Alvin From of the Democratic Leadership Council, an organization that didn't "have any power to do anything except screw up national elections every four years." "We just sort of stapled together all the shopping lists [of Democratic constituency groups], ran them through a Xerox machine, and called them a platform," Bruce Babbitt said of his party's practice in recent years, especially in 1984.

The selection of a woman as his running mate should have made Walter Mondale appear bold and decisive, but the National Organization for Women's very public pressure on him to choose Geraldine Ferraro created exactly the opposite impression. Instead of appearing courageous, Mondale wound up resembling Neville Chamberlain returning from Munich.

If the Democrats are to shake this image of being beholden to narrow interest groups, it will be necessary for their candidates to make it clear from the start that they will seek to advance the *common interests* of all Americans and will be the captives of no particular group.

America needs and wants leaders, not followers.

Democrats should be able to expect a degree of maturity from the leaders of constituency groups traditionally associated with their party. Those interest-group leaders ought to realize several facts after the 1984 debacle: First, nominating a candidate who believes in 75 percent of what your group believes in and who can win the presidency is preferable to nominating a candidate who endorses 100 percent of your program, but who can do nothing for you because he cannot be elected. Having some influence with the president is better than having a defeated candidate in your back pocket. Second, almost any Democrat is going to be more favorably inclined towards the needs of traditionally Democratic constituencies than will almost any Republican. Third, in order to win majority support, it is necessary for a candidate to make a broad, national, inclusive appeal, and this entails de-emphasizing the specific agendas of constituency groups.

Fourth, such traditional Democratic constituencies as labor, minorities, women, and the poor should be the *base* from which the party starts in its quest for a national majority. Democratic candidates should not have to spend their time trying to prove their support for the objectives of these groups; they should be able to feel that this base is secure and go out and seek other, as yet uncommitted, voters. As ADA president Barney Frank said to me, "liberals ought to be able to take their friends for granted. Walter Mondale should have been able to take peace people, blacks, feminists, and gay-rights activists for granted by July of 1984 and worry about everybody else. Because he didn't, he was damaged."

As New Progressives seek a concert of interests, they will be asking individuals to be willing to rise above narrow self-interest in order to advance the common good. What liberals ask of individuals they must also demand of groups. The interests of both individuals and organizations are often legitimate, but the New Progressivism seeks not to aid any particular group or individual. It appeals instead to our higher *national* and *human* interests and calls upon individuals and groups alike to reach for a higher standard.

"There is," Woodrow Wilson pointed out in his 1912 campaign, "a common interest which transcends every particular interest in the United States." That common interest is a major theme of the New Progressivism. Pursuing this common interest means rejecting the special pleas of particular organizations. As Wilson said in 1910, "the standard of statesmen is the common interest, and the common interest cannot be thought of interest by interest." "Government is not a warfare of interests."[1]

Each group in America, like each individual, will of course look out for its own needs, but each must also take account of the interests of the rest and seek to come, through the instrumentality of inspired political leadership, to a common understanding. This is what I have suggested might be called the New Community or the New American Family. This can be done by a leader capable of inspiring the people, and it can restore hope to Americans—not the Reagan sort of self-centered hope but genuine, *common* hope.

The New Progressive program must put national needs before

sectional, interest-group, or personal advantage. But liberals must never lose sight of the fact that the nation is the sum of its parts. There surely is a national or public interest, but it is not something distinct from the interests of the various people and groups in the nation. That is why it is possible to persuade groups and individuals that working for the common interest can be in *their* interests.

There is no reason for Democrats to turn on their friends. "The one thing you shouldn't do," Congressman Richard Gephardt rightly stresses, "is start kicking groups out of your party." The support of blacks, women, labor, Hispanics, the poor, and other traditional Democratic "interests" is needed for the party to succeed. But, as Governor Michael Dukakis puts it, there must be "a clear understanding that everybody can't get everything they want on their wish list." There cannot be an "insistent demand that if all the particular items on a particular constituency's agenda aren't met they're going to pick up the ball and go home," the Massachusetts governor told me in 1986.[2]

Liberal candidates should state at the outset of their campaigns that they will not endorse the agenda of any particular group in order to get its support. The proper way for organizations to operate in American politics is for *them* to examine the plans and proposals of candidates and decide which contender they like best. It is not the proper place of interest groups to draw up their own lists of demands and insist that candidates endorse *their* agendas. *Interest groups should endorse candidates; candidates should not endorse interest groups.*

The fact of diversity in the United States cannot be ignored, even while progressives are appealing to a higher common interest. There are different ways of putting this. Mario Cuomo says "we were never meant to be a melting pot; we are a mosaic. Our beauty derives from the harmony of our coming together in our differences." Jesse Jackson employs a different metaphor to make the same point. "Every part of a coalition is a patch in a quilt," Jackson told me. "You're patching regions together, you're patching race and sex and religion and business and management and labor. So I argue that a coalition is a quilt, many patches, many pieces, different colors, different sizes, bound by a common thread."[3]

Democrats will be emphasizing that common thread in the late 1980s and 1990s, as they seek to free themselves of the burdensome image of being appeasers of narrow interest groups. Democratic National Committee Chairman Paul Kirk took several steps after assuming his post in 1985 to erase the damaging perceptions of the past. He removed the various caucuses from direct representation on the party's standing committees. This action shows that the party is willing to incur the wrath of those who claim to speak for various interests, which is all to the good. "That's the best thing that can happen to our party right now," Chuck Robb said in a 1986 interview, "to have the chairman of the DNC willing to stand up and say 'no.' "

Most of the interest groups seem to understand the necessity for toning down their demands. "Right now," Joe Biden told me in early 1986, "they're scared to death. They're out there and they say, 'Holy God, look what our instinct for demanding purity has produced. Look who we have.' So now they're willing to go back and say, 'Well, if you'll cash in 20 percent of your agenda, I'll cash in 20 percent of my agenda.' " Biden's only worry on this score was that a good showing by Democrats in one election might lead interest groups to think that they could safely go back to the old ways, and the Democrats' success in the 1986 elections, followed by the Reagan administration's Iran debacle, increased that danger. Democrats must guard against overconfidence, but they have reason to be optimistic. They think that there is a good chance that the interest-group issue will turn against the Republicans in the near future. "I think we're in good shape," Congressman Tony Coelho told me, "as long as we don't get taken off in some wild-assed direction. I think the New Right hurts them *much* more than labor does us."[4]

The simple truth that the Republicans are the ones who are beholden to pernicious special interests is likely to be brought home to the voters in coming years. The Grand Old Party is still what it long has been: the party of the most dangerous special interests—big business and the super-rich. The huge 1986–87 Wall Street insider trading scandal could not help but have a negative effect on the political party most closely associated with the get-rich-quick ethic. Dale Bumpers notes that all the people to whom Democrats have been accused of "pandering" have very little economic clout.

It's not the Chambers of Commerce and it's not the economic royalists of this country that we're pandering to. On the other hand, this [Reagan] administration can raise millions of dollars overnight. Forty percent of the benefits of the Reagan tax cuts went to the richest 5 percent of the people in the country. But the people were so distracted by our apparent obsession with those so-called interest groups that no one paid any attention to an interest group one-tenth that size which was getting 40 percent of the pie.

But the traditional Republican interest groups in the country clubs and boardrooms may be the least of the party's worries in coming years. The Republican party has attracted all sorts of fringe groups that seek to have their zealous visions enacted into law. This is part of the price of power. Just as the Democrats had to put up with strident extremists on the left when they were in power, the Republicans of the 1980s faced similar groups on the right.

I have already noted that Pat Robertson may be to the Republicans in 1988 what Jesse Jackson was to the Democrats in 1984. The real danger that Robertson and the assorted loons and bigots of the extreme right pose to the GOP is in pulling the more mainstream Republican candidates toward their extreme positions. In 1972 George McGovern's party was fatally tagged as the party of "Acid, Amnesty, and Abortion." Columnist Richard Reeves has suggested that the Republicans of the eighties might be on their way to being dismissed as the party of "God, Guns, and the Gold Standard."

"The right-wing litmus tests are already coming fast and furious," Paul Kirk said in 1985, "pushing Republicans ever farther to the radical right." Patricia Schroeder shares the view that "the really radical, evangelical right-wing fundamentalists that want to turn the government into a theocracy are going to make the Democratic party's problems with unions look small." That opinion is hard to argue with. In fact, while the Democrats may continue to suffer to some degree from association with certain interest groups, Michael Dukakis provides the useful reminder that the party is far more unified than it was in the past: "When I think of the Democratic party in the late fifties—I mean, my God, it was part racist and part [civil-rights-oriented]. You had Richard Russell and Hubert Humphrey in the same party. We couldn't decide what we were for, what we were against. We had this *enormous* gulf. We don't have that these days. There's a far greater consensus among Democrats as to what we ought to be doing."[5]

And, despite that enormous gulf, the Democrats managed a narrow victory in 1960.

*   *   *

That 1960 election was won—despite the well-publicized intervention of candidate John F. Kennedy and his brother Robert to win the release of Martin Luther King, Jr., after his arrest in Georgia—with the electoral votes of six states that had once belonged to the Confederacy. Richard Nixon carried every state from the Great Plains west to the Pacific, with the exception of Texas, New Mexico, and Nevada. In the years since Lyndon Johnson's 1964 landslide, Democratic presidential candidates have had great difficulty carrying states in the South and the West. In fact, Hubert Humphrey's victory in Washington in 1968 was the last for a Democratic presidential nominee in any western state other than Hawaii. The rapid movement of Americans into the "Sun Belt" has given these regions greater strength in the electoral college (twenty-one more electoral votes than they had in 1968, with more to come after the 1990 census), and some analysts believe that the result is a Republican "lock" on the presidency.

Recent electoral history is not encouraging for Democrats. They won only once in the five presidential elections from 1968 through 1984. That victory by Jimmy Carter was narrow and benefited from the anti-Republican Watergate reaction. The last three Republican presidential victories, on the other hand, have been by very large margins. And, with the exception of the 1976 vote for southerner Carter, Democrats have been virtually whitewashed in the South as well as the West.

Were it true that the Republicans' strength in those two regions gave them a lock on the electoral college, the Democrats could only hope that the Republicans would defeat themselves (as they did in the mid-1970s); there would be little they could do to advance their own cause. Fortunately for Democrats, however, the Republican lock on the electoral college is far from unbreakable.

Neither the South nor the West should be considered solidly and unshakably Republican, although both have been nearly so in recent presidential elections. Both regions have frequently chosen Democratic governors. "You take the eleven Rocky Mountain states," Morris Udall pointed out to me in 1985, "and we've had an almost unbroken line of progressive, sensible, moderate Democratic governors." The same is true of most southern states, despite some Republican gains in 1986. Moreover, there are changes occurring in both areas that may make them more fertile ground for the New Progressivism.

In the early part of the twentieth century, the West was the most progressive region of the country. As late as 1948, Harry Truman carried every western state except Oregon. Since then, however, the region has become distinctly conservative and has usually gone heavily Republican. This shift in the West is one of the most remarkable in modern American political history, surpassing even the Republicanization of the South. The shift of the South was not an ideological change. When conservative southern whites got fed up with the liberalism of the national Democratic party, they began to vote for national Republicans. But they remained conservative. The shift in the West, though, appears to have been more one of ideology than of party.

Bruce Babbitt cites two factors to explain the change. Migration from the Midwest into the West brought conservative Republicans into the region, especially its urban areas, where political power came to be concentrated. The other key, in Babbitt's estimation, is that "the populism of old was antigovernment. You were outside the establishment, advocating reform." But from the 1950s onward, "reform and the existence of the federal government sort of became fused together, and the traditional western antipathy to the federal government became an issue, rather than populist policies." The former governor of Arizona told me that "one of the reasons some of us get away with being pretty liberal on a lot of things is we're not perceived as apologists for the federal status quo."

Patricia Schroeder points to some other reasons for the Democratic decline in her region. One is that westerners have strong traditional values, and the Republicans have rhetorically seized those American values and made it appear that Democrats do not believe in them. Another reason for Democratic losses in the West, Schroeder believes, is that "the party from our side of the country looks too much like it's the Rust Belt, the Northeastern-Midwest Coalition. We've never had anybody on the top of the ticket who didn't come from that part [of the country]—or the South. The party has always thought North-South; it has never thought West."

The fact that the Democrats have never had anyone on their national ticket from farther west than Nebraska, Texas, or South Dakota takes on more significance when one notices that in four of the last five presidential elections, the Republican ticket was headed by a man from California. Gerald Ford is the only non-Californian to head the GOP ticket since 1964—and the only one who lost. Tony Coelho draws from this the obvious conclusion that "we need a Californian or somebody who projects to the West as either president or vice-president. I think it's very important that we have somebody who the Pacific Coast feels comfortable with."

With the right ticket and the right theme, the Pacific Coast states of California, Oregon, and Washington are well within the Democrats' reach. Together these three states have sixty-four electoral votes, while the other eight western states have a total of only forty. California alone has more electoral votes than the eight Mountain states. The latter should not be ignored by Democrats, and there is good reason to think that several of them can be won in coming presidential elections, but it is clear that the three coastal states are the key to cracking the Republican lock on the electoral college. And the Pacific states—and, for that matter, the western states in general—do not make comfortable bedfellows for Republicans from the South. The latter tend towards fundamentalism and repression; the former are among the most libertarian areas in the country.[6]

The South presents different problems—and different opportunities—for the Democrats. Many southern whites have long been uncomfortable with the Democrats' commitment to racial justice. To the extent that this is still an obstacle to winning white votes in the region, it will have to remain so. The last thing the party should do is dilute its support for equality of opportunity, integration, and necessary assistance for those who have been victimized by pervasive racial discrimination. But those in other parts of the nation who comfort themselves with the notion that southern whites are notably more racist than their counterparts elsewhere ought to take another look at the South—and at Howard Beach, Chicago, and countless other localities in the North. There is no question that the South still harbors many unreconstructed white racists, but probably no more on a per-capita basis than do other sections. Those who fit this description and vote on that issue must be conceded to the Republicans.

The point is, however, that the percentage of those who are both racists and vote on that basis is no greater in the South than anywhere else. There are still Democratic majorities to be created across the region out of the large numbers of whites who are either not conscious racists or who can be convinced that other issues are more important, added to most of the black voters. Such coalitions have been built on the state level across the South; they can be duplicated in a national election.

It is difficult to argue with the proposition that the Democratic party has done so poorly in the South in recent presidential elections because it did not present the region with acceptable candidates. The Democrats have not won a national election without an incumbent president in this century unless they had a southerner on the ticket (if one considers Woodrow Wilson a southerner). Hubert Humphrey, George McGovern, and Walter Mondale chose running mates who were northern liberals like themselves. This is a mistake that the party cannot afford to make again.

After the 1984 election southern Democrats began to do all they could to make sure that their party does not repeat the mistake of ignoring the region. The Democratic Leadership Council, which has expanded from its principally southern beginnings, is attempting to develop policies and candidates that will appeal to moderates in the South and elsewhere. And Democratic politicians across the region engineered the first full-fledged regional primary in American history for the week of March 8, 1988. The consequences of these two moves could be very important in determining both the party's future nominees and their chances of victory.

In seeking to appeal to voters who think they dislike liberalism, the DLC shuns the term, but much of what its members are talking about is compatible with the New Progressivism described in this book. This is not to deny certain differences. Some figures in the DLC are considerably less liberal on some issues than is the program I have outlined. As I noted earlier, though, "progressive" is an even more popular political label in the South than it is elsewhere. The message is more important than the geographical origins of the candidate, but having a southerner on the ticket would be most helpful to the Democrats in winning at least part of the region.

It should not automatically be assumed that a northern "liberal" could not win in the South. Southerners have always shown a proclivity for exciting candidates and good speakers. "The South is a culture that has invented better than two dozen pepper sauces to put on its breakfast eggs," says Texas Agriculture Commissioner Jim Hightower. "That is not a moderate culture, it seems to me. And we like our politics just as spicy as that. You cannot beat pepper sauce with milk toast, and that's pretty much what these people [conservative Democrats] would have us do." There may not be many Marios in the South, but someone as exciting as Governor Cuomo should not be written off in the region just because his background differs from those of most voters in the region. It should also be remembered that Gary Hart did very well in the early southern primaries in 1984, despite the fact that he had almost no organization in the region and had paid it only a few brief visits.

Two other points about the South and the Democratic party are of great importance. One is that when both parties hotly contest their presidential nominations, many of the more conservative voters who have participated in Democratic primaries in the past will choose to vote in the Republican primaries. This may enhance the prospects of the more progressive Democratic candidates.

The most important variable in the Democratic attempt to win back majority support in the South is that changed economic circumstances may weaken the Sun Belt's allegiance to the Republicans and cause its residents to reassess their opposition to federal intervention. People in poor southern states have long worked against their own interests by opposing federal programs that redistribute wealth to poorer areas. Such programs are plainly beneficial to the entire economies of the poorest states, most of which are in the South. But that obvious truth has been denied by many in the region, who have cheered Ronald Reagan as he tried to dismantle the federal government and its income-transfer programs. Southern antipathy to the federal government has deep roots. It goes back to the days of slavery, when the federal government posed a threat to the South's "peculiar institution," and especially to the Civil War, when the "Federals" were the enemy. In more recent times, as Arkansas Governor Bill Clinton points out, southern "white folks think it's the federal government that's caused all the racial problems—busing and all that."

Such deep-seated feelings are difficult to overcome with the common sense that doing away with the sharing of resources represented by the federal government will assure that poor southern states will remain on the bottom, left with only their own meager tax bases. But two developments of the mid-eighties may make residents of the South more receptive to common sense. One is the Gramm-Rudman budget balancing act, which is likely to strike hard at federal programs that benefit the middle class. This may bring home to many people—outside as well as inside the South—the realization that *they* need federal programs, too. The other development is the rapid decline of important parts of the Sun Belt economy, particularly petroleum and agriculture. When the richer parts of the region were doing well, as Governor Clinton notes, they were attracted to the Republicans' antigovernment message because they knew they "were growing like Topsy, with taxes that were lower than the national average, because of the natural resources that *God* put here—the government didn't put them here." Relative prosperity allowed some parts of the Sun Belt to continue to think that laissez-faire was the best policy. People thought "government was the problem—it was trying to prop up the dying regions of the country," Clinton told me. But as the shoe shifted to the other foot in 1985 and 1986, many in the region had to reassess the situation. "Now we're being forced to go beyond that because New England is the most prosperous region in the country."[7]

People in the Sun Belt were left with a choice between concluding that God has chosen New England over them or admitting that government intervention in the economy, along the lines of the partnership approach used in Massachusetts and other booming states, can be beneficial. If enough people in the region come to see this, the Sun Belt will be ripe for the New Progressivism.

Eras of reform begin in a variety of ways. All are at least in part reactions against the conservatism of the preceding period, but the particular circumstances and issues of each new age of reform are distinct. In most respects the mid-eighties appear most like the late 1950s, but in one very important way they resemble the period around the turn of the century, when the Progressive era was incubating in the closing years of McKinley conservatism. At that time, as in the Reagan years, the federal government was committed to doing as little as possible to ameliorate social ills. Thwarted in Washington, progressives turned to the states and cities and began their reform efforts on those levels.

Before the Progressive movement reached the federal government, which occurred only in Theodore Roosevelt's second term, much significant reform was enacted in states and cities around the nation. Significant reforms began with South Carolina's adoption of the first statewide primary in 1896 and South Dakota's enactment of the initiative and referendum in 1898. Soon such progressives as Robert M. La Follette in Wisconsin and William S. U'Ren in Oregon were pushing a bevy of reforms, including direct primaries, the initiative and referendum, railroad commissions, state income taxes, corrupt-practices acts, and laws limiting lobbying and campaign expenditures. By the time progressivism really began to take hold in the nation's capital in 1906, reform administrations had been elected in Iowa, Arkansas, Minnesota, Kansas, Mississippi, New York, and Georgia, in addition to Wisconsin and Oregon. Many other states adopted various reform measures in the years before progressivism became national.

In addition, reform mayors had arisen in many cities, including Samuel M. ("Golden Rule") Jones in Toledo, Tom L. Johnson in Cleveland, Joseph W. Folk in St. Louis, Seth Low in New York, and Hazen S. Pingree in Detroit.

Early Progressives saw the states as "experimental laboratories" in which new ideas could be tried out and the ones that worked spread to other states and, eventually, to the federal government. The whole Progressive movement came to be called the "Wisconsin Idea," an important part of which was to have state agencies utilize the expertise of the faculty of the University of Wisconsin.

Something similar to the state antecedents of the national Progressive era was in full swing by the mid-1980s. As Ronald Reagan used the power of his two hands—decreased revenues and increased military spending—to get a firm grip around the neck of federal social policy, choking off any possibility of innovation there, activist, reforming government started to flourish in the states. President Reagan created a federal void in many areas that cried out for bold initiatives, and governors and state legislatures began moving in to fill it.

The irony is that while the Reaganites have been causing the old liberalism to wither in Washington, they have inadvertently been fertilizing the New Progressivism in the state capitals. Colorado Governor Richard Lamm calls Reagan's version of the New Federalism "buck-passing without the bucks." "The Reagan administration's abdication of federal responsibility . . . has left it up to the states," says Arizona's Bruce Babbitt. "Well, the states are Democratic, and there's been a wonderful flowering of progress."

"A great deal of the energy and vitality has moved to the states," Michael Dukakis points out. "Most governors, including Republican governors, are acting much more like heirs to the Democratic tradition than the folks in Washington, which is an interesting phenomenon."

Dukakis's Massachusetts has been to this New Progressive blossoming in the states what La Follette's Wisconsin was to the analagous development of early progressivism. His initiatives in cooperative economic development, finding jobs for welfare recipients, and collecting unpaid taxes are being widely imitated. One is tempted to say after a visit to Massachusetts that he has seen the future, and it works.

Other governors—notably Republican Lamar Alexander in Tennessee and Democrats Bill Clinton in Arkansas, Mark White in Texas, and William Winter in Mississippi—took the lead in educational reforms. Democrat Richard Riley in South Carolina pushed through an innovative preventive-health-care program for the poor, as did the Texas legislature after skillful prodding by black Democratic state representative Jesse Oliver. Democrat Booth Gardner of Washington is one of many governors of both parties who have made strong foreign-trade initiatives. Many other notable advances in such areas as maternal and child health care have been made by such governors as Thomas Kean, Republican of New Jersey, and Democrats Mario Cuomo of New York, Bob Graham of Florida, Chuck Robb of Virginia, Bruce Babbitt of Arizona, James Blanchard of Michigan, and Martha Layne Collins of Kentucky.

"I think you can just go around [the various states] and look at what's going on now," Governor Clinton told me, "and you can see the germs of it [the New Progressivism] emerging." "Government has a legitimate and proper role to play," says former Utah Governor Scott Matheson, chairman of the Democratic Policy Commission. "We are not beating up on government, as Reagan has done. We are rehabilitating it."

Clinton believes that what Reagan has done is to give the Democrats in the states "an opportunity to purge ourselves of some of our shackles of the past that we need to shed, *without giving up our values*. And the gaping holes in the national Republican policies have reaffirmed the validity of our values." Clinton maintains that if one looks at the best of what the governors have been doing, the future direction of the nation will be visible.[8]

Democrats do not have a monopoly on forward-looking programs in the states. But as the American people demand more of their government in the next few years, and as people turn more toward the New Progressivism, they are not likely to find a Lamar Alexander or a Tom Kean atop the national Republican ticket. They are almost certain to find a New Progressive at the head of the national Democratic party.

The last wave of liberalism crested in 1964, with Lyndon Johnson's overwhelming victory over Barry Goldwater. Four years later a conservative was elected, although only because of discontent over the Vietnam War. Liberalism was still dominant in domestic affairs in 1968, but that year marked the beginning of a new conservative wave. That wave broke on America's political shores in 1978 (precisely the year predicted by the elder Arthur Schlesinger three decades before). Perhaps the most significant sign of the new conservative mood in 1978 was the endorsement by the voters of California of Proposition 13, the Jarvis–Gann revenue-slashing plan. Other indications of the swing to the right in 1978 included the first proposal of the Kemp–Roth tax plan, the defeat of five liberal Democratic senators, and the Republicans' gain of eleven seats in the House of Representatives. Popular culture reflected the turn to self-centeredness, as "Dallas" became the new smash television hit, popular music was absorbed in the mindless disco craze, and readers made Robert J. Ringer's Looking Out for Number One, published the previous year, a best seller.

By 1980 the conservative movement was able to seize control of the country. It reached its peak in 1984 and soon thereafter entered the early stages of decline. Some of the reasons for the predictable swings of the political and attitudinal pendulum include the fact that conditions are never completely to the liking of most people, and they come to blame whichever party or philosophy is in power for what they don't like. "Had enough?" becomes a powerful appeal for the party that has been out of power for several years, regardless of which party that is. Another factor is that the longer a party stays in power, the farther into its agenda it gets. Usually the first objectives it tackles are the most popular ones. As time goes by, the governing group gets into the more controversial and vulnerable parts of its program. This happened to liberals in the late sixties, and it started happening to conservatives in the mid-eighties.

The cycle is also caused in part by the party in power tilting too

far toward one extreme or the other. There is what amounts to a
"Newton's Third Law of Politics," which states that in social and
political attitudes, as in physics, for every action there is an opposite
(although not necessarily equal) reaction. As Ann Lewis, the national director of Americans for Democratic Action, has said, "there
is an internal pendulum in American politics, a self-correcting
mechanism. When you go too far in one direction you have to go
back the other way." As the momentum back towards the center
picks up, the pendulum of course swings well beyond the center toward the other extreme, until a majority recoils from that extreme
and reverses direction once more.

Although this process resembles a law of physics, it is in fact
grounded entirely in social and philosophical principles. There is a
set of basic American values, in which most of us like to think we
believe. When those in power stray too far from those basic values, a
majority will desert them.

Financier Felix Rohatyn has described the most recent swing
from one extreme to the other by saying: "A liberalism incapable of
fiscal self-discipline brought about a radical conservatism conspicuous for its selfishness and insensitivity."[9]

It is precisely the selfishness and insensitivity of the Reagan
brand of "conservatism" that is proving its undoing. Among the
most important of the values for which Americans like to think they
stand are equity, decency, and compassion. "Americans have had
the most active doctrines of equality in the world," political scientist
Theodore J. Lowi said in 1985, "and, although our record of obser-
vance may have been poor, our shame gave us the urge to continue
trying. Conservatives have removed that shame." Lowi has put his
finger on the reason both for the temporary success of Reaganism's
appeal and for its ultimate rejection by the American people. The
official American motto under Reaganism might be changed from *e
pluribus unum* to "I'm O.K., and it's O.K. if you're not."

Most Americans will tolerate that sort of attitude only for so
long. We are a basically decent people. "Right now," Jim Wright
said to me in 1986, "we're in a period of self-centeredness in which
those who have been reasonably successful comfort themselves with
the thought that this is because they have applied themselves, not
because they've been fortunate or lucky. And, for the moment, perhaps, people tend to think in terms not of the fortunate and the less
fortunate, but of the winners and the losers. And to brand someone

as 'a loser' is almost to condemn him" under the standards of Reaganism. But Wright did not believe that such attitudes would last
much longer, because they run counter to the image Americans
want to have of themselves. "I think there is a strain within us of
compassion and decency and fellow feeling," he told me, "which is
going to surge back to the front."

Edward Kennedy, Jr., described the basic faith not only of his
family, but of liberalism, to a reporter in 1985 when he said, "people are essentially decent. If you can get across the needs and the
remedies to the American people, they'll act." A sufficiently determined and callous administration can hide those needs from the
public view for a time, but when the public awakens to what has
been going on, they will demand that action be taken to try to bring
our national practices more into line with our professed values.

Americans believe—at least in theory—in equal justice under
the law, but Ronald Reagan's annual attempts to "zero out" the
Legal Services Corporation made it clear that he believes that legal
assistance should be available only to those who can pay for it.
Americans believe that no one should go hungry in a land of affluence, but the Reagan administration sharply cut back funding for
food stamps and placed administrative roadblocks in the way of the
hungry. The same president who cut the funds and erected the roadblocks then said in May, 1986, that the only reason anyone in the
United States was hungry was because of "ignorance." Americans
believe that the sick deserve medical care, but Mr. Reagan's cuts in
Medicaid funding have left more than half (54 percent) of American families living below the poverty line without coverage. By
1986, at least 35 million Americans had neither government nor
private health insurance. Such medically indigent people are rou-
tinely turned away by hospitals and doctors. Americans believe that
the handicapped deserve proper care and opportunities to achieve
all that they are able to, but the Reagan administration has for years
carried out what the Supreme Court termed in 1986 a "clandestine
policy" to deny basic disability assistance to tens of thousands of
handicapped citizens.[10]

Such mean-spirited attacks on common decency grate against
the American conscience and self-image. Ronald Reagan's personal
magnetism seemed to separate him in the public mind from his policies. But the shame of what his administration has been doing is too
much for most of us to accept. Without Mr. Reagan's smiling coun-

tenance to mask what is going on, the ugliness of the Republican treatment of the less fortunate will be apparent to most voters.

In fact, Reagan's personal popularity notwithstanding, polls indicated that most Americans had already "had enough" of Reaganism by early 1986. A *Washington Post*–ABC News poll at that time found that over the first five years of the Reagan presidency, support for increased federal spending in nine domestic areas had *risen*, in many cases substantially. A few examples: support for spending the same amount or increasing funding for food stamps rose from 48 percent at the beginning of the Reagan presidency to 66 percent in 1986, for maintaining or increasing unemployment insurance funding rose from 72 percent to 81 percent, and for Medicaid from 89 percent to 94 percent. It is also instructive to see the change in the relationship between those who favor an increase in spending on specific programs and those who would cut them (or expressed no opinion—these two figures were lumped together in the reporting of the poll's results). In 1981, of those who wanted a change in spending for loans and grants to college students, 22 percent wanted an increase and 30 percent favored a cut. In 1986, 34 percent wanted an increase and 21 percent a cut. On Medicaid, the ratio went from 44 percent to 15 percent in favor of an increase in 1981 to 49 percent to 9 percent in 1986. When President Reagan took office, 23 percent favored higher spending for unemployment insurance and 28 percent wanted to cut it; five years later, 24 percent wanted more funding and only 19 percent wanted a cut in this program.

Those favoring spending at the same level or increasing spending represented at least two-thirds of all respondents on each program: Medicare, 96 percent; Social Security, 94 percent; Medicaid, 91 percent; day care for children of working parents, 88 percent; unemployment insurance, 81 percent; loans and grants to college students, 79 percent; aid to public television and radio, 67 percent; aid to arts and music, 67 percent; food stamps, 66 percent. At a time when President Reagan was trying to slash these programs, overwhelming majorities of the American people wanted to maintain or increase them. It appears that the Reagan offensive on social programs had the unintended effect of focusing public attention and increasing support for them. The only drop in support for spending increases between 1981 and 1986 was for military spending, from 72 percent when Mr. Reagan took office, to only 22 percent five years later. This, of course, is the one area in which the president has substantially increased spending. The 1986 survey found that 64 percent oppose reducing social spending as a way to cut the deficit, but 56 percent favor reducing military spending to achieve that end.

On all counts the public and the president were in sharp disagreement. The same is true on many of the "social issues" dear to the hearts of the New Right. Those favoring abortion on demand rose from 40 percent at the beginning of the Reagan term to 54 percent in 1986, when *88 percent* of all Americans surveyed said they favored abortions under at least some circumstances. Americans also demonstrated their opposition to curtailment of First Amendment rights through harsh pornography laws.

Exit polls at the 1984 election indicated that only 6 percent of the people who had voted for Ronald Reagan identified his conservatism as a reason for their votes, while a scant 5 percent of the 1984 Reagan voters said that agreement with his views was the main reason that they voted for the president.[11]

On a vast array of issues, the public's position in the mid-eighties was an essentially "liberal" one, even if many people rejected that label. Nearly twice as many Americans identified themselves as conservatives as called themselves liberals. It seems that ADA president Barney Frank was correct when he said in 1985 that "the public is a lot more liberal than it knows." It is clear that the name "liberal" still rubs many people—including many people who take liberal positions on most issues—the wrong way. But a philosophy expressing these popular beliefs and calling itself the New Progressivism would have an excellent prospect for success.[12]

The spark for a New Progressive revival could arise from any of several sources in the American populace. But when it does, will the Democratic party be able to fan it into a roaring political blaze or will the party's institutions throw a wet blanket over the flickering flame? Pat Caddell was among those in the mid-eighties who worried that the structure of the Democratic party might snuff out a new spark of idealism.

Certainly such a development is possible. The national Democratic party has been an outmoded, ineffective organization for some time. There are, however, many signs that this is changing. To be effective, the national party needs modernization, message, management, mail, money, media, and marketing. Over the past decade or so, the Republicans have been providing most of these needs and the Democrats have not. Republicans—and New-Right interest groups—got far ahead of Democrats and liberals in fund raising, direct-mail solicitation, slick media presentations, computerized voter and donor lists, and attractive packages for their message. The enormous lead that the Right enjoyed in these areas paid off handsomely in national—and some state—elections. In addition to the inherent advantages that these organizational strengths gave to the Republicans, they also created an impression that the party was efficient and could make the government work, an impression that was sorely lacking in the Democratic party at the end of the Carter presidency.

The Democrats started way behind in most of these important party functions, but under the leadership of Democratic National Committee Chairman Paul G. Kirk, Jr., Democratic Congressional Campaign Committee Chairman Tony Coelho, and Democratic Senate Campaign Committee Chairman George Mitchell, the party in the mid-eighties began modernizing its technical capabilities and jettisoning some of its most troublesome procedures and habits.

There are two basic reasons why Kirk was able to move boldly in areas that had long hampered the party. The first is that many Democrats were finally beginning to shed their "majority complex." It was slowly dawning upon them, after they lost four of five presidential elections, that they were no longer the automatic governing party. This led members of the party to become more interested in winning than in splitting ideological hairs or in struggling over the party structure. "You can see that mellowing process at work in the Democratic party right now," Bruce Babbitt told me in 1986. "Paul Kirk has been very much the beneficiary—and in some degree the initiator—of that inside the party. And you can see it in many different sectors. We've still got a long ways to go, but we're headed the right way."

The other reason that Kirk was able to introduce changes in the DNC that would have raised great outcries from various Democratic constituencies in the past is that as a former aide to Ted Kennedy, Kirk has a strong liberal identity. He "could do what I couldn't because he's got the credentials," says former DNC Chairman John C. White.

What Kirk did is remarkable. He appointed South Carolinian Don Fowler as head of the party's Fairness Commission and insisted that the commission complete its business by the end of 1985.

As a result, the party's rules were set for 1988 almost three years before the convention. He disbanded the official "caucuses" within the DNC: black, Hispanic, women's, lesbian-gay, Asian-Pacific, business and professional, and liberal-progressive. He commissioned an in-depth national poll of 5,500 voters in 1985 to get a better feel for what the voters really thought. And he jettisoned the party's midterm mini-convention in 1986, thereby avoiding public squabbles inside the party that could have weakened it and tarnished its image.

Some of Kirk's most important contributions have been in the areas of modernization and message. He identified sixteen target states for 1986 in which computerized voting lists were installed and state Democratic finance plans were developed. As he said, his principal goal was "to get the party on an irreversible course toward modernization." It will take a long time for the Democrats to catch up with the Republicans in the use of modern technology, but a significant start has been made.

Kirk has also played an important part in liberating his party from the image of being a collection of special-interest groups. "We have to be interested in affirmative action," he maintains, ". . . but the only quota I'm interested in is 51 percent of the electoral college." Kirk criticized the AFL-CIO for endorsing a candidate before the 1984 primaries and asked that they not do it again in 1988. "In my view," he said at a 1985 meeting of the Communications Workers of America, "the trade-union movement can strengthen the party's nominee by refraining from an early endorsement. Let the candidates use the primary process to develop and to demonstrate their own broad political base before giving your full and united backing." Kirk also stood up to Jesse Jackson and rejected his choices for party vice-chairman and head of the Fairness Commission. He helped begin to move the party toward the essential goal that Senator Kennedy has defined as seeking "to lead a country, not a collection of divided and contending groups."[13]

The appointment of the Democratic Policy Commission, chaired by former Governor Scott Matheson of Utah, was one of Kirk's most important contributions. The Policy Commission, composed almost entirely of elected officials (who know what sort of Democratic messages the public accepts), is playing a role in revamping the party's appeal similar to that of the Democratic Advisory Council in the late 1950s (yet another parallel of the mid-eighties to the late fifties). What emerged from the new Policy Commission in the summer of 1986 was a set of ideas somewhat similar—although muted—to the New Progressivism that has been set forth in these pages. This is no attempt to imitate the Republicans' appeal. Given a choice between the genuine article and a quick copy, people are going to choose the genuine article. But if they are offered a different article of greater quality, they are likely to buy it. Members of the Policy Commission set out to define what makes Democrats different from—and in their view, better than—Republicans. That difference is between Democratic cooperative individualism and Republican laissez-faire (except when the immediate interests of an important constituent are at stake—"in his own district," goes the saying, every congressman is a liberal").

These successful, elected Democrats know that they have to stand for something if they want the public to follow them. Polling is an essential function of modern campaigns, but its purpose should never be to determine what positions candidates will take. The party cannot become like the people Jean-Jacques Rousseau described in *Julie*, who "have to go into society every night to learn what they're going to think the next day." There is a critical difference between telling people what they want to hear and determining when they are ready to hear what you believe. Tactics cannot be allowed to determine policy.[14]

One Republican advantage that the Democrats are never likely to offset is money. This is less of a problem in the publicly financed presidential elections than it is in other races. In 1983–84, for example, the Republican Senate Campaign Committee raised $83 million, while its Democratic counterpart took in less than $10 million. This gives the GOP a great advantage. It is able to use the promise of full financing to entice candidates into races against tough Democratic incumbents, but many good Democratic candidates choose not to challenge entrenched Republicans because they cannot raise sufficient money to give them a chance to get their message across. The Democratic Senate Campaign Committee is obliged to practice a form of triage, in which it concentrates its limited resources on the candidates who appear to be in close races. The likely big winners and big losers are left with little support. This makes it very difficult for a little-known Democrat to pull off a startling upset, although the party had several pleasant surprises in the 1986 Senate races.

The Republicans' monetary advantage carries over to presidential elections, despite the apparent equality provided by public financing. Independent "conservative" groups raise large sums and spend them on negative advertising campaigns against the Democrats or on advertising for the Republicans that is not under the control of the party or the candidate.

The principal need for vast amounts of money in modern campaigns is to purchase television time and other media exposure. AFL-CIO President Lane Kirkland believes that the Democrats' "delivery system" is much more of a problem than their message. Tony Coelho points out that on most issues the Democrats are much closer than the Republicans to what the public wants and believes. "Our problem as a party," he told me in 1985, "is that we don't have the money to *market* what's going on. One of the things I'm devoted to is developing Democratic capabilities. We're not into computers. We're not into marketing analysis. We're not into direct mailing. Finally we're getting into it, but we gotta get *better* at it."

Use of the media has been one of the areas of greatest advantage for the right wing over liberals. The Republican right invested a large amount of money and time in producing radio tapes and news/opinion pieces for small radio stations and newspapers around the country. "They really put on a major PR campaign in the last twenty years," Patricia Schroeder contends, "and it was down on social programs, down on government—and they *sold* it. If you want to see how this opinion has been built over the past twenty years, drive around America and turn on the radio and listen to the pap that came out on the air." Congresswoman Schroeder also points out that the right-wingers have been very clever in "constantly screaming how 'left-wing' the media is. This puts the media in a similar position to what it was in the McCarthy era."[15] The idea that the national media are dominated by liberalism is, at best, an anachronism. No one follows the whims of a fickle public opinion more carefully than the television network executives. Their overriding motive is higher ratings; so as long as Ronald Reagan remained popular, it was to be expected that he would be treated with kid gloves by Dan Rather and company. The last thing ratings-conscious news directors want to do is to anger their viewers.

This means that liberals and Democrats face difficulties in both the news reports and with paying for commercials. The close ear that the networks keep to public opinion means, however, that if American attitudes are perceived to be swinging back in a liberal direction, the media will quickly change their tune.

All the improvements in the capabilities of the national Democratic party outlined here are important to bettering its chances for victory in coming elections. Even if, as I have argued, the national mood is moving in a liberal direction, the Democratic party can ill afford to sit and wait for its departed adherents to come home. It has to seek them out aggressively with the New Progressive message and improved political techniques.

Important as all this is, however, nothing the Democrats do as a party is nearly as crucial to their electoral prospects as finding the proper candidate to deliver their message and win the trust of the American people. An inspirational leader who can do what John F. Kennedy did at the beginning of the 1960s—inspire by his own optimistic and idealistic outlook—is worth more than all the polls and plans and position papers that the party can produce. If such a candidate emerges and presents a vision to mesh with the rising liberal idealism in the nation, a significant new era of reform will soon be upon us.[16]

Despite his loss of prestige as a result of the Iran arms scandal, Ronald Reagan will probably leave office as a popular president, just as Dwight Eisenhower did. But Eisenhower, like Reagan, was not able to transfer his personal popularity to other members of his party. In 1958, in the twilight of the Eisenhower age, the Democrats gained fifty-one seats in the House and eight in the Senate, setting the stage for a victory in the presidential election two years later.

Similar election results have been recorded in the off-year elections during the sixth year of other two-term presidencies in this century. In the elections of 1918, 1926, 1938, 1950, 1966, and 1974, the party out of power made significant gains in the congressional races in the sixth year of a presidency. In the sixth year of Woodrow Wilson's presidency in 1918, the Republicans won control of both houses of Congress. The sixth year of the Harding–Coolidge administration, 1926, saw the Democrats gain eleven seats in the Senate and twelve in the House. In 1938, Franklin Roosevelt's sixth year in office, the Republicans picked up eight seats in

the Senate and eighty-one in the House. In 1950, the sixth year of
the Truman presidency, Republicans gained five places in the Senate and twenty-nine in the House. Six years into the Kennedy–Johnson era, the Republicans added four senators and forty-seven
representatives. And in the Watergate election of 1974, the sixth
year of the Nixon–Ford presidency, the Democrats, though already
holding majorities in both chambers, added five senators and forty-
six representatives to their totals. In five of these seven sixth-year
elections, the gains by the party out of power presaged a presidential
victory two years later. The only exceptions were 1926, when Coolidge prosperity lasted long enough to elect Herbert Hoover two
years later, and 1938, a unique case because of FDR's third-term
candidacy in 1940. The Democrats would not have beaten Eisenhower in 1960, and they might never be able to defeat Reagan, but
they will not have to.[17]

The Democrats' pickup of eight seats in the Senate and five in
the House in 1986 fit the pattern of sixth-year election gains by the
party out of power. The modest Democratic increases in the House
were a consequence of the party's earlier success in holding firm
control of that chamber. The 1986 results provided no guarantee of
a Democratic victory in the 1988 presidential election, but viewed
in historical perspective they were encouraging.

One of the most important facts that both parties must consider
as they prepare for future presidential elections is that Ronald Reagan will not be a candidate. In determining their strategy for opposing the Republicans, Democrats need constantly to remind
themselves of this seemingly obvious point. As Brian Lunde, executive director of the Democratic National Committee, said after reviewing the results of the party's major poll in 1985, the voters have
"put him [Reagan] in the history books and they're moving on into
the future." Democrats must do the same. Tempting as it is to criticize all the outrageous policies that Reagan has advanced and the
errors that he has made, such personal attacks will gain the Democrats little.

The very fact that a sizable majority of Americans adored Ronald Reagan at the same time that they disagreed with his policies
will make the task of Republicans who try to succeed him a most
formidable one. They will be left with the unpopular Reagan policies but without the popular Reagan persona. The 1986 Senate
races indicated how the voters react to Reaganism without Reagan.

The less the Democrats mention the name "Reagan" and the more they talk about what the "radical rightists" (a term at once more accurate and more negative than "conservatives") stand for and want to do with the country, the better off the party will be. Contrasting a liberal program based upon what I have called the New Progressivism with the increasing extremism of the Republicans will result in a campaign in which Reagan has little effect.

As they develop their own New Progressive themes, the Democrats can watch the Republicans march farther to the right and experience increasing dissension. Senator Lloyd Bentsen tells a story to illustrate what was happening to Republicans in the mid-eighties. He says that after the Democrats regained control of the House of Representatives in 1954, Speaker Sam Rayburn told him: "Now, Lord, our troubles start. We've got a majority. We've been very united as a minority." The Republicans are in no immediate danger of facing that problem in the House, but their growing conviction that they are now the natural majority in the nation is bound to encourage extremism and disagreement within their ranks. "Success breeds dissension," Bruce Babbitt points out, "because the ideologues are never happy with success; they always want to push it another ten yards. . . . I think there's a kind of historical inevitability about the rise of all these special-interest groups who are unhappy. Their agenda has not been met; they're only going to get more shrill." And no matter how most voters feel about Ronald Reagan, they are not going to be comfortable with all the people Bob Dole has called "screwballs" who are wielding so much influence in GOP councils.[18]

Democrats have an opportunity to turn the tables on the Republicans, both on the special-interests issue and on the invocation of the heroes of America's past. In 1984 Ronald Reagan strove to link himself to every deceased liberal Democrat that he could think of. This was understandable. There are, after all, far more and far better Democratic heroes in our history than there are Republican heroes. But there have been some of the latter, as well. In coming elections Democrats can not only reclaim their own heroes, but take the Republicans' as well: Lincoln, Theodore Roosevelt, and perhaps Eisenhower.

Lincoln stood for the "plain people." How would he feel about a Republican president who cut nutrition programs at the same time he cut the taxes of the rich?

There was a time when many progressive Republicans fought for the common good and a willingness to be responsible. For the sake of future generations, Teddy Roosevelt always said we must forgo immediate rewards and rise above narrow self-interest in using natural resources. No other president has ever been more closely identified with protecting the environment against exploiters and polluters. How would TR feel about a Republican president whose main contributions to the environmental cause were James Watt and Anne Gorsuch Burford?

And how would Dwight Eisenhower, who first warned us of the threat of the "military-industrial complex" feel about a Republican president who set out to turn over $1.6 *trillion* to military contractors?

A Democratic electoral vote majority *can* be put together. If all the voters who cast their ballots for Democratic governors had supported the presidential ticket in 1984, Fritz Mondale would have won the election. The party's success in 1986 Senate races in the South and West demonstrated that the Republicans have no lock on those regions.

Democrats have often in the past been, in the words of David Broder, "resistant to the systematic application of survey research and the discipline of developing detailed strategic plans for targeting and winning the necessary 270 electoral votes." Plainly this will have to change if the party is going to be successful in coming national elections.[19]

Even if the dreary returns from the 1984 national election are examined, the outlines of a conceivable Democratic electoral-college majority can be discerned. Fourteen states and the District of Columbia gave the Mondale-Ferraro ticket at least 42 percent of their votes in 1984. Given President Reagan's incumbency, his ability to mesmerize the public, the apparent prosperity, and the weaknesses in the 1984 Democratic campaign, it does not seem unreasonable to believe that any state that gave at least 42 percent of its votes to the Democratic nominees in 1984 may be winnable by a strong Democrat who does not have Ronald Reagan for an opponent. These states, with their Mondale percentage and their number of electoral votes, are as follows:

GROUP I

	Mondale, %	Electoral Votes
California	42	47
D.C.	86	3
Hawaii	44	4
Illinois	43	24
Iowa	46	8
Maryland	47	10
Massachusetts	49	13
Minnesota	50	10
New York	46	36
Oregon	44	7
Pennsylvania	46	25
Rhode Island	48	4
Washington	44	10
West Virginia	45	6
Wisconsin	45	11
	Total	218

There is good reason to think that, with a new liberal mood in the country, different economic perceptions, Mr. Reagan not running, the unpopular agenda of the New-Right interest groups more prominently displayed by the Republicans, an attractive Democratic program grounded in the New Progressivism, and a stronger Democratic candidate, that the Democrats should substantially improve their showing in all these states. Victory in all would put the party's candidate within striking distance of the 270 electoral votes needed for victory.

If the threshold of Mondale votes is dropped to 39 percent—admittedly a very low level—an additional fifteen states with 150 more electoral votes come within range:

GROUP II

	Mondale, %	Electoral Votes
Alabama	39	9
Arkansas	39	6
Connecticut	39	8
Delaware	40	3
Georgia	40	12
Kentucky	40	9
Louisiana	39	10

	Mondale, %	Electoral Votes
Maine	39	4
Michigan	40	20
Missouri	40	11
New Jersey	40	16
New Mexico	39	5
Ohio	40	23
Tennessee	41	11
Vermont	41	3
	Total	150

It is obvious that a future Democratic nominee could not expect to win all these states. But if he or she were to sweep the 218 electoral votes in Group I, only fifty-two more would be needed for victory. And the states in Group II that offer the best prospects for a Democrat in 1988 are precisely those with the largest number of electoral votes. The necessary fifty-two votes could be obtained by winning as few as three in Group II—Michigan, Ohio, and one among New Jersey, Missouri, and Tennessee, for example. Of course it is not likely that the Democrat will win *all* the states in Group I, but Group II provides many possibilities to make up for any losses in the first category.

There is a third group of states that, despite their low Mondale totals in 1984, just might be won by a Democrat in the near future. These include:

GROUP III
Electoral Votes

	Electoral Votes
Florida	21
Mississippi	7
North Carolina	13
Texas	29
Total	70

Victory in these states is not likely, but it is, for a variety of reasons, possible. The remaining states might provide a pleasant surprise for the Democrats somewhere, but appear to be generally safe in the Republican column:

GROUP IV
Electoral Votes

Alaska	3
Arizona	7
Colorado	8
Idaho	4
Indiana	12
Kansas	7
Montana	4
Nebraska	5
Nevada	4
New Hampshire	4
North Dakota	3
Oklahoma	8
South Carolina	8
South Dakota	3
Utah	5
Virginia	12
Wyoming	3
Total	100

Even some of these "safe" Republican states might prove to be winnable by the Democrats in the near future. Seven are Rocky Mountain states, a region that has rarely elected Republican governors in recent years and that is suffering from a depressed mining industry. Five are the agricultural states of the Great Plains, which are facing serious depression, and one of those five, Oklahoma, is—like Texas and Louisiana—heavily dependent on oil, another industry that collapsed in the mid-1980s. Yet another sick industry—textiles—is a key employer in the Carolinas and Virginia. Voters in such states (and in other poor or economically depressed states) may well be receptive to the New Progressivism's message of a more affirmative government that seeks cooperation among management, labor, and the government.

Presidential elections in which there is no incumbent are usually close. It is worth emphasizing once more that the personal popularity of a president is not transferable. The Roosevelt Coalition eroded rapidly under Harry Truman. Without the FDR magic, Truman needed a near miracle, including incumbency, a very strong campaign, a weak opponent, and a solid program, to win in 1948. Most important, Roosevelt had done more than work his personal magic on people; he had actually *done* things for them. His majority

was more stable than Reagan's because it was based on something
more than charm. Even so, Truman had a hard time holding that
majority together when FDR was gone. Future Republican nominees are not likely to have any of the positive factors going for them
that Truman had four decades ago.

The Democratic prospects in the late eighties and nineties are
much better than most observers think. Governor Bill Clinton pre-
dicts,

> You may have a sort of replay of the 1960 election, where we'll
> fight out over our new ideas and pick the best fellow we can to
> be the nominee, and the Republicans will be able to say "we just
> need to do a little better with what we've been doing the past
> eight years," and you may have a fairly close race. But if we
> nominate someone who represents the things you and I are talk-
> ing about [that is, the New Progressivism], then we've got at
> least a fifty-fifty chance and maybe better.

Conservative Republican Congressman Newt Gingrich of
Georgia agrees. If the election becomes a referendum on the Reagan
presidency and the Republicans "take no risks and run on Reagan's
coattails," Gingrich told columnist Richard Reeves in 1986, "we
lose that fight because Americans always want something new. . . .
We don't buy last year's soap."

"All Kennedy really did in 1960," American Enterprise Institute for Policy Studies scholar William Schneider points out, "was
to say it was time to get the country moving again. In 1988, it could
be time again." I think it will be, but if the Democrats emphasize
the New Progressivism, they will be offering a good deal more than
just to "get the country moving again."

And if the liberal wave has not grown quite high enough yet in
November of 1988? Mario Cuomo puts it well: "If the Republicans
win in '88, then by '92, forget about it. You [the Democrats] could
run Mickey Mouse" and win.[20]

CHAPTER 8

The Springsteen Coalition

We learned more from a three minute record than we ever learned in school
—BRUCE SPRINGSTEEN (1984)

Rock and roll just used to be for kicks
And nowadays it's politics
And after 1986 what else could be new
—BILLY JOEL (1986)

Democratic pollster Patrick Caddell calculated in the mid-eighties that by 1988, those born in the baby boom and after (that is, those born from 1946 onward) will constitute 61 percent of the electorate. The nation's populace was aging, but voting power had shifted decisively to those who would be between eighteen and forty-two in 1988. Any strategy that hoped to elect a president that year or subsequently had to find a way to appeal to this majority of the electorate. Understanding the attitudes and values of this vast segment of the population will provide the key to elections for the next four decades.

This huge, relatively youthful portion of the electorate can be divided into three basic age groups: the early baby boomers, born from 1946 through 1955, the late baby boomers, born from 1956 through 1964, and the post–baby boomers, born since 1965 (and, for the purposes of the 1988 election, before November 1970). The formative experiences of these three groups were quite different, and

228

those experiences go a long way toward accounting for their widely differing general outlooks.

The early boomers reached political consciousness (age fourteen to eighteen) between 1960 and 1973—at a time when idealism and rebellion were the orders of the day. These are the people who thought they were going to change the world. Many became disillusioned in the 1970s and turned inward. Some of the more successful of them became the "yuppies" whom the media briefly confused with the entire generation. It is principally this age group (those between thirty-three and forty-two in 1988) that Caddell has in mind when he says that so much was expected of them, but so far they have not accomplished much.[1] Many of these early boomers continue to look back nostalgically toward the idealism of their youth. They have been cynical and self-centered for long enough to know how unfulfilling such attitudes are. As they recall their earlier days, many of them are susceptible to what might be termed "reillusionment."

But it would be a serious mistake to lump together everyone in this particular age group. The affluent yuppies constitute no more than 10 percent of the total baby-boom population and less than 20 percent of those born in the early boom years. They can be an important voting bloc, and Democrats should not ignore them. Emphasis on New Progressive policies of economic growth, widespread opportunity, and social liberalism may win many to the Democratic banner. But, as Texas Agriculture Commissioner Jim Hightower has pointed out, this relatively small group cannot form the basis of a political party: "We are not going to build a Democratic majority by offering more Cuisinarts and L. L. Bean gift certificates to the people of this country." Democratic pollster Mark Mellman agrees. "Most baby boomers don't drive BMW's," he notes. "They don't have Chinese dogs and they don't live in the downtown areas of major cities."[2]

Far more numerous than the yuppies are members of another subgroup within the baby boom. This group, which is struggling to make ends meet and trying to achieve a standard of living as high as that of their parents, has been dubbed the "new collars" by University of Massachusetts public service professor Ralph Whitehead, Jr. Others have called these hard-pressed young people of the middle and working classes the "Springsteen voters" because many of them live the sorts of lives about which Bruce Springsteen sings. They are facing up to the realities imposed by their numbers. Jobs, pay raises, and homes have all been made harder to come by because of the sheer numbers of people in the generation. The American dream holds that those who work hard will do better than their parents and will experience a rising standard of living. The reality has been that between 1973 and 1983 the median income of baby-boom families *declined* by 14 percent in constant dollars. "As a generation," thirty-three-year-old Chicagoan Elizabeth Newman told a newspaper reporter, "we were brought up to think that we could have tremendous jobs, wonderful houses, exotic travel, great marriages, beautiful children, . . . but for us even a hut in a distant suburb by a freeway would hopelessly tip our delicate financial balance."

These less affluent young adults have a very different outlook from that of the stereotypical yuppie. Professor Whitehead illustrates the difference by saying: "You tell a new-collar voter about a $600 toilet seat at the Defense Department and he'll want to fire the people involved. You tell a yuppie about one and he'll want to know what colors they come in."

Many baby boomers are finding that, contrary to the beer commercial, they *can't* "have it all." In 1970 three-fourths of all American families could buy an average-priced house. In 1984, only one-third could do so. During the 1950s and '60s, the average American's inflation-adjusted income increased by 100 percent between the ages of twenty-five and thirty-five. For those who were twenty-five in 1973, however, their real income had risen by only 16 percent when they reached thirty-five in 1983.[3]

"Baby-boomers had such a mesmerizing youth," says Landon Y. Jones, author of *Great Expectations: America and the Baby Boom Generation.* "Now their expectations are colliding with reality, and there are all kinds of conflicts ahead." People raised on high expectations are confronting "low mobility in the job market."

For the Springsteen voters, economic growth is not a luxury. Their numbers make a growing economy absolutely essential. Without it they face a future of downward mobility. Any party that fails to make this need a central focus of its policy will not attract this largest of all voting groups. They are concerned not merely with the number of jobs available, but with their quality and level of pay. They have liked Ronald Reagan's optimistic rhetoric, but they are likely to realize before long that most of the jobs that have been created in recent years are low-paying service jobs. As House

Speaker Jim Wright says, the Reagan administration "has updated Marie Antoinette by saying of our workforce: 'Let 'em flip hamburgers.' "[4]

It is for this reason that the New Progressivism's emphasis on an active government promoting economic growth and cushioning the shocks of economic change should appeal to a large portion of the baby-boom population. Their vast numbers leave them with little choice but to turn for assistance to an affirmative liberal government. And the problems of numbers pressing on jobs, housing, and other resources are even larger for the late baby boomers than for the early boomers. A greater portion of the late-boomer population is in the "new-collar" or Springsteen group. Fewer of those born between 1956 and 1964 will have a chance to become yuppies.

The late baby boomers did not arrive at political consciousness until 1970 to 1982. They came of age in a time of deep cynicism. Everything seemed to be going wrong. The United States was in the final stages of losing a war that most of its people had concluded we should never have been in. Revelations of lying by the highest officials in two successive administrations representing both major parties produced a climate the opposite of that in which idealism had been nurtured in the early sixties. The environment was deteriorating; energy was said to be running out; inflation was soaring; the economy was stagnating. Watergate completed the process of destroying confidence in government and cooperative action. And at the same time these late boomers were beginning to face the harsh realities that the demographics of the baby boom created in terms of jobs, housing, and opportunities.

Young people are naturally optimistic. When they grow up in an age of cynicism and are told that everything is wrong in the world, their optimism is usually not snuffed out; it is turned inward. Young people in such an age will be optimistic about *their own* futures, not those of others, or our common future. They "look out for Number One." There were few illusions left when the late boomers reached their mid-teens, so that, unlike their slightly older siblings, they never suffered disillusionment. They had never become "illusioned" in the first place. Those who came of age in the "me decade" never thought much in terms of what "we" could accomplish.

This group, ranging in age from twenty-four to thirty-two in 1988, has been very favorably inclined toward Ronald Reagan. Yet they were deprived of a portion of their normal development because there were no ideals to which they could hold when they reached the age of natural idealism. Should a new wave of idealism sweep other age groups in the late eighties and early nineties, the late baby boomers might experience a delayed version of this stage of development.

"There is in most Americans," Louis Brandeis once said, "some spark of idealism, which can be fanned into a flame. It takes sometimes a divining rod to find what it is; but when found, and that means often, when disclosed to its owners, the results are extraordinary." Such could be the case with those in their twenties and early thirties if someone identifies for them the latent and still untapped idealism of their generation.

The post–baby-boom generation was just reaching voting age in the mid-eighties. Those eligible to participate in the 1988 election will be between eighteen and twenty-three in that year. Their experiences have been very different from those of the late boomers. The oldest among them did not begin to reach political consciousness until the end of the seventies, and most of them have arrived at that age during the Reagan years. Vietnam, Watergate, and the other horrors of the late sixties and early seventies are only historical events to them. They began to notice the world around them only in the years when President Reagan's optimism was ascendant. They are not disillusioned. Why should they be? It is, after all, "morning in America."

There is an enormous irony at work here. As I have noted earlier, Richard Nixon managed through failure and disgrace to achieve the principal conservative objective of undermining public faith in government far better than he could have by succeeding in his efforts at budget cutting and impoundment. In the 1980s the irony has come full circle because Ronald Reagan's apparent success in his conservative, antigovernment program has restored the people's faith in government. In 1986 President Reagan's pollster, Richard Wirthlin, found that "Americans once again have faith that our public institutions can cope with problems." A CBS News/*New York Times* poll at the beginning of 1986 found that the percentage of Americans who thought that government creates more problems than it solves had declined from 63 percent when Mr. Reagan took office to 51 percent five years later. Confidence in government, Wirthlin's survey concluded, had returned to its 1972 level, before it was smashed by Watergate.[5] It appears that Mr. Reagan's seeming success may have hurt the conservative cause as much as Mr. Nixon's failure advanced it.

If this is true for Americans in general, it is even more the case with the young. Certainly they want to be optimistic, but if "America is back," why should they settle for the narrow, selfish, personal optimism offered by the Reaganites? If anything is possible, then why should we tolerate hunger and poverty and the threat of nuclear war?

The pessimism into which liberals fell in the early 1970s prepared the soil for the seeds conservatives were sowing. If traditionally optimistic liberals lost hope for the world, there was nothing left to do but pursue personal advancement. But the optimism of the conservatives in the eighties has produced a climate in which liberalism can once again germinate. The broader optimism of the New Progressivism is likely to attract the post–baby-boom generation away from the egoistic optimism of the Republicans.

Young people tend to be reactive. They do not like to be told by their elders what they "should be," so they rebel against such imposed identifications. Whatever is "in" will soon be "out," and vice versa. When the young of the 1950s were stereotyped as the "silent generation," those who were slightly younger became the "radical youth" of the 1960s. People who thought about the fact that the young always seek to rebel wondered how the rising generation could think of anything more outrageous than the long hair, obscenities, loud music, filth, and drugs of the youth of the late sixties. Although it may have seemed as though the youth of the seventies were not rebelling, in an important sense they were. Just when the young were pigeonholed as radicals, their younger siblings rebelled against that image by becoming more conservative (although these stereotypes are always overdone). In terms of going against expectations, going "straight" was one of the most daring things young people could do in the wake of the sixties youth rebellion.

By the mid-eighties, however, the stereotype had shifted to seeing the young as conservative, Republican, self-centered clones of the Alex character on the popular NBC sit-com "Family Ties." The image had become very much the same as that of the silent generation of the 1950s. Once the young had been classified—and sometimes castigated—as the "me generation" and career-oriented budding yuppies, it was to be expected that youth would rebel again, probably in much the same way as the "rebels without a cause" of the fifties. Columnist Ellen Goodman even suggested that "Madonna's black lace bra and white lace stockings" are a mid-eighties female version of Marlon Brando's black leather jacket.[6] But you didn't have to accept Cyndi Lauper as the new James Dean to see that a new rebellion was smoldering among the young of the mid-eighties. Of course there were enormous differences between the youth rebellion that emerged from the silent fifties and that which appeared to be developing in the quiet eighties. For one thing, the youth of the eighties did not have the demographic power enjoyed by their counterparts thirty years earlier. This may be just as well. Without the numbers to convince themselves (and many of their elders) that they have all the answers, young people in the eighties and early nineties may remain liberal and not go off into wild flights of "radicalism."

There is, in any event, no question that the young late in the Reagan conservative era were doing just what their forebears did late in the Eisenhower conservative era: moving in a liberal direction. Evidence from opinion polls through campus protests to popular culture demonstrates this. The young can usually be expected to do what is least expected of them.

While columnists and media analysts were pegging the youth as self-centered, career-oriented conservatives, the evidence showed that college-age Americans had in fact been becoming more liberal. The mid-eighties saw a significant swing among college students back to the liberal arts and away from business courses. A survey of the nation's college freshmen in 1985 found that most labeled themselves as "middle of the road," but more identified themselves as liberal or far left than conservative or far right. On a series of fourteen issues on which liberal and conservative positions are clear, majorities—often overwhelming majorities—of 1985's freshmen supported the liberal view. The only exception was abolition of the death penalty, support for which was only 26.6 percent. But 78 percent said that the government was not doing enough to control pollution, 73.3 percent said the wealthy should pay a larger share of taxes, 66 percent said that the government was not doing enough to promote disarmament, and only 26.8 percent—the lowest number in the two decades of this survey's history—said that they thought military spending should be increased. A near all-time high of 60.5 percent believed that the government should provide a national health care plan "to cover everybody's medical costs," and another record high of 54.4 percent endorsed busing to achieve racial balance. Significantly, opinion on each of these issues except national health care moved in a liberal direction from the 1984 survey to the 1985 survey. (The percentage favoring national health-care declined only slightly from its record high in 1984.)

A Carnegie Foundation survey of all undergraduates, not just freshmen, in the spring of 1984 found similar attitudes. A startling 75.6 percent of the college students sampled said that "private corporations are too concerned with profits and not enough with public responsibility." A 56.7 percent majority believed that "poverty could be eliminated within 10 years if it were given a high national priority." More than 90 percent wanted a greater effort to improve U.S.–Soviet relations; 85.7 percent said "foreign-policy decisions should be based on a strong commitment to human rights"; 75.3 percent said that "a woman should have freedom of choice on abortion"; 71 percent believed that "handgun sales and ownership should be legally controlled"; and only 36.3 percent agreed that "if people can't find jobs, it's their own fault."

Perhaps the most striking counter to the notion that the young are conservative was the finding of a 1986 *Washington Post*–ABC News survey that the eighteen-to-thirty-year-old age group as a whole (not just college students) supported *increased* governmental activism by a margin of 50 to 48 percent. None of these findings seem to support the popular notion that the young are becoming tied to Reaganism. Like other age groups, they like Ronald Reagan, but sharply disagree with his positions on most important issues.[7]

The post–baby-boom generation has no memories—positive or negative—of the great causes of the past, but it is looking for new causes of its own. Like the boomers themselves, younger Americans are yearning for something noble in which to believe and for a "hero" to lead them. "I've been starving for a strong figure ever since Kennedy," said twenty-seven-year-old Philadelphian Gary Novick in 1984, "and I don't really remember him." Many of the voters in all the subgroups within the younger electorate settled for Ronald Reagan in 1984, but he is not really what they are looking for. They want someone who is optimistic in the broadest and best sense, who sincerely believes in arms reduction, who is responsible both socially and fiscally, who will respect diverse beliefs and behavior, and who will inspire by offering them a measure of idealism.

"The only generation that would be remotely comparable to this one," sociologist Daniel Bell said in 1984, "would be the generation of the early Eisenhower years. Once again, you've got kind of an 'era of good feeling,' an older 'decent' man in the White House, reasonably good economic times—and a population that tends to be more career-oriented." The point was well-taken, and if 1984 marked the end of a period similar to Eisenhower's first term, 1988 would be analagous to 1960, and the young would be looking for an idealistic leader.

All three large age groups born since 1946 desire a blend of individual freedom and community responsibility. Neither party offered them that in 1984, and most of them chose to go with the apparent prosperity of Reaganomics. But most of the people in these age groups are afraid of the repressive right-wingers, and especially the religious Right. "The future of American politics," David Boaz of the libertarian Cato Institute has suggested, "may be determined by whether the Democrats can liberate themselves from the grip of the AFL-CIO before the Republicans break free from the Moral Majority."

The voters who will be forty-two and under in 1988 are not really satisfied with the egoism preached by the Reaganites. Most of them—not only the "new-collar" majority—have an attitude of patriotism that comes much closer to that expressed in the songs of Bruce Springsteen than to that peddled by Ronald Reagan and the Republicans. They are not Pollyannas. They love what the United States stands for, its values and principles, but they understand that we do not always live up to those values. When they see something wrong, they don't want to look the other way, they want to right it. Many of them still think their generation is destined to change the world. They would prefer to return to a community-oriented idealism, as long as that idealism includes an emphasis on economic growth and opportunity. Growth, opportunity, change, responsibility, and tolerance—these are the key political goals of the young majority of American voters. "There's a great opening here," says generational historian Anthony Esler of William and Mary, "for liberal leadership that would speak values and offer hope, and not talk about problems and limits all the time." What he has described sounds very much like a thumbnail sketch of the New Progressivism. The majority coalition that can be built around those liberal themes might justifiably be styled the "Springsteen Coalition."[8]

*   *   *

The best way to understand the moods of the three parts of the Springsteen Coalition is through their popular culture. More than any generations that came before them, these generations born after World War II have been immersed in a national popular culture. Movies and television have been prominent in that culture, but it has been dominated since the mid-1950s by a single cultural form: rock music. As Landon Jones has said of the baby boomers, "Rock was the sound track in the movie version of their lives. They discovered it, romanced to it, protested to it, and, someday, will presumably be buried to it."

Charles Reich suggested in *The Greening of America* (1970) not only that the youth of America would save the world, but that they were in the process of doing it through culture. His argument that "culture is politics," that a change in "consciousness" or "lifestyle" amounted to political change, was gravely mistaken, as the increasingly conservative politics of the early seventies demonstrated. But while culture and politics are not interchangeable, they are related. Singer-songwriter Don McLean once said that there are connections between popular music and politics because singers and politicians play to the same audiences. This may not be entirely the case, but when it comes to voters born since 1946 the assessment is close to the mark.

A change in popular culture usually reflects a change in the attitudes of the popular audience. Such a cultural change provides no guarantee that political change will follow along similar lines. It does indicate that similar political change is possible, *if* leaders arise to translate the attitudes behind the cultural changes into effective political action.

It is apparent that a cultural change accompanied the rise of the conservative era. As the conservative wave of the late seventies and early eighties was rising, the nation was on a fifties nostalgia kick, with such enormously popular new television shows as "Happy Days" and "Laverne and Shirley," reruns of such fifties staples as "Leave It to Beaver," and movies in the mold of *Saturday Night Fever* (1977) and *Grease* (1978), which highlighted a youth culture associated with the fifties.

The late seventies were characterized by what Paul Grein, an editor at *Billboard* magazine, calls "a definite absence of social comment in music." The disco craze of those years, highlighted by the likes of the Village People, Donna Summer, K. C. and the Sunshine Band, and various members of the Gibb family, amounted for the most part to "mindless bubble-gum stuff."

And, moving beyond the teeny-bopper music, the desire to return to a secure, blissful, conservative past was heralded by the great popularity of collections of new versions of love songs from the thirties, forties, and fifties. The success of Willie Nelson's *Stardust* album in 1978 was as much a sign of the changing mood of the country as was television's "Dallas." When rock superstar Linda Ronstadt teamed up with Nelson Riddle's orchestra to do a collection of old standards entitled *What's New* in 1983, the nostalgia era was in full swing. Between 1983 and 1985, Carly Simon, Toni Tennille, Barry Manilow, and again both Nelson and Ronstadt came out with what *New York Times* music critic Stephen Holden accurately described as "fifties-style torch albums." When the conservative era was at its peak, Julio Iglesias burst on the American scene as a new version of the forties-fifties Latin lover. Even Billy Joel's superb 1983 album *An Innocent Man* revived a style of rock that had flourished in the early sixties, before what we usually think of as "the sixties" began with the assassination of John F. Kennedy, the arrival of the Beatles, and the escalation of the war in Vietnam. As Joel pointed out in one of that album's songs, however, "You know the good old days weren't / Always good / And tomorrow ain't as bad as it seems."

It was, as Holden noted, "no accident that the retrograde tendencies in American pop coincide[d] with the Reagan presidency." Yet at just the time that Holden's insightful piece was appearing in the *Atlantic* in 1985, the trend that he was describing was being displaced by a sudden rebirth of the sixties style—and message.[9]

"Groovy! The '60s Are Returning" proclaimed *Newsweek* at the end of 1985. A month earlier, *Esquire* had published a piece on "The Return of the Sixties." "Far-Out! It's a '60s Revival!", exclaimed a *Seventeen* headline in 1986. Similarly titled articles appeared frequently in the mid-eighties. They suggested that the styles of the 1960s in clothing, music, furniture, jewelry, and other realms were becoming popular once again. Paisley, peace symbols, Peter Max designs, psychedelic music and art—all reminders of the most recent period of liberalism—were said to be returning to popularity.

One doubts (and hopes that the doubts are well-founded) that anyone, save perhaps *Newsweek,* will soon be saying "Like, groovy, man—far out!" again. And surely there are many aspects of the sixties that most of us would prefer to leave buried. There is a significance to the growth of sixties nostalgia, though. The fifties revival in the mid-to-late seventies heralded a turn toward conservatism. If in the mid-eighties the sixties were coming back in, can liberalism be far behind?

The first indication of a rebirth of interest in the sixties was the great popularity of *The Big Chill* in 1983, but many other signs have arisen since then. Bob Dylan's 1986 concert tour with Tom Petty and the Heartbreakers was called "the summer's main event" and "the tour of the year" by *Rolling Stone.* NBC planned a six-hour mini-series on the sixties. The title they chose ("Glory Days," from a 1984 Bruce Springsteen song) indicated the connection between the two eras. Reruns of "The Monkees" became a television hit with a new generation of teen-agers in 1986. A television special with videos done by major film makers for each of the songs on the Beatles' seminal 1967 album, *Sgt. Pepper's Lonely Hearts Club Band,* was planned for the twentieth anniversary of the album's release in 1987.

High-school- and college-age youth of the mid-eighties seemed especially intrigued by the sixties. College courses on the decade became hot items. Students often lamented that they were "born too late" and missed the "golden age." Patricia Field, proprietor of a sixties boutique in Greenwich Village, told *Newsweek* that she often overhears kids saying things like "It must have been a great time."[10]

Popular songs with references to the events and causes of the 1960s, such as the Dream Academy's "Life in a Northern Town," Bryan Adams's "Summer of '69," and Paul Hardcastle's "19," became common in the mid-eighties. Radio stations devoted to playing music from that era cropped up all over the country. Television commercials used music and scenes from the sixties to market everything from cars to breakfast cereal.

None of this meant that history was repeating itself. The sixties are gone forever, but the nostalgia switch from the fifties to the sixties can be seen as a harbinger of changing social and political attitudes.

Fashion is fickle, of course, and we should not make too much of the reappearance of mini-skirts, love beads, and wire-rimmed glasses. This is all superficial. There were, however, much more important cultural signs that the national mood in the mid-eighties was shifting away from egoism and towards a greater degree of social concern.

The largest indication that a new, less self-centered mood was arising was the series of extraordinary "mega-events" to aid the starving in Africa and assist other causes. The movement began in Great Britain late in 1984 with the recording of "Don't They Know It's Christmas?" by a group of rock stars brought together by Irish rock singer Bob Geldof and calling itself Band Aid. The makeshift group included Phil Collins, Simon Le Bon, Bono, George Michael, Sting, and more than thirty others. The purpose of the record was to raise as much money as possible for famine relief in Ethiopia. The record sold 3.5 million copies in Great Britain, making it the number-one release for the year 1984 as well as the most successful single in British history. Its success quickly jumped across the Atlantic; 2.5 million copies were sold in the United States during the 1984 holiday season.

Harry Belafonte later summed up the impact of this initial step by musicians into famine relief: "Band Aid made it fashionable to care again." Geldof himself said the effort made compassion "hip" and that the series of events that started with the Band Aid record had begun to vanquish "the New Brutalism" in modern society. He lamented the lack of any sense of community, on either side of the Atlantic, and said that we in wealthy, advanced societies "actually *need* that crowd that's dying over there as much as they need us," for our humanity.

The television pictures from East Africa in the fall of 1984 aroused something that had lain dormant for several years in many people in the Western world. The visual images brought home what was happening, Geldof has said. "Famine is just a word, and when you read that hundreds of thousands are dying you say, 'That's fucking awful.' But when you *see* it, you see a human—i.e., yourself, since you may put a personal projection on it—then . . . you have to do *something.*"

Critics have complained that mega charity events do little good, and may even be counterproductive, because they lead people to think that private charity efforts can solve massive problems. But few of the organizers of these events were under any such illusion. Geldof chose the name Band Aid to indicate that much more was needed. "There's no use putting a Band-Aid on a wound that requires twenty stitches," he said. Though putatively apolitical, Geldof understood from the start that "the only way to deal with this problem is to deal with it perhaps on the scale of a Marshall Plan for Africa. You can't get politics out of it."[11]

The process of drawing attention to social problems—what would have been termed "consciousness raising" in the sixties—was the principal accomplishment of the mega charity events of the mid-1980s. Of course the money raised saved lives, but more important was the extent to which the star-studded events focused public attention on problems that demanded commitment and action, got millions of people personally interested in and involved with those problems, and, perhaps, laid the foundation for the kind of political change that would be needed to attack the problems on a massive scale.

Soon after the success of the Band-Aid record, Harry Belafonte came up with the idea of doing a similar recording in the United States. The original idea was for a group of black music stars to create such a record. Belafonte approached Ken Kragen, who manages Lionel Richie and Kenny Rogers. Within thirty-six hours, Richie and Michael Jackson had written the song, "We Are the World," and persuaded Quincy Jones to produce it. The project rapidly expanded when Bruce Springsteen agreed to join. On January 28, 1985, following the Grammy Award ceremonies in Los Angeles, a collection of rock stars calling itself United Support of Artists for Africa (USA for Africa) held an all-night recording session. The participants were the most impressive collection of rock, country, and pop music stars ever to join in a single recording. In addition to Belafonte, Richie, Jackson, Springsteen, and Rogers, they included Kim Carnes, Ray Charles, Bob Dylan, Darryl Hall, Waylon Jennings, Billy Joel, Cyndi Lauper, Huey Lewis, Kenny Loggins, Bette Midler, Willie Nelson, John Oates, the Pointer Sisters, Smokey Robinson, Diana Ross, Paul Simon, Tina Turner, Dionne Warwick, and Stevie Wonder.

The result was a musical and human triumph. Although there were several earlier signs that a change in American attitudes, away from egoism and towards greater social concern, was beginning, the release of "We Are the World" in March 1985 is the most conve-

242   ROBERT S. McELVAINE

nient point from which to date the turn in the tide of American sentiment. The song rose to the top of the charts within two weeks of its release, sold 8 million copies, raised $44 million for African famine relief and to fight hunger and homelessness in the United States, and won four Grammy awards, including record of the year and song of the year.

But its impact far exceeded those statistics and honors. The image of the rock community was shifting from one of taking to one of giving, and with that shift began a change in the larger consciousness of America. "It's not just about raising money but raising consciousness to change priorities," Ken Kragen said. "We Are the World" did just that. Though the $44 million the record raised may not have done much in the struggle against hunger, those who criticized the effort for diverting attention from political action should note that one direct result of the success of "We Are the World" was passage of a bill by the Congress providing $800 million in famine relief. "Maybe we have to be the voice for people who have lost perspective on what life is about," suggested Stevie Wonder. Diana Ross was on target when she said of the USA for Africa project: "I've got a feeling that we're creating a shift in what's going on today."[12]

That shift in consciousness, that change in priorities, continued in July 1985 with the third in the series of rock mega-events, Live Aid. Another offspring of the churning mind of Bob Geldof, Live Aid was a joint effort of Band Aid and USA for Africa. It was far and away the largest concert in history, taking place in both London and Philadelphia, involving twenty-two acts in London and thirty-nine in Philadelphia, and seen on television by an estimated 1.9 billion people in 152 countries worldwide—the largest audience in the history of the planet. Participants read like a Who's Who of rock, including Mick Jagger, Phil Collins, Madonna, Sting, Paul McCartney, Teddy Pendergrass, Bryan Adams, Tina Turner, Eric Clapton, Sade, Bob Dylan, David Bowie, U2, Ashford and Simpson, Dire Straits, Elvis Costello, Wham!, Boy George, Billy Ocean, Patti LaBelle, the Beach Boys, and reunions of the Who, Crosby, Stills, Nash, and Young, and Led Zepplin. "This thing today is like 100,000 Ed Sullivan shows," said rock star Tom Petty.

The purpose again was to raise money to feed the starving in Africa and to raise the consciousness of comfortable people concerning the plight of millions of their fellow human beings. Both goals were accomplished. Some $70 million was donated to the relief effort.

Once more, though, the most lasting significance of the event involved not the money but the mood. "Here is a specific desire to affect consciousness," American promoter Bill Graham said before the concert. People in attendance and watching on television frequently mentioned how reminiscent the event was of "the spirit of the sixties." That link was made manifest when veteran pacifist folksinger Joan Baez began the Philadelphia part of the show by saying, "Good morning, children of the eighties. This is your Woodstock, and it's long overdue." Many of the younger people in the Philadelphia audience expressed regret at having missed the sixties when, as a *New York Times* story of the day after Live Aid put it, "people gathered regularly in support of good causes." The good feeling that comes from a sense of brotherhood and joining in an important cause was commented on by many on that long July day of music and message.

"I think this is just the beginning of a resurgence of caring for others," said Mary Travers, another folksinger closely tied to progressive causes since the sixties. "It says something about getting back to the basic human family. It's a dream, a positive dream." A sense of community that had been absent in American life for many years was apparent at Live Aid. "The spirit is just bouncing off people," a seventeen-year-old New Jersey youth told a *Times* reporter. "People are working too hard right now and it seems they don't look beyond their own houses," lamented a New York woman who watched the concert on television. "But with music it's easy to feel things. You end up thinking. Maybe people will be more aware now and think beyond just the music."

That seemed a lot to hope for, but after such a long period of self-centeredness, with so many people yearning for something worthy outside themselves in which to believe and for which to work, Live Aid and similar events were finding a ready audience. "Nothing's impossible," British rock promoter Harvey Goldsmith had told Bob Geldof when the latter approached him about the possibility of doing a transatlantic superconcert. That message and a related one on a sign in JFK Stadium during Live Aid—"If it can be done, we'll try. If it must be done, we'd better"—were important for Americans suffering from a decade of cynicism to hear.[13]

One unexpected result of Live Aid was another event in September, aimed at helping distressed American farmers. An impromptu comment by Bob Dylan near the end of the Live Aid concert, in which he expressed the wish that some of the money being raised might go to American farmers facing foreclosures, was overheard by Willie Nelson. The country-music star quickly seized upon the idea and organized Farm Aid, another day-long concert originating at the University of Illinois and focusing attention on the plight of American farm families at the same time that it raised funds to try to assist such farmers.

By the fall of 1985, it seemed that everyone who was anyone was getting onto the "aid" bandwagon. Designers held a Fashion Aid show in New York in November. Garry Trudeau started a project that persuaded the vast majority of his fellow cartoonists to do strips related to hunger on Thanksgiving 1985. An Art Aid auction featuring works by Andy Warhol, Roy Lichtenstein, and other leading artists raised $400,000 for famine relief early in 1986. Other records were cut and concerts held. They ranged from a group of heavy metal rockers ("Hear 'n' Aid") through Latino Aid and Country Aid to "A Concert of Concern" to raise money for the Red Cross's African relief program, featuring Leontyne Price, Wynton Marsalis, and others at Carnegie Hall.[14]

The causes began to expand beyond African famine, first to hunger and homelessness in the United States and the problems of American farmers. A distinguished group of American comedians put on Comic Relief in Los Angeles to raise money and concern for the homeless of America. Among the participants were Whoopi Goldberg, Robin Williams, Billy Crystal, Sid Caesar, George Carlin, Dick Gregory, Penny Marshall, and Carl Reiner. A total of $3 million was raised, enough to provide a bed for a single night to about 120,000 people—less than 20 percent of the estimated number of homeless Americans. As usual, though, awareness was a greater goal than immediate fund raising. A good deal of the humor was politically pointed. Robin Williams, for example, doing an impression of William F. Buckley, answered a question about the status of the homeless by saying: "Basically, I feel by examining it from the present administration's policy of trickle-down, I think the homeless are being pissed on pretty heavily."

A group of rock artists cut an album in 1985 to raise money for Greenpeace, the environmental activist group. Another one-time group, styling itself Artists United Against Apartheid and including

David Ruffin, Lou Reed, Jackson Browne, Miles Davis, Run–DMC, Bruce Springsteen, George Clinton, Bob Dylan, Bonnie Raitt, and Bono, got together to record "Sun City" in the fall of 1985. In terms of political statement, this record went well beyond the famine relief efforts. It took a definite partisan stance, not only against apartheid, but also against the Reagan administration's policy toward South Africa. One verse says:

> Our government tells us we're doing all we can
> Constructive engagement is Ronald Reagan's plan
> Meanwhile people are dying and giving up hope
> This quiet diplomacy ain't nothing but a joke.

Steve Van Zandt, a guitarist formerly with Springsteen's E Street Band, wrote the song as a dance record with a political message. "The beat is the first line of communication," he said. "All around the world, everybody dances. We wanted the record to communicate at that level and let everybody absorb lyrics at their own pace." In addition to addressing South African racism and the Reagan administration's policy towards it, Van Zandt said he "also wanted to refocus on racism in general, and show some of the parallels from South Africa to right here at home. They have black neighborhoods and we have black neighborhoods; they don't educate poor people, and neither do we. The Civil Rights Act twenty years ago did not cure everything."

Here was message music of the sort that had rarely been heard in over a decade. And other causes began to crop up in joint efforts by artists. Bruce Springsteen organized a group of New Jersey musicians in 1986 to do a song called "We Got the Love" to raise money for food banks. Springsteen and Willie Nelson took out newspaper ads urging the 3M company not to abandon its plant in Springsteen's hometown of Freehold, New Jersey. A twenty-five-year salute to Peter, Paul, and Mary was held in Washington early in 1986 to raise money for TransAfrica Movement, an organization that works to end South African racial laws. And as we shall see, numerous individual singers and established groups began to put out socially conscious songs on a variety of topics.[15]

One of the most impressive examples of the renewed political and social activism within the realm of rock music was the June 1986 Conspiracy of Hope tour to support Amnesty International.

This effort to publicize the nonpartisan international human rights organization called for a much greater commitment from the artists than had such earlier projects as Live Aid. This time, a full two-week tour of six American cities was scheduled. Sting, U2, Peter Gabriel, Lou Reed, Joan Baez, Bryan Adams, and the Neville Brothers participated in the whole tour. They were joined at some locations by many other acts, including Jackson Browne, Bob Geldof, Peter, Paul and Mary, Joni Mitchell, Yoko Ono, Bob Dylan, Tom Petty and the Heartbreakers, the Police (Sting's group), and Don Henley.

The result was what one reviewer of the opening concert in San Francisco called "an inspired evening of politicized rock 'n' roll that carried the spiritual scent of the '60s." The final eleven-hour concert at Giants Stadium in New Jersey was broadcast nationally by MTV and included frequent statements by music and film stars about the cause of freeing political prisoners. U2 and Sting, another reviewer said, "turned a great concert into a freedom party." "Sing it for every prisoner in every jail," U2's Bono shouted to the audience in Los Angeles, "every prisoner rotting in jail. Are you with us?" The crowd made it plain that it was. "I think it worked," an elated Bono said afterward. During the New Jersey concert, Amnesty International U.S.A. executive Director John Healy said, "It's bigger and better than anything we could have anticipated. I'm ecstatic. And the musicians are actually becoming human-rights activists." So, surely, were some in the audiences.[16]

In terms of numbers of participants, the two largest of the charity mega-events of the mid-eighties both took place on the same day, May 25, 1986. Sport-Aid, yet another of Bob Geldof's projects, enlisted an estimated 20 million runners in seventy-six countries around the world to raise money for African famine relief. This largest fund-raising event in history was nearly ignored in the United States, where it conflicted with Hands Across America, an event that received far more publicity in the American media.

While Geldof's group was planning Sport Aid, Ken Kragen and USA for Africa were coming up with a monumental plan of their own: to persuade more than 5 million Americans to join hands in a line all the way from New York to Los Angeles. Though in the end there were many gaps, somewhere between 3.5 million and 4.5 million people were said to have joined in the line. Perhaps $50 million was raised for the hungry and homeless in the United States. Such sums sound impressive, but they do not mean much in the face of enormous problems. Even if it had reached its wildest projections of $100 million, Hands Across America would only have added a bit more than 1 percent to the nearly $9 billion that charities already spend annually on the human services programs. And the $100 million goal was the equivalent of a scant eight-tenths of 1 percent of what the federal government—even under Ronald Reagan—spends on the food-stamp program.

But as was the case with the other mega-events, the message was much more important than the money. "Nobody's off the hook just because we did something terrific yesterday and called a lot of attention to the issues," Kragen said the day after the human chain was assembled. "We haven't by any means solved them, and no one would pretend that we have." "The money is really secondary," Kragen said at another point. "What an event like this does is create tremendous momentum. . . . You swing the pendulum back to the individual making a contribution in his community."

But can such events really accomplish anything significant? In an incisive article in the New Republic, Mickey Kaus condemned what he dubbed "celebritics," which he said occurs "when the celebrities become so powerful that they frame the issues and run the campaigns themselves, dispensing with the boring old politicians altogether." Kaus was exactly right when he wrote that "warm, compassionate feelings are not enough. Progress requires choices, political ones."

It is undeniable that many of those who participated in such events as Hands Across America saw it, as conservative columnist James J. Kilpatrick charged, as "a larky way to spend a Sunday afternoon." "Such events," George F. Will witheringly commented, "are the equivalent of Easter parades for people who want to dress up their consciences and take them for a stroll so other people can see how pretty they are."

Such potshots are easily taken at people who pack fancy picnic lunches to go out and hold hands for the hungry. But beyond those with designer consciences were millions of people who were made to think about others. Singing the Hands Across America theme is not political action; but is is prepolitical action. It undermines the acceptability of the uncaring attitude that was the American norm from the late seventies through the mid-eighties. It starts people thinking again about social problems. As they see that these problems are too large to be dealt with through private charitable efforts, they are likely to turn to political action. It may be especially significant in this regard that so many of the participants in these events were young—precisely the age groups that have so often been dismissed as proto-yuppies and have been thought to be utterly self-centered and immune to idealism.

"Democrats and liberals," the editors of the *New Republic* rightly commented, "should take it upon themselves to constructively channel the amorphous goodwill that was so evident" in Hands Across America. United Nations Children's Fund executive director James P. Grant, noting that either Sport-Aid or Hands Across America would by itself "rank as the largest simultaneous mass-participation demonstration ever mobilized for any cause," argued that together they constituted an unprecedented show of concern for the hungry and vulnerable. The people who participated, he said, "wait for their governments to catch up with them."

Ken Kragen's goal, Mickey Kaus complained, was "to change politics from the outside, to shift the political demand curve dramatically and then sit back and watch the politicians scramble to adjust."

As Paul McCartney once said in a different context: "What's wrong with that, I'd like to know?" Changing the political demand curve is what democratic politics is all about. Surely those who are concerned about altering social policy should not just sit back and watch while the politicans try to revamp their product to bring political supply into equilibrium with demand, but the rest of Kaus's description of the intent and impact of the mega-events of the mid-eighties is not only accurate but, it seems to me, laudatory.[17]

The great "nonpolitical" charity events—"the largest number of celebrities ever assembled" and all—amounted to a *preface to politics*, and a decidedly liberal politics at that.

Bob Dylan wrote "The Times They Are A-Changin'," the classic song of the early 1960s, in October 1963, a few weeks before President Kennedy was assassinated. Like many other protest songs by Dylan and others, this one preceded the real onset of the sixties era of reform. Certainly JFK's election in 1960 and his two-and-a-half-year presidency were important to the reform era of the sixties. The civil-rights movement was already in full swing, but little had yet been accomplished in the way of legislation or in achieving the liberal dominance of the decade.

The point is the commonplace one that artists are the vanguard of change. When Dylan told "mothers and fathers throughout the land" that their sons and daughters were beyond their command and that their "old road was rapidly agin'," he was speaking of developments that were *about to* happen, not ones that had already come to pass. By 1968, few mothers and fathers would have argued with Dylan's words, but five years earlier, most probably would have. Art is more prophecy than history. It makes sense to look to art—and particularly in a democracy to *popular* art—to get an idea of where we are going.

Rock music has become one of the most popular art forms in the modern world. And rock in the mid-eighties rather suddenly and dramatically returned to social consciousness. In the fall of 1985 the *Wall Street Journal* recognized this development with a front-page story entitled "Pop Musicians Start to Rock the Boat." "Protest music," *Journal* reporter Rick Wartzman informed readers (who, it is safe to assume, were previously unaware of the fact), "is beginning to pervade the pop scene much the way folksingers raised anti–Vietnam War protest songs to an art in the 1960s. But the social commitment today, following the lyrically numbing disco craze of the late 1970s, is cutting an even wider swath."

Indeed it is. Protest music in the early sixties was generally confined to the folk genre, and while it was to become socially significant within a few years, it was then still outside the mainstream of popular music. The 1980s revival of message music has taken place in the heart of rock 'n' roll, involves many of the era's most popular musicians, and addresses a wide range of social issues.

The new upsurge in music with a message seems to have arisen from two distinct origins. One is a group of politically conscious musicians from Great Britain and Ireland. A substantial number of the new protest songs discussed in this chapter are part of a new Anglo-Irish musical invasion of the United States comparable to the British invasion that began with the Beatles in 1964. The imported status of so many of the songs takes nothing away from their usefulness as a barometer of social consciousness and idealism in the United States, however. If the protest music is popular with American listeners—and it is—its origins are of no significance.

The other source of the new protest music is, in any case, entirely native—"born in the U.S.A.," as it were. "Bruce Springsteen's hugely popular 'Born in the U.S.A.' concert tour" in 1985, the *New Republic* correctly noted the following year, "with its combination of patriotism and sympathy for the down-and-out, was one indication" of the growing American impulse to return to idealistic causes and move beyond Reaganism.

Springsteen's importance to the new activism in music is difficult to exaggerate. By 1985 he had become much more than *the* hottest item in popular music—he had become a cultural phenomenon unmatched since the Beatles reached their peak. He has been described as a "latter-day Woody Guthrie." Politicians sought to link themselves to "the Boss." Sociologists attempted to explain the meaning of his popularity. Authors named emerging political coalitions after him.

Springsteen and those—such as John Cougar Mellencamp and John Cafferty and the Beaver Brown Band—who have used their music to take up similar causes are not "trying to fan the flames of American pride. Instead," as *Rolling Stone* writer Mikal Gilmore has said, "they're trying to say that if the nation loses sight of certain principles, it also forfeits its claim to greatness." *Newsweek* said of Springsteen in 1985, "in this summer of mindless Rambomania, the values championed in his songs offer an alternate vision of resurgent American patriotism." He is a symbol of the great *potential* of America, of its finest values and ideals, not of a blind "my country, right or wrong," "U.S.A., U.S.A.!" patriotism. Of course some of his listeners failed to understand his message, but it is "more about promises broken than promises kept. . . . These are pictures of an America gone wrong."[18]

But Springsteen's vision is also of an America that can still be saved and brought back to its true values. As novelist Richard Ford has written, Springsteen "gives a voice of consequence to the unlistened to. It's what poets sometimes do." "Born in the U.S.A.," Ford says, "stands as the rally cry for all the unrequited and unnoticed Americans who claim it." Journalist David Hinckley has rightly contended that Springsteen's great popularity is a "perhaps inevitable counterpoint to national political leaders whose tacit message is that the less visible, the less powerful, and the less fortunate can be ignored."

Springsteen won't let us forget such people. He sings of the problems of workers in dead-end jobs:

Someday Mister I'm gonna lead a better life than this
Working on the highway laying down the blacktop
Working on the highway all day long I don't stop
Working on the highway blasting through the bedrock

of class divisions:

Tonight down here in Linden Town I watch the
cars rushin' by home from the mill
There's a beautiful full moon rising above the
mansion on the hill

and of lost jobs and dying communities:

Now Main Street's whitewashed windows
and vacant stores
seems like there ain't nobody
wants to come down here no more
They're closing down the textile mill
across the railroad tracks
Foreman says these jobs are going, boys
and they ain't coming back to your
hometown

While he usually lets his music speak for him and does not like
to get directly involved in political issues, Springsteen has made it
clear that he is no fan of Reaganism and that his patriotism is very
different from the Rambo/Reagan sort. When the president attempted to link himself to the singer's burgeoning popularity during
the 1984 campaign, Springsteen was outraged. "You see the Reagan
re-election ads on TV—you know: 'It's morning in America,'" he
told a Rolling Stone interviewer, "And you say, 'Well, it's not
morning in Pittsburgh. It's not morning above 125th Street in New
York. It's midnight, and, like, there's a bad moon risin'.'" He frequently pauses in concerts—often before singing "Hungry
Heart"—to ask people in the audience to join him in making donations to local food banks. When Reagan and other right-wingers
tried to associate themselves with the Boss (maybe the nickname
misled them into thinking that he was on their side), Springsteen
complained that Americans were "gettin' manipulated and ex-

ploited." "This is a song about blind faith," he said in introducing a piece in 1984, "like when the president talks about arms control." And during one of his huge concerts in 1985, at RFK Stadium in Washington, the Boss warned his listeners about their president's policy in Central America and about the general drift of America away from the values and policies that made it great: "Go and read a history book. If you look at where we've come from and where we're going it's pretty scary. Just take a walk from the Lincoln Memorial to the Vietnam Veterans' Memorial." The first single released from the blockbuster 1986 five-record album *Bruce Springsteen and the E Street Band Live/1975–85* was "War," a 1970 song with a sharp antiwar message. On the album, Springsteen introduces the song by warning young people that "the next time, they're gonna be lookin' at you . . . In 1985, blind faith in your leaders—or in anything—will get you killed." The lyrics leave no doubt that Springsteen's patriotism is vastly different from Reagan's:

> War
> What is it good for
> Absolutely nothing
> War
> It's nothing but a heartbreaker
> War
> Friend only to the undertaker
> War is the enemy of all mankind
> The thought of war blows my mind[19]

A major question about Bruce Springsteen is why his quantum leap to the status of national symbol occurred in 1985. Not only had he been recording for a dozen years prior to that, but he had been hailed as early as 1974 as "rock and roll future," and in October 1975 he received an honor normally reserved for world leaders and mass murderers: simultaneous cover stories in *Time* and *Newsweek*. Certainly his music has changed over the years, but not *that* much. His 1978 album *Darkness at the Edge of Town* explored the gulf between the promise of America and its reality in terms not very different from those of *Born in the U.S.A.*, but made no ripples on the national consciousness. It seems likely that the main trouble was that the American mood, which was just entering the conservative, self-centered part of its cycle in 1978, was not receptive to Springsteen's message at that time. Most people were too cynical for his theme that hope must never be abandoned and too egoistic for his pleas on behalf of the down-and-out. In 1978 Springsteen was reminding us of the downwardly mobile at a time when most of his countrymen were focusing on what they expected would be their own personal success.

Jon Landau, who later became Springsteen's manager, was right when he said in 1974 that the future of rock and roll was named Bruce Springsteen, but as the nation made a sharp right turn, it was to be more than a decade before America would be ready for that future. "Like Ford Mustangs and Apple computers," Springsteen's friend and biographer Dave Marsh has suggested, "some records appear at precisely the right moment." That the mid-1980s was the right moment for *Born in the U.S.A.* is a matter of immense significance in forecasting the course of American social and political attitudes.

The Bruce Springsteen phenomenon points both to the revival of liberalism and to the basis for recreating a liberal majority. "Bruce is—he's America. He's exactly what America is all about," said a nineteen-year-old male from Pearl River, New York, at one of the singer's 1985 concerts. "My mother loves Bruce, and she's fifty-two and a librarian. She was really mad I didn't get her a ticket." If you sit through one of Springsteen's four-hour concerts, Richard Ford says, you "have the time to notice who's there with you. Everybody is—which is an adequate measure of the music's potency."[20]

It is doubtful that quite "everybody" could be brought into a Springsteen Coalition, but liberals will settle for a simple majority.

Bruce Springsteen was the most prominent example of the new popularity of socially conscious music in the waning years of the Reagan presidency, but the ranks of musicians with messages were growing rapidly. Recording artists would "start paying a price" for not having a message, Dave Marsh told the *Wall Street Journal* in 1985. "It's going to be tough to be a Duran Duran [a British group not known for meaningful lyrics] on a daily basis." Steve Van Zandt agreed: "Now as a songwriter you can't indulge in the rock 'n' roll cliches of drugs and escapism."

That, unfortunately, was not entirely true. A good deal of narcissism, hedonism, and escapism remained in rock music in the mid-eighties. But the same was certainly the case in the early sixties, as protest music arose at the beginning of another era of reform. The surfing culture of that period, for instance, with its emphasis on hot rods, "California girls," and endless summers, was every bit as socially unconscious as the yuppie culture of the early eighties. (Is it any wonder that Nancy Reagan likes the Beach Boys?) The surfers were, it is true, interested in GTOs and 409s rather than Mercedes and BMWs, but what—other than many thousands of dollars—is the difference? Yet the "little deuce coupes" and "surfer girls" shared the early sixties with another sort of music that would rouse Americans—at least young Americans—to struggle against racism, war, and a host of injustices. That started to happen again in the mid-eighties.

"People are saying again that music has the power to change the world," Bowling Green popular culture professor Jack Santino said in 1985.[21] And to change it in many ways. Several artists launched fundamental assaults on the egoism and greed of the declining conservative age of Ronald Reagan and Margaret Thatcher. In "Big Time," one of the songs on his chart-topping 1986 album, So, and a bit single in 1987, Peter Gabriel sings:

> big time
> I'm on my way—I'm making it
> big time big time
> I've got to make it show—yeah
> big time big time
> so much larger than life
> I'm going to watch it growing
> big time big time
> my car is getting bigger
> big time
> my house is getting bigger
> big time
> my eyes are getting bigger
> big time
> and my mouth
> big time
> my belly is getting bigger
> big time
> and my bank account
> big time.

And Sting's smash 1985 album, *The Dream of the Blue Turtles*—
one of the year's top sellers and one of its most political collections—included the following lines in "If You Love Somebody Set
Them Free":

> Forever conditioned to believe that we can't live
> We can't live here and be happy with less
> So many riches, so many souls
> Everything we see we want to possess.[22]

All of this was a far cry from the unrestrained materialism and
me-ism of the late seventies and early eighties. Even Madonna's
"Material Girl" (1984) apparently was intended as satire, although
it is doubtful that many of her fans understood that. With the songs
quoted above, though, as with several others from 1984 on, the
message was plain.

Several musicians in the mid-eighties were pointing out to their
listeners that the putatively booming economy left many people behind. John Cafferty and the Beaver Brown Band, a group whose
themes resemble Springsteen's, included several cuts about downward mobility and unemployment on their 1985 album, *Tough All
Over*. In the title song, they said:

> He's drinking at the bar down by the
> old boat yard
> He sits and talks to strangers
> The factory laid him off again and life's
> been getting hard
> It's enough to make a good man bad.

In his triple-platinum (that is, more than 3 million copies sold)
1985 album *Scarecrow*, John Cougar Mellencamp reminded his
fans of those who were not enjoying "Reagan prosperity." The following lines from "The Face of the Nation" are a good example:

> So many lonely people
> Damn those broken dreams
> Oh yes it could be better
> You can say that about anything
> Some got it worse than me

Some got it worse than you
You see the people starvin' underneath the tree
And you wonder what happened to the golden rule.[23]

Sting combined a plea for British coal miners with an attack on
nuclear power plants and the basics of Thatcher–Reagan economics
in "We Work the Black Seam," another of the outstanding political
songs on the 1985 album *The Dream of the Blue Turtles:*

This place has changed for good
Your economic theory said it would
It's hard for us to understand
We can't give up our jobs the way we should
Our blood has stained the coal
We tunneled deep inside the nation's soul
We matter more than pounds and pence
Your economic theory makes no sense

One day in a nuclear age
They may understand our rage
They build machines that they can't control
And bury the waste in a great big hole[24]

This song came out nearly a year before the Chernobyl nuclear accident, which served to increase its impact.

Some rock singer/songwriters of the mid-eighties did not hesitate to attack President Reagan directly. In his 1986 song, "Right
and Wrong," for example, Joe Jackson said:

Stop everything
I think I hear the President
The pied piper of the TV screen
Is gonna make it simple
And he's got it all mapped out
And illustrated with cartoons
Too hard for clever folks to understand.

Jackson Browne, perhaps the most political of all American
songwriters of the eighties, pilloried the Reagan-style blind patri-

otism in "For America," the first single released from his 1986 album, *Lives in the Balance:*

> As if freedom was a question of might
> As if loyalty was black and white
> You hear people say it all the time—
> "My country wrong or right"
> I want to know what that's got to do
> With what it takes to find out what's true
> With everyone from the President on down
> Trying to keep it from you.[25]

Racism in general, and particularly its virulent South African variety, was the target of much of the new protest music. Peter Gabriel began the musical attacks on apartheid in 1980 with his moving song, "Biko." Paul McCartney and Stevie Wonder hit the top of the pop charts in 1982 with "Ebony and Ivory," which while not particularly deep did put the idea of racial harmony before a wide audience. In 1983, Randy Newman sang about "Christmas in Capetown" on *Trouble in Paradise.* When, in 1985, Stevie Wonder released *In Square Circle,* his first album in five years, he included several songs with messages. Most notable was "It's Wrong (Apartheid)":

> You know apartheid's wrong
> Like slavery was wrong
> Like the Holocaust was wrong
> It's wrong, wrong, wrong.

"I wanted to speak out, and do it in a kind of way where people will feel the rhythm of it, but also get the message across, in a peaceful way that's also *strong*," Wonder told the *New York Times.* "And the message to the people of South Africa is, 'Hold on tight, the whole world is with us, freedom is coming.' I want to participate in anything else that's going to be meaningful for the plight of the people there." One such opportunity had already arisen. With the 1985 recording of "Sun City," discussed earlier, a large segment of the rock community took a strong stand not only against the evil of apartheid, but also against the policies of the Reagan administration toward South Africa.

In their No. 1 song of early 1987, "The Way It Is," Bruce Hornsby and the Range directly confronted American racism:

They say, Hey little boy you can't go
Where the others go
'Cause you don't look like they do
Said, Hey old man how can you stand
To think that way.[26]

Appeals for an end to racism combined with more sweeping pleas for peace in the music of one of the most significant bands of the new protest movement, U2. This remarkable group from Dublin lays hard rock infused with a nondenominational liberal Christian ethic. Inspired by their lead vocalist and songwriter, Bono (Paul Hewson), U2 espouses an idealistic but militant pacifism. "We've taken the love that was a part of '60s rock and the anger that was a part of punk," Bono explained to an interviewer in 1984. "We want a spiritual side to our music as well as a raucous and rowdy side. . . . That's what we want from our music—freedom, I suppose. And a little bit of humanity."

U2 is guided, as Christopher Connelly noted in a 1985 article in *Rolling Stone*, "by a philosophy not included in such yuppie maxims as 'feeling good,' and 'going for it': not how *might* we live our lives (what we can get way with), but how *ought* we to live our lives." U2's best-selling single, "Pride (In the Name of Love)," is a tribute to Martin Luther King, Jr.

The U2 album on which that song appeared, *The Unforgettable Fire*, was named after a group of paintings done by survivors of the atomic bombings of Hiroshima and Nagasaki, and it is against war that Bono and his associates speak most forcefully. The band's 1983 album *War* remained among the top 200 in the United States for more than two years and sold over a million copies. Horrified at the religious strife in Northern Ireland, Bono wrote "Sunday Bloody Sunday" to, he said, "take the image of Northern Ireland out of the black and white and into the gray, where it truly belongs." *War* also featured a song, "New Year's Day," about Soviet-inspired martial law in Poland, and one called "Seconds," which had a clear enough message:

Say goodbye, say goodbye,
Say goodbye, say goodbye,
It takes a second to say goodbye,
Push the button and pull the plug, say goodbye.[27]

Anti-nuclear-war songs rose in the early and mid-eighties along with the renewed fear of nuclear war brought on by statements from Reagan administration officials. German singer Nena hit number one on the American pop charts in 1983 with her "99 Red Balloons":

It's all over
I'm standing pretty
In the space that was a city
I could find a souvenir
Just to prove the world was here.

Sting (Gordon Sumner), who wrote and performed a 1983 antinuclear song called "Walking in Your Footsteps" with the Police, continued his campaign against nuclear war on his solo album with "Russians," which became a hit single in the United States in 1986:

How can I save my little boy from
    Oppenheimer's deadly toy
There is no monopoly of common sense
On either side of the political fence
We share the same biology
Regardless of ideology
. . .
There's no such thing as a winnable war
That's a lie we don't believe anymore.

In some of his earlier work, Sting had camouflaged the messages in his lyrics. "I can disguise an idea inside a curtain that is innocuous," he told an interviewer in 1985. "I like being number one on the charts, but I also like surprising people. For instance, 'Every Breath You Take' [one of the top hits of 1983]—that is a truly insidious lyric dressed in a lovely song. Everybody was going around singing it like it was *love*. But it was a song about control and ownership and surveillance." Well, perhaps. Most—although not all—of the song *could* be interpreted as a statement about Big Brother, but few fans of the Police heard it that way, and that is what matters most.

But with "Russians" and several other cuts on *The Dream of the Blue Turtles,* Sting made his message crystal clear. When the album came out, he said: "My instinct tells me it's going to be big, despite the political climate. Maybe because of it." Sting apparently realized that the times were changing in the mid-eighties and rock fans would be more receptive to overtly political songs. "We've always heard that rock 'n' roll could change the world," he commented after the 1985 Live Aid concert. "That's starting to mean something."[28]

In 1985–86 Mike and the Mechanics had a hit with "Silent Running," a song about existence after a nuclear war:

Take your children and yourself
To hideouts in the cellar
By now the fighting will be close at hand
. . .
There's a gun and ammunition just outside the doorway
Use it only in emergency
. . .
Swear allegiance to the flag
Whatever flag they offer.

In addition to the songs that warned of nuclear war, the mid-eighties saw numerous new protest songs that condemned war in general. Dire Straits' 1985 album *Brothers in Arms,* which sold more than 5 million copies, contains songs that move from apparent praise of the causes for which men fight to exposure of war as "the killing game." In "Ride Across the River," songwriter and lead vocalist Mark Knopfler begins with

I'm a soldier of freedom in the army of man
We are the chosen, we're the partisan
The cause it is noble and the cause it is just
We are ready to pay with our lives if we must,

but quickly switches to

I'm a soldier of fortune, I'm a dog of war
And we don't give a damn who the killing is for

It's the same old story with a different name
Death or glory, it's the killing game.

Knopfler believed that such issues as machismo and the causes for
which people are willing to kill and die were "worth addressing, because there's such a potential for evil and destruction in all of us."
In the title song, which is the last on the album, Knopfler closes
with his pacifist message in its most straightforward terms:

We're fools to make war
On our brothers in arms.

Jackson Browne turned his attention directly to the growing
United States involvement in Central American conflicts in the title
track from *Lives in the Balance*, in which the context was under-
scored by Latin American-style music:

With the blood in the ink of the headlines
And the sound of the crowd in my ear
You might ask what it takes to remember
When you know that you've seen it before
Where a government lies to its people
And a country is drifting to war.

With lyrics like this, it was unnecessary for Browne to add, as he did
in introducing the song at some 1986 concerts, that "This is not a
lighthearted ditty." Such themes were nothing new for him in the
mid-eighties, but his lyrics had become sharper and more plainly political than ever before—and his popularity was decidedly on the
rise.[29]
    The prominence of antiwar songs did not, of course, mean that
it would be politically wise for liberals to associate themselves with a
full-blown pacifism. On the contrary, the impression that liberals
would not fight under any circumstances was one of their major
problems. But the songs joined with opinion polls to indicate that
the public in the mid-eighties was much closer to sensible
progressive positions on arms control, Central America, military
spending, and adventurism than one would have thought by looking
at votes in Congress.
    It is worth emphasizing again that the new protest music of the
mid-eighties did not arise in an obscure genre with few adherents. It

exploded into the mainstream of rock. Springsteen's *Born in the U.S.A.* and *Live/1975–1985, U.S.A.* for Africa's *We Are the World*, Sting's *The Dream of the Blue Turtles*, Mellencamp's *Scarecrow*, Dire Strait's *Brothers in Arms*, and Gabriel's *So* were among the most popular records of 1984–87. In 1985 *Rolling Stone* chose U2 as the "band of the '80s." Many other examples could be cited. Cyndi Lauper included Marvin Gaye's classic 1971 protest song, "What's Going On," on her 1986 album, *True Colors*. Albums by Talking Heads, UB40, Paul Simon, and Simple Minds also addressed a variety of social themes. Chrissie Hynde and the Pretenders put out a sixties-style album called *Get Close* late in 1986. Included was a song titled "How Much Do You Get for Your Soul?", which sharply criticizes such black singers as Michael Jackson and Lionel Richie for making soft-drink commercials.[30]

The trend toward message music became so strong that even some of the performers most associated with the "pornographic rock" that so alarmed middle America joined the protest parade. Prince and other nihilistic performers as well joined in the rush to social consciousness. Some of the critics of pornorock might have concluded that the raunch was less dangerous than the radicalism.

No one took seriously the idea that bands that had been promoting devil worship and sadism had suddenly found their consciences. On the contrary, the popularity of such music was intimately associated with the narcissism of the late seventies and early eighties. Mistakenly equating this music with "punk," much of which actually formed the roots of the revival of social protest music, Democratic party consultant Edward Lazarus said in 1985: "Punk music involves selfism and abuse to those less well off than we are. I see all those folks beating up on people smaller and weaker in the videos and I think that's not what the Democratic party is all about."

The important point is that such degradation was on the decline in rock music and videos in the mid-eighties. It did not disappear, but as the above examples indicate, the content of rock was shifting decisively towards more positive themes. The renewed idealism, social consciousness, and antiwar sentiment in rock was of great significance in pointing toward the changing mood of the American people. In 1985 and subsequently, record company executives began again to look for songwriters and performers who took what can properly be termed "liberal" stands on political issues. And fans—"many of whom," the *Wall Street Journal* noted in 1985, "would never be exposed to the issues if they weren't taken up by the rock stars—[began] clamoring for the meaningful messages."

Yet Patrick Caddell told me in 1985 that hardly anyone in Washington seemed to understand the political significance of renewed cultural protest. The exceptions were Caddell himself and Lee Atwater, a strategist for George Bush. Caddell saw the tremendous importance of the growing identification of rock musicians and their followers with "the world's dispossessed." The message-oriented groups, Caddell said, were becoming as popular as similar groups had been in the 1960s. Atwater agreed that the idealism, fear of nuclear war, humanitarian concern, and less materialistic outlook of the teens of the mid-eighties were good signs for Democrats, but maintained that Bush was a perfect candidate to capitalize on these sentiments. It was understandable that a person in his position would make such an argument, but few others would take it seriously.[31]

Rock music during Ronald Reagan's second term left little doubt that the times they were a-changin' again—and the change was in an undeniably liberal direction.

CHAPTER 9

Back to
the Future

You can blow out a candle
But you can't blow out a fire
Once the flame begins to catch
The wind will blow it higher
    —PETER GABRIEL (1980)

Some things will never change
That's just the way it is
But don't you believe them
    —BRUCE HORNSBY (1986)

Rock music was the leading force in the new cultural protest of the 1980s, as it had been in the cultural revolution of the 1960s. But there were also signs in the eighties of the same sort of change in other sectors of American popular culture. Rock led the way both because of its historical connection with protest and because the recording and concert industry is more responsive to mood changes that are at first to be found in relatively small numbers of people. The film industry, which of necessity invests much more in each of its products, is slower and more hesitant to take chances with newly emerging ideas. Network television executives, who live or die by audience ratings, are as a rule the last to follow a developing shift in public attitudes. Yet there were definite signs of change in movies and even a few in television and other forms of popular culture in the middle 1980s.

Certain trends in motion pictures plainly ran counter to the development of a new social consciousness. Obviously those who flocked to see Sylvester Stallone in his interchangeable incarnations as Rocky and Rambo were not thereby manifesting liberal principles. The dark side of the appeal of this type of film reflected the worst of the Reagan era in the United States: the desire for American "greatness" (read as domination), revenge, bitterness, violence, racism, and chauvinism. In this respect, the Stallone cult is another example of the similarity between the conservative period of the late seventies and early eighties and that of the 1950s. In the Eisenhower era, movie audiences delighted in seeing American heroes defeat the Germans, the Japanese, and Native Americans. Heroes—of either the old West or the recent war—were what American audiences wanted to see in the fifties. It was hardly surprising that as the nation retreated into another period of conservatism in the second half of the 1970s, its craving for heroes with simple (and violent) answers to all problems rose once more to the surface. Ike's America had John Wayne; Ronald Reagan's America made do with Sly Stallone.

It was no coincidence that Stallone's breakthrough came with the first *Rocky* film in the bicentennial year of 1976, as the last traces of the liberal era were subsiding and the nation was entering the reaction that would be manifest by 1978. Stallone became more violent and more jingoistic as the national mood swung farther to the right. Others who cashed in on the new wave of Wayne-ism, such as Clint Eastwood, Charles Bronson, Arnold Schwarzenegger, and Chuck Norris kept their violence more apolitical. The 1985 success of *Rambo: First Blood Part II* and *Rocky IV* represented not something new in American popular culture, but the culmination of a reactionary trend that had been rising since the mid-seventies. Lynch law in fifties westerns was replaced by lynch law in "urbans," a newer species of the same violent genus. Similar movies were popular in the late fifties when, despite appearances, the last conservative age was actually in decline. Stallone's extremely violent 1986 release *Cobra* was a box-office disappointment to its producers, indicating the possibility that even his public's appetite for blood was beginning to lessen.

Nor were all the bloody pictures of the era briefs for right-wing causes. In James Cameron's *Aliens* (1986) the Stallone part is played by Sigourney Weaver, but the picture is much more than a feminist *Rambo*. For one thing, the "enemy" being blasted away are not fellow human beings but a host of terrifying alien creatures with acid for blood. For another, Ripley (Weaver) is no killing machine. She is just trying to save humans from horrible beasts. But the most important message in the movie comes from a despicable character named Burke, who represents the company that owns the spaceship. Burke is the epitome of me-ism. He'll do anything—including killing fellow crew members and exposing humanity back on earth to the horrible aliens—to advance his career by getting exclusive rights to the alien species, which he thinks may have great "commercial possibilities." When Ripley realizes what Burke has been up to, she condemns the philosophy of greed that dominated the Reagan years by saying that it's hard to tell which species is worse, the aliens or humans. At least the aliens "don't fuck each other over for a percentage," she declares.

The top box-office film of early 1987, Oliver Stone's *Platoon*, carried essentially the same message as Springsteen's "War"—that war is good for nothing. *Platoon* accomplished the remarkable feat of evoking sympathy for American "grunts" in Vietnam at the same time that it showed how they were dehumanized in a hopeless cause.

In addition to the emergence of some action movies with a very different message, there was another side to the repulsive Stallone movies. Beyond their jingoism and violence, *Rambo* and *Rocky IV* were part of a somewhat different development in American culture—and part of a genre with a long history in filmmaking.

Stallone portrayed not simply a violent American shooting Vietnamese or bashing a Russian; he also represented the triumph of the common man. *Rocky IV*, in particular, celebrates the populist theme of the virtues of a hard-working, simple (in this case virtually Neanderthal) man overcoming the evils of modern science. The child of nature defeats the creature of technology. "It's a matter of science," a Soviet trainer with computer printouts says in the film. "Drago [the Russian boxer] is a look at the future." It is basically the same in *Rambo*. Stallone smashes a bank of computers that represents complexity—as opposed to the simplicity and common sense of the "ordinary American." Americans are rightly ambivalent about what the scientific future may bring them, and Stallone provides reassurance that ordinary humankind can not only survive against science, but prevail.

There can be little question that a majority of the more than 50

million Americans who went to see *Rocky IV* took vicarious plea-
sure in watching their All-American ape beat the bejesus out of the
Russkie. Stallone's movies are what Russian poet Yevgeny Yevtu-
shenko dubbed "war-nograhy." Their populism is of a distinctly
right-wing variety. "So it's a right-wing fantasy," Stallone has said of
Rambo. "Like Valley Forge. They did it their way, too, against the
British. No one told them from Washington how to fight."

Certainly there are dangers in this sort of childish fantasy, with
its implication that our problems can be solved by heroic, violent action. There must be some significance to the startling fact that soon
after *Rambo's* release its Beirut distributor sent the film's producers
an excited telegram in which he crowed: "This is definitely going to
be the highest grossing film in the history of Lebanon." But indications are that most Americans, even if they enjoy the deranged violence in these films, know that they are *only* fantasies. Film critic
Pauline Kael of *The New Yorker* has suggested that the appeal of
the "comic-strip patriotism" of Stallone movies is similar to that of
professional wrestling. Fans can derive excitement at the same time
that most of them understand that the entertainment's only connection with reality is to negate it.

Polls in the mid-eighties consistently showed that most Americans had no more taste for genuine danger and foreign adventure
than Stallone himself demonstrated when he canceled a trip to the
1986 Cannes film festival because he feared terrorist attack. Watching Rambo or Rocky fight the Commies on the screen is one thing;
really fighting them is quite another. Two-thirds of the Americans
polled in one survey said they believe that "there's room enough in
the world for both" the Soviet system and ours, and that we should
make no attempt to change their system. Two-to-one majorities of
Americans in poll after poll opposed American aid to the Nicaraguan Contras, let alone actual involvement by American fighting
forces in Central America. Stallone and Reagan were popular when
they talked tough (or, in the former case, grunted tough), but most
Americans in the mid-eighties preferred to keep the military action
on the screen.[1]

Right-wing populism was also evident in other manifestations of
the renewed cold-war mentality of the Reagan era. Television commercials exploited the reborn Russophobia so reminiscent of the
1950s. The most notable such example was a spot for Wendy's
hamburgers which depicted a fashion show in the Soviet Union. A

stereotypical Russian woman of generous proportions models the same drab outfit for daytime, evening, and swim wear (no choices of toppings such as Wendy's gives its customers).

Other filmmakers also joined Stallone in peddling their own versions of war-nography. John Milius's *Red Dawn* (1984) was based upon the same sort of right-wing populism that permeated the Stallone efforts. When the Soviets, Cubans, and Nicaraguans invade the United States, it is not the government, the regular military, or our vast nuclear arsenal that rises to the occasion and fights back to defend the American way of life; it's a group of high school football players! One of them, who had seemed like a good kid, winds up responding to an inquiry about how it felt to kill a man (well, not really a man—a Commie), with: "It was good."[2]

Disconcerting as the barbarism of the right-wing populist movies is, the notion that it is up to "ordinary people" to undo the mistakes and corruption of the powerful is one of the most cherished parts of the American democratic dogma. And the populist theme that coexisted with violence and chauvinism in such films as *Red Dawn* and *Rocky IV* is one that was also regaining popularity in less objectionable vehicles in the 1980s.

WarGames, a 1983 film directed by John Badham, sees those in authority and their computers as every bit as much of a threat to "good folks" as *Rambo* does. But Badham's perspective is very different from Stallone's. A Seattle boy, David (Matthew Broderick), is a computer freak who accidentally breaks into the Norad Command's computer, which, it turns out, has been programmed to replace fallible humans and direct the launching of American missiles in the event of an attack. David does not realize at first that the game of Global Thermonuclear War he starts playing with the Norad computer is not just another Atari-like diversion. Neither, it develops, does the computer. When an alarmed David asks the machine whether what they are doing is real or just a game, the computer's response is: "What's the difference?"

David and his girlfriend have to go through a series of difficulties with adults in authority in order to save the world from nuclear holocaust. In the end, though, it is the computer that provides the film's basic, common-sense liberal message about nuclear war: "The only winning move is not to play."[3]

Hollywood populism can take many forms. Several films of the mid-1980s satirized the "lifestyle" of the beautiful people of Ronald Reagan's America. The "return of elegance" apparently did not impress Paul Mazursky, whose *Down and Out in Beverly Hills* (1986) ridicules the conspicuous consumption of the Whiteman (note the name) family. Their more-than-comfortable life is disrupted when a posthippy bum, Jerry (Nick Nolte), attempts to drown himself in their pool. The cultural commentary in this funny film is often pointed, although some of the impact is lost at the end, when Mazursky departs from Jean Renoir's 1931 film, *Boudu Saved from Drowning*, which provided the inspiration for his movie. Boudu returned to "freedom," but Jerry is tempted back to the "slavery" of luxury.[4]

One of the indications of the growing gap between rich and poor—and even between rich and "middle-class" people—in Reagan's America has been the return of an old movie theme that nearly disappeared in the years of genuine widespread upward mobility from the end of World War II into the seventies. Films during the Great Depression often depicted the yawning social gap between rich and poor. The most acceptable way for the poor to rise in the cinema of the thirties was by gaining the love of a wealthy member of the opposite sex (and in the process curing him or her of evil snobbery). Sharp class division rather suddenly reappeared in films of the eighties—as it did in real life. And the solution once again seemed to be that of Hollywood in the thirties: Make Love, Not Politics.

Such messages were contained in the skillfully crafted *An Officer and a Gentleman* (1982) and the exploitative *Flashdance* (1983), about the aspirations of a young woman who is a welder by day and a dancer by night. But the most notable of these new "class-conscious" films is John Hughes's *Pretty in Pink* (1986), which presents a suburban high school of the 1980s as a class society in which the budding yuppies are already adept at looking down their noses at the kids who don't wear and drive what they do. Our heroine from—literally—the wrong side of the tracks is Andie (Molly Ringwald). She seeks the love of the rich Blane (Andrew McCarthy) and endures the abuse of such young snobs as Steff (James Spader). The basic plot is one of the oldest in existence, but the ridicule of the rich and the strong class context make it a potentially important statement to young audiences of the eighties. The point was appropriate enough at a time when the number of American millionaires was soaring as never before, but 40 percent of the nation's population was suffering real economic decline.

Whether the exposé of the evils of class division in *Pretty in Pink* had much impact on the film's mostly youthful audience is open to question. But satirizing embryonic yuppies was a common feature of 1980s popular culture. Young Americans were coming of age watching the attitudes and beliefs of Alex (Michael J. Fox), the outwardly self-centered, greedy, future businessman of America, who was held up to ridicule week after week on NBC's "Family Ties." This sitcom was television's second most popular show during the middle of the decade. Certainly some undiscerning viewers identified with Alex's positions and did not understand the satire. (President Reagan, for instance, said in 1986 that "Family Ties" was his favorite program.) Most of the show's huge audience, though, presumably got the point.[5]

Perhaps the best satire on egoism to emerge in the mid-eighties was Albert Brooks's movie, *Lost in America* (1985). The film is an allegory of America in the Age of Reagan. David Howard (played by Brooks himself) is a very upwardly mobile young advertising executive. Advertising is, of course, exactly the right field for a symbol of an America lost in materialism and greed. David is expecting a promotion from his $100,000-a-year job to the senior vice presidency of his agency. He and his wife have just placed a down payment on a $450,000 house, and he is trying to decide on the right Mercedes and the right boat. Still, the Howards talk about the lure of "dropping out of society" the way Peter Fonda, Dennis Hopper, and Jack Nicholson did in *Easy Rider*. Like the America he symbolizes, David Howard craves success, but also yearns to get away from it all, to return to nature, to see the "real America" in Luckenback, Texas, or at Walden Pond, or wherever it may be.

David's chance to escape the successful life comes when he flips out after learning that his boss intends not to make him vice-president but to send him to New York to work on the agency's new Ford account. After David's behavior gets him fired, he tells his wife to quit her job so that they can take to the road. "I was on the road to nowhere," he exclaims. "It's the Nowhere Road—it's the carrot on the stick and the gold watch when you're seventy."

But David and Linda (Julie Hagerty) intend to be Easy Riders of a different sort. They take to the road with about $145,000 in their pockets, riding in a fully equipped luxury motor home. This mode of transportation is to the yuppie of 1985 what Captain America's Harley-Davidson was to the hippie of 1969. "We can drop out and still have our nestegg," David chortles.

Their plans for the simple life of leisure end abruptly when Linda loses all their money in a gambling spree in Las Vegas. They settle briefly in a trailer park in a small town in Arizona, where David finds employment as a crossing guard at $5.50 an hour. After one day of this unanticipated simple living, the Howards readily agree to go to New York, where he will "eat shit" so that he can get his job back.

For a thoroughly upper-middle-class, success-driven fellow like David, there was no other choice. But most of the audience was likely to understand that being a money-obsessed advertising executive and dropping out or working for $5.50 an hour are not the only possibilities. Neither road chosen by David Howard was the right one for America, but *Lost in America* made it clear which one the nation was on in the first half of the 1980s.[6]

The last liberal era arose largely out of concern over the danger of nuclear war and over racial injustice. The same areas were the cause of growing concern among many Americans in the 1980s, and that concern was reflected in the popular culture.

One of the films that heralded the end of the Eisenhower era was Stanley Kramer's *On the Beach* (1959). Such earlier movies as *Strategic Air Command* (1955) and *Bombers B-52* (1957) had peddled the notion that nuclear weapons were devices of protection, like families. In fact, General Hawkes (Frank Lovejoy) speaks in *Strategic Air Command* of "the new family of nuclear weapons." But there is no haven in *On the Beach*. There is no way to measure the impact of a movie on public consciousness, but *On the Beach* may well have changed the thinking of a substantial number of people on the subject of nuclear weapons.

As the liberal sixties came, so did a fuller understanding of the danger of nuclear war. The 1962 Cuban missile crisis led to several movies that dealt with the topic from a liberal perspective. *Seven Days in May* (1964) and *Fail-Safe* (1964) were powerful films, but Stanley Kubrick's *Dr. Strangelove, or How I Learned to Stop Worrying and Love the Bomb* (1964) was in a category by itself. General

Jack D. Ripper (Sterling Hayden) is an early nuclear version of Rambo and the other right-wing vigilantes of the eighties, but his effect on the audience is very different from that of Stallone's characters. When Kong (Slim Pickins) uses good old American ingenuity to repair his plane so that it can deliver its bomb and begin the end of the world, he rides out of the bomb bay with the nuke between his legs like a horse and shouts "Yippee" as he waves his cowboy hat. This makes him quite literally the last American hero.

For more than a decade after *Dr. Strangelove*, few American heroes were to be seen on the silver screen, and nuclear war became even more unthinkable than it had been before. Concern over it ebbed from the mid-sixties through the late seventies; most of us just put it out of our minds. Certainly we did not learn to love the Bomb, but we did stop worrying.[7]

The election of Ronald Reagan, a man whose political career was launched the same year that *Dr. Strangelove* was released (and who had defended Barry Goldwater's loose talk that year about using nuclear weapons—and who had said similar things himself in more recent years), brought the issue firmly back into the public consciousness. The president and several leading figures in his administration made statements indicating that they thought nuclear war could be limited and won. During his 1980 campaign for the presidency, Reagan was asked whether he thought the United States could survive a nuclear war. "It would be a survival of some of your people and some of your facilities that you could start again," he replied, echoing the plans of Peter Sellers as the deranged Nazi scientist Strangelove. But Reagan stressed that he did not think our society would consider it "acceptable."

It is not surprising that this sort of talk made many Americans—not to mention Russians and others—uneasy. In 1974, less than half (47 percent) the Americans surveyed by the Roper organization thought that nuclear war would "be a serious problem 25 or 50 years from now." By 1983, that figure had soared to 71 percent. In 1985, polls indicated that 38 percent of all Americans and 50 percent of those under thirty believed that an all-out nuclear war was likely to take place within the next ten years. As *Newsweek* put it in its own imitable way in 1983: "The bomb is back."

Certainly the renewed fear of nuclear war arose initially with no help from Hollywood—other than that provided by its prodigal son in the White House. A huge movement supporting a bilateral nuclear freeze arose in the early 1980s. One of the most important salvos in the new struggle to alert people to the danger of nuclear war was the publication of Jonathan Schell's *The Fate of the Earth* in 1982. Schell made clear why nuclear war differs in kind, not just in degree, from other types of mass destruction: the possibility of human extinction—even of the extinction of all life—is a danger far more frightening than the deaths of individuals, no matter how numerous and ghastly those individual deaths may be. We are all going to die eventually, anyway, but there is some comfort in knowing that the world will go on without us.

The growing concern with the possibility of nuclear war was rapidly reflected in the popular culture. We have already mentioned the spate of antinuke songs in the eighties. Films and television were quick to join. In 1983, Paramount released Lynne Littman's *Testament*, a wrenching film about the consequences of nuclear war on the residents of an upper-middle-class community outside San Francisco. This is not a typical disaster movie: There are no firestorms, no melting faces, not even many visible effects of radiation poisoning. Instead, we watch the residents of an ordinary American town slowly die from the effects of radioactive blasts that did not hit them directly. We never know who launched the attack. It really doesn't matter.

If *Testament*'s impact was small, the same could hardly be said of 1983's other major production about nuclear war. ABC's presentation of "The Day After" was one of the most significant events in the history of television. One hundred million Americans looked on as Lawrence and Kansas City—along with the rest of the world— were incinerated. Here was the ultimate disaster movie, one that attracted the twelfth-largest American television audience ever.

A generation too young to have hidden under school desks in the 1950s was given a horrible view of the effects of nuclear war. Of course most of us already knew that such an event would be unpleasant, but seeing a more-or-less realistic depiction of the consequences brought it home in a different way. At the end of the film the following words flashed across the screen, serving to increase the impact on the audience: "The catastrophic events you have just witnessed are in all likelihood less severe than what would actually occur in the event of a full nuclear strike against the United States."

ABC insisted that "The Day After" was apolitical, "a giant public service announcement, like Smokey the Bear." Even Smokey can't please everyone, though. The *New York Post* complained about the film's "unremittingly depressing vision of nuclear holocaust." A truly balanced production would presumably have shown more of the cheerful side of instant vaporization and slower radiation poisoning.

Such a film could not be apolitical. In a special edition of "Viewpoint" broadcast immediately after the movie, ABC anchorman Ted Koppel noted that "what we've all just seen is a sort of a nuclear version of Charles Dickens' *Christmas Carol.*" That is just what it was: a vision of shadows of things that might come, but that can still be prevented. The question, of course, is how? Despite the professed apolitical nature of the production, "The Day After" made it clear that those who spoke of "winnable" nuclear war were talking nonsense.

Whatever the reasons, sentiment for arms control and reduction of nuclear forces rose. This did not always accrue to the benefit of liberals or their positions. Graphically showing people what a nuclear war might be like also served to increase support for President Reagan's Strategic Defense Initiative, at least so long as people believed that a Star Wars umbrella could actually protect them from what ABC had put on their TV screens.

Other films tied to the theme of nuclear disaster were produced in the Reagan years, including the already mentioned *WarGames* and *Mad Max Beyond Thunderdome* (1985). The latter—the third and most successful of the Mad Max series—is, like *On the Beach*, set in a postnuclear apocalypse Australia. There the resemblance ends. In George Miller's *Mad Max*, almost everything has been destroyed. Physically and mentally deformed people roam about. Some are organized into a brutal, dictatorial miniature city called Bartertown. The exaggerated violence in the film both shows what survivors of a nuclear holocaust might face and satirizes the violence of other movies of the decade.

Mad Max approached the subject in a different way from the other nuclear disaster films of the eighties, but it joined with them in leaving viewers with a grim picture of what the future might bring. The political effects of the various views of nuclear apocalypse were palpable. In 1985, 75 percent of those polled favored a bilateral freeze on nuclear weapons and 61 percent endorsed a unilateral freeze by the United States for six months to see if the Soviets would respond favorably. These positions ran counter to those of the Reagan administration, which refused to respond to the Soviets' unilateral moratorium on nuclear testing in 1985–87. Plainly, the basic message of popular culture's answer to the question of nuclear war was the same in the 1980s as it had been in the late fifties and early sixties—it was a liberal one. Just as plainly, that message was getting through to most Americans.[8]

Conservative periods in our history have generally witnessed an increase in racial intolerance. Politically and socially, blacks have often seen their status decline during such times. Yet, throughout the twentieth century, stirrings among black Americans and a growth of white interest in black culture have characterized the later years of conservative periods—those leading up to the subsequent eras of reform.

In the first years of the century, as the Progressive era was rising, white racism was at a fever pitch in most of the United States. But many whites developed a taste for ragtime music, and blacks responded to the rash of lynchings and race riots by beginning to organize, first with the Niagara Movement, which led to the formation of the NAACP in 1909. In the 1920s, the second incarnation of the Ku Klux Klan pushed the idea of "100 percent Americanism," which excluded blacks and many other groups. Marcus Garvey's Universal Negro Improvement Association organized hundreds of thousands of blacks under the banners of racial pride and returning to Africa. "The world has made being black a crime," Garvey said. "I hope to make it a virtue." Whites in increasing numbers in the twenties adopted black jazz and frequented clubs in New York's Harlem and the black districts of other cities.

In the 1950s yet another version of the Klan joined with the White Citizens Council and other racist organizations to employ a variety of methods to maintain segregation. At the same time, though, a massive nonviolent civil-rights movement based upon passive resistance was developing among Southern blacks, and white listeners were tuning in to hear such black performers as Little Richard, Chuck Berry, and Fats Domino as they created rock 'n' roll. It was not long after the start of Dwight Eisenhower's second term that both the civil-rights movement and the new black music would be taken up by substantial numbers of whites and begin to change the course of the nation.

A similar phenomenon was observable in the declining years of the Reagan administration. Protests over South African apartheid and the lack of action against it by the Reagan administration became widespread. The positions taken by the Reaganites indicated that racism, like egoism, was once again acceptable. However, incidents of racial violence in the mid-eighties led to a rebirth of civil-rights protest. Early in 1987, for example, some 25,000 people marched to oppose Ku Klux Klan violence in Forsythe County, Georgia. The demonstration was the largest civil rights march since the 1960s.

Perhaps even more significant was a noticeable revival of the popularity of black musicians among whites, as evidenced by the success of Prince, Michael Jackson and his siblings, Lionel Richie, Whitney Houston, Tina Turner, Sade, Billy Ocean, and Patti La-Belle, along with many others. For several consecutive weeks in the summer of 1986 the three top-selling albums in the United States were all the products of black women (Janet Jackson's *Control*, Patti LaBelle's *Winner in You*, and Whitney Houston's *Whitney Houston*). Facing a growing loss of young listeners to black-oriented stations, mainstream radio stations were giving black artists much more airplay than they had in earlier years. In 1986 the rap music of such black groups as Run–DMC began to attract large white audiences. And early in 1987 a white group, the Beastie Boys, rose to the top of the charts with a rap album. This phenomenon was strikingly reminiscent of the white adoption of black pop music in the fifties. *Billboard* columnist Paul Grein declared in 1986 that Michael Jackson's 1982 album *Thriller* had "turned the business upside down and rendered the color barrier obsolete."

The explosion of black crossover music in the mid-eighties was impressive, but equally striking evidence of a resurgence of white cultural interest in blacks was to be found in movies and television.

In the history of American cinema, there have been only three black actors who could be called full-fledged stars. The first, Sidney Poitier, reached the peak of his popularity in the late 1960s. After he left Hollywood, no black star with mass appeal to "crossover" (that is, white) audiences arose until the 1980s. Richard Pryor's popularity soared in 1982 with the success of *Richard Pryor Live on the Sunset Strip* and *Some Kind of Hero*. He was joined late in Ronald Reagan's first term by Eddie Murphy, who achieved "superstar" status in 1984 with *Beverly Hills Cop*, the biggest nonsummer box-office hit in American film history. A survey that year found Murphy to be the most popular performer in the United States, and Paramount signed him to an exclusive $25 million contract for six pictures. That sort of deal had not been seen since the days when Ike was still in office.

Both Pryor and Murphy are comedians who specialize in satire and, as *New Republic* film critic Stanley Kauffmann has pointed out, "both of them [are] mockers of the status quo" at a time when conditions for a majority of blacks are worsening. Still, the popularity of black *comics* might not be too surprising. Serious films about blacks were in short supply through most of the seventies and early eighties. There was, in fact, a lapse of a dozen years between successful serious movies centered on blacks: *Sounder* in 1972 and *A Soldier's Story* in 1984. The latter, a low-budget film with no top stars, based upon Charles Fuller's 1982 Pulitzer Prize–winning play, *A Soldier's Play*, was a startling box-office success. The film, set in 1944, centers on the consequences of the arrival at a Louisiana army base of a black captain investigating the murder of a black sergeant. It skillfully explores not only interracial conflict, but also the stratifying effects it can have on blacks.

The success of *A Soldier's Story* led Hollywood executives to conclude that, as documentary filmmaker St. Clair Bourne put it at the end of 1984, "a black film was no longer a liability." Any remaining doubts were removed a year later when Steven Spielberg's production of Alice Walker's novel *The Color Purple* became a major hit. The mere fact that Spielberg, whose taste seems to coincide exactly with that of middle America, wanted to make a film of the Walker novel indicated that a majority of whites in the nation were ready to watch a film with a nearly all-black cast that dealt with black problems. Of course Spielberg put his usual stamp of optimism on the story, but there is a need for affirmative black films with happy endings.

The success of *The Color Purple*, much larger than that of *A Soldier's Story*, opened new possibilities not only for blacks in the film industry, but for some improvement in race relations in this country. For those who questioned whether a few movies offered signs of a realistic hope for change, there was an even larger indication of the same trend in another segment of popular culture: "The Cosby Show."

It would be difficult to overstate the significance of the leap of

Bill Cosby's sitcom to the top of the television rankings in the 1984–85 season. NBC executives had been reluctant to put the show on the air. Sitcoms were said to be a dying breed and, as Cosby recalled in 1985, when he came along "wanting to do one with an *all-black* cast, [they] had to say: 'Wrong time, wrong color.' "

Who *wouldn't* have had that thought in the midst of the Reaganite assault on the achievements of the civil-rights revolution? But, of course, those who feared that white America in the mideighties would not be interested in such a black show severely underestimated both Cosby and the American public. "The Cosby Show" quickly established itself as America's favorite television program, and by the 1985–86 season it was consistently scoring the highest Nielsen ratings that any show had recorded since the heyday of "All in the Family" in the early seventies. Even that, however, does not gauge the extraordinary impact of "The Cosby Show." In less than two years, it led NBC from its traditional last-place rating among the networks to first place. And by 1985 the TVQ survey found Bill Cosby himself to be the most popular performer in America.

The magic of "The Cosby Show" is that it depicts middle-class family life in a funny way to which most people can readily relate. Some critics have complained that the professional duo of Cliff and Clair Huxtable is far removed from the lives of most black people. Such complaints miss the two great accomplishments of the show. One is that it provides positive role models for young blacks, few of whom were likely to have been inspired to walk in the footsteps of Redd Foxx's character on "Sanford and Son." The other is that white viewers see *themselves* in the Huxtable family. Whites cannot help but realize that the only difference between their own families and Cosby's is that his family has darker skins. Harvard psychiatrist Alvin Poussaint, who reviews the script of each show, appears to have been on target when he asserted that "this show is changing the white community's perspective of black Americans. It's doing far more to instill positive racial attitudes than if Bill came at the viewer with a sledgehammer or a sermon."[9]

Perhaps most whites were not yet ready to say "black is beautiful," but they were at least learning that black people could be very much like themselves. The receptivity of white Americans to black popular culture in the middle 1980s was, in light of what had pre-

ceded earlier reform eras, one of the strongest signs that public attitudes were shifting in a liberal direction.

Although it was not so perceived at the time, *The Big Chill*
(1983) was a fitting monument to the peak of the Reagan era—and
at the same time, paradoxically, one of the most important signs
that that era was about to decline. The movie tells the story of a
group of sixties radicals who come together at the funeral of a friend
who had remained committed to his ideals until his suicide. They
all wind up pondering how far they have departed from what they
thought was important when they were in college. All had become
yuppies (though the movie was made a year before that term was
coined). Backed by a superb sixties soundtrack, *The Big Chill* was
exactly what one reviewer called it: "the feel-good movie of '83." In
this sense it was appropriate to a time when the nation was ena-
mored of a President Feelgood. It was okay to have had ideals when
you were young and foolish, but now sensible adults were making
their fortunes as television stars, "writers" for *People* magazine, corporate attorneys, running-shoe merchants, physicians, business executives' wives, or drug dealers (money is money, after all).

Yet *The Big Chill* was not lauding what those who wanted to
change the world in the sixties had become. If it was the ultimate
baby-boomer saga, the movie served to remind comfortable people
in their thirties of whence they came. It showed how the erstwhile
idealists had turned into what they used to despise. So much had
been expected of this huge generation, and *The Big Chill* made it
clear that it had yet to achieve any significant part of its potential.
Director Lawrence Kasdan appeared to some critics to be a bit too
"comfortable with the 'failure' of his generation," but what he actually did was to hold up a mirror to the generation. Many of its
members were not pleased with what they saw. This realization—
brought about, of course, by many other events in addition to Kasdan's film—started many boomers searching again for something
worthwhile in which to believe. This was evidenced by the brief
surge of support for Gary Hart and his "New Ideas" early in 1984.

The significance of *The Big Chill* lay neither in the answers it
provided (it offered none) nor in the newness of the questions it
raised. Its achievement was to force large numbers of people to confront the questions that were already in the backs of their minds. In

her review of the film in *The Nation*, Katha Pollitt charged that Kasdan did not understand that "for 1960s radicals, there's more to the 1980s than a choice between buying another Mercedes and killing yourself." Yet the real message of the film is that other choices must be found—neither suicide nor yuppiedom is a satisfactory alternative—and we have to begin to look for them.

There was nothing original in *The Big Chill*. It borrowed heavily from John Sayles's low-budget *Return of the Secaucus 7* (1980), which also dealt with seven sixties veterans and one outsider at a reunion. Similar questions had been addressed elsewhere, including Lanford Wilson's play, *The Fifth of July* (1980), Kathleen Tolan's drama *A Weekend near Madison* (1983), and several of Ann Beattie's stories. The virtue of *The Big Chill* lay in its ability to make the questions about what happened to the generation's idealism more accessible to a great number of people.

A final accomplishment of *The Big Chill* was that in addition to raising the basic problem of abandoned ideals among the baby boomers, it also hinted at the fate of the next generation. There is one outsider at the weekend gathering of sixties survivors: Chloe (Meg Tilly), who is about fifteen years younger than the others. She represents the generation that came of age after idealism had died. She is spaced-out and seems to accept whatever happens in a *que sera sera* manner. Yet the viewer can tell after a while that Chloe wishes she could believe in something. She envies the experiences of those who were on the barricades in the sixties.[10]

The problems of the postsixties generation and its relationship to the legacy of that last era of liberalism were treated in a variety of media in the eighties. The heroine of Bobbie Ann Mason's 1985 novel, *In Country*, a Kentucky girl born in the late sixties, is only vaguely aware of what went on during her childhood. But as she listens to her mother's records, she is regretful that she missed the idealism and excitement of that turbulent period.

Joel Schumacher's 1985 movie, *St. Elmo's Fire*, strives to be a sort of "Little Chill." It, too, centers on a group of four males and three females who were college friends. But this gang of seven are in their early twenties and have just left college. They are trying, with varying degrees of success, to adjust to the "real world." Unlike their counterparts in *The Big Chill*, these recent graduates never had any ideals to abandon. Some of them are plainly not pleased with the world as they find it, but none has any notion of what to do about it.

One, Billy (Rob Lowe), is decidedly rebellious, but his rebellion has no direction. In this he is similar to the Marlon Brando and James Dean characters of the 1950s. The same applies to rock stars Prince and Madonna playing characters based upon themselves in *Purple Rain* (1984) and *Desperately Seeking Susan* (1985).[11]

The link between the age of Eisenhower and the age of Reagan was made more explicitly in several other films of the mid-eighties. Herb Ross's *Footloose* (1984) took a fifties story and placed it in a fifties-like setting, but the time is actually the eighties. The Reverend Shaw Moore (John Lithgow) is a Moral Majority type who dominates a small midwestern town. He obtains bans on rock 'n' roll and "obscene" books, and the kids rebel, as they did in so many fifties movies. It is a simple plot, but its significance lies in the fact that almost all viewers were sure to identify with the "rebels" and against the repressive religious Right.

Steven Spielberg and Robert Zemeckis literally took viewers from the eighties back to the fifties in their smash hit *Back to the Future* (1985). When Marty McFly (Michael J. Fox) gets into a time machine and accidentally travels back to 1955, the dawn of the youth culture, he finds it necessary to intervene in the lives of his parents to ensure that they will get together and he will be born. The subliminal message is that if we don't take the proper action now, the future may dissolve like Marty McFly begins to. Another message, designed to appeal to youthful movie audiences, is that young people can save their elders.

Back to the Future, Pauline Kael has argued, "represents a culmination of the fifties' appeal to the youth market." Precisely right, and a culmination comes, of course, at the end of a period. American culture had its last big fling with fifties nostalgia with *Back to the Future* (and 1986's *Stand By Me* and *Peggy Sue Got Married*), and moved on more fully into sixties nostalgia.[12]

Several of the kids-in-rebellion films of the eighties borrowed freely from *Rebel Without a Cause* (1955). *Footloose* even reenacted, with tractors, the game of chicken that climaxed the James Dean movie. But none of those came close to rivaling *Rebel*'s impact on the youth of the fifties. Neither did a remarkable 1985 film from John Hughes called *The Breakfast Club*, though it came closer than the others. Hughes's films stand out as far superior to the other teen movies of the era. *Sixteen Candles* (1984) is a delightful story that captures the humorous essence of teenage existence, and *Pretty in Pink* (1986), as already noted, attempted to say something about class division.

Hughes's masterpiece is *The Breakfast Club.* The entire movie takes place at a Saturday detention session at a suburban Chicago high school. The basic point, as in *Rebel Without a Cause*, is that adults cause the problems their children face. The reason is that parents have become materialistic and success-oriented. As the introverted Allison (Ally Sheedy) says when the detainees finally get her talking: "It's unavoidable. When you grow up, your heart dies." The vice-principal in charge underlines the point by making it clear that the only thing that interests him is money.

The kid who becomes the leader in liberating the group is a rebel in the Sal Mineo mold, played by Judd Nelson. Molly Ringwald portrays a popular "princess," who pointedly complains that she never receives love from her parents, only "things." But it is left for the jock, a wrestling champion named Andrew Clark (Emilio Estevez), to state plainly their common problem with adults in the me age. It would be going too far to suggest that his monologue could be an epitaph for the Reagan era, but it amounts to one of the most powerful statements our popular culture has produced against the latest age of egoism.

Andrew explains that he is in detention because he "taped Larry Lester's buns together." "The bizarre thing is," he says, "I did it for my old man." His father always told him about all the wild things he used to do in school, and Andrew wanted his father to think that he, too, was cool. So when he saw Larry, who was "kind of skinny and weak," he thought about his father's attitude toward weakness, and then jumped on him and "started whaling on him."

Later all Andrew could think about was Larry having to go home and tell his own father what had happened to him:

And the humiliation, the fucking humiliation he must have felt—it must have been unreal. How do you apologize for something like that? There's no way. It's all because of me and my old man. My God, I fucking *hate* him. He's a mindless machine that I can't even relate to anymore: "Andrew, you've got to be *Number One!* I won't tolerate any *losers* in this family! Your intensity is for shit! *Win! Win! Win!*" You sonofabitch. You know, sometimes I wish my knee would give. Then I wouldn't be able to wrestle anymore, and he could forget all about me.[13]

These lines are one of the many declarations of independence from the late seventies–early eighties age of self-centeredness and materialism. By the middle years of the decade, American popular culture was full of such indications that the times were indeed changing again.

The signs of a new stirring of idealism that point toward the dawn of a new age of reform have been growing more numerous in the mid-eighties, not only in the popular culture, but across the American social scene. Americans gave more to charity in 1984 and 1985 than they ever had before, with the total up by nearly 14 percent over those two years. The 1985 donations to charity amounted to more than 2 percent of personal income for the first time since 1969. Of course such voluntary contributions did not nearly compensate for the Reagan budget cuts, but they did indicate that many Americans understood that the need was growing.

There were many signs that the American people were beginning to tire of what Harvard psychiatry professor Robert Coles called the "getting-rich-is-good ethos of the Reagan administration." "I think we've bottomed out of that period of narcissism and indifference to moral issues," Coles said late in 1985. For years people had listened to those in power "confuse selfishness with self-reliance," as James Reston put it. The slogan had been "Hallowed be *My* name; *My* kingdom come; *My* will be done." People will remain content only for so long with what Michael Harrington called at the end of the last such era "empty abundance." Then people will do what Harrington said some were doing in the early sixties, they will "hunger for value and belief rather than for food." Mario Cuomo noticed the return of this hunger as early as 1982. After he participated in a nuclear freeze rally that year, he wrote in his diary,

... there is a great yearning for something worthwhile to believe in. The nuclear freeze is the simplest possible morality; life is better than death; peace is better than war; love is better than stupidity. It is hardly more than an affirmation, and yet it brought nearly a million people together. I could tell, just from their faces, that everyone felt good about the day. There was none of the hostility and tension that attended the rallies of the '60s.

Cuomo told me four years later that people were "*aching* for something to believe in." They "want something to cheer—an uplifting idea. They want *desperately* to have aspirations, reaching, beautiful striving."[14]

After hearing a 1985 speech by Ralph Nader, a Tufts University senior summarized the emerging desire for something in which to believe: "One of the reasons [Nader is] important is that he tells me to be idealistic. I'm constantly told, 'Be realistic ... don't be a dreamer.' He tells me that's not true, that I can make a difference." The renewed sense of idealism was apparent in the huge increase in inquiries to the Peace Corps. Such requests rose by nearly 1,000 percent in 1986. When the Peace Corps sought 600 volunteers to go to Ethiopia in 1985, 10,000 people applied. Thousands of students jeered Vice-President George Bush's appearance at a ceremony at the University of Michigan commemorating the twenty-fifth anniversary of John Kennedy's speech calling for the establishment of the Peace Corps. And VISTA, the domestic service program, came back from the edge of the grave in the middle of the eighties to withstand the Reagan administration's efforts to dismantle it.

The number of college campuses participating in the annual Oxfam fast "to call attention to world hunger" more than doubled from 1983 to 1984. There was a sharp increase in the mid-eighties in the number of college students who volunteered for community service. The new mood was well described by Martha Jones, the director of one such program at Berkeley. "I could have stood on the steps of Sproul Hall a few years ago shouting into a microphone," she said in 1985, "and nobody would have listened. But these students [now] are so enthusiastic. Who's projecting that these kids are selfish?" Frank Newman, who wrote a 1985 report for the Carnegie Foundation for the Advancement of Teaching urging the establishment of a new federal program under which students would receive financial aid in return for community service, pointed out one of the most significant aspects of the rise in student volunteer service. In the 1960s, Newman noted, young people responded to the idealism of President Kennedy. But in the mid-eighties they regained an interest in public service on their own, without "any call at all."[15]

Students in the mid-eighties were doing more than participating in public service projects. Tens of thousands of college students, starting in the spring of 1985, joined in protest actions against

South African apartheid, American support for it, and university investments in companies that continue to do business in South Africa. These protests were reminiscent not of the bitter, often violent confrontations of the late sixties, when the chant was "Two, four, six, eight, organize to smash the state," but of the civil-rights protests of the late fifties and early sixties. The student activism of the late sixties "didn't just develop out of nothing," Stanford sociologist Seymour Martin Lipset reminds us. "If you look back at that period, there was the beginnings of student activism, a revival of it in the late '50s—in '58, '59—and it grew gradually. In the early '60s it was concerned with civil rights. . . . So that the movement of '65 and on really emerged gradually out of a growing movement that started in '59–'60." Something very similar appeared to be beginning among students in 1985 and '86.

"South Africa," veteran activist and sociologist Todd Gitlin argued in 1985, "is [in the '80s] the moral equivalent of terrorist-segregationist Mississippi of an earlier day." What made the apartheid issue so attractive to newly active students was its moral clarity. Young people raised in an age of cynicism crave ideals, but they hold back from commitment for fear of being taken in. But apartheid is unambiguous. It is hard to find people in the United States who will defend it. (This fact is in itself a testament to the remarkable success of the last liberal era.) A Gallup poll in 1986 found that among those Americans who had been following the situation in South Africa (about half the population), 73 percent said that they supported the black population there, while only 12 percent said they sided with "the South African government." Of course it is safe for Americans to oppose racism in South Africa, just as it was safe for students who stayed in the North in the early sixties to oppose racism in the American South.

The safety of the issue notwithstanding, the rise of campus demonstrations in mid-decade was an important development. In the spring of 1985, antiapartheid demonstrations spread across the nation: Berkeley, Columbia, Rutgers, Cornell, Harvard, Stanford, Syracuse, Wisconsin, Michigan, and dozens of other campuses came alive. Tactics included sit-ins, rallies, teach-ins, protest songs, and other actions of the 1960s. Between 5,000 and 7,000 students attended a rally at Berkeley. Nearly 100 students at Rutgers spent more than a week occupying a student center that sixties' activists had sought to have named for black singer-actor-political activist

Paul Robeson. The 1985 students called the building Nelson Mandela Hall, in honor of the jailed leader of the African National Congress.

Athough apartheid was the most common target of the new protests, other issues also aroused student concern. Many joined in projects to fight hunger in Africa and in this country. The first important actions in the new wave of protest came at Brown University in the fall of 1984. Students passed a referendum asking the university health service to stock cyanide pills for use in the event of nuclear war. The point was to dramatize the suicidal nature of the nuclear arms race. A month later, a group of Brown students attempted to make a citizen's arrest of a CIA recruiter visiting the campus. Their argument was that the agency was involved in such criminal activities as mining harbors in Nicaragua, and that trying to recruit people for criminal activities is itself a crime. An estimated 50,000 people marched in San Francisco in April 1985 to protest American ties to South Africa, intervention in Central America, and the arms race.

The protests spread even to the most unlikely campuses, such as the University of California at Santa Barbara, noted as a fun-in-the-sun school where more interest is usually shown in beer than in social injustice. A university spokeswoman there said of the anti-apartheid demonstrations in 1985: "Here we have it, finally. An issue for the '80s."

There were significant differences between the protests of the mid-eighties and those of the late sixties. The more recent actions placed a much greater emphasis on nonviolence and on achieving specific results. Participants in the actions of the mid-eighties were more polite and respectful of the rights of others. Indeed, when the favored tactic changed in the 1985–86 school year to building shanty towns to symbolize the desperate living conditions of South African blacks, it was right-wing students who turned to violence. At Dartmouth and a few other campuses, right-wing extremists burned the shanty towns that had been set up by opponents of apartheid. It was, in fact, notable that in the mid-eighties most of the repulsive loudmouths who tried to disrupt meetings were not leftists, as had been the case in an earlier day. At Mondale–Ferraro rallies during the 1984 campaign, as well as at other public gatherings in the following years, the people doing the disruptive shouting were anti-abortionists and fundamentalists. If the increase in obnoxious behavior by people on the left in the late sixties was a sign of the coming decline of liberalism, the rise of similar practices on the right may be presaging the decline of conservatism.

The campus demonstrations of the mid-eighties served notice that the belief that students no longer cared about social issues was mistaken. "A lot of people don't want to express their concern because they are in an environment that says it's not cool to be concerned," suggested Cornell student John Muse in 1985. "But activism could become cool again." Berkeley student Mark Lilly believed that what was happening was that "people with a lot of pent-up energy finally see a chance to do things constructively." "We believe that this spring's antiapartheid demonstrations have shown that the 'me' generation is now a generation of the past," said David Goldiner, one of the leaders of the 1985 Columbia protests. "Students are thinking about themselves and their role in American society as they have not done for a long time. The age of apathy and quiescence on America's college campuses is over."[16]

Among the other indications of a changing mood in America in the mid-1980s was a growing concern about hunger elsewhere in the world and hunger and homelessness in our own generally affluent society.

A program called Children for Children was launched in the New York City school system in 1984–85 to raise money for the starving in Ethiopia. Nearly a million children made donations, totaling $150,000 in the first month. The comments of some of the children demonstrated what a powerful experience this was in raising social consciousness. "Once you expose somebody to something like this," one student said, "They have to do something about it." "It's a terrible feeling to know that I have so much and they have so little," an eleventh grader said. "You might not have money to go to the movies or a concert," another New York teenager said, "but you've never hit rock bottom." "We might be hungry sometimes," an Hispanic child from the Lower East Side stated, "but we ain't starving." "It's not right for them to starve when we have so much," another declared. But perhaps the most significant comment came from a child of about seven or eight, who said: "I want the president to watch this . . . to make him do what we're doing."

A barrage of information on the worsening problems of poverty, hunger, and homelessness in the United States hit the American public in the mid-eighties. Early in 1985, the Physicians Task Force on Hunger in America released the results of a year-long study that indicated that "hunger is a problem of epidemic proportions across the nation" and that the hunger problem was "getting worse, not better" in the 1980s. The study's most important finding was that "the recent and swift return of hunger to America can be traced in substantial measure to clear and conscious policies of the Federal Government." Early in 1986, Bill Moyers shocked a national television audience with his report on "The Vanishing Family: Crisis in Black America." At about the same time, Daniel Patrick Moynihan's book, *Family and Nation*, was published, detailing many of the same problems. A few months later, CBS televised a dramatic movie based on the career of Mitch Snyder, head of the Community for Creative Nonviolence, an organization that works for the homeless.[17]

Taken together, these messages via different media may have helped shake the nation out of its complacency about poverty in much the way that Michael Harrington's *The Other America* did in the early sixties. The principal differences are that Harrington's book came out when there was a president in office who was sympathetic to the problems of the poor and that, bad as they certainly were becoming, the actual material conditions of most poor Americans in the eighties were not *as* bad as they had been in the early sixties. The reason was the various federal programs that had been initiated in the last liberal era.

Still, as the problems of the underclass grew worse and more visible in the mid-eighties the likelihood that they would become a major political issue increased. One area where the response was apparent was within the mainline churches. While so-called "conservatives" were making great headway with fundamentalist groups in the eighties, many of the large denominations were staking out decidedly liberal positions on social and international issues.

Most of those on the right who welcomed it, and most of those on the left who feared it, did not realize it, but the return of religion to a greater prominence in American life in the eighties was the proverbial double-edged sword. The essential Judeo-Christian values are, after all, liberal values. Some of those who rushed to religion in the eighties were motivated by personal greed ("Save *me*, Lord!" "Just Thee and me, Lord!"). But many others sought in religion something beyond themselves in which to believe, a set of worthwhile values by which to conduct their lives. There is nothing incompatible between religious people of this sort and progressives. On the contrary, they are natural allies.

One of the best examples of the confluence of liberalism and mainstream religion was the United States Bishops' Pastoral Letter on the American Economy, which went through various drafts from 1984 through 1986. "Every perspective on economic life that is human, moral, and Christian," the letter began, "must be shaped by two questions: What does the economy do *for* people? What does it do *to* people?" The document went on to state that "the poor have a special claim on our concern because they are vulnerable and needy. We believe that all—Christians, Jews, those of other faiths or no faith at all—must measure their actions and choices by what they do *for* and *to* the poor." The Roman Catholic Church, which with more than 52 million members in the United States is by far the largest single church in the nation, was taking a clearly liberal stance on economic and social policy.

In 1985 the liberal Bishop Edmond Browning was elected to a twelve-year term as Presiding Bishop of the 2.8 million member Episcopal Church, two days after Browning's predecessor, Bishop John Allin, charged that President Reagan did not understand the causes of human suffering and that the administration's policies would lead to a "chain reaction of desperately oppressed, suffering human beings, losing hope and life." Bishop Browning announced promptly after his election that he believed that Episcopalians wanted their church to take stronger action against hunger, unemployment, racism, and the arms race.

The Council of Bishops of the United Methodist Church, the third-largest church in the United States with 9.4 million members, voted unanimously in 1986 to issue a pastoral letter stating their "clear and unconditioned" opposition to the use of nuclear weapons under any circumstances.

It seemed clear as the second half of the decade got underway that many large church organizations were, like so many other Americans, beginning to move farther away from the right-wing positions espoused by fundamentalists and members of the Reagan administration. When the new age of progressivism dawned, religious Americans would be an important part of the movement, as they had been in all past eras of American reform.

The group in American society that most closely watches trends in public attitudes is the advertising industry. At the same time,

290 ROBERT S. McELVAINE

however, advertising executives must be sure that they do not get too far in front of a trend, the way artists often do. Such cultural forms as music and film are more likely to indicate where attitudes are heading in the near future, but advertising may be the most accurate gauge of where the majority is at a given moment.

It therefore seems significant that there was a noticeable change in what was coming out of Madison Avenue from 1985 to 1986. During the first half of 1985, everything was aimed at the self-centered, acquisitive yuppie. A year later a subtle shift had taken place. Certainly advertisers still sought the acquisitive, upwardly mobile consumer—Michelob Light did not stop telling people that they could "have it all"—but the industry began to insert messages of altruism and of concern for the economic difficulties faced by the non-yuppie majority of baby boomers. American Express advertised its "Project Hometown America," in which the company encourages communities to develop new solutions to their problems. IBM began running magazine ads in which it pointed proudly to a program in which the company trains physically disabled people in communities around the country.

The shift in advertising remained small as of 1986, but the fact that it was occurring at all was yet another indication that the times were a-changin' again.[18]

Cumulatively, the incidents, attitudes, and examples of culture that have been noted in these pages seem sufficient to indicate that change was in the air in the mid-eighties. But perhaps such developments as protest songs, movies with liberal themes, campus protests, liberal sentiment in opinion polls, and increases in contributions to charity and applications to the Peace Corps were merely the last echoes from two decades before. It had seemed that way at the end of the 1950s. In retrospect, however, it is apparent that the isolated signs of a liberal rebirth as the Eisenhower era ended were in fact harbingers of a new era of reform.

Are the bits of evidence presented here the last, faded blooms of autumn that were somehow missed by the Reagan frost, or are they the first buds of a new springtime of reform? At the close of his *The Rights of Man* (1792), Thomas Paine provided a statement that speaks directly to this point. The Age of Reason has something important to say to the Age of Reagan:

It is now towards the middle of February. Were I to take a turn into the country the trees would present a leafless winterly appearance. As people are apt to pluck twigs as they walk along, I perhaps might do the same, and by chance might observe that a *single bud* on that tree had begun to swell. I should reason very unnaturally, or rather not reason at all, to suppose *this* was the *only* bud in England which had this appearance. Instead of deciding thus, I should instantly conclude that the same appearance was beginning, or about to begin, everywhere; and though the vegetable sleep will continue longer on some trees and plants than on others, and though some of them may not *blossom* for two or three years, all will be in leaf in the summer, except those which are *rotten*. What pace the political summer may keep with the natural, no human foresight can determine. It is, however, not difficult to perceive that the spring is begun.[19]

It is as hard for us today to predict the pace of the political spring as it was in Paine's time, but enough swollen buds have been found to indicate that the next summer of progressivism cannot be far off.

Or, to change the metaphor, the years of right-wing egoism amounted to a drought that had by the mid-1980s left the American landscape strewn with combustible material. The only questions that remained were when someone would strike the match that would ignite the next liberal era and who that person would be.

P E R M I S S I O N S

293

NOTES

INTRODUCTION

1. John Steinbeck to Adlai Stevenson, as quoted in Eric F. Goldman, *The Crucial Decade—And After: America, 1945–1960* (New York: Vintage, 1960), p. 325.
2. "I Like Ike," lyrics by Joe Glazer and John Greenway, on John Greenway, *Talking Blues* (Folkways Records, 1958).
3. Ralph Waldo Emerson, "The Conservative"; Henry Adams, *History of the United States of America During the Administrations of Thomas Jefferson and James Madison* (New York, 1889–91), vol. VI; Arthur M. Schlesinger, Sr., *Paths to the Present* (New York: Macmillan, 1949), pp. 77–92; Arthur M. Schlesinger, Jr., *The Cycles of American History* (Boston: Houghton Mifflin, 1986), pp. 23–48; Arthur Levine, *When Dreams and Heroes Died: A Portrait of Today's College Student* (San Francisco: Jossey-Bass, 1983), p. 25.
4. Charles Forcey, *The Crossroads of Liberalism: Croly, Weyl, Lippmann, and the Progressive Era, 1900–1925* (New York: Oxford University Press, 1961), pp. xi–xiv; Robert S. McElvaine, "Liberalism Is Not Dead," *New York Times,* September 20, 1980.
5. Author's interview with Joseph L. Rauh, Jr., Washington, D.C., June 21, 1985.
6. James Simon Kunen, interviewed on ABC News "Nightline," May 3, 1985 (New York: Journal Graphics, 1985, show #1030).
7. F. Scott Fitzgerald, *This Side of Paradise* (New York: Scribner, 1920).
8. Susannah Kennedy, as quoted in the *Washington Post,* April 20, 1985.
9. Author's interview with Patrick H. Caddell, Washington, D.C., September 12, 1985.
10. Schlesinger, *Paths to the Present,* pp. 77–92.
11. Joan Baez, interviewed on ABC News "Nightline," May 3, 1985 (New York: Journal Graphics, 1985, show #1030).
12. "Material Girl," lyrics by Peter Brown and Robert Rans, 1984, on Madonna, *Like a Virgin* (Sire Records, 1984).
13. Author's interview with Rep. Morris Udall (D, Ariz.), Washington, D.C., July 16, 1985.
14. Neal Peirce, "Downtowns Gaining Esteem," *Clarion-Ledger* (Jackson, Miss.), May 16, 1986.
15. Author's interview with Gov. Michael Dukakis (D, Mass.), Boston, May 10, 1986; author's interview with Gov. Bruce Babbitt (D, Ariz.), Phoenix, March 20, 1986.
16. Mario M. Cuomo, address to Black Ministers' Association, Rochester, N.Y., August 16, 1982, in Mario Cuomo, *The Diaries of Mario M. Cuomo: The Campaign for Governor* (New York: Random House, 1984), p. 448.

17. Author's interview with Sen. Lawton Chiles (D, Fla.), Washington, D.C., February 26, 1986.
18. As quoted in Goldman, *Crucial Decade*, p. 290.

CHAPTER 1

1. Kevin P. Phillips, *The Emerging Republican Majority* (New Rochelle, N.Y.: Arlington House, 1969), p. 6.
2. Ibid., p. 23.
3. Laurily K. Epstein, "The Changing Structure of Party Identification," *PS*, 18 (Winter 1985), p. 52.
4. Everett Carll Ladd, "The GOP Upsets the Balance of Parties," *Wall Street Journal*, April 8, 1985; Phil Gailey, "From Biden to Babbitt to Nunn," *New York Times Magazine*, May 18, 1986.
5. Barry Sussman, "Yes, We May Well Be Experiencing a Major Party Realignment," *Washington Post National Weekly Edition*, December 3, 1984.
6. Ladd, "GOP Upsets."
7. Seymour Martin Lipset, "The Elections, the Economy and Public Opinion," *PS*, 18 (Winter 1985), p. 38; Kenneth E. John, "Could Kennedy Win in '88?" *Washington Post National Weekly Edition*, May 13, 1985.
8. *New York Times*, April 1, 1985.
9. Ladd, "GOP Upsets."
10. *Los Angeles Times*, November 7, 1984.
11. *New York Times*, April 1, 1985.
12. Samuel L. Popkin, "The Donkey's Dilemma: White Men Don't Vote Democratic," *Washington Post*, November 11, 1984.
13. Author's interview with Gov. Charles S. Robb (D, Va.), Fairfax, Va., January 29, 1986; *New York Times*, November 7, 1985.
14. Lipset, "Elections, Economy and Public Opinion," p. 36.
15. Martin Wattenberg, *The Decline of American Political Parties, 1952–1980* (Cambridge, Mass.: Harvard University Press, 1984).
16. Walter Dean Burnham, *Critical Elections and the Mainsprings of American Politics* (New York: Norton, 1970), p. 73.
17. Ladd, "GOP Upsets"; Lipset, "Elections, Economy and Public Opinion," p. 35; Wattenberg, *Decline of American Political Parties*; Chuck Lane, "Ronnie's Kids," *New Republic*, December 3, 1984, p. 23.
18. Lipset, "Elections, Economy and Public Opinion," p. 38.
19. Robert S. Erikson and Kent L. Tedin, "The 1928–1936 Partisan Realignment: The Case for the Conversion Hypothesis," *American Political Science Review*, 75 (December 1981), pp. 951–62.
20. David S. Broder, "No Proof Found of Realignment," *Clarion-Ledger*, March 6, 1985.
21. Ladd, "GOP Upsets."
22. Lipset, "Elections, Economy and Public Opinion," p. 32.
23. *Los Angeles Times*, November 7, 1984; David S. Broder, "Recent Boondoggles Have Shaken Reagan's Credibility," *Clarion-Ledger*, May 5, 1985.
24. Thomas Ferguson and Joel Rogers, "The Myth of America's Turn to the Right," *Atlantic Monthly*, May 1986, pp. 50, 52–53.

25. Ellen Goodman, "Another First for Ferraro: Peddling a Product on TV," *Los Angeles Times*, February 24, 1985.

26. David W. Brady and Patricia A. Hurley, "The Prospects for Contemporary Partisan Realignment," *PS*, 18 (Winter 1985), p. 64.

27. Editorial, "Franklin Delano Reagan," *New York Times*, July 20, 1980.

28. Jules Witcover, *Marathon: The Pursuit of the Presidency, 1972–1976* (New York: Viking, 1977), p. 99.

29. William E. Leuchtenburg, *In the Shadow of FDR: From Harry Truman to Ronald Reagan* (Ithaca, N.Y.: Cornell University Press, 1983), p. 213.

30. Robert S. McElvaine, "Reagan's Mellon Slices," *New York Times*, May 21, 1981; Leuchtenburg, *In the Shadow of FDR*, pp. 211, 230.

31. Robert S. McElvaine, "Roosevelt and Reagan," *Christian Century*, 99 (May 12, 1982), pp. 556–58; Lou Cannon, *Reagan* (New York: Putnam, 1982), p. 18; David McCullough, "The Legacy: The President They Can't Forget," *Parade*, January 31, 1982, pp. 4–6.

32. Editorial, "Reagan's Year," *Wall Street Journal*, July 14, 1986; "Yankee Doodle Magic," *Time*, July 7, 1986, pp. 12–16; TRB, "Blurred Vision," *New Republic*, August 4, 1986, p. 4.

33. Ferguson and Rogers, "Myth of America's Turn to the Right," p. 51.

34. Brady and Hurley, "Prospects for Contemporary Realignment," pp. 64–65.

35. Walter Lippmann, *Drift and Mastery* (New York: Mitchell Kennerly, 1914; rpt., Englewood Cliffs, N.J.: Prentice-Hall, 1961), p. 135; Robert S. McElvaine, *The Great Depression: America, 1929–1941* (New York: Times Books, 1984), p. 8.

36. Russell Baker, *Growing Up* (New York: Congdon & Weed, 1982), p. 91.

37. Richard Norton Smith, *An Uncommon Man: The Triumph of Herbert Hoover* (New York: Simon & Schuster, 1984), p. 332.

38. David S. Broder, "Reagan, Choice of a New Generation," *Washington Post National Weekly Edition*, May 20, 1985.

39. Jeffrey L. Pasley and Adam Paul Weisman, "He's Back," *New Republic*, January 19, 1987; *Wall Street Journal*, December 5, 1986.

40. John E. Chubb, William H. Flanigan, and Nancy H. Zingale, *Partisan Realignment* (Beverly Hills, Calif.: Sage, 1980), p. 166; Brady and Hurley, "Prospects for Contemporary Realignment," p. 66.

41. *New York Times*, May 15, 1985.

42. William Schneider, "Half a Realignment," *New Republic*, December 3, 1984, p. 22.

43. Kevin Phillips, "Hubris on the Right," *New York Times Magazine*, May 12, 1985, p. 48.

CHAPTER 2

1. Editorial, "The Center Rediscovered: 'Liberal' Is No Longer a Dirty Word," *New York Times*, November 4, 1982.

2. William Schneider, "What the Democrats Must Do," *New Republic*, March 11, 1985, p. 16.

3. TRB, "Democrats in Oz," *New Republic*, April 1, 1985, p. 6.
4. *New York Times*, March 30, 1985; Edward M. Kennedy, speech at the John F. Kennedy Presidential Conference, Hofstra University, Hempstead, N.Y., March 29, 1985; Gary Hart, "Toward True Patriotism: A New Course for the 1980s," speech at Faneuil Hall, Boston, February 14, 1985; Hobart Rowen, "Democratic Disarray," *Washington Post National Weekly Edition*, April 1, 1985.
5. Franklin D. Roosevelt in the *New York World*, December 3, 1925, as quoted in Frank Freidel, *Franklin D. Roosevelt: The Ordeal* (Boston: Little, Brown, 1954), p. 199.
6. TRB, "Democrats in Oz."
7. *New York Times*, February 16, 1985.
8. Hart, "Toward True Patriotism"; David S. Broder, "Have Democrats Lost Direction?" *Clarion-Ledger* (Jackson, Miss.), March 3, 1985.
9. Timothy Noah, "10 Political Words That Dare Not Speak Their Name," *New York Times*, November 19, 1986.
10. As quoted in Charles L. Wallis, *The Treasure Chest* (New York: Harper & Row, 1965), p. 175.
11. Milton Viorst, *Liberalism: A Guide to Its Past, Present and Future in American Politics* (New York: Avon, 1963), p. 12.
12. Robert S. McElvaine, "Where Have All the Liberals Gone?" *Texas Quarterly*, 19 (Autumn 1976), pp. 202–13.
13. Viorst, *Liberalism*, pp. 12–16.
14. Samuel I. Rosenman (ed.), *The Public Papers and Addresses of Franklin D. Roosevelt* (New York: Russell & Russell, 1938–50), II, 11–16.
15. *New York Times*, January 21, 1981.
16. Warren E. Miller (ed.), *American National Election Study, 1980* (Ann Arbor: Inter-University Consortium for Political & Social Research, 1982), I, 220–21; Thomas Ferguson and Joel Rogers, "The Myth of America's Turn to the Right," *Atlantic Monthly*, May 1986, p. 45.
17. "Kennedy Remembered," *Newsweek*, November 28, 1983, p. 64.
18. Kenneth E. John, " 'Don't Tax You, Don't Tax Me, Tax That Fellow Behind the Tree,' " *Washington Post National Weekly Edition*, May 6, 1985.
19. Christopher Jencks, "How Poor Are the Poor?" *New York Review of Books*, May 6, 1985, p. 41.
20. Hugh Heclo, *The Development of Welfare States in Europe and America* (New Brunswick, N.J.: Transaction, 1981), p. 403.
21. John Logue, "The Welfare State: Victim of Its Success," *Daedalus*, 108 (Fall 1979), pp. 69–87.
22. George Gilder, "Welfare State Promotes What It's Supposed to Cure," *U.S. News and World Report*, April 6, 1981, p. 53.
23. Chuck Lane, "The Manhattan Project," *New Republic*, March 25, 1985, pp. 14–15.
24. Charles Murray, *Losing Ground: American Social Policy, 1950–1980* (New York: Basic, 1984), p. 9.
25. Ibid., pp. 156–64.
26. Robert Kuttner, "Declaring War on the War on Poverty," *Washington Post*

Book World, November 25, 1984, p. 4; Robert Greenstein, "Losing Faith in 'Losing Ground,'" *New Republic*, March 25, 1985, pp. 12–13.

27. Murray, *Losing Ground*, pp. 160, 157–58.
28. Ibid., p. 165, Figure 12.1.
29. Greenstein, "Losing Faith," pp. 13–16.
30. Jencks, "How Poor Are the Poor?" p. 43, Table 2.
31. Greenstein, "Losing Faith," p. 16; Jencks, "How Poor Are the Poor?" p. 45; David Ellwood and Mary Jo Bane, *The Impact of AFDC on Family Structure and Living Arrangements* (Cambridge, Mass.: Kennedy School of Government, Harvard University, 1984); Richard C. Coe and Greg J. Duncan, "Welfare: Promoting Poverty or Progress?" *Wall Street Journal*, May 15, 1985.
32. Jencks, "How Poor Are the Poor?" p. 45.
33. "The Boxer," lyrics by Paul Simon (1969), on Simon and Garfunkel, *Bridge over Troubled Water* (Columbia, 1970).
34. Alfred Diamant, Bloomington, Ind., letter to the editor, *Washington Post National Weekly Edition*, May 13, 1985.
35. Meg Greenfield, as quoted in Lane, "Manhattan Project," p. 14.
36. Lane, "Manhattan Project," pp. 14–15.
37. *Clarion-Ledger/Jackson Daily News*, May 5, 1985.
38. John E. Schwarz, *America's Hidden Success: A Reassessment of Twenty Years of Public Policy* (New York: Norton, 1983), pp. 44–45.
39. Jencks, "How Poor Are the Poor?" p. 42, Table 1; *Statistical Abstract of the United States, 1984*; Schwarz, *America's Hidden Success*, pp. 47–48.
40. Greenstein, "Losing Faith," p. 17; Jencks, "How Poor Are the Poor?" p. 42, Table 1; *Statistical Abstract, 1984*.
41. Jencks, "How Poor Are the Poor?" p. 43, Table 2.
42. As quoted in Ernest R. House, Urbana-Champaign, Ill., letter to the editor, *New Republic*, May 20, 1985, pp. 2, 41; Schwarz, *America's Hidden Success*, pp. 32, 56; *New York Times*, September 11, 1984.
43. *New York Times*, May 23, 1985; *Clarion-Ledger*, June 4, 1985.
44. *New York Times*, February 27, 1985; Michael Harrington, "Reagan Worsens Poverty," *New York Times*, August 29, 1984.
45. Seymour Martin Lipset, "The Economy, Elections, and Public Opinion," *Tocqueville Review*, Fall-Winter 1983, pp. 431–69; Barry Sussman, "President's Popularity High Despite Doubts on Policies," *Washington Post*, January 20, 1985; CBS News/News York Times Poll, "Post-Election Poll, November 8–14, 1984," as quoted in Seymour Martin Lipset, "The Elections, the Economy and Public Opinion: 1984," *PS*, 18 (Winter 1985), pp. 28–30.
46. As quoted in Viorst, *Liberalism*, p. vii.
47. Author's interview with Sen. Edward M. Kennedy (D, Mass.), Washington, D.C., February 27, 1986; author's interview with Gov. Mario M. Cuomo (D, N.Y.), New York, January 21, 1986.
48. Adam Clymer, "A Liberal by Any Other Name May Get More Votes," *New York Times*, November 24, 1985.
49. Kennedy interview; author's interview with Sen. Gary Hart (D, Colo.), Wash-

ington, D.C., September 12, 1985; author's interview with Rep. Tony Coelho (D, Calif.), Washington, D.C., July 17, 1985.

50. *Diner* (1982, directed by Barry Levinson, MGM/United Artists); Cuomo interview; Arthur Levine, *When Dreams and Heroes Died: A Portrait of Today's College Student* (San Francisco: Jossey-Bass, 1983), pp. 103–15.

51. Mario M. Cuomo, speech at Harvard University Class Day, Cambridge, Mass., June 5, 1985; Cuomo, commencement address, Stanford University, Stanford, Calif., June 16, 1985.

52. Author's interview with Alvin From, Washington, D.C., January 22, 1986; author's interview with Rep. Patricia Schroeder (D, Colo.), Washington, D.C., September 12, 1985; Hart interview; Kennedy, speech at Hofstra University; Hart, "Toward True Patriotism."

53. Hart interview.

54. Author's interview with Joseph L. Rauh, Jr., Washington, D.C., June 21, 1985; Coelho interview; author's interview with Rev. Jesse L. Jackson, Little Rock, Ark., March 22, 1986; Cuomo, Stanford address.

55. Author's interview with Rep. Richard Gephardt (D, Mo.), Washington, D.C., February 26, 1986; author's interview with Sen. Lawton Chiles (D, Fla.), Washington, D.C., February 26, 1986; From interview; Kennedy interview; author's interview with Richard Goodwin, Bourne, Mass., July 8, 1985.

56. Hart interview; From interview; author's interview with Rep. Barney Frank (D, Mass.), Washington, D.C., July 17, 1985; Jackson interview.

57. Kennedy interview.

58. Author's interview with Gov. Bill Clinton (D, Ark.), Little Rock, Ark., April 17, 1986; author's interview with Gov. Michael Dukakis (D, Mass.), Boston, May 10, 1986; author's interview with Arthur Schlesinger, Jr., New York, July 15, 1985; Mario Cuomo, speech at the Henry Gonzalez Dinner, San Antonio, Tex., January 18, 1986.

59. Dukakis interview; Clinton interview; Richard Reeves, "Bradley Still Practicing Politics," *Clarion-Ledger*, July 10, 1986; *New York Times*, January 2, 1983; Mario M. Cuomo, "A Case for the Democrats, 1984: A Tale of Two Cities," keynote address to the Democratic national convention, San Francisco, July 16, 1984; Cuomo interview.

60. Jackson interview; Dukakis interview; Charles S. Robb, speech at the Lyndon B. Johnson Presidential Conference, Hofstra University, Hempstead, N.Y., April 12, 1986; *New York Times*, April 13, 1986; Clinton interview; author's interview with Sen. Christopher Dodd (D, Conn.), Washington, D.C., January 28, 1986.

CHAPTER 3

1. Editorial, "Mirrors and Mr. Reagan," *New York Times*, November 15, 1981.

2. Lester C. Thurow, *The Zero-Sum Society: Distribution and the Possibilities for Economic Change* (New York: Basic, 1980; Penguin, 1981), p. 9.

3. William Greider, "The Education of David Stockman," *Atlantic Monthly*, December 1981, pp. 46–47.

4. James Tobin, "Reaganomics and Economics," *New York Review of Books*,

December 3, 1981; Robert Kuttner, *The Economic Illusion: False Choices Between Prosperity and Social Justice* (Boston: Houghton Mifflin, 1984), p. 2.

5. Greider, "Education of David Stockman"; Robert Lekachman, *Greed Is Not Enough: Reaganomics* (New York: Pantheon, 1982), pp. 66–68.

6. Robert S. McElvaine, "Coolidge—What Better Model?" *Boston Globe*, June 27, 1981; Ronnie Dugger, *On Reagan: The Man and His Presidency* (New York: McGraw-Hill, 1983), p. 103.

7. Robert S. McElvaine, *The Great Depression: America, 1929–1941* (New York: Times Books, 1984), pp. 25–50.

8. Kevin P. Phillips, "The Era of Republican Ascendancy May Already Have Ended," *Washington Post National Weekly Edition*, July 28, 1986; George Anders, "Déjà Vu? The Stock Market's Surge Has Some Seeking Historical Clues," *Wall Street Journal*, April 1, 1986; Lester C. Thurow, "The 20's and 30's Can Happen Again," *New York Times*, January 22, 1986; Robert Lekachman, "The Roaring Eighties," *Harper's Magazine*, August 1986, pp. 20–22; Flora Lewis, "Money Isn't Economics," *New York Times*, December 12, 1985; *New York Times*, July 27, 1986; U.S. Dept. of Commerce, Bureau of the Census, *Current Population Reports*, P-60, No. 120 and No. 149.

9. Thomas Ferguson and Joel Rogers, "The Myth of America's Turn to the Right," *Atlantic Monthly*, May 1986, pp. 43–53; *New York Times*, October 15, 1984, July 27, 1986.

10. As quoted in Peter N. Carroll, *It Seemed Like Nothing Happened: The Tragedy and Promise of America in the 1970s* (New York: Holt, Rinehart & Winston, 1982), p. 129.

11. Barry Bluestone and Bennett Harrison, *The De-Industrialization of America* (New York: Basic, 1982), p. 97; *New York Times*, October 15, 1984.

12. *New York Times*, April 6, 1985.

13. TRB, "Blurred Vision," *New Republic*, August 4, 1986.

14. Robert J. Samuelson, "Inflation's Stubborn Hangover," *Newsweek,* August 26, 1985, p. 49.

15. Author's interview with Rep. Morris Udall (D, Ariz.), Washington, D.C., July 16, 1985; author's interview with Gov. Bill Clinton (D, Ark.), Little Rock, Ark., April 17, 1986; author's interview with Arthur Schlesinger, Jr., New York, July 15, 1985.

16. William H. Gray, III, "Compassion Without Bankruptcy," *New York Times*, May 29, 1986.

17. *New York Times*, July 11, 1985; Greider, "Education of David Stockman," p. 32.

18. Haynes Johnson, "How Reagan Won by Losing," *Washington Post National Weekly Edition*, May 13, 1985; Udall interview.

19. As quoted in Dee Brown, *Bury My Heart at Wounded Knee* (New York: Holt, Rinehart & Winston, 1970; paperback ed., Bantam, 1972), photo insert following p. 222.

20. Author's interview with Sen. Dale Bumpers (D, Ark.), Washington, D.C., January 23, 1986.

21. "Back to the Future, Again," *Time*, February 17, 1986; "Budget Fog Begins to Clear," *U.S. News and World Report*, May 26, 1986; Jim Fain, "Chicken

Little and the Deficit Doom," *St. Petersburg Times*, August 6, 1985; Billy Skelton, " 'Reagan on Rushmore' Plan May Face Granite-Like Resistance," *Clarion-Ledger/Jackson Daily News* (Jackson, Miss.), September 8, 1985.

22. Paul Craig Roberts, "Spending Rate More Important," *Clarion-Ledger/Jackson Daily News*, August 18, 1985.

23. Author's interview with Sen. Lloyd Bentsen (D, Tex.), Washington, D.C., September 12, 1985.

24. *New York Times*, July 27, 1986; Jeffrey E. Garten, "America's Economic House of Cards," *New York Times*, August 12, 1985; Barry Bosworth, "Public Still Too Unconcerned," *Clarion-Ledger/Jackson Daily News*, August 18, 1985; editorial, "Deficits Breed Deficits," *St. Petersburg Times*, August 4, 1985; Clyde H. Farnsworth, "Suddenly, the International Debt Crisis Is Close to Home," *New York Times*, March 3, 1985; Clyde H. Farnsworth, "U.S. Trade Deficit Rose to a Record in 1985," *New York Times*, January 31, 1986; Clinton interview.

25. *Atlanta Constitution*, June 14, 1985.

26. As quoted in Dugger, *On Reagan*, pp. 102–03.

27. Calvin Coolidge, as quoted in Jude Wanniski, *The Way the World Works: How Economies Fail—and Succeed* (New York: Basic, 1978), p. 120.

28. Ibid.

29. Edwin Meese, as quoted in Dugger, *On Reagan*, p. 113; Jack Kemp, as quoted in *Clarion-Ledger*, August 5, 1986.

30. Dugger, *On Reagan*, p. 107.

31. William Safire, "Only Thing to Fear," *New York Times*, August 22, 1985.

32. George F. Will, "What about Tax Reform?" *Clarion-Ledger*, May 30, 1985; Carl Rowan, "Social Change Via Tax-Reform Plan," *Atlanta Constitution*, June 7, 1985; *New York Times*, May 27, 1985; editorial, "Sneak Attack on Campaign Finance," *New York Times*, June 3, 1985; Paul Blustein, "The Reagan Tax Plan: Economics or Ideology?" *Wall Street Journal*, July 1, 1985.

33. Lekachman, *Greed Is Not Enough*, p. 58; Safire, "Only Thing to Fear"; Will, "What about Tax Reform?"; Jacob K. Javits, "The Treasury's Trojan Horse," *New York Times*, May 14, 1985; Erwin M. Yoder, Jr., "Demagoguery over a Deduction," *Washington Post*, June 18, 1985.

34. Mario M. Cuomo, testimony before the Committee on Ways and Means, U.S. House of Representatives, July 17, 1985.

35. *New York Times*, May 17, 1985, May 27, 1985; Tom Wicker, "Buchanan Opens Fire," *New York Times*, May 21, 1985; Kenneth E. John, "Don't Tax You, Don't Tax Me, Tax That Fellow Behind the Tree," *Washington Post National Weekly Edition*, May 6, 1985; Robert S. McIntyre, "Get On Board," *New Republic*, June 2, 1986; Walter W. Heller, letter to the editor, *New York Times*, August 5, 1986; "Devoted to Deductions," *Washington Post National Weekly Edition*, August 4, 1986.

36. Kuttner, *The Economic Illusion*, pp. 94–97.

37. Bob Kuttner, "The Free Trade Fallacy," *New Republic*, March 28, 1983, pp. 16–21.

38. Gary Hart, *A New Democracy: A Democratic Vision for the 1980's and Beyond* (New York: Morrow, 1983), p. 51.

39. Schlesinger interview.

40. Hart, *A New Democracy*, pp. 92–93.
41. Kuttner, "Free Trade Fallacy"; Robert E. Reich, *The Next American Frontier* (New York: Times Books, 1983), pp. 140–41; Anthony Lewis, "Angry at Success," *New York Times*, August 12, 1985.
42. Thurow, *Zero-Sum Society*, p. 7.
43. Reich, *Next American Frontier*, pp. 234, 239–40; Stuart E. Eisenstadt and William Spring, "Let's Give the Unemployed New Skills, Not Just Handouts," *Washington Post National Weekly Edition*, December 3, 1984; Hobart Rowen, "Businesses for the Jobless," *Washington Post National Weekly Edition*, May 13, 1985.
44. Thurow, *Zero-Sum Society*, p. 7; Reich, *Next American Frontier*, pp. 240–41.
45. Kuttner, *Economic Illusion*, pp. 13, 46–48; Thurow, *Zero-Sum Society*, pp. 7–8.
46. Reich, *Next American Frontier*, pp. 263–67.
47. Ibid., pp. 256–60.
48. John E. Schwarz, *America's Hidden Success: A Reassessment of Twenty Years of Public Policy* (New York: Norton, 1983), pp. 87–93; Lekachman, *Greed Is Not Enough*, p. 62.
49. Schwarz, *America's Hidden Success*, pp. 108–09, 112.
50. Bluestone and Harrison, *Deindustrialization of America*, p. 5.
51. Schwarz, *America's Hidden Success*, pp. 124–28, 139–40.
52. Kuttner, *Economic Illusion*, p. 277.
53. Author's calculations, from U.S. Dept. of Commerce, Bureau of Economic Analysis, *The National Income and Product Accounts of the United States, 1929–1976*, Table 8.1, pp. 376–79, and U.S. Dept. of Commerce, Bureau of the Census, *Statistical Abstract of the United States, 1986*, Table 720, p. 432. The year in which the White House changed parties was calculated with the party of the departing president, since economic performance in such years was probably more influenced by his policies than by those of the incoming president. If those years are included with the records of the incoming president, the results change only slightly: the Democrats' average would be 5.0% and the Republicans' 0.96%.
54. Benjamin Franklin, as quoted in Samuel Eliot Morison and Henry Steele Commager, *The Growth of the American Republic* (New York: Oxford University Press, 1962), I, 281.

CHAPTER 4

1. Author's interview with Gov. Bruce Babbitt (D, Ariz.), Phoenix, March 20, 1986; Bruce Babbitt, "The Soul of a Democrat," Chubb Lecture, Timothy Dwight College, Yale University, December 4, 1985; Michael Shanahan, "Gadfly: Arizona's Babbitt Tilts at Traditional Democratic Values," *Sacramento Bee*, March 9, 1986; Theodore J. Lowi, "What's New about Neoliberals?" *Washington Post Book World*, June 16, 1985.
2. Author's interview with Gov. Mario M. Cuomo (D, N.Y.), New York, January 21, 1986; Mario Cuomo, speech to Black Ministers' Association, Rochester, N.Y., August 16, 1982, in Mario M. Cuomo, *Diaries of Mario M. Cuomo: The Campaign for Governor* (New York: Random House, 1984), p.

448; author's interview with Sen. Joseph R. Biden, Jr. (D, Del.), Washington, D.C., September 12, 1985; Joseph R. Biden, Jr., Jefferson–Jackson Day Address, Jackson, Miss., March 1, 1986.

3. Author's interview with Gov. Charles S. Robb (D, Va.), Fairfax, Va., January 29, 1986; author's interview with Sen. Gary Hart (D, Colo.), Washington, D.C., September 12, 1985; Gary Hart, "Toward True Patriotism: A New Course for the 1980s," speech at Faneuil Hall, Boston, February 14, 1985; Lee Iacocca, with William Novak, *Iacocca: An Autobiography* (New York: Bantam, 1984), pp. 231–32.

4. Robert S. McElvaine, "Liberals Return to the Flag," *New York Times*, September 2, 1984.

5. George F. Will, "Watchdogging Institutions," *Clarion-Ledger* (Jackson, Miss.), May 23, 1985; TRB, "Democrats in Oz," *New Republic*, April 1, 1985, p. 2.

6. Richard Reeves, "Majority Exercising Tyranny," *Clarion-Ledger*, May 12, 1985; Don Edwards, "The FBI's 'Friendly Visits,' " *Washington Post National Weekly Edition*, May 13, 1985; Anthony Lewis, "Is This America?", *New York Times*, February 10, 1987; Anthony Lewis, "Yearning to Breathe Free," *New York Times*, February 13, 1987; Charles Stewart, III, Cambridge, Mass., letter to the editor, *New York Times*, May 28, 1986.

7. "A Newsweek Poll: Sex Laws," *Newsweek*, July 14, 1986, p. 38; *New York Times*, June 12, 1986.

8. William Safire, "Prove Yourself Innocent," *New York Times*, August 11, 1986; *New York Times*, September 16, 1985, December 3, 1985.

9. Ellen Goodman, "Fight over Family Planning Exported to Third World," *Clarion-Ledger*, September 3, 1985.

10. Editorial, "Senator Moynihan and the Children," *New York Times*, April 9, 1985; Daniel Patrick Moynihan, *Family and Nation* (San Diego: Harcourt Brace Jovanovich, 1986); editorial, "Who's Watching the Kids?" *New York Times*, July 12, 1985; Sylvia Ann Hewlett,"Feminism's Next Challenge: Support for Motherhood," *New York Times*, June 17, 1986; James Reston, "Broken Families: Troubling Problem That Concerns Us All," *Clarion-Ledger*, February 19, 1986; Fred M. Hechinger, "Alarm over Alienation of the Young," *New York Times*, March 25, 1986; author's interview with Rep. Patricia Schroeder (D, Colo.), Washington, D.C., September 12, 1985; Neal Peirce, "Day Care Fast Becoming Important Benefit for Employees," *Clarion-Ledger*, January 7, 1986; *New York Times*, November 11, 1985; Miriam Stein, "Helping Needy Infants," *Boston Globe*, May 11, 1986.

11. Moynihan, *Family and Nation*, p. 173; *Arkansas Gazette* (Little Rock), March 22, 1986; *Arkansas Democrat* (Little Rock), March 22, 1986; author's interview with Rev. Jesse L. Jackson, Little Rock, Ark., March 22, 1986.

12. Editorial, "The Worth of Women's Work," *New York Times*, May 13, 1985; Gary Hart, *A New Democracy: A Democratic Vision for the 1980's and Beyond* (New York: Morrow, 1983), pp. 107–08; Thomas Ferguson and Joel Rogers, "The Myth of America's Turn to the Right," *Atlantic Monthly*, May 1986, p. 46; *New York Times*, May 15, 1985; Schroeder interview.

13. William Raspberry, "Those Who View Society with Colorblind Eyes See White," *Clarion-Ledger*, February 14, 1986; Ronnie Dugger, *On Reagan: The Man and His Presidency* (New York: McGraw-Hill, 1983), pp. 197–98; Glenn C. Loury, "A New American Dilemma," *New Republic*, December 31, 1984, pp. 14–18; William Raspberry, "Jobless Wasteland," *Washington Post*, January 27, 1986.

14. Harry L. Hopkins, *Spending to Save: The Complete Story of Relief* (New York: Norton, 1936), p. 109.

15. Jackson interview; Babbitt interview; Neal Peirce, "Welfare Changes Proposed," *Clarion-Ledger*, December 22, 1985; author's interview with Gov. Michael Dukakis (D, Mass.), Boston, May 10, 1986; Kenneth A. Couch, "How Good Is ET in Massachusetts?" *Washington Post National Weekly Edition*, March 31, 1986; Neal Peirce, "Welfare Task Force May Try to Foist More onto the States," *Clarion-Ledger*, March 31, 1986; Fred Barnes, "Dukakis Rising," *New Republic*, April 14, 1986, pp. 13–15; Shawn Doherty, "The Duke Turns Things Around in 'Taxachusetts,'" *Newsweek*, March 24, 1986, p. 30; Renee Loth, "The D Team," *Boston Globe Magazine*, May 11, 1986; Charles M. Atkins, Commissioner, Massachusetts Department of Public Welfare, letter to the editor, *Washington Post National Weekly Edition*, April 14, 1986.

16. Nicholas Lemann, "The Origins of the Underclass," *Atlantic Monthly*, June 1986, pp.31–41; Mickey Kaus, "The Work Ethic State," *New Republic*, July 7, 1986, pp. 22–33; William Raspberry, "Welfare Trap Should Be Confronted," *Clarion-Ledger*, October 22, 1985; William Raspberry, "Stressing Poor's 'Deficiency' Self-Defeating," *Clarion-Ledger*, January 7, 1986; William Raspberry, "Let's Re-evaluate Welfare," *Clarion-Ledger*, February 21, 1986; William Raspberry, "Charity Blamed for Poverty," *Clarion-Ledger*, June 17, 1986; editorial, "The Work and Fairness of Workfare, *New York Times*, March 24, 1986; Ellen Goodman, "Same Old Song about Poverty," *Clarion-Ledger*, February 21, 1986.

17. *St. Petersburg Times*, August 4, 1985; Alan K. Campbell, "Restoring Teachers' Dignity," *New York Times*, August 28, 1985; James J. Kilpatrick, "New Education Report Emphasizes Preschool, Junior High," *Clarion-Ledger*, September 19, 1985; Amy E. Schwartz, "Excellence Cuts," *New Republic*, April 1, 1985, pp. 15–17; A. Bartlett Giamatti, "Short-changing Education," *New York Times*, April 24, 1985; Richard Reeves, "Education Cuts a Social Blow," *Clarion-Ledger*, March 14, 1985.

18. Michael Harrington, *The Other America: Poverty in the United States* (New York: Macmillan, 1962; rev. ed., Penguin, 1981), p. 211; *Clarion-Ledger*, May 6, 1985; editorial, "Making Sense of Gun Control," *New York Times*, July 9, 1985; Paul Simon, *The Once and Future Democrats: Strategies for Change* (New York: Continuum, 1982), p. 107; William Safire, "Friendly Disposition, *New York Times*, May 13, 1985; Sydney H. Schanberg, "Color Accountability Gray," *New York Times*, May 14, 1985.

19. Dugger, *On Reagan*, pp. 72, 77, 78, 91; *St. Petersburg Times*, August 4, 1985; *New York Times*, September 19, 1985; *Washington Post National Weekly*

Edition, December 10, 1984; author's interview with Rep. Morris Udall (D, Ariz.), Washington, D.C., July 16, 1985.

20. As quoted in Dugger, *On Reagan*, p. 299.
21. Ellen Goodman, "People Keep Getting Hungry," *Clarion-Ledger*, April 16, 1985; "Infant Mortality 'Southern Problem,' " *Clarion-Ledger*, May 20, 1985; *Washington Post*, June 21, 1985; Simon, *Once and Future Democrats*, pp. 56–57; *New York Times*, August 15, 1985; editorial, "Federal Spending That Works," *New York Times*, August 21, 1985.
22. Henry Fairlie, "Farmers and the Land," *New Republic*, April 1, 1985, pp. 14–15; author's interview with Sen. Paul Simon (D, Ill.), Washington, D.C., September 13, 1985; Simon, *Once and Future Democrats*, pp. 95–99.

CHAPTER 5

1. Author's interview with Sen. Dale Bumpers (D, Ark.), Washington, D.C., January 23, 1986; Les Aspin, "A Democratic Defense Policy: Defense Without Nonsense," speech delivered before the Coalition for a Democratic Majority, Washington, D.C., April 17, 1985; author's interview with Rep. Les Aspin (D, Wis.), Washington, D.C., February 27, 1986.
2. Regis Debray, as quoted in Richard Reeves, "Jerry Brown Offers 'New Perspectives' Worth Reading," *Atlanta Constitution*, July 29, 1986.
3. Anthony Lewis, "The Urge to Intervene," *New York Times*, December 12, 1985; Christoper Layne, "The Real Conservative Agenda," *Foreign Policy*, 61 (Winter 1985–86), pp. 73–93.
4. Jonathan Yardley, "Conservative Smugness," *Washington Post National Weekly Edition*, May 13, 1985.
5. Philip Geylin, "Voting Tough," *Washington Post*, July 16, 1985; Paul Slansky, "Reaganisms in Review," *New Republic*, January 6 and 13, 1986, p. 13.
6. Charles Krauthammer, "The Poverty of Realism," *New Republic*, February 17, 1986.
7. Dwight D. Eisenhower, as quoted in Archibald L. Gilles, "Must America Be Ugly?" *New York Times*, February 27, 1985.
8. *New York Times*, April 1, 1985.
9. David S. Broder, "A New Look for Democrats," *Washington Post*, July 17, 1985; Aspin interview.
10. Author's interview with Sen. Joseph R. Biden, Jr. (D, Del.), Jackson, Miss., March 1, 1986; author's interview with Gov. Charles S. Robb (D, Va.), Fairfax, Va., January 29, 1986; *New York Times*, June 13, 1986; author's interview with Sen. Gary Hart (D. Colo.), Washington, D.C., September 12, 1985.
11. James R. Dickenson, "The Democrats' Defense Problem," *St. Petersburg Times*, August 1, 1985; Gary Hart with William S. Lind, *America Can Win: The Case for Military Reform* (Bethesda, Md.: Adler & Adler, 1986), p. xiii; "Senator Hart and American Foreign Policy," *Congressional Record*, 99th Congress, 2d Session, Vol. 132, No. 85, June 20, 1986.
12. Elie Wiesel, remarks, April 19, 1985, transcript in *Washington Post*, April 20, 1985.

13. *Apocalpyse Now* (1979, Francis Coppola, United Artists).
14. Sydney H. Schanberg, " 'Memory Is the Answer,' " *New York Times*, April 23, 1985; Tom Wicker, "Who's Afraid of What?" *New York Times*, May 17, 1985.
15. Henry Steele Commager, "Nations Aren't Innocent," *New York Times*, June 27, 1985.
16. Author's interview with Patricia Derian, Washington, D.C., June 18, 1985.
17. Stephen J. Solarz, "It's Time for the Democrats to Be Tough-Minded," *New York Times*, June 20, 1985; Biden interview, March 1, 1986.
18. Derian interview.
19. Ibid.
20. *New York Times*, December 16, 1985; author's interview with Rep. Jim Wright (D, Tex.), Washington, D.C., February 27, 1986.
21. Donald Mann, President, Negative Population Growth, letters to the editor, *New York Times*, May 17, December 16, 1985.
22. *New York Times*, February 5, 1986, May 21, 1985.
23. Richard J. Barnet, "America Goes It Alone," *New York Times*, October 23, 1985.
24. Editorial, "Bad Ideas and Good," *New Republic*, December 3, 1984, p. 6.
25. Gregory A. Fossedal, "A Morality Test for South Africa's Opposition," *New York Times*, February 4, 1986.
26. Anthony Lewis, "Time and South Africa," *New York Times*, October 24, 1985; Michael Calabrese, "Time to Talk with Black South Africa," *New York Times*, September 4, 1985; Andrew J. Glass, "The Wrong Side of the Struggle," *St. Petersburg Times*, August 6, 1985.
27. Asa Baber, "Smack in the Middle of a Low-Intensity Conflict," *Playboy*, June 1986, pp. 104–06, 191–96.
28. Thomas Ferguson and Joel Rogers, "The Myth of America's Turn to the Right," *Atlantic Monthly*, May 1986, p. 48.
29. Paul Taylor, "On Defense, It's No More Mr. Nice Guy," *Washington Post National Weekly Edition*, April 14, 1986.
30. William Safire, "Gary Gets Engaged," *New York Times*, June 23, 1986; Biden interview, March 1, 1986.
31. Ronald Reagan, as quoted in Ronnie Dugger, *On Reagan: The Man and His Presidency* (New York: McGraw-Hill, 1983), p. 395; Aspin interview.
32. Fred Barnes, "Broken Defense," *New Republic*, July 1, 1985, p. 11.
33. Arthur Schlesinger, Jr., "Closing Down the Pentagon Follies," *New York Times*, September 28, 1984.
34. Editorial, "The Gun That Shoots Crooked," *New York Times*, August 28, 1985.
35. Barnes, "Broken Defense," p. 10; *New York Times*, May 14, 1985; Barry Sussman, "Voters Don't Back MX," *Washington Post National Weekly Edition*, April 18, 1985; Paul Taylor and Kenneth E. John, "Butter 1, Guns 0," *Washington Post National Weekly Edition*, March 3, 1986; author's interview with Sen. William Proxmire (D, Wis.), Washington, D.C., January 24, 1986.
36. Editorial, "Ike's Lesson, Unlearned," *New York Times*, January 21, 1986.

37. Editorial, "Desperately Seeking Truman," *New York Times*, June 19, 1985.
38. Robb interview; author's interview with Sen. Lawton Chiles (D, Fla.), Washington, D.C., February 27, 1986; author's interview with Rep. Richard Gephardt (D, Mo.), Washington, D.C., February 26, 1986; Jeffrey Record, "Reagan's Strategy Gap," *New Republic*, October 29, 1984, p. 18.
39. *New York Times*, October 7, 1985.
40. As quoted in Record, "Reagan's Strategy Gap," p.21.
41. Bumpers interview.
42. Aspin, "Defense Without Nonsense."
43. Bumpers interview.
44. Sen. William Proxmire (D, Wis.), speech at Millsaps College, Jackson, Miss., October 28, 1986; author's questioning of Adm. Richard Truly, associate administrator of NASA, Jackson, Miss., November 21, 1986.
45. *Atlanta Constitution*, June 6, 1985; Robert McNamara and Hans Bethe, "Reducing the Risk of Nuclear War," *Atlantic Monthly*, July 1985, pp. 43–47; *New York Times*, December 17, 1985.
46. Flora Lewis, "Soviet S.D.I. Fears," *New York Times*, March 6, 1986.
47. *New York Times*, December 17, 1985.
48. Anthony Lewis, "Silent Spring," *New York Times*, May 29, 1986; Paul Newman, "The 'G' in G.O.P. Is for Glitch," *New York Times*, February 27, 1986.
49. Flora Lewis, "A 'Star Wars' Cover-Up," *New York Times*, December 3, 1985; Richard Reeves, "Public Debate Being Hampered by Tampered-with Facts," *Clarion-Ledger*, January 2, 1986.
50. Richard Reeves, "Technology Isn't Perfect," *Clarion-Ledger*, May 12, 1986.
51. William Raspberry, "The Pentagon Budget Is Big Enough," *Washington Post*, February 28, 1986.
52. Barnet, "America Goes It Alone."
53. Anthony Lewis, "The Military-Industrial Complex," *New York Times*, November 21, 1985.
54. Tom Wicker, "The Wrong Race," *New York Times*, April 11, 1986; Mark O. Hatfield, "A 'Plan' to End the Arms Race?" *New York Times*, April 15, 1986; David S. Broder, "SALT II Decision Bad on Both Foreign, Domestic Fronts," *Clarion-Ledger*, June 4, 1986; Tom Wicker, "A Dark New Identity," *New York Times*, June 6, 1986.
55. Sen. Albert Gore, Jr., Jefferson–Jackson Day Address, Jackson, Miss., April 19, 1985.
56. Eugene J. Carroll, "A Useful Nuclear Step By Moscow," *New York Times*, August 7, 1985; Flora Lewis, "Why Not a Test Ban?" *New York Times*, January 24, 1986.

CHAPTER 6

1. George F. Will, "Rap Brown Takes Islam Seriously," *Clarion-Ledger* (Jackson, Miss.), September 23, 1985.
2. William H. Chafe, *The Unfinished Journey: America Since World War II* (New York: Oxford University Press, 1986), pp. 343–80.
3. Tom Wicker, "Has Reagan Peaked?" *New York Times*, April 23, 1985; Lou

Cannon, "Anyone Have a Magic Wand? Reagan Seems to Have Lost His," *Washington Post National Weekly Edition*, May 6, 1985; David S. Broder, "A Shaken Ronald Reagan," *Washington Post National Weekly Edition*, May 13, 1985; "Reagan's Losing Streak," *Washington Post National Weekly Edition*, June 10, 1985; Jack W. Germond and Jules Witcover, "Reagan's Support Wears Thin," *St. Petersburg Times*, August 2, 1985.

4. Richard Sennett, *The Fall of Public Man* (New York: Knopf, 1977), p. 271.

5. Author's interview with Gov. Mario M. Cuomo (D, N.Y.), New York, January 21, 1986.

6. Jim Fain, "Chicken Little and the Deficit Doom," *St. Petersburg Times*, August 6, 1985; author's interview with Sen. Christopher Dodd (D, Conn.), Washington, D.C., January 28, 1986.

7. Anthony Lewis, "Reagan Creates His Own Realities," *Clarion-Ledger*, February 3, 1985; author's interview with Gov. Charles S. Robb (D, Va.), Fairfax, Va., January 29, 1986.

8. Karl E. Meyer, "The Elusive Lenin," *New York Times*, October 9, 1985; David S. Broder, "Reagan Ignores Realities," *Clarion-Ledger*, September 1, 1985; Anthony Lewis, "Vacuum at the Top," *New York Times*, October 11, 1984; Anthony Lewis, "Out to Lunch," *New York Times*, October 1, 1984; Anthony Lewis, "The Hollow Center," *New York Times*, November 24, 1986.

9. Broder, "Reagan Ignores Realities."

10. Author's interview with Sen. Gary Hart (D, Colo.), Washington, D.C., September 12, 1985.

11. Author's interview with Rep. Patricia Schroeder (D, Colo.), Washington, D.C., September 12, 1985.

12. Author's interview with Rev. Jesse Jackson, Little Rock, Ark., March 22, 1986.

13. John Kenneth Galbraith, "Reagan's 'Facts'—Artistic License," *New York Times*, September 27, 1985.

14. Michael Rogin, "Ronald Reagan: The Movie," paper presented at the annual meeting of the American Political Science Association, New Orleans, August 1985; Martin Tolchin, "How Reagan Always Gets the Best Lines," *New York Times*, September 9, 1985.

15. James Reston, "Big Things and Little Things," *New York Times*, April 17, 1985.

16. Tolchin, "How Reagan Always Gets the Best Lines"; Mark Green and Tony Kaye, "Mr. Reagan's Slippery Words," *New York Times*, July 7, 1985; Flora Lewis, "The Big Bark," *New York Times*, July 12, 1985; David R. Burton, "If Congress Is Spendthrift, Where Are Reagan's Vetoes?" *Wall Street Journal*, September 11, 1984.

17. *New York Times*, May 12, 1985; Adele Simmons, "Reagan's Silence on Abortion Terror," *New York Times*, July 29, 1985.

18. William Safire, "Access-Selling Escalating," *Clarion-Ledger*, February 19, 1986; "Peddling Influence," *Time*, March 3, 1986; "Cashing In on Reagan," *Newsweek*, March 3, 1986.

19. Author's interview with Joseph L. Rauh, Jr., Washington, D.C., June 21,

1985; Arthur M. Schlesinger, Jr., *The Cycles of American History* (Boston: Houghton Mifflin, 1986), p. 41.

20. Cuomo interview; Anthony Lewis, "Reform or Religion?" *New York Times,* May 30, 1985; Ronnie Dugger, *On Reagan: The Man and His Presidency* (New York: McGraw-Hill, 1983), p. 113; editorial, "Reckless Reaganomics," *St. Petersburg Times,* August 1, 1985; Sen. Joseph Biden, Jefferson–Jackson Day Address, Jackson, Miss., March 1, 1986; Gov. Mario Cuomo, testimony before House Ways and Means Committee, July 17, 1985; Bruce Babbitt, "The Soul of a Democrat," Chubb Lecture, Timothy Dwight College, Yale University, December 4, 1985.

21. Robert J. Samuelson, "The Myth of Reaganomics," *Newsweek,* February 24, 1986; Geoffrey Rips, "Phil Gramm's Economics of Despair," *Texas Observer,* November 8, 1985, pp. 2–4; Dodd interview.

22. Author's interview with Sen. Dale Bumpers (D, Ark.), Washington, D.C., January 23, 1986; Tom Wicker, "After Reagan, What?" *New York Times,* October 10, 1985.

23. *Wall Street Journal,* February 26, 1986; Hart interview.

24. *New York Times,* August 6, 1985; R. Emmett Tyrell, Jr., "Conservative Grumbles," *Washington Post,* July 15, 1985; Lou Cannon, "Reagan's Actions Leave Conservatives Confused," *Atlanta Journal-Constitution,* June 15, 1985; Richard Reeves, "Republicans Are Cracking Up," *Clarion-Ledger,* August 1, 1985; George F. Will, "Pat Robertson's Mustard Seed," *Newsweek,* March 3, 1986; Jerry Falwell, as quoted in Robert Lekachman, *Greed Is Not Enough: Reaganomics* (New York: Pantheon, 1982), p. 57; "Power, Glory— And Politics," *Time,* February 17, 1986.

25. Seymour Martin Lipset, "The Elections, the Economy and Public Opinion: 1984," *PS* (Winter 1985), p. 30; *New York Times,* November 24, 1985.

26. Bumpers interview; Richard Reeves, "Post-war Politics Unresolved," *Clarion-Ledger,* May 16, 1985; "With God on Our Side," lyrics by Bob Dylan, on Bob Dylan, *The Times They Are A-Changin'* (Columbia Records, 1964); Cuomo interview.

27. Robert S. Boyd, "TV Evangelist's Political Plans Stir Controversy," *Clarion-Ledger/Jackson Daily News,* March 15, 1986; "Power, Glory—And Politics"; Diane Winston, "Robertson Mixes Media Savvy, Religious Message," *News and Observer* (Raleigh, N.C.), February 18, 1985; William Saletan, "Teflon Telepreacher," *New Republic,* January 20, 1986, pp. 9–11; "Standing Tall for Moral Principles" (interview with Pat Robertson), *Time,* February 17, 1986, p. 66; Winston, "TV Preachers' Message: For God and Country"; Cuomo interview; Will, "Pat Robertson's Mustard Seed"; author's interview with Rev. Marion G. "Pat" Robertson, Jackson, Miss., June 2, 1986.

28. Rich Jaroslovsky, "Racial Purist Uses Reagan Plug," *Wall Street Journal,* September 28, 1984; *New York Times,* May 2, 1985; William Raspberry, "An 'Actively Anti-Black' Administration," *Washington Post National Weekly Edition,* May 20, 1985; editorial, "Setback for Zealotry on Civil Rights Issue," *Kennebec Journal* (Augusta, Me.), July 5, 1985; editorial, "The Point Man for a Bad Policy," *Atlanta Constitution,* June 7, 1985.

29. James Reston, "The New Hatchet Man," *New York Times,* June 19, 1985;

Patrick J. Buchanan, "The Contras Need Our Help," *Washington Post National Weekly Edition*, March 17, 1986; Haynes Johnson, "When the Truth Becomes Treachery," *St. Petersburg Times*, June 12, 1985; *St. Petersburg Times*, August 2, 1985; Richard Hofstadter, *The Paranoid Style in American Politics and Other Essays* (New York: Knopf, 1965); Paul Greenberg, "Right-Wingers Blast Shultz," *Clarion-Ledger*, August 15, 1985.

30. *New York Times*, April 17, 1985; editorial, "Stonewalling the Disabled," *New York Times*, May 15, 1985; Anthony Lewis, "Now We See It," *New York Times*, May 16, 1985; Johnson, "When the Truth Becomes Treachery."

31. Editorial, "Justice and the 'Hysterical Right,' " *Atlanta Constitution*, June 17, 1985.

32. Richard Reeves, "Group Decries 'Birth Dearth,' " *Clarion-Ledger*, March 13, 1986; Benjamin J. Wattenberg and Karl Zinsmeister, "The Birth Dearth: The Geopolitical Consequences," *Public Opinion*, December 1985–January 1986, pp. 7–13.

33. Rowland Evans and Robert Novak, "Purity Fight Produces Split in Right," *Clarion-Ledger*, August 30, 1985.

34. Thomas P. O'Neill, Jr., Alfred M. Landon Lecture on Public Issues, Kansas State University, April 22, 1985, as quoted in *New York Times*, May 3, 1985; John E. Schwarz, *America's Hidden Success: A Reassessment of Twenty Years of Public Policy* (New York: Norton, 1983), pp. 73–75.

35. Christopher Lasch, *The Culture of Narcissism: American Life in an Age of Diminishing Expectations* (New York: Norton, 1978); Peter Marin, "The New Narcissism," *Harper's Magazine*, October 1975, pp. 45–56.

36. Sidney Blumenthal, "The G.O.P. 'Me Decade,' " *New Republic*, September 17 and 24, 1984, pp. 12–15; Leon Weiseltier, "The Poor Perplex," *New Republic*, January 7 and 14, 1985, pp. 10–12.

37. " 'Individualism Has Been Allowed to Run Rampant': A Conversation with Robert Bellah," *U.S. News and World Report*, May 27, 1985; Arthur Levine, *When Dreams and Heroes Died: A Portrait of Today's College Student* (San Francisco: Jossey-Bass, 1980), pp. 103–15.

38. "Where Reaganomics Is Going Astray: Interview with Representative Jack Kemp," *U.S. News and World Report*, August 23, 1982, p. 27; Morton Kondracke, "Beyond Reagan," *New Republic*, September 10, 1984, pp. 8–11; Rowland Evans and Robert Novak, "Is He the GOP's Future?" *Reader's Digest*, June 1982, pp. 108–12; Flora Lewis, "The Gold Standard," *New York Times*, January 28, 1986.

39. Lawrence Goodwyn, *Democratic Promise: The Populist Moment in America* (New York: Oxford University Press, 1976); C. Vann Woodward, *Tom Watson: Agrarian Rebel* (New York: Oxford University Press, 1938); Irving Kristol, "The New Populism: Not to Worry," *Wall Street Journal*, July 25, 1985; *Atlanta Constitution*, June 14, 1985; Tom Teepen, "The Whipping-Boys of Politics," *Atlanta Journal and Constitution*, June 15, 1985; *Atlanta Journal and Constitution*, June 16, 1985; George F. Will, "What about Tax Reform?" *Clarion-Ledger*, May 30, 1985.

40. James MacGregor Burns, *Roosevelt: The Lion and the Fox* (New York: Harcourt, Brace, & World, 1956), pp. 235–37.

41. William Safire, "Only Thing to Fear," *New York Times*, August 22, 1985; George F. Will, "The Soul of Conservatism," *Newsweek*, November 11, 1985; "And a Happy New Year," *New Republic*, Year-end 1982, pp. 5–6; Benjamin J. Stein, "What Happened to Republicanism?" *New York Times*, January 29, 1986.
42. *New York Times*, June 24, 1985, August 21, 1985, November 25, 1985, February 2, 1986; David S. Broder, "Republican Candidates Step Up for Their First Audition," *Clarion-Ledger*, March 5, 1986; Safire, "Over Their Shoulders"; *Washington Post National Weekly Edition*, March 10, 1986.
43. Cuomo interview; author's interview with Senator Edward M. Kennedy (D, Mass.), Washington, D.C., February 27, 1986; Pierre S. du Pont, IV, as quoted in *New York Times*, June 24, 1985; Paul Taylor and Kenneth E. John, "Butter 1, Guns 0," *Washington Post National Weekly Edition*, March 3, 1986.
44. Kevin P. Phillips, "The Era of Republican Ascendancy May Already Have Ended," *Washington Post National Weekly Edition*, July 28, 1986; *New York Times*, August 5, 1986, June 29, 1986; Richard Reeves, "Zealots Bringing Down GOP," *Clarion-Ledger*, June 5, 1986; David Broder, "Conservatives Also Anxious about Aftermath of Reagan," *Clarion-Ledger*, June 30, 1986; George F. Will, "A Cold Snap Coming?" *Newsweek*, August 18, 1986, p. 64; George F. Will, "Americans Must Decide How Much Government We Want," *Clarion-Ledger*, November 20, 1986.

CHAPTER 7

1. Author's interview with Rep. Barney Frank (D, Mass.), Washington, D.C., July 17, 1985; author's interview with Alvin From, Washington, D.C., January 22, 1986; author's interview with Gov. Bruce Babbitt (D, Ariz.), Phoenix, March 20, 1986; Woodrow Wilson, as quoted in John Milton Cooper, Jr., *The Warrior and the Priest: Woodrow Wilson and Theodore Roosevelt* (Cambridge, Mass.: Harvard University Press, 1983), pp. 167, 220.
2. Dorothy Gilliam, "A Message from Blacks to the Democrats: As You Rush to the Center, You're Alienating Friends," *Washington Post National Weekly Edition*, May 19, 1986; author's interview with Rep. Richard Gephardt (D, Mo.), Washington, D.C., February 26, 1986; author's interview with Gov. Michael Dukakis (D, Mass.), Boston, May 10, 1986; William Schneider, "What the Democrats Must Do," *New Republic*, March 11, 1985, p. 17; Babbitt interview.
3. Author's interview with Sen. Edward M. Kennedy (D, Mass.), Washington, D.C., February 27, 1986; Edward M. Kennedy, speech at the John F. Kennedy Presidential Conference, Hofstra University, March 29, 1985; Mario M. Cuomo, *Diaries of Mario M. Cuomo: The Campaign for Governor* (New York: Random House, 1984), pp. 341–42; author's interview with Rev. Jesse Jackson, Little Rock, Ark. March 22, 1986.
4. *New York Times*, April 12, 1985; author's interview with Gov. Charles S. Robb (D, Va.), Fairfax, Va., January 29, 1986; author's interview with Sen. Joseph R. Biden, Jr. (D, Del.), Jackson, Miss., March 1, 1986; author's inter-

view with Rep. Tony Coelho (D, Calif.), Washington, D.C., July 17, 1985.

5. Author's interview with Sen. Dale Bumpers (D, Ark.), Washington, D.C., January 23, 1986; Richard Reeves, "Zealots Bringing Down GOP," *Clarion-Ledger* (Jackson, Miss.), June 5, 1986; "Bygones," *Time*, December 23, 1985; author's interview with Rep. Patricia Schroeder (D, Colo.), Washington, D.C., September 12, 1985; Dukakis interview.

6. Richard Moe, "The Democrats Are Going to Have to Start Whistlin' Dixie," *Washington Post National Weekly Edition*, April 7, 1986; author's interview with Rep. Morris Udall (D, Ariz.), Washington, D.C., July 16, 1985; Babbitt interview; Schroeder interview; Coelho interview; Kevin P. Phillips, "The Era of Republican Ascendancy May Already Have Ended," *Washington Post National Weekly Edition*, July 28, 1986.

7. Moe, "Whistlin' Dixie"; From interview; *New York Times*, September 11, 1985, and April 8, 1986; editorial, "Hyping Hyper Tuesday," *New York Times*, March 28, 1986; Carl P. Leubsdorf, "New Hampshire Would Affect '88 Southern Regional Primary," *Clarion-Ledger/Jackson Daily News*, March 9, 1986; David S. Broder, "Super Primary Won't Be," *Clarion-Ledger*, March 12, 1986; Jim Hightower, speech at the National Press Club, October 17, 1985, *Texas Observer*, November 8, 1985, pp. 8–10; Dan T. Carter, "Southern Political Style," in Robert Haws (ed.), *The Age of Segregation: Race Relations in the South, 1890–1945* (Jackson: University Press of Mississippi, 1978); Dukakis interview; author's interview with Gov. Bill Clinton (D, Ark.), Little Rock, Ark., April 17, 1986.

8. David S. Broder, "Reagan's Ironic Revolution," *Washington Post National Weekly Edition*, August 26, 1985; Renee Loth, "The D Team," *Boston Globe Magazine*, May 11, 1986, pp. 12, 40–49; Dukakis interview; David S. Broder, "Education, Testing of Teachers to Be Newest Wave of Reform," *Clarion-Ledger*, May 14, 1986; Neal Peirce, "Schools Biggest Issue Occupying Minds of Governors," *Clarion-Ledger*, February 24, 1986; *New York Times*, March 31, 1986; Neal Peirce, "Texas Politician Typical of New Variety of Black Leader," *Clarion-Ledger*, March 6, 1986; Clinton interview; James J. Kilpatrick, "Meese's Calls for Renewed Federalism Music to Many Ears," *Clarion-Ledger*, February 10, 1986; *Newsweek*, March 24, 1986; David S. Broder, "A New Look for the Democrats," *Washington Post*, July 17, 1985; Neal Peirce, "States Focus on Helping Kids," *Clarion-Ledger/Jackson Daily News*, November 23, 1986.

9. George F. Will, "Hart Fights Conservative Flow," *Clarion-Ledger*, March 12, 1985; David S. Broder, "Is Political Tide Turning?" *Clarion-Ledger*, May 19, 1985; Kevin P. Phillips, "Hubris on the Right," *New York Times Magazine*, May 12, 1985; Frank interview; William Safire, "Is Support Span Shortening?" *Clarion-Ledger*, May 27, 1985; author's interview with Sen. Lawton Chiles (D, Fla.), Washington, D.C., February 26, 1986; Ann Lewis, as quoted in editorial, "A Time of Reckoning for Liberals," *Atlanta Constitution*, June 14, 1985; Felix Rohatyn, as quoted in column by Sydney J. Harris, *Clarion-Ledger*, March 3, 1985.

10. Theodore J. Lowi, "What's New about Neoliberals?" [review of Charles Peters and Phillip Keisling (eds.), *A New Road for America: The Neoliberal*

Movement], *Washington Post Book World,* June 16, 1985; author's interview with Rep. Jim Wright (D, Tex.), Washington, D.C., February 27, 1986; Dotson Rader, "What Are the Young Kennedys Up To?" *Parade,* January 12, 1986; Richard Reeves, "Reagan Mean to the Poor," *Clarion-Ledger,* June 9, 1986.

11. Paul Taylor and Kenneth E. John, "Butter 1, Guns 0," *Washington Post National Weekly Edition,* March 3, 1986; Barry Sussman, "What's the Evidence for This Shift to the Right We Hear About?" *Washington Post National Weekly Edition,* July 21, 1986; Thomas Ferguson and Joel Rogers, "The Myth of America's Turn to the Right," *Atlantic Monthly,* May 1986, p. 49.

12. Barney Frank, as quoted in James J. Kilpatrick, "Sometimes It's Hard to Tell Conservatives from Liberals," *Atlanta Journal/Constitution,* June 16, 1985; *New York Times,* November 24, 1985.

13. Author's interview with Patrick H. Caddell, Washington, D.C., September 12, 1985; Fred Barnes, "The Majority Complex," *New Republic,* August 5, 1985, pp. 12–15; Babbitt interview; David S. Broder, "Either This Party Is Getting Its Act Together—or It's Dead," *Washington Post National Weekly Edition,* July 8, 1985; *New York Times,* November 11, 1985, November 23, 1985, March 9, 1986; David S. Broder, "Kirk Revitalizing Party Forces," *Clarion-Ledger,* April 3, 1986; Paul G. Kirk, Jr., "Democrats Rebuilding Party," *Clarion-Ledger/Jackson Daily News,* January 5, 1986; Peter Perl, "Lane Kirkland's Diagnosis on the Democrats," *Washington Post National Weekly Edition,* April 8, 1985.

14. David S. Broder, "A New Look for the Democrats," *Washington Post,* July 17, 1985; Dukakis interview; author's interview with former Assistant Secretary of State Patricia Derian, Washington, D.C., June 18, 1985; Jean-Jacques Rousseau, *Julie,* as quoted in Richard Sennett, *The Fall of Public Man* (New York: Knopf, 1977), p. 119; Coelho interview; David S. Broder, "Coelho's Tactical Genius Scary," *Clarion-Ledger,* June 9, 1986.

15. Bob Kuttner, "What Money Could Do for Democrats," *Washington Post National Weekly Edition,* April 7, 1986; Sidney Blumenthal, "Meet the Democrats' Greatest Fund-Raiser—Ed Meese," *Washington Post National Weekly Edition,* June 23, 1986; Robert Kuttner, "Ass Backward," *New Republic,* April 22, 1985, pp. 18–23; Perl, "Kirkland's Diagnosis"; Coelho interview; Schroeder interview.

16. Tom Wicker, "For Want of a Horse," *Kennebec Journal* (Augusta, Me.), July 5, 1985; author's interview with Richard Goodwin, Bourne, Mass., July 8, 1985.

17. Coelho interview; Kuttner, "What Money Could Do for Democrats."

18. *New York Times,* November 23, 1985; author's interview with Sen. Lloyd Bentsen (D, Tex.), Washington, D.C., September 12, 1985; Babbitt interview; Richard Reeves, "Democrats Need a Leader," *Clarion-Ledger,* April 3, 1986.

19. Loth, "The D Team," p. 41; David S. Broder, "Campaign '84 Post-Mortems," *Washington Post National Weekly Edition,* December 17, 1984.

20. Clinton interview; Newt Gingrich and William Schneider, as quoted in

Reeves, "Democrats Need a Leader"; author's interview with Gov. Mario M. Cuomo (D, N.Y.), New York, January 21, 1986.

CHAPTER 8

1. Author's interview with Patrick H. Caddell, Washington, D.C., September 12, 1985.
2. *Atlanta Constitution*, June 6, 1985; Jim Hightower, speech to the National Press Club, October 17, 1985, *Texas Observer*, November 8, 1985; Sara Rimer, "Experts Study the Habits of Genus Baby Boomer," *New York Times*, April 21, 1986.
3. Phil Gailey, "Yuppie Is Dead, Long Live the 'New Collar' Voter," *New York Times*, July 19, 1985; Rimer, "Genus Baby Boomer"; Phillip Longman, "The Downwardly Mobile Baby Boomers," *Wall Street Journal*, April 12, 1985; Jim Wright, "No, You Can't Have It all," *New York Times*, February 3, 1986; *New York Times*, March 6, 1986.
4. "Here Come the Baby-Boomers," *U.S. News and World Report*, November 5, 1984; Landon Y. Jones, *Great Expectations: America and the Baby Boom Generation* (New York: Coward, McCann & Geoghegan, 1980; paperback ed.: Ballantine, 1981); Richard Reeves, "Baby Boomers' Disillusionment Will Make Them Liberal," *Clarion-Ledger*, January 6, 1986; Wright, "No, You Can't Have It All."
5. Louis Brandeis, as quoted in Sydney H. Schanberg, "The Possible Is Possible," *New York Times*, May 21, 1985; Hugh Sidey, "Readings in the Roosevelt Room," *Time*, June 2, 1986; Thomas Ferguson and Joel Rogers, "The Myth of America's Turn to the Right," *Atlantic Monthly*, May 1986, p. 45.
6. Ellen Goodman, "What Does Parental Tolerance Get You? Madonna," *Atlanta Constitution*, June 7, 1985.
7. Edward B. Fiske, "Liberal Arts Rising from Ashes," *Commercial Appeal* (Memphis, Tenn.), November 9, 1986; Colin Campbell, "Campus Scenes: Seeing Light at the End of the Liberal Arts Tunnel," *New York Times*, November 17, 1986; Thomas J. Meyer, "Freshmen Are Materialistic but Not Conservative, Study Finds," *Chronicle of Higher Education*, January 16, 1985; Thomas J. Meyer and Gaynelle Evans, "Most of This Year's Freshmen Hold Liberal Views, Study Finds," *Chronicle of Higher Education*, January 15, 1986; Robert Jacobson,"Most Students Satisfied with Their Education, Survey Indicates, but Frustrations Are Widespread," *Chronicle of Higher Education*, February 5, 1986; Paul Taylor and Kenneth E. John, "Butter 1, Guns 0," *Washington Post National Weekly Edition*, March 3, 1986.
8. Jones, *Great Expectations*; Reeves, "Baby Boomers' Disillusionment"; Rich Jaroslovsky, "Reagan Appeals to Young Voters," *Wall Street Journal*, October 16, 1984; Gordon Rayfield and Julian Baim, "Don't Take Yuppies for Granted," *New York Times*, November 16, 1984; Roger Hickey, "Redefining 'Baby Boomers,'" *New York Times*, July 9, 1985; David Boaz, "In '88, Who'll Win the Baby Boomers?" *New York Times*, November 7, 1985.
9. Jones, *Great Expectations*, p. 72; Charles A. Reich, *The Greening of America* (New York: Random House, 1970); Paul Grein, as quoted in Rick Wartz-

man,"Pop Musicians Start to Rock the Boat for Activist Causes," *Wall Street Journal*, September 12, 1985; Stephen Holden, "Pop Nostalgia: A Counter-revolution," *Atlantic Monthly*, April 1985, pp. 121–22.

10. "Groovy! The '60s Are Returning," *Newsweek*, December 16, 1985; Frank Rose, "The Return of the Sixties," *Esquire*, November 1985, pp. 25–26; "Far-out! It's a '60s Revival!" *Seventeen*, July 1986, pp. 66–67; "Rolling Stone 1986 Summer Music Guide," *Rolling Stone*, July 3, 1986; David Fricke, "Dylan on HBO," *Rolling Stone*, July 17–July 31, 1986, p. 21.

11. Stephen Holden, "45 Against Famine," *New York Times*, February 27, 1985; Harry Belafonte, on "We Are the World: A Year of Giving," CBS television, November 19, 1985; David Breskin, "Bob Geldof: The Rolling Stone Interview," *Rolling Stone*, December 5, 1985, pp. 28–34, 60, 63–67.

12. Holden, "45 Against Famine"; *Washington Post*, February 26, 1986; Ken Kragen, as quoted in *Washington Post*, June 19, 1985, and in Holden, "45 Against Famine"; "A New Spirit of Giving," *Newsweek*, June 2, 1986; Stevie Wonder and Diana Ross, on United Support of Artists for Africa, "We Are the World," Home Box Office, 1985.

13. *New York Times*, July 14, 1985, July 15, 1985, November 12, 1985; *Washington Post*, July 14, 1985; Mary Travers, as quoted in *New York Times*, July 15, 1985; editorial, "From Woodstock to Philadelphia," *New York Times*, July 16, 1985; Tom Petty, Bill Graham, and Harvey Goldsmith, as quoted in Michael Goldberg, "The Day the World Rocked," *Rolling Stone*, August 15, 1985; Sting, as quoted in "Playboy Interview: Sting," *Playboy*, November, 1985, pp. 51–66.

14. *New York Times*, November 8, 1985, March 28, 1986, May 28, 1985; *Clarion-Ledger/Jackson Daily News*, November 28, 1985.

15. Robin Williams, on "Comic Relief," Part I, Home Box Office, 1986; "Sun City," lyrics by Little Steven (Steve Van Zandt), on United Artists Against Apartheid, *Sun City* (Manhattan Records, 1985); Steve Van Zandt, as quoted in *New York Times*, October 21, 1985; *Clarion-Ledger*, April 25, 1986; *New York Times*, December 4, 1985; *Washington Post*, February 26, 1986.

16. *USA Today*, June 6, 1986; Bono, as quoted in Michael Goldberg, "Amnesty's Rock & Roll Roadshow," *Rolling Stone*, July 17–July 31, 1986; John Healy, as quoted in *New York Times*, June 16, 1986.

17. *New York Times*, May 26, 1986; "A New Spirit of Giving"; "Lending a Helping Hand," *Time*, June 2, 1986; Ken Kragen, as quoted in *Clarion-Ledger*, May 27, 1986, and in "A New Spirit of Giving"; Mickey Kaus, "Age of Celebritics," *New Republic*, February 24, 1986, pp. 15–17; James J. Kilpatrick, "Hand-holders Did Nothing Compared to Salvation Army," *Clarion-Ledger/Jackson Daily News*, June 1, 1986; George F. Will, "Moral Exhibitionism No Help," *Clarion-Ledger*, April 14, 1986; "Hands Across America," lyrics by M. Blatte, J. Carney, L. Gottlieb, recorded by Voices of America (EMI Records, 1986); editorial, "Hand Jive," *New Republic*, June 16, 1986, p. 8; James P. Grant, executive director, United Nations Children's Fund, letter to the editor, *New York Times*, June 6, 1986; "Silly Love Songs," lyrics by Paul McCartney, on *Give My Regards to Broad Street* (MPL/Columbia, 1984).

18. "The Times They Are A-Changin'," lyrics by Bob Dylan, on Bob Dylan, *The Times They Are A-Changin'* (Columbia Records, 1964); Wartzman, "Pop Musicians Start to Rock the Boat"; "Hand Jive"; Robert Palmer, "Springsteen Echoes Mood of America," *New York Times*, August 6, 1985; "He's on Fire," *Newsweek*, August 5, 1985; Mikal Gilmore, "Positively Dylan," *Rolling Stone*, July 17–July 31, 1986, p. 135; Bill Bradley, " 'He's New Jersey and He Is Ours,' " *USA Today*, August 5, 1985.

19. Richard Ford, "The Boss Observed," *Esquire*, December 1985, pp. 326–29; David Hinckley, "Suddenly, Springsteen Rules Rock 'n' Roll Roost," *Clarion-Ledger*, August 30, 1985; "Working on the Highway," lyrics by Bruce Springsteen, on Bruce Springsteen, *Born in the U.S.A.* (Columbia Records, 1984); "Mansion on the Hill," lyrics by Bruce Springsteen, on Bruce Springsteen, *Nebraska* (Columbia Records, 1982); "My Hometown," lyrics by Bruce Springsteen, on *Born in the U.S.A.*; K. Loder, "Bruce Springsteen," *Rolling Stone*, December 6, 1984; "He's on Fire"; *Washington Post*, August 6, 1985; "War," lyrics by Barrett Strong and Norman Whitfield, on *Bruce Springsteen and the E Street Band Live/1975–85* (Columbia Records, 1986).

20. "He's on Fire"; Hinckley, "Suddenly, Springsteen Rules"; Ford, "The Boss Observed"; Jefferson Morley, "The Phenomenon," *Rolling Stone*, October 10, 1985; Merele Ginsberg, "The Fans," *Rolling Stone*, October 10, 1985.

21. Dave Marsh, Steve Van Zandt, and Jack Santino, as quoted in Wartzman, "Pop Musicians Start to Rock the Boat."

22. "Big Time," lyrics by Peter Gabriel, on Peter Gabriel, *So* (Geffen Records, 1986); "If You Love Somebody Set Them Free," lyrics by Sting, on Sting, *The Dream of the Blue Turtles* (A & M Records, 1985).

23. "Tough All Over," lyrics by John Cafferty, on John Cafferty and the Beaver Brown Band, *Tough All Over* (Scotti Brothers Records/CBS, 1985); "The Face of a Nation," lyrics by John Cougar Mellencamp, on John Cougar Mellencamp, *Scarecrow* (PolyGram Records, 1985).

24. "We Work the Black Seam," lyrics by Sting, on Sting, *The Dream of the Blue Turtles*.

25. "Right and Wrong," lyrics by Joe Jackson, on Joe Jackson, *Big World* (A & M Records, 1986); "For America," lyrics by Jackson Browne, on Jackson Browne, *Lives in the Balance* (Elektra/Asylum Records, 1986).

26. "Biko," lyrics by Peter Gabriel, on Peter Gabriel, *Peter Gabriel* (Geffen Records, 1980); "Ebony and Ivory," lyrics by Paul McCartney and Stevie Wonder, on Paul McCartney, *Tug of War* (Columbia, 1982); "Christmas in Capetown," lyrics by Randy Newman, on Randy Newman, *Trouble in Paradise* (Warner Brothers, 1983); "It's Wrong (Apartheid)," lyrics by Stevie Wonder, on Stevie Wonder, *In Square Circle* (Tamla/Motown, 1985); Stevie Wonder, as quoted in Robert Palmer, "Stevie Wonder's Message of Love and Protest," *New York Times*, October 7, 1985 "The Way It Is," lyrics by Bruce Hornsby and the Range, *The Way It Is* (RCA, 1986).

27. Christopher Connelly, "Keeping the Faith," *Rolling Stone*, March 14, 1985, pp. 25–30, 60; Jim Miller, "Stop in the Name of Love," *Newsweek*, December 31, 1984, p. 61; "Pride (In the Name of Love)," lyrics by Bono, on U2, *The Unforgettable Fire* (Island Records, 1984); "Sunday Bloody Sunday,"

"New Year's Day," and "Seconds," lyrics by Bono, on U2, *War* (Island Records, 1983).

28. "99 Red Balloons," by J. U. Fahrenkrog-Petersen-C. Karges, English trans. by K. McAlea, on Nena, *99 Luftballons* (CBS Records, 1984); "Walking in Your Footsteps," lyrics by Sting, on the Police, *Synchronicity* (A & M Records, 1983); "Russians," lyrics by Sting, on Sting, *The Dream of the Blue Turtles*; "Playboy Interview: Sting"; "Every Breath You Take," lyrics by Sting, on the Police, *Synchronicity.*

29. "Silent Running," lyrics by Michael Rutherford and B. A. Robertson, on Mike and the Mechanics, *Mike and the Mechanics* (Atlantic, 1985); "Ride Across the River," lyrics by Mark Knopfler, on Dire Straits, *Brothers in Arms* (Warner Brothers, 1985); Stephen Holden, "Dire Straits Stirs Dispute with Irony," *New York Times*, September 4, 1985; "Brothers in Arms," lyrics by Mark Knopfler, on Dire Straits, *Brothers in Arms*; "Lives in the Balance," lyrics by Jackson Browne, on Jackson Browne, *Lives in the Balance*; Stephen Holden, "Rock: Jackson Browne," *New York Times*, June 2, 1986; James Hunter, "The Bold New Browne," *Rolling Stone*, July 3, 1986.

30. Cyndi Lauper, *True Colors* (Portrait, 1986); Talking Heads, *True Stories* (Sire, 1986); UB40, *Rat in the Kitchen* (A&M, 1986); Paul Simon, *Graceland* (Warner Brothers, 1986); Simple Minds, *Once upon a Time* (Virgin, 1985); Stephen Holden, "Pretenders and Rock's Direction," *New York Times*, November 11, 1986.

31. Kathy Stroud, "Stop Pornographic Rock," *Newsweek*, May 6, 1985; Robert Friedman, "Sex, Drugs 'n' Rock 'n' Roll," *St. Petersburg Times*, August 4, 1985; William Raspberry, "Filth on the Air," *Washington Post*, June 19, 1985; Robert Palmer, "Records: From Prince, 'Around the World.'" *New York Times*, April 22, 1985; Caddell interview; Edward Lazarus and Lee Atwater, as quoted in Maureen Dowd, "Why Are All the Politicians Watching Rock Video?" *New York Times*, April 19, 1985.

CHAPTER 9

1. *Rambo* (1985, Sylvester Stallone, MGM/UA); *Rocky IV* (1985, Sylvester Stallone, MGM/UA); *Aliens* (1986, James Cameron, 20th Century-Fox); *Platoon* (1986, Oliver Stone, Orion); Ellen Goodman, "High-Tech Morality Misplaced," *Clarion-Ledger*, December 25, 1985; editorial, "War-nography," *New York Times*, January 8, 1986; "Rocky and Rambo," *Newsweek*, December 23, 1985; "An Outbreak of Rambomania," *Time*, June 24, 1985; "Blood, Sweat and Cheers," *Newsweek*, June 3, 1985; Jack Kroll, review of *Rambo*, *Newsweek*, May 27, 1985; Richard Schickel, review of *Rambo*, *Time*, May 27, 1985; Richard Schickel, review of *Rocky IV*, *Time*, December 9, 1985; Jack Kroll, review of *Rocky IV*, *Newsweek*, December 9, 1985; Stanley Kauffmann, review of *Rambo*, *New Republic*, July 15 and 22, 1985; Pauline Kael, review of *Rambo*, *The New Yorker*, June 17, 1985; Thomas Ferguson and Joel Rogers, "The Myth of America's Turn to the Right," *Atlantic Monthly*, May 1986, p. 48.

2. "Rocky and Rambo"; *Red Dawn* (1984, John Milius, MGM/United Artists);

Andrew Kopkind, review of *Red Dawn, The Nation,* September 15, 1984; Richard Corliss, review of *Red Dawn, Time,* August 27, 1984.

3. *WarGames* (1983, John Badham, MGM/UA); Pauline Kael, review of *War-Games, The New Yorker,* June 13, 1983; Richard Schickel, review of *War-Games, Time,* May 30, 1983.

4. *Down and Out in Beverly Hills* (1986, Paul Mazursky, Buena Vista); Janet Maslin, review of *Down and Out in Beverly Hills, New York Times,* January 31, 1986; Pauline Kael, review of *Down and Out in Beverly Hills, The New Yorker,* February 10, 1986.

5. Pauline Kael, review of *Pretty in Pink, The New Yorker,* April 7, 1986; *An Officer and a Gentleman* (1982, Taylor Hackford, Paramount); *Flashdance* (1983, Adrian Lyne, Paramount); *Pretty in Pink* (1986, John Hughes, Universal); Richard Corliss, review of *Pretty in Pink, Time,* March 3, 1986; "Family Ties" (NBC Television).

6. *Lost in America* (1985, Albert Brooks, Geffen/Warner Brothers); Pauline Kael, review of *Lost in America, The New Yorker,* April 8, 1985; Stanley Kauffmann, review of *Lost in America, New Republic,* March 18, 1985.

7. *On the Beach* (1959, Stanley Kramer, United Artists); *Strategic Air Command* (1955, Anthony Mann, Paramount); *Bombers B-52* (1957, Gordon Douglas, Warner Brothers); Peter Biskind, *Seeing Is Believing: How Hollywood Taught Us to Stop Worrying and Love the Fifties* (New York: Pantheon, 1983), pp. 343–47, 67; *Seven Days in May* (1964, John Frankenheimer, Seven Arts/Joel Productions); *Fail-Safe* (1964, Sidney Lumet, Columbia); *Dr. Strangelove; or How I Learned to Stop Worrying and Love the Bomb* (1964, Stanley Kubrick, Columbia).

8. Ronnie Dugger, *On Reagan: The Man and His Presidency* (New York: McGraw-Hill, 1983), p. 400; "TV's Nuclear Nightmare," *Newsweek,* November 21, 1983, pp. 67–71; Rogers and Ferguson, "Myth of America's Turn," pp. 48–49; Jonathan Schell, *The Fate of the Earth* (New York: Knopf, 1982); *Testament* (1983, Lynne Littman, Paramount); Stanley Kauffmann, review of *Testament, New Republic,* November 28, 1983; "The Day After" (ABC Television, November 20, 1983); "Fallout from a TV Attack," *Time,* December 5, 1983; "The Nightmare Comes Home," *Time,* October 24, 1983; *New York Post* article quoted in Lawrence Weschler, "ABC Drops the Big One," *The Nation,* November 26, 1983; Paul Attanasio, "Big Bang, Little Box," *New Republic,* December 5, 1983; Michael Kinsley, "The Morning After," *New Republic,* December 12, 1983; Robert Karl Manoff, "The Week After," *The Nation,* December 10, 1983; *Mad Max Beyond Thunderdome* (1985, George Miller and George Ogilvie, Warner Bros.); Richard Schickel, review of *Mad Max Beyond Thunderdome, Time,* July 22, 1985.

9. Author's interview with Patrick H. Caddell, Washington, D.C., September 12, 1985; Marcus Garvey, as quoted in Lawrence W. Levine, "Marcus Garvey's Moment," *New Republic,* October 29, 1984, p. 26; "The New First Ladies of Soul," *Newsweek,* July 21, 1986, pp. 60–61; Stanley Kauffmann, review of *Beverly Hills Cop, New Republic,* December 31, 1984; *Beverly Hills Cop* (1984, Martin Brest, Paramount); "Crazy Eddie," *Newsweek,* January 7, 1985, pp. 48–55; *A Soldier's Story* (1984, Norman Jewison, Columbia); Jack

Kroll, review of *A Soldier's Story, Newsweek,* September 10, 1984; Stanley Kauffmann, review of *A Soldier's Story, New Republic,* October 15, 1984; "A Revival of Black Movies?" *Newsweek,* January 7, 1985, p. 50; *The Color Purple* (1985, Steven Spielberg, Warner Brothers); Stanley Kauffmann, review of *The Color Purple, New Republic,* January 27, 1986; Janet Maslin, review of *The Color Purple, New York Times,* December 18, 1985; "The Cosby Show" (NBC Television); "Cosby's Fast Track," *Newsweek,* September 2, 1985, pp. 50–56.

10. *The Big Chill* (1983, Lawrence Kasdan, Columbia); Richard Corliss, review of *The Big Chill, Time,* September 12, 1983; David Ansen, review of *The Big Chill, Newsweek,* September 26, 1983; Katha Pollitt, review of *The Big Chill, The Nation,* October 22, 1983; Pauline Kael, review of *The Big Chill, The New Yorker,* October 17, 1983; Stanley Kauffmann, review of *The Big Chill, New Republic,* October 31, 1983; *Return of the Secaucus 7* (1980, John Sayles, Libra); Lanford Wilson, *The Fifth of July* (New York: Hill & Wang, 1978); Michael Weller, *Loose Ends* (Garden City, N.Y.: Doubleday, 1979).

11. Bobbie Ann Mason, *In Country* (New York: Harper & Row, 1985); *St. Elmo's Fire* (1985, Joel Schumacher, Columbia); *Purple Rain* (1984, Albert Magnoli, Warner Brothers); *Desperately Seeking Susan* (1985, Susan Seidelman, Orion).

12. *Footloose* (1984, Herbert Ross, Paramount); Pauline Kael, review of *Footloose, The New Yorker,* March 5, 1984; David Ansen, review of *Footloose, Newsweek,* February 20, 1984; *Back to the Future* (1985, Robert Zemeckis, Universal); Richard Corliss, review of *Back to the Future, Time,* July 1, 1985; Jack Kroll, review of *Back to the Future, Newsweek,* July 8, 1985; Pauline Kael, review of *Back to the Future, The New Yorker,* July 29, 1985.

13. *Rebel Without a Cause* (1955, Nicholas Ray, Warner Brothers); *Sixteen Candles* (1984, John Hughes, Universal); *The Breakfast Club* (1985, John Hughes, Universal); Pauline Kael, review of *The Breakfast Club, The New Yorker,* April 8, 1985.

14. *New York Times,* May 17, 1985; "A New Spirit of Giving," *Newsweek,* June 2, 1986, pp. 18–20; Robert Coles, as quoted in *New York Times,* October 17, 1985; James Reston, "The Class of 1985," *New York Times,* May 19, 1985; Michael Harrington, *The Other America* (New York: Macmillan, 1962, rev. ed., Penguin, 1981), pp. 91–92; Mario M. Cuomo, *The Diaries of Mario M. Cuomo: The Campaign for Governor* (New York: Random House, 1984), p. 222; author's interview with Gov. Mario Cuomo (D, N.Y.), New York, January 21, 1986.

15. Editorial, "One Person Can Make a Difference," *St Petersburg Times,* August 3, 1985; "A New Spirit of Giving"; *New York Times,* October 8, 1985, July 9, 1985, October 17, 1985.

16. Todd Gitlin, "Divestment Stirs a New Generation," *The Nation,* May 18, 1985; Seymour Martin Lipset on ABC News, "Nightline," May 3, 1985 (New York: Journal Graphics, 1985, show #1030), p. 5; Kenneth E. John, "South African Blacks Win Friends," *Washington Post National Weekly Edition,* April 21, 1986; "A New Breed of Activism," *Newsweek,* May 13, 1985, pp. 61–62; *New York Times,* February 14, 1985, April 25, 1985, April

5, 1985, April 15, 1985, April 17, 1985, April 19, 1985, April 23, 1985, May 9, 1985, January 24, 1986, February 12, 1986, February 13, 1986; *Washington Post*, April 20, 1985, January 24, 1986; "Shanties on the Green," *Newsweek*, February 3, 1986, p. 63; *Chicago Tribune*, April 11, 1986, April 13, 1986; David A. Goldiner, letter to the editor, *New York Times*, May 31, 1985.

17. ABC News, "20/20," repeat broadcast, May 4, 1985; *New York Times*, February 27, 1985, February 3, 1986, March 3, 1986; Physicians Task Force on Hunger in America, *Hunger in America: The Growing Epidemic* (Middletown, Conn.: Wesleyan University Press, 1985); "The Vanishing Family: Crisis in Black America" (Bill Moyers, CBS Television, January 25, 1986); Daniel Patrick Moynihan, *Family and Nation:* The Godkin Lectures Harvard University (San Diego: Harcourt Brace Jovanovich, 1986); "Samaritan: The Mitch Snyder Story" (1986, CBS Television); editorial, "Hand Jive," *New Republic*, June 16, 1986, p. 8.

18. "First Draft—Bishops' Pastoral, Catholic Social Teaching and the U.S. Economy," *Origins: NC Documentary Service*, November 15, 1984; *New York Times*, September 11, September 9, September 12, 1985, April 30, 1986, May 20, 1986, November 14, 1986.

19. Thomas Paine, *The Rights of Man* (1791, 1792; New York: Dutton, 1951), p. 286.

INDEX

Abortion, 112–13, 215
Adams, Bryan, 239
Adams, Henry, 4
Advertising
  altruistic messages in, 289–90
  for me generation, 8
Affirmative action, 118–19, 120
Agriculture, 75–76, 95
  New Progressive program for,
    134–35
Alexander, Lamar, 210
Aliens, 265–66
Allin, John, 289
American Enterprise Institute,
  188
Amnesty International, 245–46
Anderson, John, 72
Anderson, Reuben, 18
Apocalypse Now, 148
Arms control, 168–70. *See also*
  Nuclear weapons
Art Aid, 244
Artists United Against Apartheid,
  244–45
Aspin, Les, 64, 139–40, 146,
  159, 164
Atwater, Lee, 263

Babbitt, Bruce, 9–10, 105, 180,
  198, 204, 209, 210, 216,
  222
Baby boomers, 6, 7, 228–32
Back to the Future, 281
Badham, John, 268
Baez, Joan, 8, 243

Baker, James, 193
Baker, Russell, 29
Balance of payments, 87–88
Baliles, Gerald L., 18
Band Aid, 240, 241
Bane, Mary Jo, 51
Beastie Boys, 276
Beatles, 239, 249
Beattie, Ann, 280
Beaver Brown Band, 250,
  255
Belafonte, Harry, 240, 241
Bell, Daniel, 236
Bellah, Robert, 191
Bentsen, Lloyd, 87, 222
Beverly Hills Cop, 276–77
Biden, Joseph R., Jr., 106, 146,
  159, 179–80, 201
Big Chill, The, 239, 279–80
"Big Time," 254
"Biko," 257
Bill of Responsibilities, 138
Birth control
  and sex education, 116
  in Third World, 113–14,
    152–53
Blacks
  call for moral revival, 116–17
  in conservative periods,
    275–76
  cultural influence of, 275–79
  and Democratic party, 16–17
  election of, 18
  infant mortality rate for, 53
  in motion pictures, 276–77

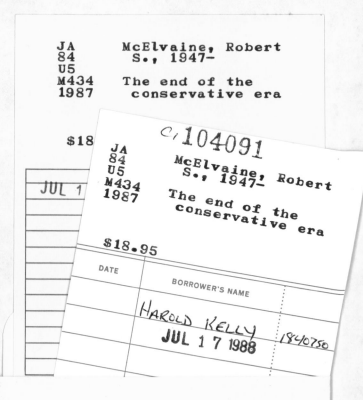